*Liberalism
and the Origins of
European Social Theory*

Liberalism and the Origins of European Social Theory

STEVEN SEIDMAN

University of California Press
Berkeley   Los Angeles

University of California Press
Berkeley and Los Angeles, California

© 1983 by
The Regents of the University of California
Printed in the United States of America

1 2 3 4 5 6 7 8

Library of Congress Cataloging in Publication Data

Seidman, Steven.
  Liberalism and the origins of European social theory.

  Bibliography: p.
  Includes index.
    1. Sociology—Europe—History.   2. Socialism—Europe—
History.   3. Liberalism—France—History.   4. Liberalism—Germany—
History.   I. Title.
HM22.E9S44 1983   301'.094   82-21802
ISBN 0-520-04741-9
ISBN 0-520-04986-1 (pbk.)

Contents

Preface   ix

Acknowledgments   xii

General Introduction   1

PART ONE: The Origins of European Social Theory

1. The Enlightenment   21
2. The Counter-Enlightenment: Analytical Continuities and Ideological Shifts in European Social Thought   42

   Summary of Part One   74

PART TWO: Marx

   Introduction to Part Two   81

3. Romantic and Enlightenment Presuppositions of Marxian Social Theory   87
4. The Revolutionary Motif: Revolution as the Vehicle of Democracy   101

v

5. The Critique of Capitalism and the Problematics
    of Socialism   120

    Summary of Part Two   140

PART THREE: *Durkheim*

Introduction to Part Three   145

6. The Liberal Tradition in France and the Crisis of
    the 1890s   152

7. Democracy and Sociology: Durkheim's Synthesis
    of Liberalism and Revolution   161

8. The Individual and Society: The Problem of
    Collective Life   179

    Summary of Part Three   198

PART FOUR: *Weber*

Introduction to Part Four   203

9. Prussian Hegemony and the Failure of German
    Liberalism: Weber's Early Materialism   207

10. The Prospects for Liberal Democracy: Weber's Turn
    to Idealism   213

11. Universal History and the Problem of Rationality
    and Modernity   235

    Summary of Part Four   269

General Conclusion   273

Appendix: Beyond Presentism and Historicism:
Understanding the History of Sociology   281

Notes   299

Works Cited

      Preface and Introduction   367

      Part One   371

      Part Two   378

      Part Three   382

      Part Four   385

      Conclusion and Appendix   392

Index   397

Preface

In an important essay on Marx and Weber, Karl Löwith remarked: "Social science, like the society it studies, is divided into two branches: *bourgeois sociology* and *proletarian Marxism*."[1] Löwith's essay was published almost fifty years ago, but scholarly opinion, in the main, has not changed.[2] In a recent book on *The History and Nature of Sociological Theory*, Daniel Rossides repeats this piece of conventional wisdom: "Despite the similarity between Marxism and sociological thought, Marx worked outside the main assumptions and methods of both liberalism/capitalism and sociology."[3] A consistent historical articulation of this thesis maintains that sociology, from Comte through Durkheim and Weber to functionalism, developed as a reaction against the revolutionary tradition as that was elaborated from the philosophes through utopian socialism to Marxism. In this spirit, Alvin Gouldner writes: "If the key polemical target of Positivist Sociology had been the *philosophes* and the French Revolution, the common polemical target of the thinkers of the Classical period was Marxism. . . . Classical Sociology was the great achievement of the middle class of Western Europe . . . when in general, the middle class was increasingly threatened by the rise of Marxist Socialism."[4] One of my main aims is to criticize the thesis of the social and intellectual polarization between

Marxian social theory and sociology by way of a general historical interpretation of the development of European social theory.

The thesis of the bifurcation of Marxism and sociology has had negative theoretical and practical consequences. First, it has led to bad intellectual history. The history of modern social theory is reconstructed as two separate and competing lines of development—Marxism and sociology—reflecting the antagonistic class divisions of modern Europe. Not only must we object to the reductionist bias of this thesis—of theory to ideology and of ideological development to social class—but this thesis misses the crucial feature of Marxism and sociology: Marx arrived at a revolutionary standpoint not—as in the orthodox French revolutionary tradition—by abandoning liberalism, but by working through liberalism to a democratic ideology. Similarly, in their effort to revitalize liberalism, Durkheim and Weber found in the revolutionary tradition both a cogent critique of the classical doctrines of liberalism—natural law and utilitarianism—and a consistent extension of liberalism's initial commitment to social justice and democracy. Second, the assertion of the antithesis between Marxism and sociology has promoted the contemporary isolation of Marxists and sociologists. This, I believe, has led to the ideological hardening of social theory and its decreasing theoretical penetration. Third, this thesis has contributed to the widening political gap between liberalism and social democracy, which, as in the past, is conducive to conservatism and irrationalist movements.

It is one of my principal theses that nineteenth-century European social theory, chiefly that of Marx, Durkheim, and Weber, departs from both the liberal and the revolutionary orthodoxy. Their ideas combine central elements of liberal and revolutionary thought, and it is precisely this broad intellectual synthesis that is a major source of the creative and enduring power of their theories. Too much of contemporary social theory is marked by ideological orthodoxy and its consequent intellectual petrification. We need to renew the dialogue that nurtured the best of classical social theory. This revitalization of an intellectual tradition has important practical as well as theoretical consequences: as we survey contemporary politics, we observe, on the one hand, the retreat of liberalism from the democratic heritage of the revolutionary tradition; on the other hand, and equally dismaying, we find the crassest illiberalism parading as a revolutionary politic. My aim is to contribute to the existing dialogue between liberalism and revolution by detailing the movement of liberalism and revolution within the tradition of European social theory.

Acknowledgments

During the years when my thoughts were maturing, I had the good fortune of being exposed to a number of teachers, scholars, and friends, some of whose passion and ideas inform this book. There are three individuals whose lectures and/or friendship proved enduring: Kenley Dove, the late Benjamin Nelson, and Michael Gruber. In addition, I want to extend my gratitude to the following scholars who commented on earlier drafts of this manuscript: Robert Bierstedt, Thomas Burger, Randall Collins, Lewis Coser, Anthony Giddens, Colin Loader, Jack Mendelson, Gianfranco Poggi, Joel Telles, Friedrich Tenbruck, and R. Stephen Warner. To my good friend Jeffrey C. Alexander, who exemplified the calling of scholarship through his enthusiasm, openness, and forthright criticisms, thank you. I dedicate this book to Komluk.

General Introduction

GEOFFREY HAWTHORN HAS posed the initial and elementary problem facing all historians of social theory: "The sociologist who begins a history of social theories is at once very tempted to stop. To write such a history, he has first to decide what social theories are."[1] Pursuing this further, I argue that the historian does more than "decide what social theories are"; the historian actively *promotes* social theory. Stated as a concise thesis: every history of social theory presupposes and projects a theory of social theory.

The historian of sociology, economics, or psychology appears to be in the same situation. Thus, Raymond Aron, in his excellent study *Main Currents in Sociological Thought*, begins by saying, "to write a history of sociology one must arrive at a definition of what is to be called sociology."[2] However, the problem is more apparent than real for the historian of sociology. The historian of sociology can restrict the concept of sociology to that thought-product so designated by the author. Moreover, from the beginning of the twentieth century, sociology can be defined by its institutional practice. Followed consistently, this line of argument points to an "historicist" resolution to the problem of defining sociology. Historicism holds that to identify the meaning of sociology, the historian must study what past and present authors in their social context understand as sociology.[3] An historicist historiography of sociology would recognize that the very meaning of sociology would vary among societies and perhaps change within the history of particular societies.

Although the historicist approach may adequately resolve the problem of defining sociology, it cannot do the same for the identification of social theory. This follows from the fact that social theory is a broader concept than sociology, extending beyond institutionalized disciplinary boundaries. We cannot therefore define the nature of social theory by recourse to authorial designation or institutional practice. The specification of social theory is unavoidably a present and theoretical task. It follows that every history of social theory will be theoretically informed and significant in a double sense. First, our operative concept of social theory will determine the formal or structural properties of our history—for example, what is to be included in the history, the emphases and direction of our interpretation of the past. Second, the concept of social theory embedded in the written history will serve as a standard for contemporary definitions of social theory.[4] Hence, as a necessary preliminary to historical inquiry, we need to ask: what is social theory?

A full discussion of the nature of social theory is well beyond the scope of this Introduction. Nevertheless, drawing upon the recent work of postpositivist interpretations of science, we maintain that the most valid concept of social theory is a multidimensional one.[5] According to Jeffrey Alexander, who has systematized the idea of a postpositivist view of science into perhaps its most elaborate form, social theory consists of propositions which span the spectrum from high empirical content to high-level background assumptions and presuppositions of a nonempirical nature.[6] Furthermore, Alexander points out that the nonempirical dimension of social theory is composed of different aspects—for example, methodologies, models, political ideologies, moral beliefs, and metaphysical and epistemological presuppositions. Because each dimension has its own ideational character and impacts uniquely in the formation of social theory, the identification of social theory exclusively with one dimension yields an unacceptable reductionist account of social theory. It follows that insofar as a history of social theory is informed by a reductionist theoretical standpoint, it will be flawed in its initial conception and rudimentary structure. It is a chief contention of mine that nearly all existing historical works are formally defective because informed by a reductionist concept of social theory.

A survey of historical works reveals that they may be somewhat roughly grouped according to whether they exhibit a "positivist" or "ideological" theoretical disposition. Positivism, in this context, refers to the identification of social theory with ideational dimensions of a high empirical content—for example, methodologies, models, and explanatory propositions. Ideological reductionism links social theory with politically, morally, and affectively charged high-level background assumptions and presuppositions. To substantiate my thesis, or at least to make it plausible, I intend to discuss the underlying theoretical disposition of some recent historical works.

Turning first to an historical work informed by a positivist disposition, we may single out the fine study by Jonathan Turner and Leonard Beeghley, *The Emergence of Sociological Theory*.[7] According to Turner and Beeghley, theory functions at two levels. At the first level, theory consists of the elaboration of concepts and typologies. Though concept formation and typological construction are necessary for classification, the goal of theory is explanation. The second level of theory aims at developing explanatory propositions, ranging from the causal explanation of sociohistorical particulars to the elaboration of theoretical models and covering laws. Adopting the nomological ideal of the natural sciences as their model, Turner and Beeghley hold that the ultimate goal of theory is the formulation of abstract, timeless, and context-free laws.[8] On the basis of this positivist view of theory, Turner and Beeghley reconstruct the early history of sociological theory as successive efforts to elaborate such an explanatory science. Thus, in their analysis of early sociological theorists, the authors select only those texts that articulate or permit the articulation of abstract concepts, theoretical models, and laws. The strictly formal limitation of this historical approach reflects its exclusion of the ideological dimension of theory. Turner and Beeghley are, to be sure, aware of ideology as a component of the social milieu of early sociological theory. However, their positivism leads them to view ideology either as a part of the originating context but distinct from theory itself, or as a residue of a prescientific mode of theory, or as an impediment to the development of a genuine explanatory theory.[9] Positivistically grounded historical works such as *The Emergence of Sociological Theory* tend towards a Whiggish view of the history of social theory as a progressive movement from an ideological to a scientific mode of theorizing.[10]

The rise of the sociology of knowledge, the sociology of sociology, and the sociology of science, as well as the ideologically charged atmosphere of the 1960s, have contributed to the appearance of numerous historical works founded upon an ideologically reductionist view of social theory. An important precursor and paradigmatic figure is Karl Mannheim. In his own historical works, Mannheim, despite his intention, reduces the emergence, structure, and direction of social theory to the theorists' collectively structured political interest in changing or maintaining the existing social arrangement.[11] In *Ideology and the Development of Sociological Theory*, Irving Zeitlin interprets the historical development of sociological theory as a bourgeois response initially to the critical rationalism of the philosophes and later to Marxism and socialism.[12] Zeitlin thereby reduces sociological theory to an ideological reflex of bourgeois class interests. Zeitlin's argument has recently been restated by Daniel Rossides in *The History and Nature of Sociological Theory* and by Göran Therborn in *Science, Class, and Society*—both of whom reconstruct the development of sociological theory in terms of the changing ideological needs of capitalism and the middle classes. Ros-

sides unabashedly displays his reductionism: "My major assumption is that the stages of development in sociological
theory follow the stages of capitalist development within national and international contexts."[13] In an equally revealing
passage, Therborn underscores the reductionism informing
his historical interpretation: "It [sociology] developed and
became decisively established as an attempt to deal with the
social, moral, and cultural problems of the capitalist economic order, under the shadow of a militant working-class
movement and a more or less immediate threat of revolutionary socialism. The sociological approach to politics and
economics was rooted in a bourgeois point of view. . . ."[14]

Not all historical works which are ideologically reductionist are so one-dimensional. In *The Sociological Tradition*,
Robert Nisbet proposes as an alternative to positivism a concept of social theory which, by highlighting its intuitive and
imaginative character, renders social theory closer to moral
philosophy or an art form than to science.[15] Accordingly, in
his historical reconstruction Nisbet fastens onto "unit-ideas"
which, because they represent broad perspectives at once
philosophical, political, moral, and aesthetic—in terms of
which we grasp social reality—disclose the deep ideological
structure of social theory.[16] Although Nisbet avoids conflating
the ideological realm to simply political ideology, his work
suppresses the analytical dimension.[17] An even more nuanced
historical work but ultimately equally reductionist is Alvin
Gouldner's *The Crisis of Western Sociology*. In principle,
Gouldner distinguishes between an ideological dimension of
"background assumptions" and an analytical realm of "postulations."[18] However, in the course of both his theoretical
discussion and historical reconstruction, the analytical dimension virtually disappears before the determining power
of the ideological "infrastructure of social theory."[19] Like
Nisbet and Gouldner, who operate with a much more differentiated concept of the ideological realm, Geoffrey Hawthorn,
in *Enlightenment and Despair*, evades a crude identification
of theory with political ideology, only to end in a similarly

reductionist view of theory. Modern social theory, Hawthorn argues, emerged in the aftermath of the demise of the Christian-feudal cosmos. Its main aim was to elaborate a new cosmology that was resonant with the secular, utilitarian, and utopian character of modernity.[20] In other words, Hawthorn identifies social theory with a philosophical quest for an ordered universe. Accordingly, Hawthorn's history of social theory is confined to recounting sociologists' successive efforts to elaborate a new synthetic world-view, integrating humankind, nature, and society. Hawthorn's history screens out the analytical project of social theory.

My critical comments are of course limited to the formal structure of these historical works. However, my point is that historical works informed by a reductionist view of social theory are flawed and misleading in their initial conception and structure. Because historical works are theoretically significant, our histories must reflect the most elaborate and valid conception of social theory available. I contend that this is a multidimensional social theory.

The Development of European Social Theory

Simplifying matters, we may speak of a multidimensional social theory as two-tiered. Following our previous discussion, the analytical level refers to methodology, models, and explanatory propositions. By the ideological realm, I mean those nonempirical assumptions of a political, moral, metaphysical, and epistemological nature. Proceeding from this abbreviated model of a multidimensional theory, I have proposed an historical interpretation that outlines the main lines of development of European social theory.

This work presupposes a distinction between a European and Anglo-American theoretical tradition. Talcott Parsons long ago systematized the idea of two classical theoretical traditions.[21] Parsons maintained that in the Anglo-American tradition, from Hobbes and Locke to the classical economists, utilitarians, and social evolutionism, the controlling analytical disposition was individualistic (notwithstanding the collectivist aspects of Spencer's sociology), instrumentalist, and rationalist, and tended towards ahistorical conflict models of society. By contrast, the European tradition, influenced by the powerful counter-Enlightenment, was characterized by collectivist, idealist, and historicist assumptions and inclined towards organic models of society. In addition, historians have frequently observed parallel ideological differences between the two traditions—for example, the former's possessive or egoistic individualism, moral utilitarianism, anti-statism, and competitive pluralism is in striking contrast to the latter's moral individualism, statism, and communitarianism. This work focuses upon the development of the European tradition, although my characterization differs somewhat from that of Parsons.

It is widely recognized that the combination of an emerging secular world-view and revolutions in the political, social, and economic orders in the eighteenth century represent the originating context of European social theory.[22] It follows that the proper starting point for any historical interpretation of social theory must be the Enlightenment. Unfortunately, our standard histories hold to a stereotyped view of the Enlightenment. This perspective may be stated succinctly. The Enlightenment initiated the project of modern social theory by conceiving of the possibility of applying scientific principles to the study of human affairs. However, the philosophes were primarily moral philosophers speculating about the natural origin and universal normative principles of social life; they were political activists and critics who subordinated rigorous empirical analysis to utopian reflection, social criticism, and the agitation for social change.[23] The philosophical and critical intentions of the philosophes, as reflected in the rationalistic and moral character of their thought, impeded the full emergence of a scientific social theory.[24] The excessive rationalism of Enlightenment social thought underscores its origin in the premises of social contract theory: atomistic individualism, mechanical determinism, uniformitarianism, and ahistorism. Though these contractarian premises underlie the Anglo-American social scientific tradition, the Enlightenment did not give rise to classical European social theory. In this reading, the classical European tradition, which features holism, idealism, and historicism, marks a decisive break from Enlightenment social thought and from the Anglo-American tradition—both of which are rooted in the premises of social contract theory.[25] The analytical origins of nineteenth-century European social theory, it is argued, lie in the counter-Enlightenment, whose holistic, idealistic, historicist, and anti-normative orientation form a proto-sociology.[26] Robert Nisbet is perhaps the strongest proponent of the thesis of the counter-Enlightenment origins of European social theory:

> The paradox of sociology . . . lies in the fact that although it falls, in its objectives and in the political and scientific values of its principal figures, in the mainstream of modernism, its essential concepts and its perspectives place it much closer, generally speaking, to philosophical conservatism. Community, authority, tradition, the sacred: these are primary conservative preoccupations in the age. . . . One will look in vain for significant impact of these ideas and presentiments on the serious interests of economists, political scientists, psychologists, and ethnologists in the age. But in sociology they are—transfigured of course, by rationalist or scientific *objectives* of the sociologists—at the very core of the discipline.[27]

This thesis is qualified in one crucial way: the materialism, rationalism, progressivism, and utopian and critical orientation of Marx is a continuation of the analytical project of the Enlightenment and therefore a fundamental departure from the main lines of development of the sociological tradition.[28]

Drawing on a revisionist line of Enlightenment historiography, proceeding from Dilthey through Meinecke, Cassirer, Gay, Crocker, and Ernest Becker, I reinterpret Enlightenment social thought. My thesis is that in addition to contractarianism there is a second current of Enlightenment social thought. Following a tradition of the time, I call this the "science of man." The science of man developed in the context of a critique of social contract theory and the holistic idealism of the Catholic tradition. As the philosophes abandoned social contract theory, they turned to the study of sociohistorical development as well as a general utilitarianism to legitimate the emerging liberal natural law tradition. It is in this turn to a more synthetic social theory, combining individualism and holism, materialism and idealism, rationalism and historicism, and science and critique, coupled to their shift towards a sociohistorical and utilitarian account and justification of liberal values, that we find the analytical origins of European social theory.[29]

The second and *the major concern* of this work is the ideological origins and development of European social theory. My discussion is directed against the thesis of the polarization of Marxism and sociology. This thesis is so entrenched in contemporary thought that it perpetuates the theoretical and practical isolation of Marxists and sociologists. Yet, as I will show, in its strong formulation the thesis is historically and theoretically wrong, and even in its weaker version it is misleading.[30]

The thesis of the polarization of Marxism and sociology is argued at a theoretical and historical level. Theoretically, the above thesis states the ideological and analytical opposition of Marxism and sociology. Streamlining the argument to its essential and common core, it is argued that Marxian social theory is at variance with sociological theory in the following, admittedly overdrawn, ways. Marxism is a dialectical and historical theory (asserting a dynamic unity between subject and object and theory and practice), while sociology is positivistic (subject-object and fact-value dualism) and disposed to ahistorical formalisms.[31] Marxism is "materialistic" in the sense of proceeding from the anatomy of the political economic structure to the social totality, whereas sociology is "idealistic" in its retreat from economics. It substitutes a focal concern for "superstructural" factors, particularly the role of common beliefs and values in history.[32] Marxism is a critical science (an *Oppositionswissenschaft*), in contrast to sociology, which is a science of order or a *Stabilisationswissenschaft*.[33] Marxism expresses the revolutionary interests of the working class, whereas sociology articulates the needs and interests of the middle classes.[34]

Underpinning these systematic differences between Marxism and sociology is an historical interpretation tracing their divergent intellectual lineages. Marxism and sociology, it is argued, have common intellectual roots in the Enlightenment. However, as they emerged and assumed their systematic form in the nineteenth century, they followed two distinct intellectual trajectories.[35] Marx's intellectual development is traced from the Enlightenment, particularly the critical and activist orientation of the materialists, to the utopian socialists, particularly Saint-Simon, who sustained the critical and scientific orientation of the philosophes. Finally, the scientific orientation was reinforced by the scientific rationalism of the bourgeois economists, while the critical side was further stimulated by the historico-critical idealism of the German idealists and Young Hegelians. Marxism is thus conceived as a unity of science and critique. Though sociology originates in the eighteenth century as well, it is the positivistic or noncritical aspects of the Enlightenment that are its true inheritance. Similarly, though Saint-Simon was a key figure in French sociology, it was his scientism and concern with moral order that was featured in sociology. The interest in moral order was reinforced by the formative and sustaining impact of the conservative and romantic reaction on sociology.[36] Thus, sociology reveals, as its essential standpoint, an uneasy balance between the scientific and liberal values of the Enlightenment and the implicit conservative disposition of its concepts and perspectives derived from the counter-Enlightenment. This pattern of differential development is considered the major axis for interpreting the history of social theory. The decisive historical juncture in the "binary fissure" of theory into Marxism and sociology was the industrial and French revolutions, which yielded a class system wherein ideological allegiances were divided between working-class revolution and the bourgeois liberal ideology of order.[37] The divergence between Marxism and sociology reflect the theoretical manifestations of the class and ideological divisions between the proletariat and the bourgeoisie.[38]

There are two qualifications to this thesis that make it resistant to the more obvious criticisms. First, the above thesis does not deny periods of dialogue and even cross-fertilization, for example, between 1890 and 1920 or in the 1960s. This dialogue and reciprocity, it is argued, does not substantially alter the essential differences between Marxism and sociology. Second, the fact that in its subsequent development Marxism has functioned as a conservative ideology signals its vulgarization and betrayal, not its core values and theoretical disposition.

Leaving aside the adequacy of these arguments, I offer an alternative line of criticism. I contend that Marx shares with sociology a common analytical program, stemming from their similar roots in the Enlightenment. The project of Marxism and sociology may be defined, in broad analytical terms, as the integration of materialism and idealism, individualism and holism, rationalism and historicism, and science and critique.[39] Interestingly enough, it is the contemporary Left, in search of a critical theory, that has pointed to and criticized the excessively bourgeois character of Marxian social theory as exhibited in its reductionist tendencies. This critique of Marxism has been made forcefully by the Frankfurt School, whose members perceive in the "latent positivism," instrumentalism, and the tendency towards economism the bourgeois makeup of Marxism.[40] Similarly, French theorists such as Jean Baudrillard, Jean-Joseph Goux, Gilles Deleuze, and Felix Guattari point to Marx's utilitarian concept of labor, his productivism and suppression of the symbolic, as well as his scientism as evidence that Marx ultimately capitulated to the bourgeois values and ideas that he claimed to oppose.[41] In pointing to convergences, I do not deny important divergences between Marx and particular sociologists at the level of epistemology and sociohistorical analysis.[42]

I insist, moreover, that it is a mistake to differentiate Marxism and sociology as representing an opposition between a revolutionary and a liberal ideology. Indeed, it is my principal contention that, while the liberal and revolutionary orthodoxies continued to find theoretical expression in the nineteenth century, Marx and the classical sociology of Durkheim and Weber sought to synthesize liberalism and revolution. Historians of Marxism have frequently observed that Marx shared with liberalism the belief that industrialism is the key to historical progress.[43] Developing this argument further, I hold that Marxian social theory had its roots in liberalism and exhibits a quite ambivalent position towards bourgeois society. Marx's advocacy of the revolutionary ideology of communism was intended to preserve the ideological core of liberalism, namely the doctrine of autonomy and democracy. We have not hitherto understood that in the European context of the late eighteenth and early nineteenth centuries, the revolutionary tradition referred to the French tradition, beginning with the Egalitarians and continued in Babouvism, Blanqui, Proudhon, and the anarcho-syndicalism of the Third Republic. Though Marx's encounter with the revolutionary tradition was formative, its anti-liberalism and anti-modernism were quite alien to him. In contrast to the French revolutionaries, for whom the revolutionary ideology was the antithesis to liberalism, Marx came to a revolutionary standpoint by working through and transcending the limitations of liberalism.

Our view of the sociology of Durkheim and Weber is no less in need of revision. Rather than perceiving classical sociology as a bourgeois response to Marxism and socialism, we must recognize that classical sociology incorporated into its ideological outlook a good deal of the critical and constructive project of the revolutionary tradition. Specifically, I argue that the absence of a strong democratic tradition in Germany led Weber, as well as Tönnies, Simmel, and the early Sombart, all of whom were aware of the shortcomings of liberalism but ideologically removed from philosophical conservatism and romantic anti-modernism, to adopt a positive attitude towards Marxism. In the German context, Marxism represented both a theoretical alternative to the idealist tradition of German *Wissenschaft* and a democratic alternative to Prussian conservatism and the anti-democratic liberalism of the middle classes. France, as I indicated above, had its own revolutionary tradition, which by the mid-nineteenth century had been integrated with at least one current of the liberal tradition to form a uniquely French democratic tradition. Durkheim falls squarely within this French democratic tradition.

My contention that Marxism and sociology sought to fuse liberalism and revolution is connected to what is ultimately the organizing theme of this work: whereas Anglo-American social theory emerged as part of the triumph of liberal civilization, European social theory was elaborated in the context of the failure of liberalism and developed, in part, as its critique. Though the reasons accounting for this historical divergence are complex, we may single out the persistence of powerful sociocultural traditions and strata in France and Germany that were hostile to modern civilization. This created a culture of bourgeois opposition, which generated ideological traditions betraying an anti-liberal and anti-modernist disposition—for example, conservatism, romanticism, and the French revolutionary tradition. We do not deny, of course, the establishment of a liberal tradition in France and Germany. However, the continued strength of the church, the landed aristocracy, hierarchical and statist traditions, and an educated and cultural elite rooted in aristocratic values, and the related persistence of oppositional ideologies, resulted in a weak and defensive liberal tradition.[44] In other words, we find in France and Germany a social and cultural milieu that supported and valued ideologies opposed to liberalism and bourgeois society.

It is in this context of the failure of liberalism and a widespread social and ideological opposition to it that Marxism and sociology originate. Specifically, the social theory of Marx, Durkheim, and Weber proceeds from a two-sided perception. On the one hand, they believe that liberal society is a progressive movement in Western history to the extent that it articulates the idea of individual freedom and creates the conditions of its realization. Accordingly, they repudiate the one-dimensional critiques of liberalism advanced by oppositional ideologies. On the other hand, they recognize that the oppositional ideologies have underscored substantial deficiencies in liberal civilization. Thus, we find this critical posture towards liberalism articulated in the concepts of alienation, anomie, and reification. However, the critique of liberalism and bourgeois society by Marxism and sociology—unlike that by conservatives, romantics, and French revolutionaries—was founded upon liberal values and modernist presuppositions. The intention of Marx, Durkheim, and Weber was to preserve the progressive heritage of liberalism while reconstructing it.

The Dilemma of European Liberalism

Defined in general terms as concern with the individual, liberalism appears as the distinctive tradition of the Occident.[45] However, this position is misleading. First, a number of historians and social thinkers, beginning perhaps with Hegel and including Marx, Durkheim, Henry Sumner Maine, and, more recently, Bruno Snell, Isaiah Berlin, Eric Havelock, and Colin Morris, have argued that the concept of the autonomous individual or modern subjectivity is substantially lacking in the Graeco-Roman and Christian epochs.[46] Thus, though a process of individuation is apparent in the Graeco-Roman and Christian periods, the concept of the individual was still quite undeveloped. Second, it is incorrect to identify liberalism with individuation. Individualism can assume diverse forms, some quite illiberal, as, for example, the corporate individualism of German idealism.[47] It seems necessary, therefore, to restrict the notion of liberalism to a uniquely modern ideological tradition.

The distinguishing feature of liberalism as a world-view is the value placed upon individual freedom, whether defined as freedom from coercion, as moral self-determination, or as the right to individual happiness.[48] Liberals have sought to defend individual freedom through a variety of idioms—for example, the doctrine of natural rights (Locke), utilitarianism (Bentham), moral idealism (Kant), historicism (early Humboldt), or fallibilism (Mill). Linked to this core liberal value is the argument that the realization of individual freedom presupposes a condition of sociocultural and political pluralism. Pluralism refers to the idea that the maintenance of individual freedom implies an institutional condition of competition and conflict. The gravest threat to freedom is monopoly and absolutism, which suppress self-determination with external coercion; which suppress competition and diversity in a regimented and uniform order; and which substitute authoritarian means for conflict and consensus as the primary problem-solving mechanisms.

Liberalism arose as a reaction against a static hierarchical and absolutist order, which suppressed individual freedom. Liberals sought a program of social reconstruction founded upon their pluralistic and voluntaristic theory of institutions. However, the economic, political, and cultural terms in which classical liberalism was specified reveal its limited articulation of individual freedom. A few examples must suffice to illustrate my point. Liberals in the eighteenth and early nineteenth centuries uniformly agreed that, given what they perceived as the voluntary, pluralistic, and dynamic nature of capitalism, private property was a necessary condition of individual liberty. They failed to grasp what became the core of the socialist critique, namely that the other side to the voluntarism, competition, and dynamism of capitalism was heteronomy for the laborers and the poor, and a developmental process towards monopoly and static hierarchy. Or, to take another example, liberals clearly recognized that individual freedom implies a democratic social order. Yet, almost uniformly, classical liberals not only restricted political rights to the propertied or educated but opposed extending equality into the social and economic spheres. Again, they did not perceive that freedom without equality and a program of social justice translates into the very type of static, hierarchical, and absolutist order they initially opposed. As a final example of the limited specification of the liberal principle of individual freedom, there is the struggle for voluntarism in the cultural sphere associated with the idea of toleration. Toleration, which was initially a struggle for religious freedom (Locke) and later a struggle for free thought (Kant) and individuality (Mill), was linked to the doctrine of fallibilism. However, as is well known, liberals were not hesitant to impose severe censorship laws. Thus, Locke, after arguing for religious toleration, denies the same to atheists and, in effect, excludes all dissent that criticizes the core social institutions and the political status quo. Kant was prepared to suppress public debate as long as academic freedoms were safeguarded. It was precisely these limitations on toleration that justified the suppression of democratic working-class movements during the nineteenth century.

The economic, political, and cultural terms in which liberalism was specified were inconsistent with the general claims attached to the principle of individual freedom. There inheres in liberalism an uneasy balance of universalism and particularism, and this points to what I call the liberal dilemma. Given its universalistic claims, liberalism represents a critique of unnecessary and nonconsensual constraints upon individual freedom. However, this universalistic disposition of liberalism is belied by its specific ideological form, which not only imposes formal restrictions on freedom but projects a nonconsensual authoritative structure of domination. This contradiction, I believe, reflects the interpenetration of bourgeois class interests and liberal ideology. My point is not that liberalism's universalistic claims are a mere subterfuge for particular class interests. Rather, I hold, that in its mix of universalism and particularism, liberalism discloses, on the one hand (expressing its universalistic aspect) a tendency of transcendence, and, on the other hand (expressing its particularism) a tendency to function as a legitimation of class domination. Specifically, its universalism projects an egalitarian and democratic order, which implies a critique of bourgeois society; yet, because liberalism legitimates bourgeois class interests, its particularistic nature tends to render it an ideology of order.[49] In the course of the nineteenth century, these tensions were manifested, on the one hand, by liberalism's transformation into a conservative ideology of class domination and, on the other, by attempts to preserve its universalistic and critical core by reconstruction and supersession.

By the mid-nineteenth century, European liberalism was discredited as a progressive practice and ideology. In France and Germany, liberal parties were allied with the forces of traditional conservatism in opposition to the democratic demands of the propertyless for equal political, civil, and social rights.[50] Highlighting the triumph of particularism in liberal ideology in the second half of the nineteenth century was its ideological simplification, manifested in so-called vulgar economics, Social Darwinism, and various forms of mechanical materialism. In general, throughout the nineteenth century in France and Germany, liberal doctrine suffered a massive assault on its analytical premises, social theory, and as a political ideology. It is in the context of this critique and reconstruction of liberalism that Marxism and classical sociology originate.

The critique and reconstruction of liberalism occurred along three dimensions. First, the liberal interpretation of Western history articulated in the later phases of the Enlightenment, as the progressive unfolding of liberty propelled by scientific enlightenment and culminating in the "end of history" was revealed as a self-serving bourgeois myth.[51] Moreover, the liberal analysis of modern society as a contractual society of individual voluntary exchanges and associations was directly refuted by the development of monopolistic enterprises, bureaucracy, state intervention, etc. Second, the rationalist and individualistic presuppositions of liberal social theory, particularly classical economics but also liberal political theory, were discredited from a variety of theoretical and ideological perspectives as an inadequate foundation for social science. By the end of the nineteenth century, liberalism was no longer seriously considered as a theory of history or social theory; liberalism stood or fell as a normative theory of individual freedom. Even in this regard, however, the defense of individual liberty by recourse to a version of natural rights doctrine or utilitarianism or evolutionary theory had lost its credibility and legitimating power. The paradox of European liberalism is that at the moment of its practical triumph, if one can speak of such in Germany, classical liberal doctrine had few supporters even among the middle classes. The alignment of liberal theory and practice required a revision and transcendence of orthodoxy. Though by no means alone in this project, Marx, Durkheim, and Weber represent three momentous efforts at liberal reconstruction and transcendence.

This book is divided into four parts. Part One furnishes the details of my interpretation of the early history of European social theory. The three subsequent parts feature my interpretation of the fate of liberalism in the social theory of Marx, Durkheim, and Weber. The conclusion recapitulates the polemical context and some results of my research. As a final note, this work is written with the conviction that, in the present climate of ideological dogmatism and technocratic instrumentalism, there is a "third way." I speak, of course, of liberalism, with its tradition of individualism, pluralism, and secularism, coupled with and fortified by the revolutionary tradition, with its utopianism, communitarianism, and vision of a just and democratic society.

Part One
The Origins of
European Social Theory

1. *The Enlightenment*

MY INTERPRETATION OF the intellectual formation of modern social theory begins with a consideration of the Enlightenment.[1] On the basis of a revised conception of the Enlightenment, I argue that the main lines of development of European social theory proceed from the Enlightenment "science of man." I elaborate the analytical presuppositions of Enlightenment social theory. In addition, I define the ideological aspects of Enlightenment social theory by connecting the movement towards science to the articulation of a liberal world-view.

The Enlightenment advanced a critique of the fundamental assumptions of social contract theory. Regarding the contractarian premise of a pre-social natural man, the philosophes substituted the notion that we are by nature social or, as Montesquieu said, "formed to live in society."[2] Responding to the contractarian elements in Rousseau's early "Discourses," Voltaire maintained: "I do not think this solitary life, which our forefathers are supposed to have led, is in human nature."[3] Instead, Voltaire maintained: "The foundation of society ever existing, there has therefore ever been some society. . . ."[4] Similarly, Hume spoke critically of the "philosophical fiction of the [pre-social] state of nature," and declared: "Men are necessarily born in a family-society. . ."[5];

or again: "Human nature cannot by any means subsist without the association of individuals."[6] Unlike contract theory, which assumes an antinomy between natural man and artificial society, the philosophes sought a perspective which asserted the social nature of the individual.

By advancing the notion of the interpenetration of the individual and society, the philosophes developed the beginnings of a theory of socialization. In contrast to contract theory, which viewed society as a negative force suppressing our natural reason, Voltaire, for instance, underscored the decay of our reason in an asocial context: "Whosoever lived absolutely alone, would soon lose the faculty of thinking and expressing himself; he would be a burden to himself, and it would only remain to metamorphose him into a beast."[7] Hume made a similar point regarding moral development: "Were all society and intercourse cut off between man and man, . . . it seems evident, that so solitary a being would be as much incapable of justice, as of social discourse and conversation."[8] Finally, in the social theory of Adam Ferguson, disciple of Hume and Montesquieu,[9] we find a highly advanced statement of a theory of socialization:

> From society are derived not only the force, but the very existence of man's happiest emotions; not only the better part, but almost the whole of his rational character. Send him to the desert alone, he is a plant torn from its root: the form indeed may remain, but every faculty droops and withers; the human personage and the human character cease to exist.[10]

We are, the philosophes argued, born and subsist in society. Though the Enlightenment did not develop the details of a social psychological theory of internalization, it is clear that their view of the individual becoming human in society was a major departure from contractarianism with its antinomy of natural pre-social man and external society.

The philosophes not only pointed to our social nature but, in their critique of the atomistic individualism of contractarianism, pointed to a concept of society as something more than the summation of separate self-subsisting individuals. In *The Spirit of the Laws*, Montesquieu articulated a holistic view of society; the individual is considered only as a member of a group or institution, which, in turn, is analyzed as a reality *sui generis*. The critique of atomistic individualism is evident as well in the thought of Hume when, for example, he objects to representing social life as an aggregate of solitary individuals: "I cannot forbear condemning this sentiment, and should be sorry to think, that human affairs admit of not greater stability, than what they receive from the casual humours and characters of particular men."[11] Hume proceeded to draw attention to the structural aspects of society: "So great is the force of laws, and of particular forms of governments, and so little dependence have they on the humours and tempers of men, that consequences . . . may sometimes be deduced from them. . . ."[12] Building upon the social theory of Montesquieu and Hume, Ferguson stated this theme in a more direct fashion: "Mankind are to be taken in groups, as they have always subsisted. The history of the individual is but a detail of the sentiments and the thoughts he has entertained in the view of his species: and every experiment relative to this subject should be made with entire societies, not with single men."[13] In the view of the philosophes, human nature is social. Society is a positive agency in the formation of the cognitive and moral capacities of the individual. Finally, society must be viewed as an association of individuals from which emerge group-specific properties, which can be analytically studied as the subject-matter of a special humanistic or social science.

By adopting the perspective of the individual-in-society, the Enlightenment science of man disavowed the aim of contract theory as that of elaborating a universally valid, ideal social order. Condorcet, for example, viewed modern contract theory as an extension of the *a priori* rationalistic systems of the ancients: "Hobbes imitated Plato, in deducing from certain general principles a plan for a whole system of social order and in constructing a model to which all practice was supposed to conform."[14] It is not, of course, that the Enlightenment disclaimed moral law or repudiated a critical attitude. The philosophes were committed, as I have said, to natural law. However, they distinguished between universal moral laws and their diverse concrete realizations in positive law and social institutions. The philosophes maintained that these universal laws had to be fitted to the unique natural and social conditions of specific societies. Montesquieu provided an exemplary statement of this blend of rationalism and historicism:

> Law in general is human reason, inasmuch as it governs all inhabitants of the earth: the political and civil laws of each nation ought to be only the particular cases in which human reason is applied. They should be adapted in such a manner to the people for whom they are framed that it should be a great chance if those of one nation suit another. They should be in relation to the nature and principle of each government. . . .
>
> They should be in relation to the climate of each country, to the quality of its soil, to its situation and extent, to the principal occupation of the natives. . . . They should have relation to the degrees of liberty which the constitution will bear; to the religion of the inhabitants, to their inclinations, riches, numbers, commerce, manners, and customs.[15]

Even Condillac, the so-called archetype of Enlightenment rationalism, insisted that the application of moral laws be mediated by knowledge of particular sociohistorical conditions.

> In order to make a system, . . . he [the legislator] should not seek the most perfect government in his imagination. . . . He must study the character of the people, investigate their usages and customs. . . . Then he will preserve what is found to be good, and replace what is found to be bad, but only by means which conform most to the *moeurs* of the citizens.[16]

We, as humans, are by nature social. Furthermore, the structure of a particular society is contingent upon natural and historical conditions. Thus, principles of moral law have to be flexible in their application and accord with the historical singularity of social life. Following this line of reasoning, the philosophes could be critical, in the sense of preserving a transcendent standard, and yet remain sensitive to historical particularity.

The Methodological Critique of Contract Theory and Historiography: Towards an Integration of Rationalism and Empiricism

To the extent that the idea of natural man is a conjectural or imaginative construct, social contract theory proceeded by means of introspection. In the "Author's Introduction" to *Leviathan*, Hobbes stated this methodological principle of introspection. On the basis of the uniformity of human nature, "whosoever looketh into himself, and considereth what he doth, when he does *think, opine, reason, hope, fear,* . . . he shall thereby read and know, what are the thoughts and passions of all other men. . . ."[17] Introspection, according to contract theory, yields a concept of human nature, which, in turn, is the basis for elaborating a general theory of the origins and nature of society. Contract theory is therefore rationalistic in that its main aim is to specify universal principles deduced from *a priori* reason. The rationalistic structure of contract theory implies a disregard for the historical record or, more generally, empirical sources. In his early "Discourses" which bear the imprint of contractarianism, Rousseau underscored the rationalist premises of contract theory: "Let us begin, then, by laying all facts aside, as they do not affect the question."[18]

The Enlightenment science of man reacted against the excessive rationalism of contract theory. Adam Ferguson, echoing the sentiments of most philosophes, wrote:

> Among the various qualities which mankind possess, we select one or a few particulars on which to establish a theory, and in framing our account of what man was in some imaginary state of nature, we overlook what he has always appeared within the reach of our own observation and in the records of history.[19]

In opposition to contract theory, Ferguson recommended an empirical study of human affairs founded upon "the character of man, as he now exists."[20] The commitment to a form of social analysis based upon empirical sources was derived, in the main, from the developing tradition of a narrative and "fact-critical" historiography. Though the philosophes criticized historiography, it was a positive critique. They attacked historiography for its narrow preoccupation with political and military events and, more generally, for its lack of sociological insight.[21] Nevertheless, the tradition of historiography conferred on the philosophes a respect for facticity and critical-historical scholarship. "We demand today," proposed Voltaire, "more minute details, facts more completely authenticated, exact dates, precise authorities. . . ."[22] The Enlightenment science of man emerged in the context of a two-pronged critique of the rationalist legacy of contract theory and the empiricist tradition of narrative historiography.

At the level of epistemology, the aim of the Enlightenment science of man was to develop a *new conceptual ordering of human affairs*. We must recall that historiography and contract theory are specific ways of constituting or conceiving the realm of human affairs. Historiography singles out the unique historic "event" as its rudimentary unit of analysis and employs "narration" as the means to achieve conceptual order. On the other side, contract theory abandons the historical record and asserts a "natural order" accessible to pure or *a priori* reason. The science of man sought to integrate the concern for facticity and historical particularity of historiography with the theoretical orientation of contract theory.

By way of documenting this thesis, we may single out the formulations of Montesquieu and Hume—both of whom set the standards for the Enlightenment science of man. In *The Spirit of the Laws*, we can discern a deliberate effort by Montesquieu to mediate between the empiricism of historiography and the rationalism of contract theory. Human affairs, Montesquieu argued, can be ordered "by discovering principles or models which form an immediate level between meaningless diversity [empiricism] and a scheme which is universally valid [rationalism]."[23] Models—what we today call typological concepts—form a conceptual order combining facticity and historical particularity with the generalizing theoretical interest of contract theory. In principle, type concepts or models can be developed at different levels of generality— embracing the historically unique configuration as well as processes common to diverse historic societies.

Turning to Hume, we find a similar attempt to articulate a science of man which integrates empiricism and rationalism. In *A Treatise on Human Nature*, Hume suggested the idea of an experimental science of man. On the basis of a "cautious observation of human life," and "where experiments . . . are judiciously collected and compared," Hume concludes, "we may hope to establish . . . a science [of man]. . . ."[24] In Hume's view, the science of man proceeds from the observation of particular effects, observed in different situations, to experimentation which establishes general principles or laws of cause-effect relations. Hume made it clear that these general principles must be empirically grounded: "And though we must endeavor to render all our principles as universal as possible, . . . it is still certain we cannot go beyond experience. . . ."[25]

Prior to the Enlightenment, human studies were divided between the empiricism of historiography and the rationalism of contract theory, or, to put it in more contemporary terms, between empirical research and theory.[26] Historiography lacked a theoretical interest, while contract theory lacked an empirical foundation. Moreover, to the extent that historiography rested upon the aesthetic principle of narration and contract theory operated according to an introspective methodology, knowledge of human affairs was subjective. At this epistemological level, the Enlightenment science of man was a decisive breakthrough to the modern idea of social science. The science of man provided a conceptualization of human affairs that integrated empiricism and rationalism, or fact and theory. By developing modes of empirical generalization such as models, type concepts, casual analysis, and experimentation, the Enlightenment made social inquiry into a public or intersubjective form of systematic knowledge.

The Object and Aim of
the Enlightenment Science of Man

What, then, was the nature of the Enlightenment science of man? In *The Spirit of the Laws,* Montesquieu specified the object of the science of man: "I have first of all considered mankind . . . amidst . . . an infinite diversity of laws and manners."[27] The science of man, as Voltaire indicated in his *Essay on the Manners and Spirit of Nations,* was to be a universal historical inquiry. "For the first time," Condorcet declared, "man knew the globe that he inhabited, was able to study in all countries the human race modified by nature and social institutions."[28] The Enlightenment science of man posed as its object *all the peoples of the earth, from antiquity to modernity, from East to West.* Furthermore, the science of man was to study *all spheres of the social life of man*—economy, polity, social structure, and culture. In his "Discourse on Universal History," Turgot claimed: "This universal history encompasses . . . the early beginnings of mankind; the formation and intermingling of nations; the origin of governments and their revolutions; the progress of language, of natural philosophy, of morals, of manners, of the arts and sciences."[29] The science of man proposed to study human nature as it developed and assumed diverse forms in history.

The aim of the science of man can be stated in the form of two related problems. First, the problem of social development: how to account for the historic differences in sociocultural development. In the *Preliminary Discourse to the Encyclopedia of Diderot,* d'Alembert stated the problem of social development:

> How men, having separated into various great families, so to speak, have formed diverse societies, how these different so-

cieties have given birth to different types of governments, and how they have tried to distinguish themselves both by the laws that they have given themselves and by the particular signs that each has created in order that its members might communicate more easily with one another.[30]

In addition to the sociological problem of social development, the science of man posed the anthropological problem of human nature: to discover the common properties or the "natural" basis of the unity of mankind. One of the chief aims of the science of man, wrote Hume, "is . . . to discover the constant and universal principles of human nature, by showing men in all varieties of circumstances and situations, and furnishing us with materials, from which we may form our observations, and become acquainted with the regular springs of human action and behavior."[31] The science of man was conceived as a comprehensive study of the constant and variable elements of the human condition.[32]

This twofold project presupposed a distinction between humans as natural and as social beings. As natural beings, there is a certain uniformity and constancy to our actions. As sociocultural beings, human affairs partake of a remarkable diversity. As Hume stated the matter: "There is a general course of nature in human actions as well as in the operation of the sun and the climate. There are also characters peculiar to different nations and particular persons."[33] Regarding this dialectic of natural unity and sociocultural diversity, Voltaire argued:

> It is clear that everything which belongs intimately to human nature is the same from one end of the universe to the other; that everything that depends on custom is different. . . . The empire of custom is much more vast than that of nature; it extends over manners and all usages, it sheds variety on the scene of the universe; nature sheds unity there; she establishes everywhere a small number of invariable principles. Thus, the basis is everywhere the same, and culture produces diverse fruits.[34]

The philosophes maintained that human beings participate in a natural and sociocultural order, which gives to experience an aspect of constancy and uniformity as well as diversity. Within the sociocultural order itself, the philosophes asserted that, although there is diversity and change, there is sufficient regularity to permit a science of man.[35]

The doctrine of the malleability of human nature underlies the distinction between our natural and social sides. In effect, the philosophes maintained that human beings have, as it were, an opening or natural disposition to diversify. Montesquieu referred to humankind as that "flexible being"; even more pointedly, Hume declared: "Man is a very variable being, and susceptible of many different opinions, principles, and rules of conduct."[36] Because human beings exhibit an essential nature in the form of structural constancies and uniformities of experience as well as sociocultural variation, the science of man may be defined, more or less, as a structural and cultural study of history.

Two Strains of Enlightenment Social Theory: Instrumentalism and Multidimensionality

Enlightenment social theory evolved in the context of a reaction against Christianity. An important aspect of the philosophes' attack upon Christian dogma was their critique of its pessimistic view of human nature. The philosophes replaced the doctrine of original sin with the notion of a primeval amoral human nature. An individual, Voltaire reasoned, is "born neither good nor wicked; education, example, the government into which he is thrown—in short, occasion of every kind—determines him to virtue or vice."[37] In addition, the philosophes substituted a positive view of our nonlogical side—human passions, desire, will, and sensuality—for the negative beliefs of Christian dogma.[38] In direct opposition to the Christian tradition, Voltaire argued that the passions are "the principal cause of the order we see today in the world."[39]

In a similarly defiant vein, Diderot asserted: "It is the passions alone . . . that can elevate the soul to great things."[40] In their reaction against the ascetic anti-naturalism of Christianity, the philosophes sought to integrate into their concept of human nature the nonlogical component.

Though the concern with nonlogical motivations was characteristic of the philosophes, they developed two theoretical ways of treating nonlogical action. We must distinguish two analytical strains—instrumentalism and multi-dimensionality—which are related to two divergent metaphysics of human nature: materialism and dualism. From Hobbes and Spinoza through Mandeville, La Mettrie, Holbach, Helvétius, Bentham, and the classical economists, we find a dominant current of analytical instrumentalism linked to a materialist metaphysic. Regarding this materialist conception of human nature, Holbach wrote:

> Man is a being purely physical: the moral man is only this physical being considered under a certain point of view. . . . His visible actions as well as the invisible motions internally excited, deriving from his will or thoughts, are equally the natural and necessary consequences of his peculiar mechanism. . . .[41]

From this materialist standpoint, the nonlogical sources of motivation are identified with organic drives and instincts, such as self-preservation or sexual need. Human conduct is viewed as a consequence of fixed principles that are built into our material nature and operate according to a hedonist psychology. Of this strict natural determinism, Bentham said: "Nature has placed mankind under the governance of two sovereign masters, *pain* and *pleasure*. . . . They govern us in all we do, in all we say, in all we think. . . ."[42] By explaining human action as a process of adaptation to either internal conditions of human nature (instincts, drives) or constraining external conditions (the competitive mechanism of the market), the voluntary and expressive aspect of human experience is entirely suppressed. Following a recent tradition in social theory, I call this model of social action analytical instrumentalism.

Paralleling the current of materialism running from Hobbes through the eighteenth century is a dualistic view of human nature. Although dualism has religious roots in Christianity, there is a secular tradition proceeding, on the one hand, from Shaftesbury and Hutcheson, and, on the other hand, from the humanistic French tradition, for example, Montaigne and Bayle. Like the materialists, the dualists sought, not always successfully, to return to the natural basis of our spiritual existence without, however, eliminating moral autonomy.[43] Montesquieu proposed the following combination of naturalism and idealism: "Man, as a physical being is like other bodies governed by invariable laws. As an intelligent being he incessantly transgresses the laws ... and changes those of his own instituting. He is left to his private direction. ..."[44] In a letter to Condorcet, Turgot enunciates in no uncertain terms his opposition to all mechanistic forms of materialism:

> I do not wish to investigate how pleasure and pain, desire and aversion, influence the determination of the will. I merely state that we find in experience only one principle productive of movement, and that is the will of intelligent beings which is not primitively determined but which determines itself, not by motions but by motives, not by mechanical causes but according to *final causes*. I maintain that these feeling, thinking, and willing beings, proposing their own ends and choosing their own means, constitute an order as real and as certain as that of entities considered purely material and agitated by purely mechanical causes.[45]

It was Kant, above all, who stated and ultimately offered the most forceful argument for the duality of human nature:

> In meditating on the nature of man, I thought I discovered two distinct principles; one of which raised him to study of eternal truths, to the love of justice and moral beauty, to the regions

of the intellectual world whose contemplation is the delight of the sage, the other of which lowered him into himself, enslaved him to the empire of the senses, to the passions which are their ministers and through them frustrated all that the first feelings inspired in him.[46]

The rise of materialism in the eighteenth century was vigorously opposed by the majority of philosophes, who sought to uphold a secular theory of moral autonomy.[47]

This dualistic view of human nature had important consequences for Enlightenment social theory. Because we are both physical and moral beings, the science of man had to consider both the "material" (or structural) and "ideal" (or voluntary) factors implicated in human conduct. A satisfactory account of human affairs had to refer, on the one hand, to the material conditions constraining social action, and, on the other, to the internal relation between the "free" individual and a symbolic world of moral order, beauty, and truth. I call this synthesis of instrumentalism and "voluntarism" a multidimensional model of social action.[48] My contention is that the philosophes began the difficult task of translating a dualistic view of human nature into a multidimensional social theory.

The beginnings of a multidimensional theory can be seen in Montesquieu's *The Spirit of the Laws*. In characterizing the different types of societies, Montesquieu distinguished between a materialistic component—the number of people, climatic and topographical conditions, division of labor, economic development—and an idealist aspect, the cultural system of a society. In determining the conditions necessary to sustain a republic, for instance, Montesquieu included, on the materialist side, a small population, close physical proximity, or simple division of labor, and, on the idealist side, a "virtuous" citizenry, i.e., a populace embued with strong patriotic values, the "spirit" of public service, self-denial, and moral probity. In an important programmatic formulation, which indicates the commitment to multidimensionality but, at the same time, its nonsystematic character, Montesquieu stated: "Mankind are influenced by various causes: by the climate, by the religion, by the laws, by the maxims of government, by precedents, morals, and customs; whence is formed a general spirit of nations."[49] The idea of cultural idealism as a counterbalance to materialism is found in Voltaire's historical inquiry into the "spirit and customs of men" as well as in Hume's focus upon the "spirit of the age."[50] Regarding Voltaire, one commentator writes:

> For whilst Voltaire is becoming more deterministic, another concept is also becoming increasingly important in his historical writing: the concept of custom or opinion.
>
> Under this heading he includes all the views, feelings, and beliefs of men which cannot be shown to be determined either by man's moral nature or by his physical situation. . . . The concept is one which arises naturally as a reaction against the general deterministic tendency of Enlightenment historiography, and it is also to be found in Hume.[51]

It must be emphasized that I am not saying that the Enlightenment achieved a satisfactory theoretical synthesis of materialism and idealism. In the social theory of Holbach and Helvétius, as well as in the emerging economic doctrines of the physiocrats and the classical economists, there is, as Talcott Parsons has demonstrated, a pronounced strain of methodological individualism and analytical instrumentalism.[52] In fact, these premises dominated the nineteenth-century theoretical tradition of Anglo-American social science. However, my contention is that many of the philosophes reacted against analytical individualism and instrumentalism, and it is in this alternative theoretical tradition that we find the beginnings of a multidimensional social theory. It is these latter strains of Enlightenment social thought that, through the mediation of the counter-Enlightenment, form the point of departure of classical European social theory.

From Science to a Modern-Liberal World View

The Enlightenment science of man is a major breakthrough in social science. In its critique of contract theory, the Enlightenment reoriented the focus of human studies from questions regarding the origins of society and the ideal social order to an empirically oriented inquiry combining a sociological interest in sociocultural development and an anthropological interest in the structure of human nature. To the extent that contract theory was integral to the movement of modern rationalism associated with Descartes, Leibniz, and Spinoza, the critique of contract theory implied a more general critique of rationalism. The philosophes, I will argue, saw in modern rationalism a disposition towards intellectual closure and dogmatism, not unlike that of dogmatic religions. Science, with its empirical, fallibilist, and therefore "open" character, was interpreted as inherently critical and resonant with liberal values. The commitment to science was connected to the philosophes' ideological struggle for a modern and liberal order. In this final section, I want to shift the discussion to an ideological level and propose a broad interpretation of the originating ideological context of Enlightenment social theory.

In the view of the philosophes, the commitment to an empirically based science of man and nature implied a commitment to critical reason. The truth of all opinions, beliefs, and traditions was to be examined in light of the twin canons of science: experience and analytical-experimental reason. Science was therefore a critical enterprise, and, in more general terms, it was precisely the idea of critique that defined the Age of the Enlightenment.[53] Expressing the spirit of the Enlightenment, Kant wrote: "Our age is, in special degree, the age of criticism, and to criticism everything must submit."[54] Although the critics of the Enlightenment imputed to Enlightenment criticism a wholly negative and destructive intent, in fact, critique had a double sense: to tear down and rebuild, to destroy and construct. To grasp the project of the Enlightenment, we must examine the dual meaning of critique.

What was the target of the critical reasoning of the Enlightenment? To put the matter in somewhat schematic form, the Enlightenment opposed the organization of conduct and knowledge into closed and dogmatic systems. The philosophes maintained that practical and theoretical closure fosters intolerance, fanaticism, and authoritarianism.[55] The philosophes singled out two contemporary forms of closure and dogmatism: metaphysical systems and the Judeo-Christian tradition.

Contrary to the myth of the Enlightenment as the Age of Reason, the philosophes were actually tireless critics of those metaphysical systems characteristic of the Western intellectual tradition. Time and time again, the philosophes observed, philosophers, including their own immediate predecessors, Descartes and Leibniz, attempted to construct inclusive metaphysical systems founded upon "self-evident" principles or *a priori* reason. This "spirit of system," as the philosophes designated this form of bad metaphysics, yields only error, myth, superstition, and intellectual despotism. "Abstract philosophy," Hume wrote, is "the inevitable source of uncertainty and error." Metaphysics, he continued, "arises either from the fruitless efforts of human vanity . . . or from the craft of popular superstitions, [and] . . . lie[s] in wait to break in upon every unguarded avenue of the mind, and overwhelm it with religious fears and prejudices."[56] In the view of the philosophes, the "spirit of system" is inseparable from the creation of myth and superstition—both of which perpetuate ignorance and domination.

In place of the "spirit of system," with its unsupported hypotheses, imaginative constructions, and metaphysical abstractions, the philosophes advocated a return to knowledge of general principles based upon sense evidence, facts, analysis, and experimentation. This "systematic spirit," as the philosophes called their fusion of rationalism and empiricism,[57] implied the limitations of human reason.[58] Reason, the philosophes argued, could yield certainty only by remaining within the realm of sense experience. In this regard, Kant was simply reflecting the "systematic spirit" when he asserted the inability of "pure" reason to acquire certainty concerning the most basic metaphysical problems: the existence and knowledge of God, the immortality of the soul, and free will. Instead of constructing closed metaphysical systems, the philosophes called for an inquiry into the scope and powers of the human mind.

The philosophes repudiated the assumption of a transparently ordered universe fully accessible to the powers of the human mind.[59] Moreover, the attempt by pure reason or the imagination to go beyond the limits of the human understanding—i.e., to penetrate to first principles, final causes, and ultimate meanings—invariably leads to error, myth, and dogmatism. Accordingly, the philosophes abandoned the efforts of reason to articulate an inclusive and closed system of knowledge.

The Enlightenment waged a war on two fronts: against the "spirit of system" represented especially by modern rationalism; and against religion, particularly Catholicism. Although modern rationalism tended towards intellectual closure and dogmatism, the philosophes expended most of their critical energies on religion. This was so for two reasons. First, metaphysical systems were, in the main, confined to small groups of philosophers, whereas religion had mass appeal and influence. Second, the philosophes could refer to the actual history of religion for documentation of the "evils" of closure and dogmatism.[60]

From this perspective, the philosophes' critique of the particular doctrines of Christianity—original sin, immortality of the soul, miracles—represented a fundamental criticism of Christianity as a closed and dogmatic system. The world as represented by Christianity was a cosmos: human beings, nature, and the divine were integrated into a finite, hierarchical, and harmonious world order, wherein each being had a fixed place and purpose. The church hierarchy transmitted the revealed word of God—the cosmic order—to the general society in the form of a complete deductive system or casuistry of ethics, politics, and social practice. The philosophes did not oppose the ethical or spiritual core of Christianity. In fact, aside from certain materialists, they upheld the need for some form of metaphysical belief or "natural" religion.[61] Kant, we recall, criticized the pretensions of pure reason to acquire certainty, but viewed metaphysics and religion as necessary modes of thinking and belief.[62] Even more pointedly, d'Alembert recognized the need for a transcendentally anchored ethic:

> Thus, nothing is more necessary than a revealed religion. . . . Designed to serve as a supplement to natural knowledge, it restricts itself to the things which are absolutely necessary for us to know. The rest is closed for us and apparently will be forever. A few truths to be believed, a small number of precepts to be practiced; such are the essentials to which revealed Religion is reduced.[63]

The philosophes opposed the closed and dogmatic character of Christianity, which, in their view, sanctioned hierarchy and an authoritarian social order.

In the final instance, the philosophes embraced critical-scientific reason as a means to destroy intellectual closure and dogmatism. But to what positive and constructive end did the philosophes engage in critique and science? Diderot stated the goal of critique as follows: "to change the general way of thinking."[64] The Enlightenment proposed to affect a change from closed systems of thought—metaphysics and dogmatic religion—to an "open" mode of reasoning (science) that incorporated such liberal values as tolerance, criticism, and consensus based upon rational discussion. This new form of reason was to be open to the degree that it rested upon premises such as the limits of the human mind, the empirical basis of knowledge, and uncertainty in ultimate questions. There is, however, a more elementary aspect to the Enlightenment critique of closure and dogmatism. Underlying the critique of closed systems is the idea that their dogmatic character reflects cosmological presuppositions. To the extent that the world is viewed as an ordered cosmos, fully accessible to reason or revelation, to that extent there evolves completely closed and dogmatic systems. In this regard, we can see that implicit in the structure of Enlightenment criticism of closed systems is an attack upon cosmological presuppositions, i.e., external fixity, finiteness, hierarchy, and teleology. In place of cosmological presuppositions, the philosophes sought an alternative configuration of presuppositions or a world-view that coincided with their commitment to liberal values. These world-defining presuppositions I call secularism.

The notion of a secular order is the antithesis of the idea of a cosmic order.[65] Moreover, each of these concepts is related to a contrasting type of sociocultural order. Cosmological presuppositions underlie a "conservative" value configuration and, more generally, are linked to a "traditional" type of society. Secular presuppositions are integral to a "modern" social order. The concept of modernity is therefore more comprehensive than secularism as it refers to values—individualism, equality, legal-rational authority—and to social structural factors—industrialism, urbanism, and the rise of the nation-state. Of course, these are ideal typical concepts; in reality we find diverse mixes of secular and cosmological presuppositions, modern and traditional values and social structural factors.

Secularism refers to a set of assumptions about the world. In contrast to cosmological presuppositions, a secular order projects a universe that places all entities on the same level of being, and is changing, infinite, and governed by efficient, nonteleological causality.[66] Translated into sociocultural terms, secularism reveals a pronounced drift towards liberal values and orientations: progress, tolerance, egalitarianism, and empiricism.

In the presuppositions of secularism, the philosophes found a standpoint well suited to their sociopolitical aims. The modern world-view signaled an attitude marked by openness, tolerance, individualism, and progress; in a word, modernism was embraced as part of the philosophes' struggle for a liberal social order. Stated in a concise, programmatic manner, the Enlightenment articulated the presuppositions and sociocultural principles of a modern and liberal order.

Conclusion

I have proposed a reinterpretation of Enlightenment social theory. There are two sets of premises in Enlightenment social theory: contractarianism and the science of man. In the course of the eighteenth and nineteenth centuries, these two currents of Enlightenment social theory were elaborated into two distinct social scientific traditions. On the one hand, contractarianism functioned as the controlling premises of Anglo-American social science. Reacting against contractarianism, the science of man articulated the rudimentary presuppositions, problems, and themes that were featured prominently in nineteenth-century European social theory.

The deep structure of the Enlightenment science of man lies in its synthesis of empiricism and rationalism. At an epistemological level, the science of man combined the empiricist orientation of historiography with the rationalist theoretical premises of contract theory. A similar fusion of empiricism and rationalism is reflected in the philosophes' dual concern with the sociological problem of the variability of sociohistorical development and the anthropological problem of the unity of humankind. Underlying this dual orientation toward sociocultural diversity and natural unity is the more fundamental dualism, we recall, between humans as social and as natural beings. The very identification of Enlightenment social theory as a critical and scientific enterprise highlights its intention to synthesize empiricism and rationalism.

The development of a science of man is linked to a far-reaching critique of all forms of intellectual and social closure and dogmatism. The philosophes maintained that completely closed intellectual systems yield error and superstition, which in turn reflect and help to sustain hierarchical and authoritarian societies. At bottom, as the critics of the Enlightenment were correct in perceiving, the philosophes mounted a devastating assault upon the traditional sociocultural order. There was, however, a positive aim underlying Enlightenment criticism: to promote a more humane and rational society. Towards this end, the philosophes sought to substitute secular presuppositions for cosmological ones, and science for metaphysics and dogmatic religion, as new principles of knowledge and social organization. The ideological affinity between secularism and science lies in their representation of basically liberal values. The advocacy of scientific reason in the Enlightenment was therefore necessarily connected to the philosophes' ideological and practical struggle for a modern and liberal order.

2. The Counter-Enlightenment

Analytical Continuities and Ideological Shifts in European Social Thought

SITUATED BETWEEN TWO epochs—the retreating traditional social order and the oncoming modern civilization—the counter-Enlightenment attempted to safeguard traditional values and orientations in a hostile social context.[1] Inevitably, there occurred an accommodation to modernism. Thus, Maistre and Bonald were forced to enunciate their orthodox Catholicism in the language of secular rationalism. Similarly, the German Historical School combined the belief in a providential order and design with the modern historical attitude. The romantics were torn between a radical modernist subjectivism and a nostalgia for the Christian-feudal era of spiritual transcendence and organic unity. The Enlightenment critics reacted to and often against the philosophes, but unwittingly employed the language and premises of Enlightenment modernism.

The blend of traditionalism and modernism among the critics of the Enlightenment suggests that, though they frequently defined themselves as opponents of the philosophes, in fact they were as much their heirs as critics. This line of reasoning seriously challenges the long-standing thesis, found prominently in Troeltsch, Mannheim, and Nisbet, that the counter-Enlightenment signaled a complete intellectual reorientation in European thought in direct opposition to the Enlightenment.[2]

Recent historical scholarship supports my contention that intellectual bonds exist between the Enlightenment and its critics. On the general intellectual continuity between the eighteenth and nineteenth centuries, Ernst Cassirer surmises: "There is no break in continuity . . . between the eighteenth and nineteenth centuries, that is, between the Enlightenment and Romanticism."[3] Even of such harsh critics of the Enlightenment as Maistre and Bonald, Professor Jack Lively states: "Many of the charges they brought are unreal, and many of the characteristics of their own thought find parallels and roots in that eighteenth-century thinking which nurtured revolutionary attitudes. . . ."[4] Following the analysis of Dilthey, Meinecke, and Cassirer, Peter Gay observes a similar continuity in the development of modern historicism: "The historians of the Enlightenment were not quite so different from Ranke as Ranke and his followers liked to believe."[5] Considering these revisionist historical accounts of the relationship between the Enlightenment and its critics, we are led to pose the following questions: At what level do we encounter intellectual continuity and discontinuity between the Enlightenment and its critics? How does a rethinking of this historical relationship alter the interpretation of the development of European social theory?

Analytical Continuities Between the Enlightenment and the Counter-Enlightenment

In the last chapter, I sought to recast the role of the Enlightenment in the development of social theory. I argued that the

Enlightenment science of man was a fundamental analytical departure from social contract theory. In place of the abstract and deductive rationalism, atomistic individualism, instrumental model of action, and a mechanistic view of society, characteristic of contractarian premises, the Enlightenment science of man entailed a dual focus upon the uniformity and historicity of human affairs, a view of the interpenetration of the individual and society, the inclusion of normative action, and the idea of emergent aspects of social groupings. The commonplace thesis that attributes to the counter-Enlightenment the "discovery" of history, nonlogical action, a collectivist view of society, methodological empiricism, and objectivity, is mistaken. My analysis compels us to reconsider just exactly what the counter-Enlightenment contributed to the development of European social theory.

I want to discuss, in an admittedly schematic fashion, three dimensions of the social theory of the counter-Enlightenment. First, while the Enlightenment critics were not the originators of the European social scientific tradition, they served, nevertheless, as its carriers. Building upon the critique of contract theory already initiated in the Enlightenment, the Enlightenment critics adopted the premises of the Enlightenment science of man and insinuated them into the center of the intellectual milieu of the nineteenth century. In short, the counter-Enlightenment formed a bridge between the eighteenth and nineteenth centuries which was of immense significance in preparing the way for the notable development of modern social theory in Germany and France after 1850.

Second, the Enlightenment critics elaborated the premises of the Enlightenment science of man: to take but two examples, the idea of organicism and historical individuality. I have maintained that the Enlightenment science of man identified emergent properties of group life—for example, legal systems, institutions, and cultural factors. Implicit in Montesquieu's analysis of the relation of law to other social factors, in Voltaire's examination of the sociocultural milieu of Louis XIV, and in Ferguson's consideration of the economic, political, and cultural aspects of social development is a concept of society as a collective unit composed of interrelated structural and cultural components. On the one hand, the counter-Enlightenment stated this holism in a programmatic manner. On the other hand, the Enlightenment critics took methodological holism to its furthest logical conclusion: organicism. In its organic version, holism tends towards a social realism, whereby entities are viewed as self-sufficient monads susceptible only to intuitive knowledge. It is this type of holism that we find, for instance, in the later Fichte, in Adam Müller, in Savigny, in the early founders of the German Historical School of Economics, in Rankean historiography, as well as in Hegelian emanationism. As Marx, Durkheim, and Weber were to argue by way of criticism, such organic social theories were invariably coupled to an anti-scientific epistemology.

Turning to the idea of historical individuality, my reasoning follows a similar logic. The Enlightenment science of man represented a twofold relation to history. First, the philosophes sought a constant human nature amidst historical variation. Second, because the philosophes believed that human nature is subject to differential development, sociocultural diversity represented the manifold forms human nature assumed in history. What the philosophes called "character" reflects the interpenetration of human nature and history. Knowledge of humankind implied understanding both the *permanent* features of human nature and its *variable* expression (character) exhibited in historical development. Methodologically speaking, the problem of conceptualizing historical individuality entailed a combination of empiricism, with its orientation to historical particularity, and a rationalist commitment to theoretical systematization. Without the latter, historical diversity would be theoretically inaccessible. "The multiplicity of forms," writes Ferguson, "which different societies offer to our view, is almost infinite." This near-infinite historical particularity, continues Ferguson, gives "to human affairs a variety in detail, which, in its full extent, no understanding can comprehend and no memory retain."[6] The Enlightenment science of man sought a general theoretical framework in order to conceptually organize historical diversity.

It is arguable that the conceptualizations proposed by the science of man were inadequate. For instance, as Voltaire surveyed world history, his principle of reducing historical complexity is obviously methodologically questionable: "All that you seek to learn in this immensity of matter [historical diversity], is only that which deserves to be known; the genius, the manners and customs of the principal nations, supported by facts. . . ."[7] Voltaire begs the question: how do "we" determine which are the "principal nations"? Similarly, we can perhaps object to Montesquieu's three generic social types as a gross violation of the idea of historical individuality. In fact, this is precisely the point at which the Enlightenment critics protest against the science of man. They view Enlightenment rationalism as a violation of the integrity of historical particularity. Confronted with the histories of Voltaire, Hume, and Gibbon, Herder complained:

> How then can one survey an ocean of entire peoples, times and countries, comprehend them in one glance, one sentiment, or one word. . . . A whole *tableau vivant* of manners, customs, necessities, particularities of earth and heaven must be added to it, or precede it; you must enter the spirit of a nation before you can share even one of its thoughts or deeds.[8]

In making a valid point, Herder exaggerated. It was, after all, Montesquieu who said: "When I have been obliged to look back to antiquity I have endeavored to assume the spirit of the ancients, lest I should consider those things as alike which are really different, and lest I should miss the difference of those which appear to be alike."[9] And even Voltaire, speaking of Muslim culture, affirmed the principle of historical individuality and interpretive understanding: "Here are moeurs, customs, facts, so different from everything we are used to that they should show us how varied is the picture of the world, and how much we must be on guard against the habit of judging everything by our customs."[10] Hume went so far as to make this idea the elementary premise of cultural interpretation: "A critic of a different age or nation, who should peruse this [Hume's] discourse, must have all these circumstances in his eye, and must place himself in the same situation as the audience, in order to form a true judgment of the nation. . . . A person influenced by prejudice, complies not with this condition; but obstinately maintains his natural position, with placing himself in that point of view, which the performance presupposes."[11] Notwithstanding Herder's exaggeration of his own originality, a vital problem is unattended to by Herder and other Enlightenment critics: how are historical particulars to be placed within a conceptual order without violating their individuality? To the extent that the Enlightenment critics do not return either to some version of a philosophy of history or to a metaphysic of providential design and historical teleology, the logical end point of historicism would be an equally objectionable empiricist historiography.

The Enlightenment critics were correct to point to the inadequacies of the philosophes' treatment of historical individuality. However, their own approach was in many ways a regression; by abandoning a rationalist concern with conceptual order, the Enlightenment critics ended up embracing a metaphysic of divine order or a rather aimless empiricism.

I have indicated two ways in which the counter-Enlightenment played an important role in the analytical development of modern social theory. First, the critics of the Enlightenment transmitted the achievements of the Enlightenment science of man to the succeeding generations. Second, they refined and explicated a number of premises and orientations of the Enlightenment—for example, methodological holism, historicism, normative action, cultural idealism, and the problem of understanding. We now come to the third contribution of the Enlightenment critics to the development of social theory: the themes of alienation and social order.

It would be misleading to attribute to the Enlightenment

a simplistic belief in historical progress. Advocates though they were of enlightenment and progress, the philosophes coupled the progress of individual liberty to negative effects on the individual and social order. Nonetheless, the intimations of the problems of alienation and social order are offset by their abiding belief in progress, particularly in the later Enlightenment. It would be equally misleading to identify the counter-Enlightenment with a pessimistic and tragic view of history. Critics though they were of the Enlightenment idea of progress, they maintained a vital faith in a coming era of social and spiritual renewal.[12] Progress was as much a part of the agenda of the counter-Enlightenment as of the Enlightenment.

What divides the philosophes from their critics are their quite different interpretations of the idea of progress. For the philosophes, progress meant the historical movement towards a social order founded upon liberal or secular, pluralistic, and individualistic premises. The Enlightenment critics projected as an ideal society a spiritually unified, communal, and group-centered order—for example, the Greek *polis* or the Christian-feudal order.[13] From the perspective of the Enlightenment critics, the emerging liberal European order represented a drastic departure from their communitarian ideal. It is in the context of this fundamental ideological shift—to be discussed shortly—that the Enlightenment critics posed the problems of alienation and social order.

I am suggesting that the communitarian ideology of the Enlightenment critics is the basis for raising the problems of alienation and social order. On the assumption that unity between the individual, nature, and community is the precondition for individual happiness, freedom, and social solidarity, the Enlightenment critics underscored the divisions and conflict within the individual and in society originating from a condition of separation and conflict between the individual, nature, and the community.

The philosophes were not simpleminded enthusiasts of the emerging liberal civilization. The progress of science and technology had its drawbacks, and the philosophes were not reluctant to assume a critical posture. Almost all of the philosophes, for instance, perceived that the obverse of the hegemony of scientific-technical reason is the mediocrity of aesthetic creation. "I liked physics," declared Voltaire, "as long as it did not attempt to oust poetry; now that it is crushing all the arts I refuse to consider physics as anything else than an unsociable tyrant."[14] It is well known that the Scottish philosophes perceived in the enormous productive machinery of capitalism not only its potential for wealth and social progress but its destructiveness towards certain natural impulses, virtues, and critical intelligence. If the critical side of Enlightenment liberalism was overshadowed by its affirmation of sociohistorical progress, then this reflected the philosophes' continuing, and still undecided, struggle for a liberal order. Accordingly, the philosophes spent most of their critical energies attacking the structural and cultural supports of traditionalism, e.g., the clergy, dogmatic religion, hierarchy, and authoritarianism.

It was in the post-Enlightenment period that a fully developed critique of liberalism and social progress originated. The theme of alienation was central to this ideological critique of modern civilization. The alienation perspective entered into the orientations of Marx, Durkheim, and Weber stripped, however, of its anti-modernist disposition. In one form or another, the alienation theme functioned in the social theory of Marx, Durkheim, and Weber as a basis for criticizing aspects of the bourgeois version of modernity.

Recent historical scholarship has seriously challenged the assertion of a strictly antithetical relation between the Enlightenment and its critics. I have sought to specify elements of this intellectual continuity at the analytical level. However, my concluding argument regarding the origins of the problems of alienation and social order points to significant ideological discontinuities between the Enlightenment and its critics. In the following section, I want to develop this argument and link the ideological critique of Enlightenment liberalism to my interpretation of the development of European social theory.

Ideological Discontinuities Between the Enlightenment and the Counter-Enlightenment

The philosophes initiated an analytical perspective which asserted the interpenetration of the individual and society and identified emergent aspects of collective life. Yet, the philosophes were ideologically committed to a social order in which the constraints of collective life would permit maximum individual freedom. There is no contradiction here. The analytical claim that the individual is a part of society, and therefore constrained and "determined" in individual conduct, leaves unresolved the question of the content and the actual historical modes of social determination. The substantive relation between the individual and society is not an analytical question but an historical and ideological issue. Put simply, one can identify various forms which the social determination of the individual has historically assumed; similarly, one can advocate one or another mode of relation between the individual and society according to one's ideological standpoint.

The philosophes were partisans of the idea that individual liberty prospers only under conditions of minimal external constraint which is consensually based. In the eighteenth century, the philosophes articulated their doctrine of individual liberty chiefly in the idiom of natural rights. It is at this ideological level that the natural law pronouncements of the philosophes must be understood. In this way, the philosophes were able to maintain both the analytical view of the social determination of the individual and the ideological commitment to individual natural rights. As is well known, the reaction to the Enlightenment took the form of a critique of natural law. However, it should be evident from the preceding exposition that the actual historical departure from the Enlightenment in this regard was less analytical than ideological. The natural law doctrine served the philosophes as, so to speak, the available idiom in which to articulate their liberal ideology. Accordingly, the critique of natural law by the Enlightenment critics represented an all-out assault on Enlightenment liberalism. My principal concern here is with determining the way in which the ideological critique of liberalism entered into the ideological formation of nineteenth-century European social theory.

The ideology of the counter-Enlightenment represented a virtual inversion of Enlightenment liberalism. In place of modernist premises, we can detect in the Enlightenment critics a strong anti-modernist sentiment which, in certain currents of Enlightenment critique, revived cosmological presuppositions. A striking feature of the Enlightenment critics was their replacing a pluralistic order with the ideal of communitarianism: division, conflict, and competition were supplanted by the ideal of a uniform and common culture which integrates and harmonizes the interests of the individual and the community. The anti-modernist and communitarian orientation points to the central premise of the counter-Enlightenment: the affirmation of a group-centered society. This entailed a basic redefinition of the meaning of individualism. In the group-centered, communitarian society, the emphasis was not upon maximizing individual self-satisfaction or self-determination. The autonomous self was replaced by the ideal of the public or corporate individual. Instead of the secular, pluralistic, and individualistic assumptions of liberalism, the counter-Enlightenment gravitated towards the antithetical image of a group-centered, organic, and spiritually unified social order.

In order to link these general assumptions of the Enlightenment critics to the ideological development of nineteenth-century social theory, it is necessary to specify the actual historical sense of Enlightenment criticism. This is so for two reasons. First, these general assumptions—anti-modernism, communitarianism, and group-centeredness—were, in fact, manifested in heterogeneous ideological strains of Enlightenment criticism. To identify the precise ideological meaning of these assumptions therefore requires that they be understood as part of distinct ideological configurations. To put it differently: abstracted from their specific context, these general assumptions are open to various possible ideological connotations. For example, the idea of communitarianism assumes a very different significance as it is used, let us say, by Maistre, Herder, or Babeuf. Once, however, these general ideas are structured into coherent intellectual traditions, they assume a very precise ideological meaning. Second, to ascertain the historical relationship between the counter-Enlightenment and nineteenth-century social theory, we must be able to discriminate between the diverse ideological strains of Enlightenment criticism. How else could we determine whether, for example, Durkheim's communitarian orientation is derived from and sustains the meaning of the French conservatives, the German romantics, or the French revolutionary tradition? To determine the impact of the ideological critique of liberalism in European social theory, we need to specify the variants of Enlightenment criticism.

Admittedly, these distinctions will be somewhat arbitrary and to some, no doubt, objectionable. Considering, however, that there exists little consensus among intellectual historians regarding a satisfactory way to conceive these disparate countermovements, we must proceed as best we can. I propose that we distinguish three strains of counter-Enlightenment thought: Conservatism, Romanticism, and Revolution. Among conservatives, I include, at the extreme reactionary end of the spectrum, Bonald and Maistre; a more moderate conservatism is found in the Historical School of Jurisprudence. At the "more liberal" end of the continuum, we may single out such conservatives as Burke. In discussing the romantics, we will leave aside the English romantic poets and concentrate on the German romantics—by whom I refer to Schiller, Schelling, the Schlegels, Novalis, Fichte, and Schleiermacher. Among the romantics, as we shall see, there is an individualistic aspect which in many respects coincides with Enlightenment modernism. In addition, there is a more collectivist romantic current—for example, in the later Fichte—which, at the far extreme, is virtually indistinguishable from the ideology of the conservatives. Finally, the revolutionary ideology has its origins in the French Enlightenment. In speaking of a revolutionary tradition, I refer to the fissure in the Enlightenment first sounded by Rousseau but simultaneously echoed by the egalitarians. From Rousseau and the egalitarians to Babeuf and Blanquism, there is a marked continuity signifying a unique revolutionary tradition.

These distinctions are not without problems. Where, for example, do we place Hegel? In my view, Hegel defies categorization, at least along the lines I have suggested.[15] Again, in their critique of dualisms and divisions, the romantics overlap in important ways with the revolutionary ideologues. Despite these difficulties, once it is acknowledged that there are different strains of counter-Enlightenment thought an attempt must be made to conceptualize them. What follows are such ideal typical conceptualizations which invite further refinement and critique.

Conservatism*

The animating and sustaining impulse behind Conservatism is its opposition to modernism. "I believe we can best understand conservatism," writes Robert Nisbet, a sympathetic commentator, "as the first broad-gauged attack on modernism and its political, economic, and cultural elements."[16] The conservatives viewed the philosophes as the bearers of modernity and therefore set against their liberal and modernist ideology an alternative standpoint: philosophical conservatism.

The principles of philosophical conservatism reflect quite simply a return to the underlying religio-cosmological assumptions of medievalism. Translated into the language of social and political ideology, the conservatives advocated a

---

*Whenever "Conservatism" is capitalized, I am referring specifically to the ideas of philosophical conservatism.

static communal order, social hierarchies, the control of the individual by tradition, religion, and authoritarian associations, and a collective order in which the identification of individual and communal interests rested upon the annexation of religious dogma to the temporal power of the state. Regarding the need for establishing a theocracy, Joseph de Maistre remarked:

> There should be a state religion just as there is a state political system; or rather, religion and political dogma, mingled and merged together, should together form a *general* or *national mind* sufficiently strong to repress the aberrations of the individual reason which is, of its nature, the mortal enemy of any association whatever because it gives birth to divergent opinions.[17]

The communitarian ideal of the conservatives was, as the above quotation makes obvious, articulated in direct opposition to Enlightenment liberalism.

Aside from the reactionary conservatism of Bonald and Maistre, the more moderate conservatives like Burke and Savigny accepted the inevitability of accommodating to modernity. Although an historical restoration of the Christian-feudal order was unattainable, the conservatives advocated that the principles of philosophical conservatism—social fixity, hierarchy, nonconsensually founded authority, religious dogmatism, and repression of voluntarism—remain the underlying structural and cultural basis of the European order. It is this moderate or accommodating conservatism which has endured as a vital element of the European ideological milieu in the nineteenth and twentieth centuries.

The fact that philosophical conservatism has maintained its ideological appeal in Europe leads us to ask: what role, if any, has philosophical conservatism played in the ideological development of European social theory? There exists a rather formidable body of historical scholarship which suggests that philosophical conservatism has had a considerable impact on the development of sociological theory.[18]

The argument regarding the conservative ideological disposition of sociological theory may be stated briefly. The classical European sociologists spoke, of course, the language of modernist political and cultural values. The blatantly theological and ideological pronouncements of the conservatives were, no doubt, repugnant to sociologists in search of scientific legitimation and, lest we forget, rational truths. However, through the various highways and byways of intellectual history, the principles of philosophical conservatism entered into the very center of sociological theory. The influence of philosophical conservatism is manifested in sociology's abiding interest in, and underlying advocacy of, social order and stability, hierarchy, religion and moral order, social control, anti-utopianism, and an ethic of obedience and resignation. As an historical argument, the conservative interpretation of sociology is especially cogent when applied to the development of French sociology—in particular, Durkheimian sociology. To the extent that the collectivist aspects of Romanticism overlap with Conservatism, this line of reasoning could refer to German sociology as well. I leave to the next section, the examination of the relationship of Romanticism to German sociology.

In brief fashion, I want to indicate the essentials of a critique of the conservative interpretation of Durkheimian sociology.[19] Perhaps the most serious flaw in this argument is *its lack of any textual or historical evidence.* Though Durkheim speaks at length about the liberal, revolutionary, and German historicist traditions, there is no discussion, hardly even a mention, of the conservatives.[20] The argument is made, however, that philosophical conservatism entered into the mainstream of French sociology by means of Comte. It is undeniable that philosophical conservatism forms a dominant ideological strain of Comte's sociology. Two facts, though, need to be noted. First, as Anthony Giddens has perceptively observed, the Comtean influence was exerted mainly through the methodological and analytical portions of *The Positive Philosophy.*[21] Second, as will be demonstrated in the Durkheim chapters, Durkheim's critique of Comte is targeted precisely at his conservative presuppositions. The proponents of the conservative view of Durkheimian sociology offer another argument. They contend that Durkheim's communitarian assumptions betray a conservative derivation. It will be argued later in this chapter, and further documented in the Durkheim chapters, that the historical origin and ideological meaning of Durkheim's communitarianism stem from the revolutionary tradition. It is of course conceivable that Durkheim was a conservative without adopting the ideology of philosophical conservatism. Lewis Coser, for instance, has suggested that, although Durkheim's ideological commitments fall within the modern and liberal tradition, nevertheless, his liberalism itself reveals an abiding conservatism in its implicit legitimation of the status quo and in its general avoidance of the issues of social conflict, radical change, and power politics.[22] In the subsequent pages, I will argue that this interpretation is misleading. My analysis points out that Durkheim drew considerably from the native French revolutionary tradition in his effort to revitalize liberalism as a critical ideology resonant with a changing European order.

Philosophical conservatism was significant in the ideological development of European social theory only, I contend, in Comtean sociology and in the social theory embedded in the early movement of the German Historical School. In neither case did philosophical conservatism yield a viable and sustaining tradition of social theory. In the "classical phase" of sociology beween 1890 and World War I, Conservatism failed to find a place in mainstream sociology and reappeared in blatantly ideological and sometimes theological forms— for example, in the *Action Française*, the "Catholic Renaissance" prophesied by Henri Massis and Alfred de Tarde (son of the famous sociologist), or in the vulgar romanticism of Lagarde and Langbehn.[23] The inability of philosophical conservatism to generate a stable and vital tradition of social theory reflects its fragile commitment to scientific rationalism as well as the dissonance between its ideological principles and the sociocultural features of modern life.

Romanticism*

It is frequently said, and rightly so, that Romanticism was a very complex and heterogeneous cultural movement.[24] To simplify matters, I want to single out two ideological aspects of romantic thought. On the one hand, in its commitment to an active subject and dynamic view of mind as well as in its opposition to tradition, established authority, and formal order, Romanticism presents itself as a vanguard modernist movement.[25] On the other hand, in its retreat into collectivism, teleology, and objective idealism, Romanticism begins to blend imperceptibly with philosophical conservatism.[26] These two aspects of Romanticism are found in all the romantics, with the collectivist side triumphing in its later phases.[27]

The ideological core of Romanticism is revealed in its critique of the dualistic structure of Enlightenment thought. The Enlightenment, we recall, managed to evade materialism only to succumb to a series of dualisms: spirit/matter, mind/body, freedom/determinism, moral will/instinct. In this dualistic representation of reality, spirit or mind was a residual part of the universe, i.e., confined to individual subjectivity. In opposition to the Enlightenment, the romantics posited a universe infused with spirit: mind and body, reason and intuition, and subjective and objective nature are one and indivisible.

In the philosophical articulation of Romanticism—for example, the transcendental idealism of Fichte and the early Schelling—this spiritualized cosmos assumed the form of a postulated identity between spirit and matter, subject and object, founded upon the constitutive activity of self-consciousness.[28] The two poles of Romanticism, i.e., its individualistic and collectivistic modes, can be distinguished clearly in its idealist philosophy. On the individualistic pole,

---

*By "Romanticism" I refer to the ideas of the romantic movement between 1770 and 1830. Whenever the term is used in its historical sense, I will capitalize it.

we encounter elements of a subjective idealism. The primary world-constituting principle is no longer God or mechanical nature but the spiritual activity of the imagination or a self-positing reason. This is apparent, for example, in the "magical idealism" of Novalis and in the infinite striving of Fichte's moral subject. The aim of transcendental idealism, wrote Fichte in his "Second Introduction" to the *Wissenschaftslehre*, is the "complete deduction of all experience from the possibility of self-consciousness."[29] We may turn to the verse of Wordsworth for a poetic statement of the very same subjective idealism:

> I had a world about me; 'twas my own,
> I made it; for it only liv'd to me. . . .[30]

What makes this subjectivist mode of romantic thought a sort of vanguard modernism is the idea implicit in it that order, value, meaning, and identity are creations or projections of the imaginative, reasoning, or moral activity of the free subject. Gone is the idea, so much a part of the natural law tradition, of an objective order of being and value. Although this radical subjectivism evokes the later modernist-nihilist problematics of Nietzsche and German expressionism, it would be a mistake to read this into the original romantic movement. In fact, as I have suggested, this subjectivist tendency was invariably submerged in a collectivist and objective idealism. Thus, Fichte's self-generating subject merges the empirical individual and the "Absolute" or collective self. Similarly, when one considers Hegelian idealism, the notion of *Geist* partakes of the same supra-individualist conception, and, though history replaces a static conception of natural order, Hegel's hidden teleology reflects an objective order as fixed as the classicism of modern rationalism. Finally, in the literary and historical writings of the Schlegels and Novalis, the same disposition reveals itself in their evident desire to resurrect an organic society along the lines of the late Christian-feudal order. In their critique of dualisms, the romantics embraced philosophical idealism. Moreover, their idealism betrayed a tension between a modernist and a traditional conservative disposition.

At an anthropological and societal level, the romantics' opposition to dualism was reflected in their communitarian ideal. Underlying philosophical idealism was the idea of the free or autonomous individual. The concept of the self-directing individual was the accomplishment of the Enlightenment. However, the romantics were not satisfied with the formalistic character of the Enlightenment idea of autonomy, i.e., the self who confronts a separate world of content and produces cognitive, moral, and practical order. The Enlightenment notion of autonomy did not address the internal life of the individual. The autonomous, particularly Kantian individual, the romantics argued, is still a *divided being* living in a *fragmented society*. The free self of the Enlightenment is polarized within by the duality between reason and sensuality, moral will and instinctual gratification, and polarized without in his or her relations to a mechanical external nature and to a conflict-ridden society. True individualism, the romantics believed, required the cultivation of our multiple capacities into a unified personality in harmony with a conflict-free communal order. The expressive unity unfolded within each individual personality must coincide with an equally unified and harmonious cultivation of the societal community.

Aside from an idea of harmony within individual personalities and between the individual and community, the precise nature of this communitarian order was never really spelled out. Invariably, however, the romantics' communitarian ideal draws its images from pre-modern epochs, in particular the Greek *polis* (Schiller, Humboldt) or the feudal estate system (Novalis, Schlegels, later Fichte). Again, we perceive in Romanticism a definite strain of modernism—subjectivism, autonomy, and the ideal of the fully developed individual— united with and, ultimately, submerged in a more conservative, anti-modernist ideology.

The reference to Nietzsche and German expressionism suggests the sustaining impact of romantic ideas on German culture throughout the nineteenth century. It is curious to note, however, that there does not exist a detailed historical examination of the relations of Romanticism to German social theory.[31] In this brief discussion, I will limit my comments to the affiliations between Romanticism and German sociology, and in particular the relation of Romanticism to Weber's sociology.

Regarding the linkage between Romanticism and German sociology, two arguments stand out. First, Hans Freyer and Helmut Schelsky trace the origins of German sociology to the postromantic turn towards "social realism" initiated in Hegel's critique of Romanticism. "The sociology of the nineteenth century is rightly called realism. Realism is the opposite of romanticism." Freyer concludes: "Not the romantics . . . but the realistic systems which derive from Hegel are the legitimate origins of German sociology."[32] Similarly, Schelsky points to the combination of classical economics and Hegel as the twin sources of German sociology: "The theory of bourgeois society and Hegel, these are the two chief roots of German sociology."[33] This interpretation is severely flawed in two respects. First, neither Freyer nor Schelsky furnishes any evidence to substantiate this crucial historical bond between Hegel and German sociology. Furthermore, it is highly questionable to accept at face value, as Freyer and Schelsky seem to, Hegel's self-understanding as a critic of Romanticism. It is characteristic of postromantic German thinkers— e.g., Marx and Nietzsche—to repudiate Romanticism while continuing to rely upon romantic ideas. Second, the basic conceptual distinction between Romanticism and Hegelianism, resting as it does upon the idea of "realism," is hardly an adequate basis on which to construct an interpretation of German sociology. Yet, the remarks of Freyer and Schelsky regarding the relation of Hegel to the development of German sociology remain an interesting, and still unexamined, issue in the history of sociology.

There is a second approach to the question of the relation between Romanticism and German sociology. In this view, represented by Arthur Mitzman, Romanticism is identified as an anti-modernist ideology, but fundamentally different from philosophical conservatism.[34] Whether on the basis of either a "Faustian" image of the individual, characterized by the unceasing struggle to master a resistant world, or an "Apollonian" notion of the cultured and harmonious personality integrated into a communal order, the romantics criticized modernity as inherently "reifying" or "alienating." In early Romanticism, two solutions to the problem of modernity were offered: the restoration of traditional corporate forms of Germanic culture, or the establishment of state socialism. The sociologists of the 1890s—Tönnies, Sombart, Simmel, and Weber—absorbed romantic anti-modernist values and social ideals but rejected the utopian regenerative prospects of reviving Gemeinschaft through some form of medieval restoration or state socialism. During the 1890s, the resurgence of liberalism and the rise of revisionist Marxism provided a political outlet for criticizing Prussian authoritarianism and modern Gesellschaft. Hopes were raised for the possibility of a general social and cultural reformation. Thus, in these formative years of German sociology one finds an accommodation to modernism by the sociologists, i.e., a commitment to modernist political and social values—for example, science, liberalism, and industrialism—as possible vehicles for overcoming alienation.

By the early 1900s, so Mitzman argues, the prospects for a political and modernist solution had all but expired. The modernist accommodation of the 1890s was swept away in an environment increasingly dominated by a variety of neo-romantic, anti-modernist ideologies such as the *Völkish* ideology, the cultural pessimism of the Nietzsche cults, the German expressionist movement, and the more restrained anti-modernism of what Fritz Ringer calls the "orthodox mandarins." Lacking a political and modernist critical outlet, and in an intellectual milieu dazed by romantic notions of mysticism, spiritual transcendence, and aristocratic heroic ideals, the German sociologists vented their critique of German Gesellschaft in the critical idiom of romantic anti-modernism, although in a somewhat more sophisticated and milder version.[35] The anti-modernism of the sociologists, Mitzman further contends, found its way into the analytical core of sociology. Thus, Weber's post-breakdown absorption of anti-modernism is reflected in his discovery of charisma, mysticism, and eroticism. The significance of Mitzman's argument for us lies in identifying the ideological roots of German sociology in a unique form of romantic anti-modernism.

In many respects, Mitzman's writings are a *tour de force*, replete with profound insights into the interpenetration of personal life, values, and social theory. They are a much needed corrective to the "westernized" interpretations of Weber offered by Parsons and Bendix, both of whom tend to suppress this critical ideological orientation. Though Mitzman seems to have intended his work as a corrective, the end result is unmistakably a complete reinterpretation asserting the *dominance* of romantic assumptions in the origins of German sociology. In brief fashion, I want to suggest that Mitzman's errors go beyond enthusiastic overstatement. These critical notes refer only to Mitzman's interpretation of Weber.

First, Mitzman exaggerates the scope and depth of these currents of anti-modernism.[36] This is important because the modernist features of Weber's milieu *continued to serve as a rationalist outlet for critique and change.* I am thinking particularly of neo-Kantianism, liberal historicism, the Protestant social reform movement, and English currents of trade unionism, democracy, and liberalism. My claim, which will be elaborated in the Weber chapters, is that these liberal-democratic and rationalist movements were the *controlling* ideological features of Weber's sociology. Second, Mitzman confuses Weber's openness to certain manifestations of neo-romanticism with acceptance of its anti-modernism. The evidence relating to Weber's meetings, for instance, with Stefan George and his disciples repeatedly shows their irreconcilable differences and Weber's aversion to their sweeping, one-dimensional anti-modernism.[37] Third, though Weber absorbed aspects of the romantic criticisms of modern life, these criticisms were integrated into a modernist framework. To put it differently, Weber did not criticize modernity *per se* but only particular aspects of modern society.

Weber's repudiation of romantic anti-modernism is to be found, first, in his essays on Roscher and Knies, and, again, in his late essays, "Religious Rejections" and "Science as a Vocation." In the later essays, Weber distinguishes a secular perspective on the problems of rationalization, meaning, and modernity from a religious perspective. I will show that Weber unequivocally identified with the secular standpoint, though he remained respectful of a genuine religious perspective as exhibited, for example, by the religious humanism of Tolstoy.[38]

Finally, Mitzman collapses the two currents of Romanticism and thereby fails to recognize that the individualistic side—what Mitzman calls the Faustian ideal—coincides very closely with Western modernist traditions of individualism found in Puritanism and the Enlightenment. I would say that it is precisely this side of Romanticism, with its ethos of individualism, autonomy, struggle, conflict, and pluralism, and stripped of its collectivist and metaphysical underpinnings, which forms a central dimension of Weber's world-view.

Romanticism is an incredibly heterogeneous cultural movement. Its near-protean character should warn us against cut-and-dried historical interpretations. We must not forget, in addition, that Romanticism virtually died out by 1830. From the 1840s through the turn of the century, the prestige of materialism and science soared.[39] Marx was part of the original reaction against Romanticism, even though, as we will see, the expressivism and communitarianism of Romanticism was a permanent ideological feature of Marxian social theory. Weber came of age when the currents of materialism and science were peaking. Weber's early writings, I will argue, bear the strong imprint of this. Though Weber experienced a decisive intellectual reorientation after the breakdown period, it was not, as Mitzman suggests, away from modernism and rationalism but towards neo-Kantianism as a liberal-democratic ideology. It is true that shortly after his break-down Weber became more pessimistic regarding the prospects for liberal reforms in Germany. No doubt this provided a certain receptiveness to romantic criticisms of modern Gesellschaft. Nevertheless, it is impossible to read Weber's scholarly and political writings during these years without being impressed by his deep and abiding commitment to rationalism and secularism in the face of the mass flight from modernity on all sides of the political spectrum.

Revolution: Between the Enlightenment and Its Critics

In *The Rise of Totalitarian Democracy*, J. L. Talmon argues that the Enlightenment spawned two distinct, even contradictory ideologies: liberal democracy and totalitarian democracy. Although Talmon's thesis is misleading in its historical application, he states in a dramatic fashion what other scholars have alluded to for some time—namely, that there is an ideological current in the Enlightenment which departs fundamentally from mainstream liberalism. There has always been the problem of Jean-Jacques Rousseau, who is conceived alternatively as a proto-romantic,[40] proto-Marxist,[41] proto-totalitarian,[42] or proto-anarchist.[43] Fortunately, it is unnecessary to consider the welter of Rousseau-interpretations. There is another line of scholarship, predominant among historians of socialism and Marxism, which points to basic affinities between Rousseau and an emergent anti-liberal ideology associated with such contemporaries as Meslier, Mably, and Morelly. This counter-liberal movement found its eighteenth-century doctrinal and practical culmination in the revolutionary communism of Babeuf and Babouvism. I call this nonliberal ideology the revolutionary tradition.

The break from Enlightenment liberalism was sounded loud and clear in Rousseau's early discourses. In these essays,

Rousseau uncouples the advancement of science, technology, and the increasing complexity of sociocultural development from automatic human progress, in the sense of the positive unfolding of human sensual, moral, aesthetic, and cognitive powers. In this regard, however, Rousseau is really echoing the philosophes' argument that social progress exacts its costs in the form of certain negative human consequences. Rousseau's retreat from liberalism lies not in the repudiation of the idea of progress, but in his critique of the particular form of the liberal doctrine of progress and individual liberty.[44] The philosophical liberals of the eighteenth century maintained that the advancement of enlightenment and civilization constitutes social progress in that sociohistorical development points to the emergence of a secular, pluralistic, individual-centered social order which, in their view, is conducive to maximizing individual liberty. Within the context of the eighteenth century, the philosophes pointed to such developments as private property, the market economy, republicanism and the division of governmental powers, modern science, and naturalistic moralities as representing an emergent liberal society. Despite setbacks and contemporary obstacles, history reveals as its evident pattern, they argued, the progressive realization of individual freedom.

Rousseau disputed the liberal doctrine of freedom and so refused to read history as the story of individual liberty. His criticisms of private property, commerce, and the doctrine of political representation and division of powers bear witness to Rousseau's critical attitude toward liberal ideology. The significance for us of his critique of liberalism lies less in its details than in its collectivist opening. In contrast to liberalism, Rousseau linked the constitution of liberty to *egalitarian and communitarian premises*. Without social equality, liberty yields hierarchy, domination, and heteronomy. Social equality entails communitarianism: collective property, a unified and common culture, and the identification of the private with the public individual.

Whether Rousseau sacrificed individual liberty by adopting egalitarian and communitarian assumptions is a question for Rousseau scholars. Though it seems to me that Rousseau's critique of liberalism was in part an internal debate over the constitution of the conditions of liberty, it is nonetheless the case that, in substituting collectivist premises for those of liberalism, Rousseau paved the way for the articulation of a revolutionary ideology. Rousseau served as a bridge between liberalism and revolution.

The revolutionary tradition found its initial expression in the egalitarian communism of Meslier, Mably, and Morelly. Like Rousseau, the egalitarians centered their critique of the emerging liberal order on private property. Private property, they argued, perverted our natural and beneficent self-love into avarice and vanity; it created a debased culture of egoism, neediness, conflict, and hedonism. "Riches produce *need* . . . or *luxury*, which gives to riches all the vices of property and to the poor a covetousness which they cannot satisfy except by crime or the vilest dastardliness. Voluptuousness comes in the wake of luxury, and while they soften and enervate the soul of the rich . . . they throw the people into a misery which makes them ferocious and stupid."[45] However, unlike Rousseau, the egalitarians traced *all* the contemporary evils to private property. Mably wrote: "Do you want to know what is the principal source of all the misfortunes which affect history? It is ownership of wealth."[46] In addition, the egalitarians criticized private property not simply on account of its negative social and moral consequences, but as a violation of the natural or cosmic order of things. In direct opposition to the liberal doctrine of the natural right to property, Morelly substituted an egalitarian natural law doctrine: "The eternal laws of the universe are that nothing belongs privately to man except what his actual needs require. . . . Even the product of his own labors does not belong to him except for the portion which he is to consume; the balance, like his person, belongs to the whole of society."[47] This is a formulation not to be found in Rousseau. The egalitarians considered private property a breach of the first principle of the natural order—namely, equality.

The egalitarian first principle, translated into social terms, meant a social order founded upon communitarian premises. Not only were property, family, and childrearing to be communal, but the community, conceived of as an organic-spiritual unity, was to suppress all divisive and anarchistic elements. Essentially, the revolutionary ideology entailed the denial of the liberal notion of individual liberty. In its place was substituted the idea of public service. "Morelly and Mably completely rejected the [liberal] current of individualism and declared that happiness is to be found only in an organized society where individual satisfaction is subordinate to the public good," writes one commentator.[48] To achieve the production of the corporate or public individual, property and its culture of egoism and hedonism had to be destroyed. "Destroy property, the blind and pitiless self-interest which accompanies it, wipe out all the prejudices and the errors which support them, and . . . there are no more furious passions, ferocious actions, notions or ideas of moral badness." All this, Morelly tells us, ought to be the work of an enlightened elite: "To accomplish that, first allow full liberty to the really wise men to attack the errors and prejudices which maintain the spirit of property."[49] Once private property is abolished and its spirit effectively rooted out, the state will serve as a vehicle for the moral regeneration of the people: "Is it not certain that the polity ought to make us love virtue and that virtue is the only object which legislators, laws, and magistrates ought to have in view?"[50] Combined with the coercive and moral power of the state, the egalitarians saw the need for a "civil religion" capable of limiting egoistic desire and yielding a stable sociocultural equilibrium.

There is some debate as to whether the egalitarians are really modern revolutionaries, or rather moralists and utopians in the tradition of Plato, Thomas More, and Campanella. For instance, the noted historian of socialism, G. D. F. Cole, argues that the egalitarians made no attempt to link their criticisms to the existing socioeconomic conditions and did not translate their ideas into practical reforms.[51] Even in this regard there is some disagreement. Talmon argues that

"Morelly's *Code de la Nature* . . . was the first book in modern times to put full-fledged communism on the agenda as a practical program, and not merely a utopia."[52] The Curé Meslier, as another commentator has observed, "suggested that communism was the natural order to be established after the probable revolution."[53] Again, Mably, who like Rousseau rejected a return to the original state of nature, considered revolution a possibility dependent upon the will of the people: "Choose between revolution and slavery, there is no halfway house."[54] The issue, I believe, cannot be settled in the form of an either-or proposition.

In *Socialism*, Emile Durkheim proposed that the egalitarians be viewed as transitional figures, yet originators, of a revolutionary ideology. Durkheim observed that the egalitarians were different from traditional moralists and utopians in two respects. First, the sheer abundance of communist ideas in the eighteenth century marks them off from traditional utopianism, which characteristically finds historic expression only sporadically. This concentration of communist ideas, reasoned Durkheim, suggests that egalitarian communism resonated with sociocultural changes and sentiments deeply rooted in European society. Second, Durkheim further intimated that because communist ideas had sedimented into the collective social body, the egalitarians expressed a deeply felt tension in experience. This gave to the egalitarian ideology a this-worldly and practical aspect lacking in traditional utopianism. Durkheim noted the practical turn of egalitarian communism in the criticisms, for example, of Simon-Nicolas-Henry Linguet.[55] Finally, Durkheim felt that, in fact, egalitarian communism had become the spiritual or moral core of modern socialism. Durkheim was correct in suggesting that modern socialism reflects the practical turn of egalitarian communism.

Within the context of eighteenth-century France, it is, I believe, correct to remark that the highest expression of revolutionary ideology was achieved in Babouvism. Babeuf himself has recently been called "the First Revolutionary

Communist."[56] This is true if we mean that Babeuf self-consciously united theoretical and practical criticism on the basis of the egalitarian communist ideology.

My argument clearly suggests that the intellectual roots of Babouvism are in egalitarianism. The primeval law of human association, stated the Babouvist *Manifesto of Equals*, is equality: "Equality is the first principle of nature, the most elementary need of man, the prime bond of any decent association among human beings."[57] Regarding the link between equality and a communitarian order, Babeuf wrote: "The only way to [establish an egalitarian order] . . . is to organize a communal regime which will suppress private property."[58] The *Manifesto of Equals* declared point-blank: "Our demand is for the communal ownership of the earth's resources."[59]

The revolutionaries criticized the contemporary European order because it violated the twin ideals of equality and community. Revolution was necessary to restore the natural order. Babeuf reasoned that in the present system "a general upheaval in the system of property becomes inevitable and . . . the revolt of the poor against the rich becomes an inevitability that nothing could prevent."[60] The revolution will be carried out by the "suffering people":

> The hour for decisive action has now struck. The people's suffering has reached its peak; it darkens the face of the earth. . . . Now the time has come to mend matters. We, who love justice and who seek happiness—let us enter the struggle for the sake of equality. The time has come to establish the Republic of Equality.[61]

The aim of revolution was to restore the primeval condition of equality and community. The means to accomplish the "Republic of Equality" were armed insurrection, terror, and a temporary dictatorship by the revolutionary vanguard. Because of the intellectual and political immaturity of the people, and the resistance to change by the propertied classes, conspiracy, terror, and dictatorial means were considered legitimate vehicles of revolution. "All opposition," declared Babeuf, "will be crushed at once by force; hostile elements will be executed."[62] The state would play a vital role in shaping the people into a virtuous and democratic citizenry, bereft of all residues of egoism linked to the regime of private property and inequality.

We may enumerate the chief ideas of the revolutionary ideology as follows. First, social and economic equality and social justice are the necessary preconditions of individual happiness and social solidarity. Second, social equality presupposes a communal order founded upon collective property and a common culture. Third, the origins of human misery are equated with private property and its attendant effects of inequality, divisive conflict, and a culture of egoism and hedonism. Hence, the necessity of a political revolution by the propertyless against the sociopolitical order founded upon private property. Fourth, in the face of the political backwardness of the masses, the revolution will be a minority revolution directed by a vanguard party. Fifth, to establish an egalitarian and democratic order, the state must be organized into a temporary dictatorship whose main aim is to subdue opposition and, in unison with a civil religion, produce an enlightened and virtuous citizenry.

Conventional wisdom asserts the ideological polarity between Marx (revolution) and sociology (liberalism), which presumably reflects the equally polarized class divisions between the proletariat and the bourgeoisie.[63] Unfortunately, such neat classifications rarely coincide with the complexity of history. As it turns out, Marx, as his biographers tell us, was very much a bourgeois, and, as I will demonstrate, his social theory remains embedded in the presuppositions and ideals of liberalism. Despite their unmistakably bourgeois self-image, Durkheim and Weber were harsh critics of the legacy of liberalism. Their critique of liberalism does not reflect the anti-modernism of either Conservatism or Romanticism but rather their turn to the revolutionary tradition in an effort to reconstruct a liberal ideology attuned to a changing European order. In contrast to the philosophes, for whom liberalism and revolution were either/or premises, and in contrast to the nineteenth-century bearers of either the liberal or the revolutionary tradition, Marx, Durkheim, and Weber were among the few nineteenth-century thinkers who synthesized liberal and revolutionary ideological principles.

As we move from the egalitarian communism of eighteenth-century France to the revolutionary ideologies and movements of the nineteenth century, we must discriminate between two currents of revolutionary ideology. The French revolutionary tradition was rooted in the egalitarian and primitivist communitarian ideals of the French peasantry and petty bourgeois artisans. Accordingly, we can detect in it a pronounced anti-modernism manifested, for example, in its hostility towards liberalism, urban-industrial development, legal-rational authority, and political centralization.[64] The combination of its·hatred for modernity and liberalism, and the political backwardness and reactionary disposition of the peasants and artisans, was highly conducive to the conspiratorial, elitist, and terrorist strategies characteristic of the revolutionary politics of the Jacobins. Despite the French Revolution and the beginnings of urbanization and industrialization in the nineteenth century, the peasant and artisan culture of eighteenth-century France survived.[65] Thus, it is not surprising to find that the nineteenth-century heirs to the French revolutionary tradition—Fourier, Cabet, Blanqui, Proudhon, and the diverse currents and fusions of anarchism and syndicalism during the Third French Republic—remained very much advocates of the egalitarian communist ideals of Rousseau, the egalitarians, and Babouvism.[66]

Despite Marx's immersion in the ideas and history of the French revolutionary tradition, and despite the impact of the French experience on his early development, Marx's intellectual and political commitment to revolution departed in two fundamental ways from the French tradition. First, unlike the French revolutionaries, Marx shared with the liberals a thoroughly positive attitude toward modern civilization. In part, this is exhibited in the profound impact of Saint-Simon on Marx. The significance of Saint-Simon for Marx's development arises from the fact that Saint-Simon criticized liberalism without repudiating modernist premises. To put it another way, Saint-Simon opened up the possibility of coupling a revolutionary critique of liberalism and bourgeois society to modernist presuppositions.[67]

Second, unlike the French revolutionaries, who conceived of communism as simply a negation of liberalism and bourgeois society, Marx projected communism as simultaneously the realization and transfiguration of the principles of liberalism and bourgeois society. In contrast to the French revolutionaries, Marx, as will be detailed shortly, came to revolution and communism *through* liberalism, i.e., as a consequence of a positive critique of the limitations of liberalism and bourgeois society. The modernist and liberal underpinnings of Marx's revolutionary ideology, I believe, are the basis of its intellectual and political success in advanced industrial societies.

By the 1880s, when it was becoming apparent to progressive thinkers that orthodox liberalism was intellectually and politically defunct, Marx's critique of liberalism, a critique that preserved the rational and ethical kernel of liberalism, proved attractive to disillusioned liberals. Thus, unlike the Jacobin French tradition, Marxism had appeal to the educated bourgeoisie, many of whom were all too aware of the practical failure and theoretical simplicity of classical liberalism.

Durkheim and Weber came of age precisely at that historical juncture when classical liberalism had lost all explanatory power and, on account of its recent history of supporting the Right and counterrevolution, had ceased to be a progressive ideology. In the sociohistorical context of Wilhelmian Germany and the Third French Republic, it was no longer possible for historically sensitive and future-oriented thinkers to rally behind the outdated doctrines of classical liberalism. In addition, all the existing idioms of liberalism—natural law, utilitarianism, and social Darwinism—were historically and intellectually discredited. In the revolutionary tradition, particularly in Marxism with regard to Germany and with regard to egalitarian communism in France, Durkheim and Weber found an intellectually compelling critique of classical liberalism. Moreover, the revolutionary tradition consisted of a configuration of ideas and themes which could be selectively used, Durkheim and Weber thought, as the basis for a revitalized liberalism.

Marx, Durkheim, and Weber recognized and criticized the limitations of liberalism and bourgeois society. Marx extended liberal and bourgeois premises to their furthest conclusion: revolution and communism. Durkheim and Weber sought to work through the revolutionary tradition, appropriating its critique of liberalism and bourgeois society, in order to return to a reconstructed liberalism. Marx, Durkheim, and Weber, each in his own way, attempted to combine liberal themes—autonomy, pluralism, and industrial development—and revolutionary themes—equality, community, and social democratic control.

Summary of Part One

THIS IS A good place to pause and restate the contours of my argument. Social theory is linked to practical forms of life and contains multiple categorical levels, from high-level background assumptions and analytical models to research methodologies rich in empirical content. An historical reconstruction of social theory, therefore, must preserve this multidimensionality and recognize the possibility of disparities between levels and avoid reductionism in any one direction.

Enlightenment social theory consists of two analytical strains. First, the analytical individualism and instrumentalism of the materialists and economists extend contractarian premises and form the basis of Anglo-American social science. Second, the Enlightenment science of man must be understood as a reaction to materialism and the analytical premises of contractarianism. In the programmatic statements of the science of man, as well as in their historical and proto-sociological studies, we perceive the beginnings of the classical tradition of European social theory. The European tradition is characterised by its effort to integrate individualism and holism, materialism and idealism, and its comparative historical focus coupled to a thematic interest in the irony or dialectic of historical progress.

On the basis of my revised conception of Enlightenment

social theory, we needed to reinterpret the social theory of the counter-Enlightenment. I argued that, at an analytical level, the diverse currents of counter-Enlightenment thought served as carriers and developers of the science of man; in addition, the Enlightenment critics, from their own nonliberal stand-point, were able to arrive at a perspective on alienation and social order that was of major importance to the tradition of European social theory.

The analytical history of nineteenth-century social theory is, of course, immensely complex. The English theoretical tradition, particularly Spencer and the economists, continued to theorize within the framework of an instrumentalist theory of social action and order. In France and Germany, however, it was the premises of the science of man, as mediated by the Enlightenment critics, that formed the dominant perspectives of nineteenth-century social theory.

In addition, I contend that the social theories of Marx, Durkheim, and Weber find their *chief* ideological origins in the coalescence of liberalism and revolution. In answer to the question, so often posed either implicitly or directly, as to why it is that Marx, Durkheim, and Weber are still vital in contemporary theoretical debate, I have suggested, in part, the following conjecture: in uniting liberal and revolutionary ideas, Marx, Durkheim, and Weber avoided the intellectual petrification that fell upon the conservative, liberal, and revolutionary orthodoxies.

These diverse ideological orthodoxies, to pursue this further, did, it is true, yield moments of theoretical fructification. Conservatism found theoretical articulation in Comte's sociology, although, as we have seen, Conservatism was not able to preserve an ongoing social theoretical tradition. Almost simultaneously with its completion, Comte's social theory assumed an extra-academic cult status. By the end of the nineteenth century, the ideas of philosophical conservatism were unable to gain a foothold in mainstream academic social theory and reappeared as vulgar ideological and theological standpoints.

By and large, the French revolutionary tradition shared the same fate. In its most productive theoretical phase, the revolutionary ideology yielded theoretical formulations of some significance—for example, those of Fourier and Proudhon. However, by the turn of the century, the anarchist and syndicalist revolutionary ideologies had given up any presumption of scientific respectability.

Unquestionably, classical liberalism fared better in translating its ideological tenets into a social theoretical tradition. Though classical liberalism found a hostile environment in Germany, there was a great deal of support for English-styled liberalism, and its individualistic and evolutionary orientations in France. Nevertheless, the dominant social theoretical forms in France drew from its native collectivist, idealist, and democratic traditions.

It was, of course, in England that classical liberalism flourished. Classical economics, utilitarian moral theory, and Spencer's evolutionary social theory were diverse yet quite consistent expressions of classical liberalism. Even here we need to introduce an important qualification. Though the English economic and utilitarian traditions continued largely intact until World War I, Spencerian social theory, virtually the only general social theory in England, had few supporters by the turn of the century. The successors to Spencer's social theory, Hobhouse and Westermarck, reflect an initial attempt to combine collectivist and idealist orientations with classical liberal ideas. It is curious to consider that English social theory perhaps found its highest, most lasting expression, not in economics or sociology, but in its anthropological traditions.[1]

The modern intellectual milieu in Europe was defined more or less by these intellectual traditions: Enlightenment, Conservatism, Romanticism, and Revolution. As part of this environment, European social theory took root and was shaped by these broad intellectual traditions. To merely link modern social theory to these general traditions, however, would be unhistorical. As these intellectual traditions were carried into the nineteenth century, they underwent alterations. We must therefore specify, in the context of our analysis of Marx, Durkheim, and Weber, the diverse forms these traditions assumed in France and Germany during the nineteenth century.

In the chapters to follow, I relate the subsequent history of liberalism and revolution as they were articulated in the social theories of Marx, Durkheim, and Weber. One of my main themes is that many nineteenth-century thinkers, including Marx, Durkheim, and Weber, were motivated by the defects of liberalism and bourgeois society. They looked to the experience of the working class and its expression in revolutionary ideology for direction in order to reconstruct a modern ideology. Towards this end, Marx, Durkheim, and Weber sought and partially achieved a synthesis of liberalism and revolution.

Part Two
Marx

Introduction to Part Two

DURING THE FORMATIVE years of Marx's intellectual development, he imbibed the liberal spirit of the Enlightenment.
Marx's liberalism, like that of his predecessors, Lessing, Kant,
and Humboldt, was articulated in the language of idealism.
However, between 1843 and 1844, Marx reacted against both
liberalism and idealism. By 1844, Marx embraced a revolutionary politic, and by 1846 he had abandoned an idealist
view of sociohistorical reality. In the following pages, I re-
count the outlines of Marx's early intellectual development.

Karl Marx was reared in Trier, a city in the far western
province of the Rhineland. Its proximity to France, and its
temporary rule under Napoleon, allowed the critical rationalism of French culture to function as an alternative to the
conservatism of Prussian-dominated Germany. In fact, Trier
was permeated with the progressive philosophy of the Enlightenment.[1] In its public works projects, for example, the
young Marx could directly observe the benevolent impact of
enlightened reason. In addition, Karl's father, Heinrich Marx,
and his father-in-law, Baron von Westphalen, were well read
in the literature of the French liberals.[2] The extent to which
the liberal ethos had settled into the environment of the young
Marx is illustrated by the fact that the principal of his high
school was a disciple of Kantian liberalism. The papers Marx

wrote while attending high school in Trier indicate his absorption of the Enlightenment legacy of liberal humanism as well as the Christian idealism of his religious upbringing.[3]

In 1835, Marx began his university studies at Bonn. He attended the historical and literary lectures of the romantic, A. W. Schlegel. Although ostensibly preparing for a career in law, Marx spent much of his time reading and writing romantic poetry. Marx's infatuation with romantic poetry continued as he transferred to the University of Berlin in 1836. His poetry reveals the chief themes and ideas of the romantics: idealism, expressionism, and the search for spiritual renewal and unity. By 1839, Marx no longer composed poetry. Nevertheless, the romantic concern for individual and collective struggle, personal and societal integration, persisted as a central component of Marxian social theory.

At the University of Berlin, Marx gravitated from poetry to law to philosophy. It was during the period 1836–1837 that Marx underwent an intellectual conversion: from the unsystematic idealism of the romantics, to the transcendental idealism of Kant and Fichte, to Hegelian idealism. All this is dramatically detailed in a letter Marx wrote to his father in 1837:

> A curtain had fallen, my holy of holies had been shattered, and new gods had to be found. Setting out from idealism—which, let me say in passing, I had compared to and nourished with that of Kant and Fichte—I hit upon seeking the Idea in the real itself. If formerly the gods had dwelt above the world, they had now become its center.[4]

Marx repudiated that form of idealism which preserved the separation between Idea and reality, form and content, value and fact. In Hegelian idealism, the Idea or Reason is immanent to natural and historical reality. Humanity and nature are viewed as a dynamic unity whose essence, reason and freedom, develops through specific historical epochs. There were two factors which prepared Marx for this change. First, Hegelian idealism dominated Berlin; it was inevitable that Marx would eventually be challenged to seriously study Hegel. Second, Marx was strongly influenced by historically and empirically oriented social theories—for example, those of Saint-Simon and Savigny.[5] By adopting an Hegelian viewpoint, Marx could not remain satisfied with a formal and transcendental approach to the problems of philosophy and the human sciences. Thus, Marx discarded his youthful project of elaborating a "Metaphysics of Law" precisely because of its formal, dualistic, and ahistorical character. Marx's turn to Hegelianism, however momentous for his overall intellectual development, did not signify an ideological rejection of his early liberalism.

Marx's turn to Hegel was monitored by the older members of the Doctors' Club; they later formed the core of the so-called Young Hegelians. Between 1839 and 1842, Marx was a Young Hegelian and drew from the fund of their ideas—particularly those of Bruno Bauer, Moses Hess, and Ludwig Feuerbach.[6] It is necessary to recall that what the Young Hegelians found in Hegel was a form of critical rationalism that resonated with their own idealist presuppositions. In Marx's doctoral dissertation on post-Aristotelian Greek philosophy, composed between 1840 and 1841, we find this typical combination of idealism and liberalism. In the idealist spirit of the Young Hegelians, Marx declared that "idealism is no illusion, but the true reality."[7] Marx's idealism was critical and oriented to the "reform of consciousness." Marx wrote: "The *practice* of philosophy, however, is itself *theoretical.* It is *criticism* which measures individual existence against its essence or the particular reality by the Idea."[8] Reality was to be confronted with the Idea or the rational ideal immanent to it. Because Marx assumed that reason was an inherent part of the societal community, he felt that this critical encounter between concept and existing reality would serve as a catalyst of social change. Marx shared with the Young Hegelians the belief in the power of ideas to alter reality.[9] As a Young Hegelian, Marx embraced the liberal humanism and reformist politics that were the legacy of the philosophes.

Marx received his doctorate in 1841. Henceforth, he was to sever all official ties to the university. During the ensuing years, Marx found his chief source of employment, and main intellectual forum, as a writer for and editor of various progressive newspapers. Considering the sum of articles written by Marx in 1842, it is evident that he had not abandoned a basically reformist politics and liberal bourgeois outlook.[10] In these various newspaper articles, Marx fought for such liberal principles as free public discussion and the self-regulating censorship of individual conscience; asserted that the aim of the state was to guide individuals to a moral life; and affirmed social conflict, critical reason, and progress. In a word, these early writings reflect the level of criticism represented by Enlightenment liberalism.

The decisive "turning point" in Marx's intellectual development was his break from the Young Hegelians and his critique of liberalism effected between 1843 and 1844. Between the summer of 1843 and the summer of 1844, Marx composed a series of essays—*Critique of Hegel's Doctrine of the State,* "On the Jewish Question," "A Contribution to the Critique of Hegel's Philosophy of Right: Introduction," and the *1844 Paris Manuscripts*—that signaled the beginnings of his revolutionary world-view. Several factors contributed to Marx's "revolutionary turn" between 1843 and 1844. Mention should be made of Marx's encounter with Feuerbach's materialist radicalization of Hegel, and also of Marx's assimilation of the French revolutionary tradition.[11] In the various essays cited above, Marx asserted the limitations of liberal ideology and bourgeois society. He argued that the idea of autonomy translated into reality presupposes equality and democracy; and that sociocultural pluralism, to avoid its breakdown into anarchism or authoritarianism, must be coupled to a communal framework of moral consensus. Applied to social reality, Marx's newly gained revolutionary standpoint pointed to the irrationality of the bourgeois order, the class-determined character of bourgeois individualism, the self-interested foundation of bourgeois politics, and the merely formal universality of bourgeois natural rights and the constitutional state. In May 1843, in words recalling the Babouvist *Manifesto of Equals*, Marx alluded to a "suffering humanity" as the basis of a revolutionary movement:

> The system of profit and commerce, of property and human exploitation, leads ... to a rift inside contemporary society that the old society is incapable of healing. ...
>
> On one side the old world must be brought right out into the light of day and the new one given a positive form. The longer that events allow thinking humanity time to recollect itself and suffering humanity time to assemble itself, the more perfect will be the birth of the product that the present carries in its womb.[12]

Although Marx's notion of critique still retained an idealist dimension, the connection between "the system of profit and commerce" and a "suffering humanity" discloses a strong materialist aspect.[13] In 1845–1846, Marx collaborated with Engels on *The German Ideology* to give his new revolutionary posture a programmatic form. The result was the so-called materialist theory of history joined to the revolutionary politics of communism.[14]

During the years 1839–1844, Marx underwent a series of intellectual transformations: from the idealism of Kant and Fichte to that of Hegel; from the idealism of Hegel to the Young Hegelian critical rationalism; and finally, to a philosophy of practice tied to materialist premises. At another level, Marx shifted from the politics of reform to those of revolution. By 1846, Marxian social theory assumed its mature programmatic form as a materialist theory of society and history coupled to a revolutionary practice.

In the following chapters, I examine the controlling and abiding features of Marxian social theory. Three themes or motifs form the point of departure. The romantic motif refers to Marx's commitment to the fully developed, internally harmonious personality. From this romantic premise, Marx criticized bourgeois society as a divided and fragmented order;

revolution was to restore integral unity while sustaining sociocultural differentiation. The Enlightenment motif reflects
Marx's belief in the autonomous individual. Reflecting the
Enlightenment ideal of autonomy, Marx criticized bourgeois
society for its suppression, or at least its only formal and
limited realization, of autonomy. Revolution was to establish
autonomy on a truly universal basis by completing the process
of democratization begun in bourgeois society. The third motif
which informs and structures Marx's entire thinking is revolution. The revolutionary motif follows from the romantic
and Enlightenment presuppositions of Marxian social theory:
revolution was the vehicle for realizing the autonomous and
fully developed individual. My contention is that, unlike the
French revolutionary tradition, Marx's revolutionary orientation proceeds from and preserves the vital liberal heritage
of the Enlightenment. Marx turned against liberalism and
bourgeois society in a one-sided and negative way only during
those periods when bourgeois society suppressed its liberal
principles—for example, during periods of alliance between
the bourgeois and traditional right, or during counterrevo-
lutionary repression.[15]

3. Romantic and Enlightenment Presuppositions of Marxian Social Theory

IN THIS CHAPTER, we examine the romantic and Enlightenment themes which underlie Marx's critical analysis of bourgeois society.

The Romantic Motif: Towards the Integral Individual

The dominant model of reality in the Enlightenment was dualistic: it posited the antithesis of idealism and materialism at every level of experience. Like the romantics, Marx attempted to overcome this dualistic world-view. Reacting against both materialism and idealism, Marx sought a metaphysic that asserted the dynamic unity of the ideal and material. We find a similar quest for integral unity at the level of personality and social order. This attempt to surmount dualism and division is the deep romantic structure of Marxian social theory.[1]

Marx confronted the dualistic world view in its most sophisticated form: Kantian idealism. Marx reasoned that since Kantian dualism gave expression to the ideal of the autonomy of the individual, Kant's philosophy embodied the progressive liberal humanism of the philosophes. Nevertheless, the Kantian duality between intellect and sensuous nature, moral will and desire, and freedom and necessity was unacceptable to the romantics and to Marx. In addition, Kant's radical dissociation of the life of the spirit or ideas from material existence or interests limited his critique to the various modalities of reason: understanding, willing, and judging.[2] Kant, in other words, was unable to develop a critique of social, cultural, and political practice.

Marx's repudiation of the dualistic world-view did not, however, result in a materialist monism. Marx objected to the mechanical materialism of Hobbes, La Mettrie, and Holbach. In Hobbes and La Mettrie, for example, all ideational reality was reduced to "but phantoms of the real world, more or less divested of its sensuous form."[3] Even Feuerbach's humanistic materialism ultimately spoke only of the "real" corporeal or biological individual, and it ends in a natural determinism. In these various forms of materialism, the individual loses his or her quality as an active, dynamic, and free agency.

In his first "Thesis on Feuerbach," Marx stated that the active side of epistemology and anthropology was developed by idealism.[4] In the transcendental idealism of Kant and Fichte, mind was the active agency in the production of cognitive and practical order. The really decisive breakthrough in German idealism, Marx contended, was Hegel's integration of idealism and historical development. "Hegel conceives the self-creation of man as a process, conceives objectification as loss of object, as alienation and as transcendence of this alienation; that he thus grasps the essence of *labour* and comprehends objective man—true, because real man—as the outcome of man's *own labour*."[5] Since Hegel viewed history as the process by which human nature evolves through practical activity, he was a progressive and critical thinker.[6] However, because Hegel defined practical activity as mental labor and objectification, alienation, and transcendence as occurring only in the ideal realm of thought, his dialectical idealism left the empirical world intact. "In Hegel's *Phänomenologie* the *material, sensuously perceptible, objective* foundations of the various estranged forms of human self-consciousness are allowed to *remain*. The whole destructive work results in the *most conservative philosophy* because it thinks it has overcome the *objective world* . . . by transforming it into a 'Thing of Thought'. . . ."[7] Even the Young Hegelians, for all their critical consciousness, "remain within his [Hegel's] speculation and each represents only *one* side of his system."[8] Notwithstanding a critical impulse in its notion of an active subject, an historical conception of human development, and the dialectic of objectification and alienation, idealism's retreat from a critique of practice pointed to its abiding conservatism.

Marx's intention was to achieve a reconciliation of materialism and idealism; to combine the critical and scientific aspects of materialism with the dynamic and historical components of idealism. In opposition to monistic and dualistic theories, Marx sought a dialectical theory which he first called "Naturalism" or "Humanism" and later designated "Historical Materialism."[9] In Marx's dialectical approach, mind and matter, spirit and nature, constitute the unified structure of reality. In the *1844 Manuscripts*, Marx stated his position, in somewhat misleading metaphysical terms, as follows: "It is true that thought and being are *distinct*, but at the same time they are in *unity* with one another."[10] At a social theoretical level, Marx's dialectical methodology meant that, in principle, material and ideal factors or structural and cultural factors form a reciprocal, mutually causative not unilinear, mechanical relationship.[11] Marx's dialectical position regarding the unity between thought and being, structural and cultural factors, was connected to a normative model of the individual and the social order, centering upon the development and harmony within and between individuals. This romantic epistemology and anthropology is the basis of Marx's critique of the dualistic world-view of liberalism and the frag-mented nature of personal and social life in bourgeois society.

Marx argued that the dualistic world-view of liberalism was based upon the divided character of modern capitalism. Regarding classical liberal theories which separate civil so-ciety and the state, Marx wrote: "These theories, however, are right in that they express a *consequence* of modern society, for here the Estates are nothing more than the factual expression of the real relationship between the state and civil society, namely one of separation."[12] Marx criticized bourgeois society because it fragments internal personal development and cre-ates sustained opposition and polarity in civil life. Bourgeois society consists of self-interested individuals opposed to one another and internally divided between the egoistic interests of economic life and the altruistic concerns of political affairs. In capitalism, the individual and the community, self-interest and general interest, and civil society and politics stand in perpetual conflict.[13] The divisive nature of bourgeois society is one of its essential or defining features. Its structural basis, Marx argued, lies in the dualistic nature of its capitalist so-cioeconomic system: in the twofold character of the com-modity form, the dichotomous class structure, and the separation of mental and manual labor.

Marx criticized the dualisms of liberal thought and its basis in the divisive socioeconomic organization of capital-ism. Nonetheless, Marx did not simply unilaterally oppose liberalism or capitalism. Marx claimed that capitalism cre-ates the necessary conditions for the realization of the ideal of the integral individual. Marx pointed to the dynamics of capitalism, which propel the development of the division of labor and engender the expansion and enrichment of human needs and capacities. Regarding the "civilizing" character of capitalism, Marx wrote:

> Capital's ceaseless striving towards the general form of wealth drives labour beyond the limits of its natural paltriness, and thus creates the material elements for the development of the

rich individuality which is as all-sided in its production as in its consumption, and whose labour also therefore appears no longer as labour, but as the full development of activity itself. . . .[14]

Marx believed that the idea of a fully developed individual was immanent in the internal dynamics of capitalism—specifically, in the idea of modern industry. Of this positive side of capitalist development, Marx said:

Modern Industry, indeed, compels society, under penalty of death, to replace the detail-worker of to-day, crippled by life-long repetition of one and the same trivial operation, and thus reduced to the mere fragment of a man, by the fully developed individual, fit for a variety of labours, ready to face any change of production, and to whom the different social functions he performs, are but so many modes of giving free scope to his own natural and acquired powers.[15]

Though modern industry projects the ideal of the integral individual, in a capitalist system, modern industry assumes the form of a rigid division of labor producing one-sided and stunted forms of individuality. Of this negative side of capitalism, Marx wrote: "But if Modern industry, by its very nature, therefore necessitates variation of labour, fluency of function, universal mobility of the labourer on the other hand, in its capitalist form, it reproduces the old division of labour with its ossified particularizations."[16] As capitalism is an historical agency in the development of modern industry—and therefore anticipates the ideal of a fully developed individual—it is a progressive stage in social evolution. However, because capitalism entails a specific social organization of modern industry—instantiating the individual as one-dimensional and fragmented—it simultaneously obstructs social progress. Marx spoke of this as the "absolute contradiction between the technical necessities of modern industry, and the social character inherent in its capitalist form . . . ."[17]

Marx criticized the divisive character of bourgeois society.

Moreover, he opposed the liberal ideologues who claimed that bourgeois society is the terminal point of history. Because liberal social theory freezes historical development at the bourgeois stage, it functions as a conservative ideology of order. In opposition to liberalism's ideologically motivated suspension of the historical process, Marx maintained that bourgeois society was but one phase of historical development. Nevertheless, bourgeois society, Marx urged, has world historical importance because it creates the universal conditions for the realization of harmonious development within the individual and between individuals, nature, and the community. In the *1844 Manuscripts*, Marx specified the romantic ideal of integral unity in terms that he later toned down considerably. "It is the *genuine* resolution of the conflict between man and nature, and between man and man, the true resolution of the conflict between existence and being, between objectification and self-affirmation, between freedom and necessity, between individual and species."[18] The romantic structure of Marxian social theory lies in the struggle against dualisms and divisions and his quest for a fully developed and integrated humanity.

I am not, of course, alone in pointing to the romantic presuppositions of Marx's work. However, scholars such as Karl Löwith, Eric Voegelin, Robert Tucker, and M. H. Abrams tend to identify the romantic ideal of integral unity with the Millenarianism of the Judeo-Christian tradition.[19] They maintain that the notion of the reintegration of humanity is part of a broader philosophy of history—rooted in religious and mythical images—which operates according to a simple triadic scheme: first, there is paradise, an original condition of unity and harmony; second, the fall, a period of division and alienation; and third, redemption, in which the primeval condition of unity is restored at a higher level by incorporating the intermediate sociocultural developments. Marx's notion of primitive communism, the divisions and alienation of civil society, and the higher unity of industrial communism is interpreted as a secularized version of the Christian millenarian pattern of paradise, fall, and redemption. This raises a serious question concerning the intellectual status of Marxian social theory. If the above reading is correct, then Marx's social theory would have to be situated in relation to premodern or anti-modern presuppositions. This would mean that Marx's critique of bourgeois society and his revolutionary world-view would have a dogmatic and utopian status. This interpretation undercuts the legitimacy of Marxian social theory by denying its claim of advancing a critique founded upon modernist presuppositions.

The issue is far from unambiguous. Romanticism, as I previously remarked, does combine Enlightenment modernism with aspects of traditional idealism. The pattern of unity–division–higher unity is built into romantic thought.[20] The romantics looked to the past for models of integral unity. They criticized Enlightenment modernism for its dualisms and divisions. The romantics anticipated a coming era of renewal, harmony, and unity. Yet, we may wonder, is it not the case that such religious or mythical images are structured into Western culture so profoundly that one cannot help discovering them in one form or another in all Western intellectual traditions? The crucial question, I believe, is the meaning given to these images and schemes in the context of their usage.[21] With regard to Marx, I have argued that since he perceives the many-sided development of individuality as inherent in the sociocultural dynamics of industrialism, the concept of integral unity retains a modern ideological sense. Naturally, one may reason that as a utopian thinker Marx simply reads this concept into contemporary realities, although it is without an empirical basis. Whether or not we can find an empirical justification for the romantic ideal of the fully developed individual and the related communitarianism depends upon our interpretations of contemporary realities; this, I would suggest, is as much an issue of ideological presuppositions as of "factual" conditions.

The Enlightenment Motif:
Capitalism and Autonomy

The ideological impulse behind the dualistic metaphysic of the Enlightenment was the claim of individual liberty. By asserting an independent realm of subjective will, the Enlightenment developed the modern notion of autonomy—of a morally free and responsible individual. Moreover, the idea of autonomy assumed a legal and institutional form in the doctrine of political and civil rights and the rule of law. Although Marx repudiated the dualistic metaphysic of the Enlightenment, his dialectical perspective preserves its individualistic principle. Marx consistently opposed materialism—be it the materialism of Democritus, Hobbes, Holbach, or Feuerbach—because of its heteronomous model of the individual. Marx never abandoned the idealist notion of subjectivity as a free moral agency. Nevertheless, Marx's commitment to autonomy differs from the Enlightenment's in two significant ways. First, Marx refused to translate substantive or ideological individualism into methodological individualism. Second, whereas the Enlightenment believed that autonomy is inherent in the rise of science, republicanism, and commerce, Marx underscored the systematic sources of heteronomy intrinsic to bourgeois society. Thus, while the ideal of autonomy was an integral ideological component of Marxian social theory, Marx gave to the concept a unique formulation and meaning.

The critique of methodological individualism—the standpoint which takes the self-sufficient individual as the basis for constructing models and explanations of social actions, order, and change—commenced in the Enlightenment critique of contract theory. Nevertheless, methodological individualism was structured into the premises of classical political economy and utilitarian moral theory. Moreover, in Marx's early theoretical efforts against German idealism, we find strains of analytical individualism.

In his *Critique of Hegel's Doctrine of the State* and, to a lesser extent, in "On The Jewish Question," Marx developed a model of modern civil society that recalls the individualistic formulations of classical political economy. In the modern world, the individual lacks any organic ties to the community. "The present state of society is different from preceding forms of civil society in that modern civil society does not sustain the individual as a member of a community, as a communal being. . . ."[22] Modern society appears as "a fluid division of masses whose various formations are arbitrary and *without* organization."[23] Corresponding to the standpoint of political economy, Marx viewed modern social life as an aggregate of self-interest and hedonistic individuals. "Modern civil society is the principle of *individualism* carried to its logical conclusion. . . ."[24] How is social order possible? "The only bond which holds them [individuals] together is natural necessity, need, and private interest, the conservation of their property and their egoistic person."[25] In his effort to disengage himself from the methodological holism of idealism, Marx found the individualistic model of classical economics to be a viable alternative.

In his subsequent writings, Marx discarded methodological individualism without embracing holism.[26] Marx insisted that society must not be thought of as an independent collective "personality" endowed with its own interests, drives, and laws.[27] It is true, Marx said, that in bourgeois society private property, the division of labor, technology, and social organization appear to be aspects of "society" which operate separately from individual motivations. But this perception is erroneous: "these factors are only real forces in the intercourse and association of these individuals. . . ."[28] As Marx was to say in his polemic against the holistic features of Proudhon's muddled Hegelianism: "Men are the actors and authors of their own history."[29] However, Marx cautioned that this does not entail analytical individualism: "Individuals have always proceeded from themselves, but of course from themselves within their given historical conditions and relations, not from the 'pure' individual in the sense of the [liberal] ideologists."[30] Marx sought a position intermediate between individualism and holism. "Above all we must avoid postulating 'society' again as an abstraction *vis-à-vis* the individual. The individual *is the social being.* His manifestations of life . . . *are* therefore an expression and confirmation of *social life.*"[31]

Marx's repudiation of methodological individualism is highlighted in the *Grundrisse.* Reacting against classical political economy, which projected the ideal of individualism into the past as a presupposition of history, Marx contended that "human beings become individuals only through the process of history. He appears originally as a *species being,* a clan being, herd animal. . . ."[32] Specific historical conditions are necessary before the modern conception of the individual can arise. Marx pointed, for instance, to "the dissolution of the feudal form of society; on the other side, the new forces of production developed since the sixteenth century."[33] In fact, Marx argued that individualism is a very recent historical product. "Only in the eighteenth century, in 'civil society,' do the various forms of social connectedness confront the individual as a mere means towards his private purposes, as external necessity."[34] However, the modern individual is not, in fact, an isolated, self-sufficient individual. Even private interests are "already socially determined interest" in which "its content as well as the form and means of its realization, is given by social conditions independent of all."[35] In place of the private, self-sufficient, natural individual of the economists, Marx asserted a social individual bound to a context of quite determinate social relations. "But the epoch which produces this standpoint, that of the isolated individual, is also precisely that of the hitherto most developed social . . . relations.[36] Society is not the atomistic civil society of the classical economists; it is composed of well-organized social groupings, structured into a coherent whole. From this uniquely sociological perspective, the needs, interests, sentiments, and values of the individual are social and fused with collective ends.[37]

Although an analytical commitment to the idea of the social determination of individual conduct is not inconsistent with ideological individualism, it does raise the question of how Marx reconciled the ideas of autonomy and social determinism. Naturally, the individual is not thoroughly determined in every aspect of personal life. The individual retains a critical capacity to judge and choose, however, within socially defined limits. This hardly amounts, in any event, to a very substantial notion of autonomy. Marx reconceptualized the idea of autonomy by arguing that, given the social nature of individualism, autonomy is possible only in a democratic society. Substantive autonomy is possible if the individual participates, through a consensually organized process, in the founding, ongoing formation, and legitimation of social institutions. True autonomy, Marx suggested, entails a thoroughgoing democratization of social, economic, and political institutions. By connecting autonomy to the democratic organization of society, Marx could disclaim methodological individualism, yet uphold the ideal of substantive autonomy.

Because Marx linked autonomy to a democratically instituted social order, his view of bourgeois society differed from that of the Enlightenment. For the philosophes, the conjunction of science, republicanism, and commerce signaled the near-automatic progress of individual freedom. Though it is true, Marx reasoned, that these developments contain a liberating aspect for the individual, they simultaneously obstruct full individuation. Marx did not, to repeat, simply oppose bourgeois society. As I have insisted, bourgeois society assumed a positive and a negative significance for Marx.

Marx argued that capitalism is a major historical agency unleashing a number of progressive sociocultural processes: secularization, rationalization, and universalization. Capitalism dissolves pre-modern cosmologies and traditional religious views of life: "All that is holy is profaned, and man is at last compelled to face with sober senses his real conditions of life. . . ."[38] Marx held that secularism directly contributes to autonomy. As a disenchanted cosmos, a secular order implies a homeocentric universe in which human freedom and dignity assume the force of a categorical imperative. Paralleling and grounding secularism is the rationalization of the socioeconomic order. The idea of a fixed order of nature no longer acts as a norm restraining want-satisfaction; needs and wants expand in accordance with the rate and extent of the transformation of nature into utilities. As capitalism is a driving force behind rationalization, it augments people's mastery over nature and extends our capacity for self-governance. Finally, the development of socioeconomic complexity and the expansion of human needs dissolve the traditional constraints stifling human development. Capitalism is an agent creating the conditions of universalistic sociocultural forms.

> Capital drives beyond national barriers and prejudices as much as beyond nature worship, as well as all traditional, confined, complacent, encrusted satisfactions, of present needs, and re- productions of old ways of life. It is destructive towards all of this, and constantly revolutionizes it, tearing down all the barriers which hem in the development of the forces of production, the expansion of needs, the all-sided development of production, and the exploitation and exchange of natural and mental forces.[39]

The universalizing tendency of capitalism signifies the replacement of particularistic social and cultural forms by more universal ones.[40] In this regard, Marx pointed to the rise of a world literature, international social groupings and movements, and universalistic legal and moral norms. In Marx's view, this marks a substantial gain in human freedom. Thus, as a carrier of secularism, rationalization, and universalization, capitalism functions unintentionally as an historical vehicle of individual freedom and social progress.

The philosophes believed that there was an inherent link between the secular, pluralistic, and competitive premises of capitalism and autonomy. Without gainsaying the progressive role of capitalism and the bourgeois epoch as a bearer of secularism, rationalization, and universalization, Marx main-

tained that capitalism suppresses full and universal autonomy and ultimately derails the march of social progress. Of
this curious inversion, Marx wrote:

> In our days everything seems pregnant with its contrary. Ma-
> chinery, gifted with the wonderful power of shortening and
> fructifying human labour, we behold starving and overworking
> it. The new-fangled sources of wealth, by some strange weird
> spell, are turned into sources of want. The victories of art seem
> bought by the loss of character. At the same time that mankind
> masters nature, man seems to become enslaved to other men
> or his own infamy. Even the pure light of science seems unable
> to shine but on the dark background of ignorance. All our in-
> vention and progress seem to result in endowing material
> forces with intellectual life, and in stultifying human life into
> a material force. This antagonism between modern industry
> and science on the one hand, modern misery and dissolution
> on the other hand; this antagonism between the productive
> forces and the social relations of an epoch is a fact, palpable,
> overwhelming, and not to be controverted.[41]

Capitalism brings forces of social progress into world history, but simultaneously subverts their liberating potential:
the rationalization of social life does not only yield our increased control over natural and social forces, but augments
the irrationality of social life (for example, the frequent cycles
of economic crises and open class conflict). Instead of the
world perceived as a humanly constituted and demystified
order, it assumes the form of a fetishized, object-centered, and
opaque system of commodity relations; the movement towards universalistic social and cultural forms, and its inherent potential for promoting critical reason and a higher form
of individuality, begets new, more rigid particularisms and
class divisions which suppress individuality. In short, capitalism posits the individual more as a heteronomous than an
autonomous being. Marx's final judgment of capitalism was
that it is a transitional social form in which we are still in
the process of creating the conditions for individual autonomy: "The alien and independent character in which it [cap-

italism] presently exists *vis-à-vis* individuals proves only that the latter are still engaged in the creation of the conditions of their social life, and that they have not yet begun, on the basis of these conditions, to live it."[42]

This chapter has attempted to specify the twofold ideological character of Marxian social theory. We have pointed to the romantic notion of the integral individual and the Enlightenment doctrine of autonomy. On the basis of these ideological presuppositions, Marx's attitude towards bourgeois society necessarily presents both a positive and a negative side. Marx viewed bourgeois society as a progressive historical development in that it coheres around the principles of individual development, freedom, and democracy and creates the preconditions of their realization. Yet, Marx was critical of bourgeois society to the extent that it maintains a system that perpetuates sociocultural division and personal heteronomy. Marx believed that bourgeois society is a transitional historical phase whose positive and progressive character can be maintained only by its supersession.

4. *The Revolutionary Motif*

Revolution as the Vehicle of Democracy

MARX INHERITED A legacy of criticism towards bourgeois society. In the early post-Enlightenment era, liberalism and capitalism were under considerable attack from the conservatives, romantics, and the revolutionary wing of the French Enlightenment. From a broad historical perspective, the critique of capitalism extends back to Aristotle's critique of commerce.[1] The specifics of Marx's critique were derived in the main from the French revolutionary tradition. Marx departed from these various ideological currents of anti-Enlightenment in one fundamental sense: he insisted upon the progressive character of liberalism and bourgeois society. Whereas the conservatives, romantics, and revolutionaries proposed a one-dimensional negation of liberalism and bourgeois society, Marx, by contrast, sought revolutionary change as a precondition for the realization of liberal ideals and the sociocultural principles (secularism, universalism, and rationalization) implied in the bourgeois order. This chapter examines Marx's political treatment of the problem of the transition from capitalism to socialism by way of detailing the premises and strategies of Marx's idea of revolution.

Marx's transition from his early liberalism to revolutionary communism coincides with his encounter with the French revolutionary tradition. We must ascertain, therefore, the historical importance of this relationship for the development of Marx's idea of social change and revolution.

The evidence points to the fact that Marx's revolutionary ideology was not, as Shlomo Avineri intimates, simply a logical extension of the materialist turn of German idealism.[2] Though prior to 1842, Marx doesn't seem to have read the original works of French socialists, the French revolutionary tradition penetrated into his environment through several agencies. Of the highest importance is Moses Hess, perhaps the first publicly acknowledged communist in Germany, of whom George Lichtheim writes: "Hess was Marx's precursor and, so to speak, his John the Baptist."[3] Hess, as it turns out, was steeped in the French egalitarian communist tradition, and was a major contributor to the *Rheinische Zeitung* and later the *Deutsche-französische Jahrbücher*—both of which Marx served as editor. Marx assimilated Hess's coupling of Hegelian dialectics to egalitarian communism.[4] Aside from Hess, Wilhelm Weitling's several publications prior to 1843 and, in particular, Lorenz von Stein's *Socialism and Communism in Present-Day France* (1842)—both of which were reviewed in the *Rheinische Zeitung* by Hess—compelled Marx to confront the French revolutionary tradition.[5] From the summer of 1844 through his stay in Paris (February 1845), Marx undertook an intensive study of the French revolutionary tradition.[6] In addition, we know that Marx had extensive contacts with various working-class associations and met several of their leading spokesmen, including Proudhon. From Marx's polemic *The Holy Family* (composed between September and November 1844), in which he traced basic aspects of his own revolutionary standpoint to the ideas of French materialism and egalitarian communism, it is evident that the French revolutionary tradition was a key component of Marx's social and political thought.

Though the evidence establishes historical ties between

Marx and the French revolutionary tradition, the meaning of this historical relationship is less unequivocal. Perhaps the most interesting and important argument is that of Talmon, who contends that Marx inherited the full ideological apparatus of the Jacobin tradition. Among its principle tenets are "the idea of an irresistible advance to some preordained denouement, the decisive role of the enlightened vanguard in the task of realization, and the expectation of the spontaneous self-identification of man with the ultimate scheme of things—to the cessation of all conflict."[7] Following and building upon the interpretation of Marx and the revolutionary tradition by Karl Popper, Talmon reasons that the revolutionary tradition provided an unintended legitimation of totalitarian democracy.[8] Unintended because, as Talmon insists, the values of the revolutionary tradition were individualism, egalitarianism, and democracy. However, by coupling humanism to such assumptions as the belief in an imminent total change in the social order, the need for a provisional revolutionary dictatorship to educate the unenlightened masses, the need for permanent revolution and terror, and the ideal of a perfect harmony between the individual and the community, the revolutionary tradition ended up justifying an authoritarian order of coercion and centralist control over human affairs.

Applied to the French revolutionary tradition, Talmon's thesis accords very well with our own interpretation outlined in Part One. Aside from the modernist turn of Blanqui and the non-Jacobin "socialism" of Saint-Simon, the French revolutionaries, from the egalitarian communists and the Babouvists to Blanquism, betray a remarkable coherency on just the beliefs Talmon ascribes to totalitarian democracy. Talmon's thesis breaks down, however, when applied to Marx. From his very earliest to his later writings on the problem of social change and revolution, the *dominant impulse* of Marx's ideas are nondogmatic, anti-teleological, and democratic.[9] There are, I believe, two features of Marx's social and political thought that prevented him from succumbing to the "totalitarian temptation."

First, whereas the French revolutionaries flatly asserted an antithetical relation between liberalism and bourgeois society and communism, Marx understood the future socialist order as the fulfillment of the promise of liberalism and bourgeois society to institute freedom and democracy.[10] The French revolutionaries had a hatred of liberalism and bourgeois society equal to that of the reactionaries Bonald and Maistre. Politically this was manifested in their refusal to cooperate with bourgeois parties. Invariably, this propelled the French radicals into elitist, conspiratorial, and terrorist politics; what Marx called the politics of the will. As we have seen, Marx was an early advocate of bourgeois institutions and never discarded liberal values. In Marx's view, the bourgeois epoch was progressive. It articulated and initiated the institutionalization of the principles of individual autonomy and political democracy. Marx's criticism of bourgeois society reflected his belief that, given private property, autonomy and democracy could achieve only a formal instantiation, e.g., legal recognition of personality. Furthermore, Marx argued that in its natural course of development, bourgeois society suppresses its liberal and democratic principles and becomes destructive of civil life in general.[11] To the extent, however, that liberal ideology remains a vital ingredient of the bourgeoisie, Marx counseled the political and educational gains to be had from working-class alliances with liberal-bourgeois elements.[12] It is no wonder that within French revolutionary circles Marx was considered a moderate and was suspected of bourgeois tendencies.[13]

Second, unlike the French revolutionaries, who conceived of communism as the "natural order of things," Marx defined communism as a sociopolitical movement emerging from the historical development of bourgeois society. "Communism is for us," Marx and Engels wrote by way of contrasting their position with French radicalism, "not a *state of affairs* which is to be established, an *ideal* to which reality [will] have to adjust itself. We call communism the *real* movement which abolishes the present state of things. The conditions of this movement result from the now existing premise."[14] To put this differently, whereas the intellectual standpoint of the French revolutionaries was modern natural law with its idea of a fixed order, Marx assumed the historical and dialectical standpoint of Hegel.[15] In political terms this meant that liberalism and bourgeois society was not simply to be confronted with the abstract ideal of egalitarian communism—thereby making revolution an act of political determination against a resistant sociohistorical reality. Marx's dialectical approach suggested that communism was historically emergent and revolution presupposed definite objective and subjective conditions established by bourgeois society. Communism was, so Marx thought, the true heir to liberalism and bourgeois society—preserving their positive content in a transfigured form.

The theoretical premises of Marx's theory of revolution are a major departure from the French tradition. I have indicated that in part this is a consequence of Marx's Hegelian perspective on human development.[16] From an Hegelian perspective, history is viewed as a gradual and progressive movement detailing our self-transformation through a dialectic of objectification, estrangement, and supersession. The level of human or sociohistorical development sets the limits of effective sociopolitical change. Any attempt to transcend historical conditions or short-circuit sociocultural development by means of political determination alone is ineffectual. The failure of the French Revolution and its degeneration into Jacobin terror and dictatorship, Marx argued, followed from the effort to overcome the insufficient maturation of social and cultural conditions by strictly political means. The Jacobins, Marx reasoned, operated under the following false premise:

> The principle of politics is the *will*. The more one-sided and, therefore, the more perfected the political mind is, the more does it believe in the *omnipotence* of the will, the more it is blind to the *natural* and spiritual *limits* of the will, and the more incapable is it therefore of discovering the source of social ills.[17]

Marx's criticism was direct and devastating: political power can only realize possibilities given in the existing social and cultural conditions. Revolutionary terror is a testament to the impotence of the idol of political will.

Marx's Hegelianism led to a set of quite different premises for a revolutionary theory: "Men build a new world for themselves . . . from the historical achievements of their declining world. In the course of their development they first have to *produce* the *material conditions* of a new society itself, and no exertion of mind or will can free them from this fate."[18] Marx insisted, moreover, that in its natural course of development bourgeois society creates the material preconditions of a new society as well as the agents of revolution: the working classes. Capitalism "provides along with the [material] elements for the formation of a new society, the forces for exploding the old one."[19] Political power is effective only to the extent that it releases the developing material and cultural forces. "We are dealing here with a communist society . . . as it *emerges* from a capitalist society."[20]

Marx and the Politics of Revolution

Leaving aside for the moment the theoretical issues raised in the problem of the transition from capitalism to socialism, I want to discuss the much-debated problem of revolutionary strategy. Throughout his lifetime, Marx anticipated at least the beginnings of revolutionary upheaval. The material conditions were ripe and the "impoverishment" of the working classes as well as their large numbers and concentration seemed favorable for revolutionary change.[21] Marx's model of revolution was the French Revolution and the July Revolution of 1830—both popular, democratic, and violent insurrections by the majority. I want to examine several facets of Marx's "theory of revolution."

First, Marx's notion of a spontaneous majority revolution precluded the Blanquist idea of a minority revolution directed by a conspiratorial, elitist, vanguard party. The Blanquist tradition sought to justify the minority revolution/vanguard party concept on the basis of the political immaturity and backward tendencies of the working classes. By contrast, Marx's commitment to a majority revolution reflected his belief that the proletariat would of its own accord develop new needs and a critical orientation that would furnish the active drive towards a new society. After meeting with several worker associations in Paris, Marx observed:

> When communist *artisans* associate with one another, theory, propaganda, etc., is their first end. But at the same time, as a result of this association, they acquire a new need—the need for society—and what appears as a means becomes an end. In this practical process the most splendid results are to be observed whenever French socialist workers are seen together. Such things as smoking, drinking, eating, etc., are no longer means of contact or means that bring them together. Association, society and conversation, which again has association as its end, are enough for them; the brotherhood of man is no mere phrase with them, but a fact of life, and the nobility of man shines upon us from their work-hardened bodies.[22]

In the proletariat, Marx perceived not only a material force of potentially immense power but a moral agent. "The proletariat," he wrote in 1847, "needs its courage, its self-confidence, its pride and its sense of independence even more than its bread."[23] The crucial point is that in the Marxian schema a revolutionary movement would crystalize spontaneously and independently from the life-conditions of the proletariat.

Though the party has an educational function, it does not exist apart from or above the worker associations. In *The Communist Manifesto*, Marx repudiated the vanguard party concept:

> The Communists do not form a separate party opposed to other working class parties.

> They have no interest separate and apart from those of the proletariat as a whole.

> They do not set up any sectarian principles of their own, by which to shape and mould the proletarian movement.[24]

During the founding years of the International, Marx was even more direct in his rejection of the elitist vanguard party concept: "When the International was formed, we expressly formulated the battle-cry: the emancipation of the working class must be the work of the working class itself. We cannot ally ourselves, therefore, with people who openly declare the workers are too uneducated to free themselves and must first be liberated from above. . . ."[25] Marx's commitment to the idea of the "proletarian movement as a self-conscious, independent movement of the immense majority" signaled a repudiation of the minority revolution/vanguard party concept so prominent in the French revolutionary tradition (and later in Leninism).

In conjunction with the idea of a popular majority revolution, Marx insisted upon a democratically organized working-class movement and one committed to democratic values and institutions. In the course of Marx's political career, he participated in several revolutionary organizations, the most important being The Communist League (1847–1852) and the International Working Men's Association (1864–1872). It is not possible to delve into the historical details of Marx's role and politics in these two organizations. However, a few words are in order. Regarding the Communist League, it is now recognized that it was composed of two factions: the Communist Correspondence Committee, represented by Marx and Engels, and the League of the Just, a conspiratorial, elitist association with roots in Blanquism.[26] It is also known that, from the standpoint of Marx and Engels, the Communist League's central role was to be a propaganda association— spreading socialist ideas and facilitating the national and international organization and cooperation of the working class. It was not, in Marx's view, a conspiratorial vanguard party organized on centralist and authoritarian principles; nor was its role the "making of revolution." This idea is conveyed very clearly in Marx's pamphlet on "Revelations Concerning the Communist Trial in Cologney":

> There is no doubt that here too the members of the proletarian party would take part once again in a revolution against the *status quo*, but it was no part of their task to prepare this revolution, to agitate, conspire or to plot for it. They could leave this preparation to circumstances in general and to the classes directly involved. . . .
>
> The *"Communist League,"* therefore, was no conspiratorial society, but a society which secretly strove to create an organized proletarian party because the German proletariat is publicly debarred, *igni et aqua*, from writing, speaking and meeting.[27]

As a propaganda society, the Communist League's organization was to be democratic and nonauthoritarian. In 1877, Marx recalled that "the first entrance of Engels and myself into the secret Communist League took place only on the condition that everything conducive to authoritarian superstitions be removed from the statutes."[28] Though Marx and Engels achieved some notable success in democratizing the League, their efforts were frustrated at every turn by the petty bourgeois artisan supporters of conspiracy, authoritarianism, and immediate revolution. We will leave aside for now the issue of Marx's so-called capitulation to Blanquism in the stormy days of 1848–1850.

Between the dissolution of the Communist League in 1852 and the formation of the International in 1864, Marx almost completely withdrew from organized politics. However, his involvement in the International was extensive, and many of its organizational features and statutes bear his imprint. Marx's ideas concerning a democratic organization of the proletariat dedicated to propaganda and cooperation remain unchanged. He continued to insist that "the International was . . . established by the working men themselves and for themselves."[29] The main function of the International was to disseminate ideas and information and facilitate cooperation among the different national and international working-class movements.[30] Its organizing principles were to be thoroughly democratic: "This International Association and all societies and individuals adhering to it, will acknowledge truth, justice, and morality, as the basis of their conduct towards each other, and towards all men, without regard to colour, creed, or nationality."[31] Instead of pursuing this in more detail, I want to turn to the issue of the democratic values projected in Marx's notion of revolution.

I have maintained that, according to Marx, communism was viewed as the fulfillment, and simultaneously the transfiguration, of the ideals and principles of liberalism and bourgeois society. This is further supported by the fact that communism was not to be viewed as a reversal of bourgeois democracy but its genuine substantiation. In the language of the early Marx, communism is "true" democracy. In his *Critique of Hegel's Doctrine of the State*, Marx translates the meaning of true democracy as the self-governance of a people. Marx's advocacy of universal suffrage extended beyond universal civil and political rights to the demand for a democratic organization of society itself, i.e., popular sovereignty as the ruling principle of social and political institutions.[32] In the *Communist Manifesto*, Marx placed democracy as the highest priority in the revolution. "The first step in the revolution by the working class, is . . . to win the battle of democracy."[33] In the preliminary draft of the *Manifesto*, Engels was even more explicit: "The first fundamental condition for the introduction of community of property is the political liberation of the proletariat through a democratic constitution."[34] The model of a democratic constitution was the French Constitution of 1793, about which, echoing Marx's idea of true democracy, Engels wrote: "Universal suffrage, direct elections, paid representation—these are the essential conditions of political society: Equality, liberty, fraternity—these are the principles which ought to rule in all social institutions."[35]

By far the clearest illustration of Marx's equation of communism and democracy is his discussion of the Paris Commune. The Commune appeared to Marx as an exemplar of the democratic reorganization of society. The relevant passages deserve to be quoted at length:

> The Commune was formed of the municipal councillors, chosen by universal suffrage in the various wards of the town, responsible and revocable at short times. The majority of its members were naturally working men, or acknowledged representatives of the working class. The Commune was to be a working, not a parliamentary body, executive and legislative at the same time. Instead of continuing to be the agent of the central government, the police was at once stripped of its political attributes, and turned into the responsible and at all times revocable agent of the Commune. So were the officials of all other branches of administration. From the members of the Commune downwards, the public service had to be done at *workmen's wages.* . . .

> Having once got rid of the standing army and the police, the physical force elements of the old government, the Commune was anxious to break the spiritual force of repression, the "parson-power," by the disestablishment and disendowment of all churches as proprietary bodies. . . . The whole of the educational institutions were opened to the people gratuitously, and at the same time cleared of all interference of church and state. Thus, not only was education made accessible to all, but science itself freed from the fetters which class prejudice and governmental force had imposed upon it. . . . Like the rest of public servants, magistrates and judges were to be elective, responsible, and revocable.

> The Paris Commune was, of course, to serve as a model to all the great industrial centres of France. The communal regime once established in Paris and secondary centres, the old centralized government would in the provinces, too, have to give way to the self-government of the producers. . . . The rural communes of every district were to administer their common affairs by an assembly of delegates in the central town, and these district assemblies were again to send deputies to the

national delegation in Paris, each delegate to be at any time revocable.... The few but important functions which still would remain for a central government were not to be suppressed ... but were to be discharged by Communal, and therefore strictly responsible agents. The unity of the nation was not to be broken, but, on the contrary, to be organized by the Communal constitution.... While the merely repressive organs of the old governmental power were to be amputated, its legitimate functions were to be ... restored to the responsible agents of society. Instead of deciding once in three or six years which member of the ruling class was to misrepresent the people in parliament, universal suffrage was to serve the people.... On the other hand, nothing could be more foreign to the spirit of the Commune than to supersede universal suffrage by hierarchic investiture.[36]

Marx's final assessment of the Commune: "Its special measures could but betoken the tendency of a government of the people by the people."[37]

Throughout Marx's life, he maintained that the way to achieve democracy was through revolution. Thus, the third noteworthy feature of his idea of revolution is that of a violent revolution. Marx's position may be stated directly: "Material force must be overthrown by material force...."[38] In an article attacking Ruge, Marx asserted that "*socialism* cannot be realized without *revolution*. It needs this *political* act insofar as it needs *destruction* and *dissolution*."[39] And finally, turning to *The German Ideology*, Marx developed his justification for violence: "The revolution is necessary, therefore, not only because the *ruling* class cannot be overthrown in any other way, but also because the class *overthrowing* it can only in a revolution succeed in ridding itself of all the muck of ages and become fitted to found society anew."[40] Violence is a necessary part of revolution, Marx argued, on account of the resistance of the ruling class and as a means to reorganize society.

From a contemporary standpoint, Marx's legitimation of violence is considered objectionable and perhaps directly totalitarian. Contemporary social democrats try to make the case that Marx's belief in the necessity of violence reflects a youthful infatuation with the Jacobin notion of popular insurrection. In his later writings, so the argument goes, Marx replaced this Jacobin model with a gradualist and peaceful strategy. Thus, Michael Harrington writes: "In the years leading up to 1850, Marx was a democrat in the Jacobin sense. He saw the coming revolution as a gigantic popular explosion from below, as a democratic insurrection. But in the 1850s and 1860s, he had to revise his most strategic notions. The working-class movement was changing, it was organizing itself into unions. . . . At that point, Marx's perspective . . . increasingly envisioned the non-violent and electoral conquest of power."[41] Even more pointedly, George Lichtheim declares that, by the time of the International, Marx "had ceased to be a communist in the sense of the 1848 *Manifesto* and transformed himself into the theoretician of what came to be known thereafter as democratic-socialism."[42] There is no doubt but that after the debacles of 1848 Marx gave more attention to the rise of parliamentary and democratic institutions, trade unions, the cooperative labor movement, and the internal structural changes in capitalism—all of which held out the potential for a more protracted and peaceful transition to socialism. Moreover, it is important to emphasize that Marx applauded the Paris Commune for carrying out the class struggle "in the most rational and humane way."[43] However, Marx never reneged on his belief in the use of violence and forceful repression as a legitimate vehicle of revolutionary transformation.

Marx believed that in most countries either the absence of parliamentary and democratic institutions or the resistance of the military, governmental bureaucracy, or propertied classes would necessitate violence in a revolutionary situation. In France, for instance, Marx was convinced that violence was unavoidable. "In France a hundred laws of repression and a mortal antagonism between classes seem to necessitate the violent solution of social war."[44] In another passage, also written in the 1870s, Marx allows for the possibility of a peaceful transition to socialism in America and England, but he concludes: "That being the case, we must recognize that in most continental countries the lever of the revolution will have to be force; or resort to force will be necessary one day in order to set up the rule of labour."[45] In a much neglected "Circular Letter to Bebel, Liebknecht, Bracke, et al.," Marx, interestingly enough, expressed serious objections to a strictly gradualist and ballot-box transition. The Social-Democratic Party, he wrote in a tone of disbelief and criticism, devotes "its whole strength and energy to those petty-bourgeois patchwork reforms which could provide the old social order with new supports and hence perhaps transform the final catastrophe into a gradual, piecemeal and, as far as possible, peaceful process of dissolution."[46]

It simply will not do to assimilate Marx to the contemporary disposition of social democrats. Marx remained very much in the French revolutionary tradition by continuing to believe in popular insurrection and the use of violence and forceful repression. He believed, as did most democrats and revolutionaries, that in the face of the bourgeoisie's uninhibited use of violence, so well illustrated in the counterrevolutions of 1848–1850, violence was a necessary means to achieve revolutionary ends. To restrict revolutionary strategy to parliamentary and legal means, to forego the use of violence in the hope of a wrong generosity or a falsely directed sense of justice, was, in the face of the recurring barbarism of bourgeois society, a costly failure of nerve. Let us, however, be perfectly clear: Marx rejected the Blanquist notion that revolutions can be *made* by means of force and terror.

The Totalitarian Temptation: 1848–1850

My preceding analysis has shown that though Marx opposed the idea of a minority revolution directed by a conspiratorial elite party, he continued to maintain the belief in popular insurrection and the legitimate use of violence in revolutionary situations. I believe that by his not specifying the precise conditions under which violence is legitimate, and the extent and form of violence, an ambiguity is built into Marx's idea of revolution, an ambiguity which comes to the fore in his ultraradicalism during the "revolutionary period" of 1848–1850.[47]

The key text here is the "Address of the Central Committee to the Communist League" (March 1850) drafted by Marx and Engels. The context is (1) the failed revolutions of 1848 and (2) the imminent seizure of power by the German petty bourgeoisie. The discussion revolves around revolutionary strategy. At the present time, Marx said, the petty bourgeois are not in power and will try to make the proletariat "a mere appendage to official bourgeois democracy." Marx advised that "the League must work for the creation of an independent organization of the worker's party, both secret and open, alongside the official democrats. . . ."[48] Marx's advocacy of secrecy was fully justified in light of the absence of legal guarantees to the right of association, freedom of the press, universal suffrage, etc. When the moment of revolutionary struggle begins, Marx continued, the proletariat must form a temporary alliance with the petty bourgeois democrats and direct the struggle along revolutionary lines. "Above all, during and immediately after the struggle the workers . . . must oppose bourgeois attempts at pacification and force the democrats to carry out their terroristic phrases. . . . Far from opposing so-called excesses—instances of popular vengeance against hated individuals . . .—the workers' party must not only tolerate these actions but must even give them direction."[49] Marx believed that the petty bourgeois democrats would try to forestall the revolution before it benefited the proletariat. Thus, Marx declared: "It is our interest and our task to make the revolution permanent . . . until the proletariat has conquered state power. . . ."[50] The vehicle for conquering state power and effecting a transition from bourgeois democracy to communism is the "dictatorship of the proletariat."[51] In April 1850, the *Société Universelle des Communistes Révolutionaires* was formed, and in its statutes, signed by Marx, was the following declaration: "The aim of the Association is to make an end to all the privileged classes, to subject these classes to the dictatorship of the proletariat by maintaining revolution in permanence until the realization of communism."[52]

To critics of Marx as well as to contemporary Communists, these formulations clearly exemplify the Jacobin and Blanquist revolutionary tradition and represent the essential Marx. Regarding the latter claim, this interpretation cannot be justified by textual evidence. Prior to 1848, and from at least May 1850, Marx repudiated the minority revolution/vanguard party concept with its ideology of immediate revolution, conspiracy, and blood-spilling riots and terrorism. In May 1850, Marx reiterated his dissociation from Blanquism and his commitment to a working-class party whose main aim is propaganda or "theoretical enlightenment" and the organization of the proletariat:

> It need scarcely be added that these conspirators do not confine themselves to the general organizing of the revolutionary proletariat. It is precisely their business to anticipate the process of revolutionary development, to bring it artificially to crisis-point, to launch a revolution on the spur of the moment, without the conditions for a revolution. For them the only condition for revolution is the adequate preparation of their conspiracy. They are the alchemists of the revolution and are characterised by exactly the same chaotic thinking and blinkered obsessions as the alchemists of old. They leap at inventions which are supposed to work revolutionary miracles: incendiary bombs, destructive devices of magic effect, revolts which are expected to be all the more miraculous and astonishing in effect as their basis is less rational. Occupied with such scheming, they have no other purpose than the most immediate one of overthrowing the existing government and have the profoundest contempt for the more theoretical enlightenment of the proletariat about their class interests. . . .

To the extent that the Paris proletariat came to the fore itself as a party, these conspirators lost some of their dominant influence, they were dispersed and they encountered dangerous competition in proletarian secret societies, whose purpose was not immediate insurrection but the organization and development of the proletariat.[53]

On September 15, 1850, Marx officially broke from the Blanquist wing of the Communist League. His repudiation of Blanquism was final:

In place of the materialist standpoint of the *Manifesto*, they substitute idealism. Instead of real conditions they make naked *will* the driving force of the revolution. What we say to workers is: You must go through 15, 20, 50 years of civil war in order to change existing conditions, in order to make yourselves fit to exercise power; whereas they say, we must come to power *at once* or we may as well lay ourselves down to sleep.[54]

These passages seem to throw a different light upon the March 1850 "Address." The permanent revolution, as Marx observed in the concluding passages of the "Address," is a "protracted revolutionary development" requiring "15, 20, 50 years of civil war." This idea is in full accord with Marx's earlier notions of a majority revolution and an open, democratic, working-class party oriented to the enlightenment and organization of the proletariat—not to immediate, minority revolution by a sectarian, conspiratorial, elite party. This, of course, is the interpretation recommended by contemporary social democrats. Thus, though Harrington sees the 1848–1850 period as Marx's "anti-democratic temptation," he insists that permanent revolution implied a long-term peaceful revolutionary struggle.[55] Similarly, Avineri claims that the violent language of the *Manifesto* and "Address" was Marx's attempt "to pay lip-service to the Blanquist elements. . . ."[56] In fact, several letters exchanged between Marx and Engels support the interpretation that Marx's Blanquist rhetoric was merely a necessary concession to maintain solidarity in a revolutionary situation. On February 11, 1851, Marx wrote to Engels: "I'm greatly pleased by the public, authentic isolation in which we two, you and I, now find ourselves. It corresponds completely with our position and our principles. The system of mutual concessions, the halfway positions tolerated for appearances' sake, and the duty in the eyes of the public of assuming responsibility for a share of the nonsense of the party along with all these asses—all that has now come to an end."[57]

However, there are problems with this interpretation. The very *language* of Marx's formulations betrays an ambiguity at the conceptual core of his idea of revolution. Although a case can be made for a non-Blanquist reading of certain passages on permanent revolutions, the fact remains that this reading is strained or in tension with Marx's language and its apparent meaning. For example, in the *Manifesto*, Marx wrote: "The Communists turn their attention chiefly to Germany, because that country is on the eve of a bourgeois revolution . . . and because the bourgeois revolution will be but the prelude to an immediately following proletarian revolution."[58] The language is most obviously that of Blanquism: immediate revolution and by implication minority revolution, vanguard party, and terror. Can the language (immediate and permanent revolution) be so at odds with Marx's "intended" meaning (protracted revolutionary struggle)? Or consider just one of Marx's many declarations of the need for violent retribution and terror: "The very cannibalism of the counter-revolution will convince the nations that there is only *one means* by which the murderous death agonies of the old society and the bloody birth throes of the new society can be *shortened*, simplified and concentrated—and that is by *revolutionary terror.*"[59] To Richard Hunt, author of a very fine book on *The Political Ideas of Marx and Engels*, such pronouncements are "clearly a temporary aberration, born in the anguish and helplessness of defeat."[60] But we find similar "aberrations" prior to the defeats of 1848 and the admittedly shocking brutality of the counterrevolution. In the closing passage of *The Poverty of Philosophy*, Marx quoted George Sand approvingly: "Combat or death, bloody struggle or extinction. Thus the question [of revolutionary change] is inexorably put."[61] Even more revealing is the following passage from the *Manifesto* (written between December 1847 and January 1848): "In short, Communists everywhere support every revolutionary movement against the existing social and political order of things."[62] The crucial point here is this: Marx's language—"Communists support every revolutionary movement"—covers and legitimates any and all forms of self-proclaimed revolutionary movements. Marx failed to discriminate between legitimate and illegitimate forms and means of revolution; he failed to specify precisely just what constitutes a "revolutionary situation," and under what conditions and in what form violence and terror are a legitimate vehicle of revolution. In a word, Marx's ambiguity was not simply one of language and wording but one of concept. This betrays, I believe, the sustaining impact of French revolutionary tradition on Marx's politics and idea of revolution.

5. The Critique of Capitalism and the Problematics of Socialism

FROM THE FRENCH revolutionary tradition, Marx acquired many specifics of his critique of capitalism.[1] In particular, two features of the revolutionary critique were of lasting significance for him. First, what we might call the sociocultural critique of private property. The egalitarians, we recall, argued that *all* the evils of contemporary society—inequality, egoism, hedonism—stem from the existence of private property. Because the egalitarians adopted a primitivist communitarian ideal, their solution was to negate private property. Marx criticized the reactionary, anti-modernist disposition of this "crude communism," which would suppress individuality and cultural development.[2] Nevertheless, although Marx's argument was more intricate, one finds a similar chain of reasoning from private property to structural inequality on the one hand, and, on the other, from private property to a debased culture of egoism and hedonism.[3] Private property must be eliminated, Marx reasoned, but sociocultural complexity and differentiation must be preserved in a socialist order.

In the later phases of French revolutionary thought, Marx perceived a more historically informed and advanced critique of capitalism. In Sismondi, Fourier, the Saint-Simonians, and Proudhon, revolutionary critique converged upon the *capitalist organization* of industrialism. A quotation from Sismondi illustrates this quite well:

> We shall take society in its actual organization, with its workers deprived of property, their wage fixed by competition, their labor dismissed by their masters as soon as they no longer have need of it—for it is to this very special organization that we object.[4]

Though this more mature revolutionary standpoint served as the point of departure for Marx's critique of capitalism, he remained highly critical of its petty bourgeois and utopian proclivities. Remarking on the petty bourgeois socialism of Sismondi, Marx noted, "Its last words are: corporate guilds for manufacture; patriarchal relations in agriculture."[5] Marx was no less critical of Saint-Simon and Fourier—both of whom retreat from political struggle into utopianism and, in their successors, succumb to the sterile politics of sectarianism.[6]

Marx's critique of French revolutionary utopianism was twofold. First, "utopian socialism" failed to establish a link between the critique of capitalism and its historical transformation. Second, in its preoccupation with denouncing capitalism and constructing utopian alternatives, the French revolutionary tradition turned away from the analysis of capitalist development. Instead of developing a critical analysis of capitalism which would critically appropriate classical political economy, they renounced this more rigorous science for a "fantastic social science," as Marx called the efforts of Saint-Simon and Fourier. Revolutionary critique, Marx insisted, needed to elude utopianism and a mere moral critique and return to the scientific standpoint of political economy. Revolutionary critique must complete, rather than oppose, the science of political economy by disclosing the beginning, middle, and end of capitalism.

Revolutionary Critique Returns to the Scientific Standpoint of the Enlightenment

Although the revolutionary critics of liberalism and bourgeois society rightly attacked the classical economists, they abandoned the latter's scientific orientation for moralizing criticisms and utopian constructions of possible futures. In this regard the revolutionary tradition regressed behind the scientific standpoint of classical political economy. For all their shortcomings, Smith, Ricardo, and the other economists had striven to uncover the economic and political mechanisms of capitalist development. Moreover, notwithstanding the vulgar economists, the classical economists had not failed to face the stark and unpleasant realities of capitalism. Marx's descriptive portrayal of capitalism proceeds from the analysis of the classical economists:

> From political economy itself, using its own words, we have shown that the worker sinks to the level of a commodity, and moreover the most wretched commodity of all: that the misery of the worker is in inverse proportion to the power and volume of his production; that the necessary consequence of competition is ... the restoration of monopoly ...; that finally ... the whole of society must split into the two classes of *property owners* and propertyless *workers*.[7]

Classical political economy, according to Marx, had a critical edge. The economists pointed to the class character of capitalism; the material and spiritual impoverishment of the working classes; the tendency of capitalism to evolve monopolies and require state intervention. However, the economists forfeited their critical insights by failing to conceive of the possibility of overcoming these structural limitations by transcending capitalism. In Marx's view, this reflects their bourgeois class character.

It is precisely this ahistorical character of classical political economy that reveals its scientific limitations and hidden ideological conservatism. Marx argued that the economists conceived of capitalism as if it were an unchanging part of the natural order. Even Ricardo, the most advanced representative of the economists, "in the end, consciously makes the antagonism of class interests, of wages and profit, of profits and rent, the starting point of his investigations, namely taking this antagonism for a law of nature. But by this start the science of political economy had reached the limits beyond which it could not pass."[8] Because of the bourgeois class character of the economists, they viewed the essential features of capitalism—class division, social inequality, egoism, and hedonism—as permanent attributes of the nature of the individual and society. Consequently, while the science of political economy could furnish a rich descriptive portrait of capitalism, its ahistorism prevented it from arriving at a truly explanatory critical perspective on capitalism.

To go beyond the classical economists, it was necessary, Marx thought, not simply to describe capitalism, but to explain it by discovering its historical origins and development—its "law of motion":

> Political economy proceeds from the fact of private property. It does not explain it. It grasps the *material* process of private property, the process through which it actually passes, in general and abstract formulae which it then takes as *laws*. It does not *comprehend* these laws, i.e., it does not show how they arise from the nature of private property. Political economy fails to explain the reason for the division between labour and capital, between capital and land . . . ; it assumes what it is supposed to explain.[9]

The originality of Marx's critique of capitalism and his alleged scientific advance over the economists is founded upon his explanation of the origins, development, and end of capitalism. Marx claimed to have uncovered the developmental logic of capitalism and the necessity of its supersession by a classless society.[10] Marx's original insight was not, then, simply that capitalism is a transitional historical phase, an insight already offered by the revolutionary utopians; rather, it is that the laws of capitalism, as disclosed by the critical science of political economy, necessitate its own destruction. "It is a question of these laws themselves, of these tendencies working with iron necessity towards inevitable results."[11]

It is true that almost all of the French revolutionaries—e.g., Fourier, Proudhon, and Blanqui—claimed scientific status for their critique of capitalism. However, this presumption, Marx argued, is undermined by the blatantly metaphysical, moralistic, and utopian character of their critical theory.[12] A "genuine" scientific-critical analysis of capitalism must begin from the most advanced level of scientific development—namely, the bourgeois science of classical economics. Starting from the science of classical economics, Marx's intention was to reconstruct in a highly simplified form the developmental logic of capitalism, thereby "completing" the science of political economy and demonstrating the historical nature of capitalism. In his various economic studies, the *1844 Manuscripts*, the *Grundrisse*, and *Capital*, Marx sought an explanatory schema that would prove that the "laws of motion" of capitalism pointed to its historical progression into a socialist order.

The Three Models
of Capitalism's Breakdown

The details of Marx's critique of political economy need not concern us. I am not interested in providing yet another exposition of Marx's theory of capitalist development.[13] What follows is a skeletal outline of three theoretical strategies Marx utilized in accounting for the transition from capitalism to socialism.

Marx's first attempt to couple the development of capitalism to an emergent socialist order is found in his early writings, particularly in the *1844 Manuscripts*. Marx insisted that these notes were a "wholly empirical analysis based on a conscientious critical study of political economy."[14] In the first section of the *Manuscripts*, Marx analyzed the logic of capitalist development through an examination of the concepts of wages, profit, capital, and rent, concluding: "We proceed from an *actual* economic fact. The worker becomes all the poorer the more wealth he produces, the more his production increases in power and size. The worker becomes an ever cheaper commodity the more commodities he creates. The *devaluation* of the world of men is in direct proportion to the *increasing value* of the world of things."[15] From the "actual economic fact" of increased productivity, Marx inferred that the *economic impoverishment* of the worker increases; that the increased power of capital yields the worker's increased *political subjection* to the bourgeoisie; that the increased wealth of material goods finds its counterpart in the increased *spiritual deprivation* of the worker. In the famous section on "Estranged Labour," Marx's aim was quite simply to show that the development of capitalism translates into the economic, political, and spiritual debasement of the working class. The logic of capitalism's supersession by a socialist order is a necessary outcome of the alienated existence of the working classes.

This is so, in Marx's view, because human suffering in capitalist society is embodied in the dehumanized existence of the proletariat. Since their suffering represents general or universal deprivation, their opposition to capitalism carries with it the promise of general emancipation. "From the relationship of estranged labour to private property it follows further that the emancipation of society from private property . . . is expressed in the *political* form of the *emancipation of the workers* . . . because the emancipation of the workers contains universal human emancipation—and it contains this, because the whole of human servitude is involved in the relation of the worker to production. . . ."[16] According to Marx, the very meaning of the proletariat, from a world-historical perspective, lies in its revolutionary activism: "When the proletariat announces the *dissolution of the existing order,* it only declares the secret of its own existence. . . ."[17]

Between the drafting of the *1844 Manuscripts* and the publication of *The Communist Manifesto* in 1848, Marx's model of political economy became more complex, but the coupling of capitalist development to the creation of a revolutionary proletariat remained the centerpiece of Marx's theory of the transition from capitalism to socialism. In his subsequent economic studies, however, there is a definite shift to a more mechanical model of capitalist development. One still finds, to be sure, elements of the early voluntaristic model of social change—for example, in the "immiseration thesis" contained in the sections of *Capital* on "Machinery and Modern Industry" and "The General Law of Capital Accumulation." The rhetoric of the early writings is equally unmistakable: the proletariat is still "the class whose vocation in history is the overthrow of the capitalist mode of production."[18]

Without exaggerating Marx's reorientation, my argument is supported by the following points. First, in both the *Grundrisse* and *Capital*, Marx failed to articulate the relation between the developmental logic of capital and the formation of a revolutionary proletariat. Aside from a few undeveloped passages in the sections on "Machinery" and "Capital Accumulation," the problem of the emergence of class consciousness and revolutionary activism is virtually unexamined. This reflects, I believe, Marx's preoccupation with the objective, material development of capitalism and his tendency to view, in a fairly simplistic way, the subjective development of the proletariat as a mere appendage to material progress.[19] Second, Marx's attempt to translate his earlier voluntaristic thesis on "Estranged Labour" into the economistic language of the "immiseration thesis" is inconsistent with his own insights concerning the advancements made by the proletariat—for example, the achievement of the ten-hour workday.[20] Third, in his political writings of this period, Marx repeatedly observed the absence of the necessary subjective conditions of revolutionary change. What makes these much-neglected writings especially fascinating is that Marx singled out, as the decisive issue, the problem of worker solidarity. In several articles and addresses, written during the founding years of the International, Marx argued that the increase in the number of workers and their concentration must be combined with a "bond of brotherhood" or a "fraternal concurrence," whose basis must be "the simple laws of morals and justice."[21] The emancipation of the working classes had failed, Marx observed, because of their lack of solidarity: "All efforts aiming at that great end have hitherto failed from the want of solidarity between the manifold divisions of labour in each country, and from the absence of a fraternal bond of union between the working classes of different countries. . . ."[22] Sometime during the 1850s and 1860s, Marx became increasingly doubtful that the working classes would develop the revolutionary consciousness and activism he ascribed to them in earlier writings. It is not surprising, then, to find that in the *Grundrisse* and *Capital* Marx's theory of the transition from capitalism to socialism focused upon the automatic mechanisms of capitalist development.

Without going into detail, we can discern two such mechanistic explanations detailing the internal logic of capitalism's breakdown. First, in the *Grundrisse*—which hardly even mentions the working classes—the problem of capitalist development and the transition to socialism is reduced completely to the progressive automation of the labor process. In very schematic terms, Marx argued that the labor process *in general* is a form-giving, nature-shaping process based upon purposive action. The general aim of the labor process is to yield utilities or use-values. Under capitalism, labor assumes the form of abstract labor, which makes production simultaneously a valorization process. Because the *capitalist* labor process consists of concrete and abstract labor, its products have a twofold character, i.e., use-values and exchange-values. In the *Grundrisse*, the breakdown problem is reduced to the question of whether there is a systematic tendency towards abolishing the value form of labor. Marx argued that in the development of capitalism, science is pressed into its service and the labor process undergoes successive changes culminating in the "automatic system of machinery." Individual labor is productive only as social labor or as the labor of the scientific community. Science replaces unskilled labor power as the basis of the labor process and as the primary source of wealth. This symbolizes, Marx said, the limits of the labor theory of value and the end of capitalism.

> Its [capitalism's] presupposition is—and remains—the mass of direct labour time, the quantity of labour employed, as the determinant factor in the production of wealth. But to the degree that large industry develops, the creation of real wealth comes to depend less on labour time and the amount of labour employed . . . but depends rather on the general state of science and on the progress of technology. . . . Labour no longer appears so much to be included within the production process; rather the human being comes to relate more as a watchman and regulator to the production process itself. . . . He steps to the side of the production process instead of being its chief actor. . . . The *theft of alien labour time, on which the present wealth is based*, appears a miserable foundation in face of this new one, created by large-scale industry itself. As soon as labour in the direct form has ceased to be the great well-spring of wealth, labour time ceases and must cease to be its measure and hence exchange value [must cease to be the measure] of use value. . . . With that, production based on exchange value [i.e., capitalism] breaks down. . . .[23]

As is evident, the transition from capitalism to socialism is conceptualized entirely in terms of the continuous expansion of scientific-technological rationality.[24]

In Volume 3 of *Capital*, Marx proposed another mechanistic model of the transition from capitalism to socialism. With the increasing concentration and centralization of capital, promoted by the falling rate of profit, recurring crises, and the establishment of an effective national credit system, capitalism enters a "corporate" phase of development—characterized by "socialized property" in the form of joint-stock companies:

In stock companies the function [of the manager] is divorced from capital ownership, hence also labor is entirely divorced from ownership of means of production and surplus value. This result of the ultimate development of capitalist production is a necessary transitional phase towards the reconversion of capital into the property of producers, although no longer as private property of the individual producers, but rather as the property of associated producers, as outright social property. . . . This is the abolition of the capitalist mode of production itself. . . .[25]

In the joint-stock company, the social character of property is apparent in the limited form of public shareholding companies, although property continues to appear as the property of particular capitalists. Paralleling the formation of socialized property is the emergence of socialized labor in the form of cooperative factories:

The co-operative factories of the labourers themselves represent within the old form the first sprouts of the new. . . . But the antithesis between capital and labour is overcome within them, if at first only by way of making the associated labourers into their own capitalist, i.e., by enabling them to use the means of production for the employment of their own labour. They show how a new mode of production naturally grows out of an old one, when the development of the material forces of production and of the corresponding forms of social production have reached a particular stage. Without the factory system arising out of the capitalist mode of production there could have been no co-operative factories. Nor could these have developed without the credit system arising out of the same mode of production. The credit system is not only the principle basis for the gradual transformation of capitalist private enterprises into capitalist stock companies, but equally offers the means for the gradual extension of co-operative enterprises on a more or less national scale.[26]

Marx concluded: "The capitalist stock companies, as much as the co-operative factories, should be considered as transitional forms from the capitalist mode of production to the associated one."[27] In comparison to the early writings, with their voluntaristic model of social change, the above model, no less than that of the *Grundrisse*, betrays a decidedly mechanistic bias. In the later writings, it is the internal logic of the system—the processes of capital accumulation, the concentration and centralization of capital, the falling rate of profit, and scientific-technological rationalization that Marx invoked to explain capitalism's transition to socialism.

Although Marx utilized different theoretical strategies in accounting for the transition from capitalism to socialism, one theme remains constant and dominant: the transitional historical character of capitalism. By conceiving capitalism as a transitional social formation, Marx gained a perspective on capitalism that had been absent in classical political economy. The economists, Marx stated, viewed capitalism as the expression of human nature—our propensity to barter and pursue our economic self-interest. Consequently, Marx reasoned, capitalism was considered a natural and eternal condition of social life. This meant, of course, that the condition of heteronomy, and personal and social fragmentation, which Marx perceived as inseparable from capitalism, was viewed as an inherent part of the human condition. Marx's critique of classical economics centered upon demonstrating the historicity of capitalism. Capitalism, he argued, has a definite beginning, development, and end point. It follows, he thought, that the divisions and heteronomy characteristic of capitalism entail only an historical and therefore temporary significance. The postcapitalist epoch is a mode of individual and communal life without "alienation":

> The bourgeois economists are so much cooped up within the notions belonging to a specific historic stage of social development that the necessity of the *objectification* of the powers of social labour appears to them as inseparable from the necessity of their *alienation*. . . . But with the suspension of the immediate character of living labour, as merely *individual* . . . with the positing of the activity of individuals as imme-

diately general or *social* activity, the objective moments of production are stripped of this form of alienation.[28]

Though Marx pointed to the transitional character of capitalism, he did not deny its progressive historical significance. From a general historical perspective, the "inherent purpose" of capitalism is the development of the sociocultural conditions to a point at which we can assert ourselves as autonomous and fully developed individuals. Capitalism "forces the development of the productive powers of society, and creates those material conditions, which alone can form the real basis of a higher form of society, a society in which the full and free development of every individual forms the ruling principle."[29] Capitalism pointed to socialism, and socialism held out the promise of realizing the Enlightenment ideal of autonomy and the romantic ideal of integral unity or human wholeness.

Integrating the Enlightenment and Romanticism: The Return to Utopia

The combination of romantic and Enlightenment themes in social thought is not uncommon during the first half of the nineteenth century. One finds such amalgamations in Hegel, Comte, and John Stuart Mill—to name but three prominent social thinkers prior to 1850.[30] Yet, aside from Hegel, Marx differs from other social theorists who sought to blend romantic and Enlightenment orientations by the fact that his entire life-work seems to cohere around the project of systematically integrating Enlightenment and romantic ideas. More than any other social theorist, Marx seems to have sought and achieved a lasting intellectual synthesis. This is highlighted if, for example, we compare Marx's achievement with Comte's failure as illustrated in his utter inability to integrate the Enlightenment thrust of *The Positive Philosophy* with the conservative-romantic orientation of *The Positive Polity*. Nevertheless, the recent intellectual and social history of Marxism indicates that in certain fundamental ways Marx's synthesis was a failure. The bifurcation of Marxism into Critical and Scientific Marxism points up the analytical tensions within Marx between a romantic-idealist and an Enlightenment-scientific disposition.[31] The interminable debates between the mechanistic and the voluntaristic or praxis-oriented interpretations of the transition problem reflect, once again, the deep tensions between the Enlightenment and romantic sides of Marxian social theory. The controversy surrounding the early versus the late Marx is, in its essentials, a debate concerning the balance of romantic and Enlightenment emphases in Marx. In this final section, I want to examine a similar tension between romantic and Enlightenment presuppositions in Marx by treating Romanticism and Enlightenment as different principles of philosophical anthropology and relating these to Marx's projection of their reconciliation in a socialist future.

In the following pages, the Enlightenment ideal of autonomy refers to humanity's orientation toward gaining control over the forces of nature and society by means of purposive action. The romantic ideal of human wholeness can be translated into the expressivist ideal of the full development of our sensory and intellectual powers into a coherent whole. Stated in more traditional philosophical terms, the problem of reconciling Enlightenment and romantic presuppositions may be posed as the problem of harmonizing reason and nature.[32] Reason, understood here as a mode of subjecting nature to moral imperatives, is antithetical to the natural, spontaneous, and many-sided expression of desire, impulse, and human neediness. Whether Marx's concept of socialism effectively integrated Enlightenment and romantic presuppositions depends upon whether it succeeds in uniting reason and nature, or autonomy and human wholeness.

One can discern in Marx's writings two attempts to achieve this reconciliation. The first attempt can be found most prominently in the *1844 Manuscripts*. Here the utopianism of Fourier and the aesthetic writings of Kant and

Schiller played a major role. The second attempt was worked out in his later economic studies, particularly *Capital*. I briefly discuss each of these attempts and argue that neither one furnished a satisfactory model.

The problem of harmonizing autonomy and integral unity was posed, in the *Manuscripts*, directly as an anthropological problem. This reflects the fact that the *Manuscripts* contain a fully developed philosophical anthropology in the tradition of Kant, Feuerbach, and Stirner. In the *Manuscripts*, Marx posited an active subject whose nature is formed in the unique constellation of his or her dual relations to external nature and other subjects. The problem of harmonizing reason and nature was formulated in the following anthropological way: given the mastery of nature as an anthropological condition of modernity, is it possible to avoid the simultaneous deformation of human nature? The instrumental reason intrinsic to social progress and individuation appears to be destructive of the naturalism, expressivism, and wholeness implied in the romantic ideal. Is there any way to reconcile the mastery of external nature with the free and full development of individuality?

Following the lead of Kant's *Critique of Judgement*, which attempted to furnish an epistemological resolution to the problem of reason and nature, and Schiller's *On the Aesthetic Education of Man*, in which aesthetic reflection already assumed an anthropological character, Marx considered the aesthetic principle as the distinctively human trait.

> Animals produce only according to the standards and needs of the species to which they belong, while man is capable of producing according to the standards of every species and of applying to each object its inherent standard: hence man also produces in accordance with the laws of beauty.[33]

The aesthetic constitutes the principle whereby the instrumentalism inherent in the mastery of external nature and the expressivism of our naturalistic aspect are integrated and form an harmonious unity. The imagination—the cognitive basis of the aesthetic—serves as a medium for our spontaneous and instinctive desires, while allowing for the systematization and ordering constitutive of reason. To the extent that labor—humankind's distinctive life-activity—assumes an aesthetic character, the sphere of production is transformed from a realm of domination into a sphere of freedom.[34]

Marx collapsed the sphere of production and the realm of freedom. By elevating labor to the status of our unique species activity, Marx reversed a tradition dating back to the ancients.[35] For the ancients, the sphere of production was a realm of necessity. Freedom presupposed the sphere of production but inhered in practical activity (politics) and the contemplative life outside the sphere of production. Marx's reversal implied one further notion: the supersession of the division of labor. Without the overcoming of a rigid division of labor, labor could never assume its aesthetic, hence free, multifaceted form.

The problem with this formulation is that it appears to imply a pre-modern condition. The model of labor as aesthetic activity is an ideal associated with handicraft production and seems to be excluded by industrial technology. Similarly, the occupations Marx cited in considering the abolition of a fixed division of labor—fishing and hunting—are notably of a non-industrial, nonagricultural kind. In this respect, Marx preserved a residual ambivalence about modernity that was characteristic of the romantics and the utopian socialists. This formulation was discarded by Marx in his later writings.

In the *Grundrisse*, Marx wrote: "Labour cannot become play as Fourier would like. . . ."[36] In rejecting play as a model of labor, Marx was likewise abandoning Schiller's aesthetic reformulation of human nature in which play becomes the model of free activity. Yet, an ambivalence still remained. Marx appears to retain the notion that in a socialist society "labour becomes attractive work, the individual's self-realization. . . ." Marx went on to say what attractive work stripped of its character of "fun" would be: "Really free working, e.g., composing, is at the same time precisely the most damned serious, the most intense exertion."[37] Although Marx rejected Fourier's belief that labor can become "play" or "fun," he seemed to adhere to the assumption that labor can be free activity; thus, the sphere of production continues to be viewed as a realm of freedom. However, his model of free laboring activity—composing music—is irrelevant to industrial production. The break with the earlier formulation becomes evident in *Capital*. Marx sheds the residues of his early utopianism by reintroducing the separation between the sphere of production—as a realm of necessity or domination—and the noneconomic institutional sphere—as a realm of freedom. I quote Marx at length:

> In fact, the realm of freedom actually begins only where labour which is determined by necessity and mundane considerations ceases; thus in the very nature of things it lies beyond the sphere of actual material production. Just as the savage must wrestle with nature to satisfy his wants, to maintain and reproduce life, so must civilized man, and he must do so in all social formations and under all possible modes of production. . . . Freedom in this field can only consist in socialized man, the associated producers, rationally regulating their interchange with nature; and achieving this with the least expenditure of energy and under conditions most favorable to, and worthy of, their human nature. But it nonetheless still remains a realm of necessity. Beyond it begins that development of human energy which is an end in itself, the true realm of freedom, which, however, can blossom forth only with this realm of necessity as its basis.[38]

My contention is twofold: first, that this formulation is a significant reversal of the earlier one; second, that it is also defective.

The one line of continuity between the early and later formulations is the claim that the interchange beween humanity and nature is a necessary and universal condition of our existence. However, in the *Manuscripts*, the sphere of production was to become a realm of freedom; hence, the reconciliation of purposive action and human wholeness. In the later argument, the sphere of production—excepting the element of social control and the improvement of work conditions—remains a realm of necessity. This points, I believe, to another shift in Marx's thought: labor is no longer the constitutive human activity, but is a mere means to survival.[39] The truly human activity of the individual now lies in the expressive and free activity outside the sphere of production. This noneconomic institutional context of social life is the sphere whose end is human development. Marx reintroduced the Aristotelian distinction between labor and action or necessity and freedom. In the *Grundrisse*, Marx temporalized these spheres—labor time, idle time, free time—in a manner paralleling Aristotle precisely: occupation time, recreation time, leisure time.

The reestablishment of the separation between the sphere of production and the realm of freedom proves equally unsuccessful. Marx succumbs to a dualistic formulation analogous to Kantian formalism. In Kant's view, nature signifies a universal principle of causality or determinism, to which we are invariably subject in our natural or phenomenal existence. To assert a realm of freedom, Kant was compelled to posit a nonempirical or noumenal self. The problem of the relation between the phenomenal and noumenal self, between the realm of nature and freedom in Kant, is posed, once again, in Marx's dualism between the realm of necessity (labor) and the realm of freedom (action). What is the relation between the individual *qua* laborer—subject to the necessity of production and treated as a means—and the individual *qua* moral subject—autonomous and expressive and treated as an end? Marx appeared to be vaguely aware of the problem and advanced the following argument: "Free-time—which is both idle time and time for higher activity—has naturally transformed its possessor into a different subject."[40] Marx's claim was that human nature is *primarily formed* outside the sphere of production: a "different subject" develops in the institutional sphere, to which the sphere of production is subject.

Yet, is not the reverse also true? Does not the time spent in the sphere of production as a mere instrumentality, subject to strict determinism and internal repression, enter into the formation of subjectivity? To say it differently, would not the mastery and repression of internal nature in the sphere of production limit or thwart the capacity for naturalistic, many-sided expression in the institutional sphere? Would not the experience of being a passive instrument of production, a means subject to strict determinism, enter into one's capacity to be an active, autonomous individual in the institutional sphere? To argue otherwise would invariably necessitate positing Kant's noumenal self: subjectivity detached from all natural existence. To accede to the claim would pose the relation between the individual *qua* laborer and the individual *qua* moral subject as problematic.

In fact, according to Marx's own statements regarding laboring activity under socialism, the relation *is* problematic. The sphere of production under socialism is characterized by the relation of humans and machinery. This condition involves very definite effects on human development. Of this relation between ourselves and machinery, Marx wrote:

> Rather, it is the machine which possesses skill and strength in place of the worker, is itself the virtuoso, with a soul of its own in the mechanical laws acting through it. . . . The worker's activity, reduced to a mere abstraction of activity, is determined and regulated on all sides by the movement of the machinery, and not the opposite. The science which compels the inanimate limbs of the machinery, by their construction, to act purposefully, as an automaton, does not exist in the worker's consciousness, but rather acts upon him through the machine as an alien power, as the power of the machine itself.[41]

What we seem to have here are elements of a new conceptualization of the problem of alienation. Alienation is not identified solely with capitalist social organization. Alienation appears to inhere in the system of machinery. This, of course, raises a serious question: what is the meaning of freedom under socialism? Marx's original claim was that capitalism created nonlabor time (disposable time) which formed the basis for human development. Marx criticized capitalism because it transformed disposable time into surplus labor time, thereby preventing the greater part of humanity from pursuing the end of human development. Under socialism, disposable time would become free time—time for the unfolding of a fully developed individuality. Freedom was to assume a dual meaning: common control and regulation of socioeconomic production according to the consensually agreed upon needs and values of society, and the extension of the realm of freedom where individuals could develop their many-sided capacities. However, to the extent that alienation is inherent in the sphere of production, the projected realization of autonomy and human wholeness in the institutional sphere is a false utopia. Either Marx has retained a latent idealism or, in his later writings, he was prepared to admit of a "social reality" principle which identified elements of heteronomy and division with the conditions of modern society.

Marx's failure to articulate an image of the socialist future that would harmonize the dual ideals of autonomy and human wholeness highlights the tension between Enlightenment and romantic themes in his social thought. This same tension, I believe, reappears in the uneasy balance in Marxian social theory between a conception of ourselves as a tool-making animal oriented to the mastery of nature, and as a symbol-using expressive animal oriented to meaning; between analytical instrumentalism and voluntarism; between a mechanistic and a praxis-oriented model of social change. Within at least one dominant current of Marxism, the tension has been resolved by a one-dimensional reduction of humans to the level of the tool-making animal; of practice to labor; of social development and history to natural laws; of the ideal of socialism to state control. The result has been another example of what Weber called the irony of history: Marxism has become a force of heteronomy and human fragmentation.

The revitalization of Marxism, if such is possible or desirable, as a social theory and progressive revolutionary movement presupposes that it recover its romantic and idealist legacy without, however, returning to the false standpoint of the Young Hegelian philosophy of consciousness.

Summary of Part Two

MARXISM IS, AND has been for some time, in a state of crisis. The reasons are not hard to find. First, Marxism has proved well suited to function as a conservative ideology. This reflects, it is true, its transplantation into national contexts lacking an indigenous liberal and democratic tradition. Such an authoritarian translation of Marxism was made easier, however, because of the residues of Jacobinism and positivism in Marx's work. This brings us to the second source of the crisis of Marxism. Marx's analytical social theory and sociohistorical analysis has been subject to a massive critique not only from "bourgeois" critics but from within the left as well. At the analytical level, despite his intention to synthesize materialism and idealism, and individualism and holism, Marx systematically suppressed the symbolic realm of culture and failed to satisfactorily integrate a reflexive concept of individual action into his structural analysis of society. In addition, the theoretical core of Marxism—the critical analysis of capitalism and his conceptualization of bourgeois society—has been judged, again by members both of the mainstream and critical establishments, to be outdated.[1]

This analysis raises an interesting question. Given the ideological and analytical discreditation of Marxism, how are we to account for its resiliency among Western intellectuals?

Two positions have been articulated in relation to the crisis of Marxism. On the one hand, there is the argument—found, for example, in the writings of Popper, Talmon, and Lewis Feuer, as well as such representatives of the left as Ernst Bloch—that Marxism persists because it functions as a quasi-religion fulfilling the need for a meaningful and redemptory world.[2] This argument, however, is flawed on two accounts. First, it wrongly assumes that Marxism is different from other social theories in that the former appeals to nonrational needs while the latter are validated on strictly logical and empirical grounds. This positivist assumption has long been abandoned. Moreover, the attempt to account for the persistence of Marxism by referring to its hidden program of redemption fails to explain the failure of stronger versions of modern redemptory world-views such as that of Comte or Fourier. In addition, many who embrace Marxism explicitly renounce any residues of Marx's early millenarianism and seek to identify Marxism as a rigorous positive science of society.

On the other hand, it is argued that though Marx's ideas, in their concrete empirical specificity, are antiquated, there is an epistemological or analytical core that remains unrefuted and contemporary. This position received its paradigmatic statement in Lukács's "What Is Orthodox Marxism?" "Let us assume . . . that recent research had disproved once and for all every one of Marx's individual theses. Even if this were to be proved, every serious 'orthodox' Marxist would still be able to accept all such modern findings without reservation and hence dismiss all of Marx's theses *in toto*—without having to renounce his orthodoxy for a single moment. . . . Orthodoxy refers exclusively to *method*."[3] As the multiplicity of neo-Marxisms illustrate, however, there is no consensus as to just what constitutes orthodoxy or method in Marx. For Lukács, who appropriated Marxism in the context of working through German idealism, it was the notion of totality—of the interpenetration and unity of subject and object, nature and history, and theory and practice—that is the essence of Marxism. For French structuralists, who interpret

Marx within the tradition of Cartesian rationalism, the analytical core of Marxism lies in its analysis of those world-constituting principles which underlie the flux of historic experience. For English and American Marxists, raised in an empiricist and positivist tradition, Marxism represents an empirically fruitful methodology. In all these efforts to articulate orthodoxy, Marx is assimilated to wider theoretical traditions; the uniqueness of Marxism is thereby eradicated.

The persistence of Marxism among Western intellectuals reflects, I believe, its peculiar integration of a critical project with its scientific disposition and modernist presuppositions. The attraction of Marxism does not lie simply in its being a revolutionary ideology, as opposition to bourgeois society is characteristic of philosophical conservatism, romanticism, and the French revolutionary tradition as well. It is Marxism's synthesis of revolution and modernism that separates it from other oppositional and revolutionary movements. Similarly, it is not the critical disposition alone that distinguishes Marxism but its attempt to unite critique and science. Marxism, both Critical and Scientific Marxists agree, is a critical science of society, i.e., an analysis aimed at uncovering the factors blocking autonomy and individuality, which simultaneously identifies the prospects and agencies of liberation.

To summarize, among oppositional ideologies, only Marxism combines a critique of liberalism and bourgeois society with modernist premises. This is manifested in Marx's commitment to, and radicalization of, the liberal notions of secularism, individual freedom, and democracy; his affirmation of industrialism as the basis for an ideology of progress; and his coupling of critique to the premises and goal of an empirical science of society. Marxian social theory has endured, I suspect, because by formulating a revolutionary ideology that preserved the Enlightenment heritage, Marxism resonates with the critical and scientific, yet also underlying bourgeois, disposition of Western intellectuals.

Part Three
Durkheim

Introduction to Part Three

THE HISTORIES OF sociology and Marxism in the nineteenth century intersect at many crucial junctures, yet remain distinct moments of intellectual history. Sociology "originated" in Comte's *Positive Philosophy*, which was completed in 1842. In 1844, the young Marx was in Paris beginning his own "critical philosophy." Comte lived until 1857, but doesn't appear to have noticed Marx, a rather minor figure at the time. In his later writings, Marx mentioned Comte's sociology but had "a very poor opinion of it."[1] Although the sociology of Comte had no influence upon Marx, there is a thematic convergence: both Comte and Marx were responding to the shortcomings of liberalism and bourgeois society. However, whereas Comte's departure from liberalism led to the holistic idealism and conservatism of *The Positive Polity*, Marx embraced a "materialist" and revolutionary world-view.

Some historians maintain that the development of Marxism and a socialist movement signaled a far-reaching opposition to liberalism and bourgeois society and that late-nineteenth-century sociology was a response to this revolutionary challenge.[2] Applied to Durkheim, this thesis argues, in the words of Irving Zeitlin, that Durkheim "remained throughout his life opposed to socialism" and that his sociology was "an effort to construct a model of society essentially antithetical to that of Marx."³ In its present form, Zeitlin's thesis is easily discredited by Durkheim's well-known advocacy of a version of guild socialism.⁴ In fact, at one point in his life, Durkheim was to declare: "Our salvation lies . . . in the formation of a new Socialism which goes back to the French tradition."⁵ In addition, recent studies have pointed to basic parallels between Durkheim's and Marx's theories of society.⁶

At the extreme opposite pole from Zeitlin with regard to the weight given Marx are such interpreters of Durkheim as Parsons, Harry Alpert, and Nisbet, all of whom entirely disregard or belittle the Marxian and socialist influence.⁷ Regarding the Marxian influence on Durkheim, recent commentary indicates that, in fact, it was minimal. Anthony Giddens states this position concisely and, I believe, correctly: "He [Durkheim] had first become directly acquainted with Karl Marx's works during his first visit to Germany but had not previously studied Marx in any detail. By the time he came to do so, most of his basic views were well formed. . . ."⁸ By way of providing supporting arguments and evidence for the lack of a significant encounter between Marxism and Durkheim, I want to point to the following considerations.

First, from his very earliest to his later writings, Durkheim nowhere singled out Marx as a main polemical target or positive influence. There are no prolonged discussions and hardly even a mention of Marx in Durkheim's major sociological studies. Moreover, none of his major or minor writings can be said to proceed from the ideological or analytical questioning of Marx. Throughout his lifetime, Durkheim denied, when compelled by accusations of materialism, any positive influence from Marx.⁹ What Durkheim perceived as theoretically positive in Marx was, in his view, already part of the general intellectual milieu of Europe.

Second, Durkheim tended to identify Marxism as a branch of revolutionary socialist ideology. Durkheim consistently denied the scientific status of Marx's theory of class conflict, theory of value, law of wages, etc.¹⁰ Insofar as Durkheim didn't relegate the fundamentals of Marxian social theory to unsubstantiated and outdated hypotheses, he classified Marxism as a genuine expression of the moral demand for social justice.

Third, though socialism became integral to French politics from the 1880s on, Marx's influence on socialist doctrine and organization was minimal until the 1930s.[11] The organized socialist movement was, even after its putative unification in 1905, highly fragmented and heterogeneous, consisting of strains of cooperative socialism, trade unionism, revolutionary syndicalism, and Marxist socialism. Intellectually, French socialism was very eclectic, mixing Blanquism, Proudhonism, Sorelian syndicalism, and Marxism.[12]

Fourth, there was no major Marxist theoretician in France to present a serious challenge to Durkheimian sociology. The chief advocate of Marxism, Jules Guesde, was, by all accounts, a weak thinker who had only a slight understanding of Marx's theory. Sorel, who in his early writings flirted with Marxism, never escaped the more profound impact of Proudhon. Durkheim doesn't appear to have seriously considered the German Marxists, and his only encounter with a Marxist of any stature, Antonio Labriola, reveals Durkheim's offhand dismissal of Marxism.

For good or bad, Durkheim's sociology was not shaped in any significant way by an encounter with Marx. The contrast between Durkheim's "avoidance of Marx" and "Max Weber's open reckoning with Marx," to quote Dominick LaCapra, is striking and must be fully noted.[13] From his earliest investigations of Roman agrarian conditions and the East Elbian labor situation, through the study on Protestantism and capitalism, to his 1920 Munich lecture, "A Positive Critique of Historical Materialism," Weber's ideas were shaped in a significant and positive way by his theoretical reckoning with Marx. In part, the impact of Marx on German sociology was a consequence of the absence of a native theoretical tradition that coincided with a democratic orientation. For the young Weber, Marx provided a democratic alternative to the romantic and conservative social theories and politics that dominated Germany. In marked contrast to the situation in France, Marxism quickly took hold of German socialism and, in addition, found major theoretical spokesmen in, among others, Kautsky and Bernstein. The combination of the intellectual and political penetration of Marxism and the conservatism of romantic and historicist social theory led intellectuals like Weber, Sombart, Tönnies, and Simmel, who were opposed to Prussian authoritarianism, to assume a receptive and positive attitude towards Marxism.[14]

In France, Marxism was not the intellectual and political force that it had become in Germany between 1890 and World War I. But, as I have maintained in Part One, France had its own revolutionary tradition, and its impact on Durkheim has been completely neglected. Despite the disparities between individual representatives of the French revolutionary tradition, there are unifying principles and themes which form a central analytical and ideological component of Durkheim's sociology.

Pivotal to Durkheim's intellectual outlook was the commitment to social equality and justice as the precondition for individual freedom, happiness, and social solidarity in the modern world. It is hard to exaggerate the extent to which the French revolutionary tradition, from Rousseau to the egalitarians, Babeuf, Blanqui, and Proudhon, made social equality and social justice the centerpiece of its ideology. I have already demonstrated this with regard to the eighteenth-century revolutionary tradition. The same ideal is at the core of Proudhon's revolutionary ideology: "Justice is the central star which governs society, the pole on which the political world turns, the principle and rule of all transactions." In the absence of just sociopolitical relations, all "our institutions [would be] vicious, our politics erroneous: consequently, there would be disorder and social evil."[15] From the ideal of social justice, which in the French tradition meant reciprocity of respect and services and the abolition of gross inequities, there followed the particulars of the revolutionary critique of bourgeois society: the critique of private property, inequality, possessive individualism, and cultural hedonism. From the communitarian but anti-statist ideal follows their revolutionary program: decentralized worker associations, either collective property or property without inheritance, socioeconomic equality, and a morally unified order.

The revolutionary opposition to bourgeois society entailed an analytical critique of liberal social thought. Though highly unsystematic, two features of the analytical premises of revolutionary social theory further indicate the affiliation between the revolutionary tradition and Durkheim. First, the tendency in French revolutionary thought to conceive of society as an autonomous unit of social analysis. "Social science," wrote Proudhon, "is the . . . systematic understanding of what . . . society . . . is in its whole life, that is, in its totality of successive manifestations, for it is only thus that there can be reason and system."[16] Besides individual reason, Proudhon referred to a collective reason, a reason attached to group life: "The organ of collective reason is the same as that of collective force: it is the . . . group. . . ."[17] Individual reason and moral sensibility develop only in the context of collective life, and, as such, social solidarity (a term Proudhon frequently employed) is the precondition of individual liberty. In words that recall Rousseau's earlier pronouncements and anticipate Durkheim's own stated intentions, Proudhon reasoned:

> What new generations require is a unity which expresses the soul of society: spiritual unity, intelligible order, which joins us together through all the powers of our consciousness and our reason, and nevertheless leaves us our free thought, free will, free heart. . . . What we need today is a unity which, adding to our liberties, grows in its turn and fortifies itself with these liberties themselves. . . ."[18]

Durkheim's analytical commitment to methodological holism and social idealism and his concern with social solidarity fall squarely within the theorizing of the French revolutionary tradition. The impact of revolutionary ideas on Durkheim's social theory is in evidence in that these analytical premises are coupled to Durkheim's advocacy of social justice and moral community, and to his critique of hierarchy, inheritance, and bureaucratic state centralization.

There were, Durkheim thought, severe limitations, both analytical and ideological, to the revolutionary tradition. Durkheim denied scientific status to all but Saint-Simon, who in any event departs in crucial ways from the egalitarian tradition. The blatantly ideological orientation of the revolutionary tradition, Durkheim argued, led to a simplistic understanding of modern history and often inappropriate demands for social change. Durkheim was repelled by the narrow class-character, violent disposition, and elitist tendencies of revolutionary ideology and organization. No doubt, Durkheim found the anti-bourgeois and anti-modernist proclivities of the revolutionary tradition equally distasteful.

The other major component of Durkheim's social theory derives from the idealist and democratic strains of French liberalism. Almost fifty years ago, Henry Alpert argued that before Durkheim had ever read Comte, he had immersed himself in the neo-critical idealism of Renouvier.[19] More recently, Steven Lukes has stated Renouvier's influence on Durkheim in the strongest possible terms:

> One can discern what Durkheim valued in Renouvier: his uncompromising rationalism; his central concern with morality and his determination to study it "scientifically"; his neo-Kantianism emphasizing the compatibility of the determinism of nature with the freedom presupposed by morality; his Kantian concern with the dignity and autonomy of the individual together with his theory of social cohesion based on the individual's sense of unity with and dependence on others; his preference for justice over utility, and denial that the first can be derived from the second; his notion of existing society being in a state of war and his view of the State's role being to establish "social justice" in the economic sphere; his advocacy of associations, such as producers' co-operatives, independent of the State; his case for secular, republican education in state schools; and his underlying purpose of reconciling the sacredness of the individual with social solidarity.[20]

Aside from Renouvier, the idealist and democratic tradition of French liberalism continued to serve as a formative context in Durkheim's intellectual development through the writings of and direct contact with Jules Lachelier, Emile Boutroux, and Octave Hamelin. This has led Alpert to argue that "in spite of many appearances to the contrary, it is not to Comte as much as to Boutroux and Renouvier that Durkheim is closely related."[21]

In the writings of the neo-critical idealists, Alpert and Lukes point to what can only be called an indigenous intellectual and political tradition of liberal democracy in France: scientific but idealist in its insistence upon moral autonomy; individualistic but equally concerned with social solidarity; utilitarian but oriented to social justice; pluralistic but seeking moral community; committed to decentralization but attributing to the state a positive moral role in society; reformist but radical in its commitment to broad structural and cultural change. Although Alpert and Lukes are correct to point to the impact of these strains of idealism and democracy on Durkheim, they fail to notice the extent to which the ideas of neo-critical idealism coincide with and bear the mark of the French revolutionary tradition. It was in the merging of the liberal and revolutionary traditions into an essentially democratic and moral idealistic world-view, rooted in the spirit of the French Revolution, that we find the intellectual origins of Durkheim's social thought.[22]

In the chapters to follow, I argue that Durkheim's efforts to work out a reconciliation of the liberal and revolutionary traditions—to synthesize individualism and community, liberty and equality, pluralism and solidarity, collectivism and decentralized community autonomy, and economic progress and democratic planning—originated in the midst of a crisis in liberal France. The resolution of that crisis, Durkheim thought, required an ideological and social alliance of liberalism and revolution around the republican ideals of 1789.

6. *The Liberal Tradition in France and the Crisis of the 1890s*

THE OUTSTANDING FEATURE of French liberalism prior to the Third French Republic was its failure to achieve a lasting sociocultural and political dominance. Either liberalism passed into radicalism, as in the Jacobinism of 1789–1790, the radical democratic movement of 1848, and the Communards of 1870, or liberalism merged with conservatism, as in the various authoritarian regimes associated with Napoleon, the July Monarch, or the Bourbon, Orleanist, and Bonapartist dynasties. Numerous factors contributed to the instability of French liberalism: the persistence of a strong rural and agrarian social structure with ties to traditionalism; the continued presence of a powerful church and the ideological hegemony of Catholicism; and the tradition of a strong centralized state authority. However, there is one factor which we want to single out as of immense significance: the incongruity between the Lockean liberalism embraced by the French bourgeoisie and the indigenous social and intellectual conditions.

Historians have frequently pointed out that the philosophes drew their inspiration and ideology from the English

liberal tradition.[1] The towering figures for the French Enlightenment were Newton and Locke; the French philosophes
looked to the English constitution and its pluralistic social
order as a model of a good society. English liberalism penetrated into French social theory through the writings of Montesquieu, Holbach, Helvétius, Turgot, and Voltaire. What
characterizes their social and political thought are English
liberal themes: the doctrine of the constitutional balance of
powers, parliamentary government, economic individualism,
the ideal of a market economy, and a minimalist state conception. Similarly, when one examines the chief spokesmen
of French liberalism through the 1870s—Royer-Collard, Benjamin Constant, Jean-Baptiste Say, Frédéric Bastiat, Guizot—
it is the ideas of Lockean liberalism that are conspicuous.[2]

By embracing Lockean liberal ideas, the French bourgeoisie enunciated a world-view whose premises were antagonistic to native French culture. Both conservatives and
revolutionaries assailed the economic individualism, the commercial ideal, the noninterventionist state, the doctrinaire
utilitarianism, and the materialism of Lockean liberalism. By
upholding the doctrine of Lockean liberalism, the French
bourgeoisie were unable to forge the necessary social and
ideological underpinnings of a liberal social order. The result
was that French liberals ended up forming alliances with the
powerful forces of conservatism to stem the tide of revolution.
The memory of Jacobinism and its association with the Reign
of Terror led liberals to oppose the French revolutionary tradition. The liberal historian and statesman Guizot, for example, viewed revolution as the single most important threat
to a French republic. "What matters," Guizot said, "is to expel
the revolutionary spirit which is still tormenting France and
to practice the free régime she now possesses. . . ."[3] Of course,
the "free régime" Guizot spoke of was the monarchy dominated by the Crown, the church, the aristocracy, and the army;
liberal only in its constitutionalism and its encouragement
of industrialism.

The alliance between conservatism and liberalism defined

the politics and culture of French society for over half a century. The bourgeoisie sustained the illusion that in the long run radicalism would peter out and conservatism would shed its more reactionary disposition. The ideal was a basically conservative society in which the alliance of monarchy and constitution—or order and progress, as Comte expressed it— would replace the divisiveness of its revolutionary past.[4]

Two events in the formative years of the Third Republic shattered this illusion. First, the rise of the Communards manifested the continued vigor of the revolutionary tradition. The violent suppression of the Paris Commune indicated the equally sustained antipathy to the revolutionary tradition among liberals and conservatives. Second, the Boulanger and the Dreyfus Affair signaled the unyielding opposition of conservatives to the republican ideal. The idea of a gradual reconciliation of class divisions, of unity between conservatism and liberalism while suppressing radicalism, seemed increasingly utopian. The years between 1880 and World War I proved to be the crucial test of whether a liberal social order could prosper on French soil.

The combination of these divisive social, political, and intellectual factors forms the immediate context of Durkheim's sociology. I call this context the "crisis of liberalism." Prior to the Third Republic, a crisis of liberalism was not possible for the very reason that liberalism, as I have argued, had not achieved anything resembling hegemony. The Third Republic marked, in effect, the establishment of a liberal social order. It was during these years, historians inform us, that France became an industrial nation. From the 1880s on, France witnessed the rise of a national modern secular educational system, a working parliamentary government, a plurality of organized political parties spanning the full political spectrum, and the extension of civil and political rights.[5] If, as I argue, a liberal social order was instituted for the first time in France, in what sense can we speak of a crisis of liberalism? I believe there are two sets of factors which support my interpretation.

First, although a liberal order was in the making, the Republic and the very idea of liberalism were subject to relentless attacks from conservatives and radicals. The industrialization of France weakened the traditional forces of conservatism, but they remained vociferous and powerful due to their strategic locations in the universities, church, military, newspapers, and government bureaucracy. Moreover, after the defeat suffered in the Franco-Prussian War, the fusion of traditional conservatism and militant nationalism proved attractive to a humiliated France. The conservative presence spans the Third Republic, as witnessed by the Dreyfus Affair, the *Action Française*, and the "Catholic Renaissance" heralded by the popular writings of Henri Massis and Alfred de Tarde.[6] The conservatives were against the Republic and its association with scientific rationalism, individualism, democracy, and industrialism. They sought to revive the traditional supports of a conservative social order: the authoritarian state, social hierarchy, clerical education, and the central role of the church and Catholicism.[7]

Equally hostile to the Republic were the diverse movements of the French revolutionary tradition. Prior to the 1880s, French radicalism was highly fragmented and, aside from the more reformist cooperative labor movement, tended towards sporadic and intense eruptions of social violence and utopianism. Radicalism was tainted, moreover, by its historic connection to the Reign of Terror, the mob riots of 1848, and the blood-spilling of the Paris Commune. The bourgeoisie supported the conservatives in suppressing those social reforms which might have integrated elements of radicalism. As a result, there developed a condition of overt and fierce class antagonism. During the 1880s, socialism became organized: political parties, newspapers, and voluntary trade associations were formed. By the 1890s, socialism was a major social and political force in French society. Although it is true that certain elements of French socialism were early supporters of the Republic, after the dissolution of the alliance between the Radical Party (left-liberals) and the socialists, French socialism intensified its critique of liberalism and the Republic. By 1905, French socialism found itself inexorably linked to revolutionary ideologies: Marxist socialism, syndicalism, and anarchism.

The idea of a liberal France was being challenged, once again, by the polarization of the social and political forces for order and change. The threat to a viable liberal French society was magnified in that the Republic lacked a doctrine which could unify its liberal and democratic supporters and legitimate the republican ideal. Although Lockean liberalism still had its supporters, it was incapable of unifying the diverse social and political currents of French society. In fact, not only did it elicit the hostility of the conservatives and radicals, but it was increasingly discredited within the ranks of the progressive middle class.

In the face of the conservative and revolutionary critique of the Republic, and in the absence of a viable liberal doctrine, the Republic seemed destined to relapse into anarchy or authoritarianism. Durkheim came to intellectual maturity precisely when the crisis of liberalism was peaking. Durkheim's sociology aimed at articulating a doctrine that could furnish a unifying social and ideological basis for the Third French Republic. Unlike the tradition of Lockean liberalism, which turned its back on the "Principles of 1789," Durkheim believed that the task of the Republic was to complete the revolution.[8] Durkheim sought a reconstructed liberalism that would fulfill the French revolutionary heritage.

Before moving on to discuss Durkheim's sociology and its relation to the crisis of liberalism, I want to specify some of the broader cultural dimensions of the crisis. The crisis of liberalism did not only reflect the social and political instability of the Third Republic. The secular, rationalist, and individualist premises of liberalism were openly being disputed. From all sides of the political spectrum, scientific rationalism was exposed to a political and idealist critique. Durkheim frequently remarked on this rising tide of anti-science and irrationalism.[9] Durkheim referred to the "assault on reason" by the widely read American Pragmatist William James and the intuitionist philosophy of Bergson; the resurgence of the "nascent mysticism" of French idealists; the irrationalist currents linked to the Catholic revival of Henri Massis and Alfred de Tarde; the racialist, anti-Semitic nationalism of Maurras and Barrès; and the anti-intellectualism of certain forms of syndicalism and anarchism which, like the conservative *Action Française*, endorsed violence and terrorism as legitimate modes of political activity. Linked to the assault on reason, Durkheim noted an undercurrent of anti-modernism: "The anarchist, the aesthete, the mystic, the socialist revolutionary, even if they do not despair of the future, have in common with the pessimist a single sentiment of hatred and disgust for the existing order, a single craving to destroy or to escape from reality."[10] Even the noted essayist and poet Charles Péguy could write: "The modern world debases everything. Other worlds have other occupations . . . ; other worlds idealized or materialized, built or demolished. . . . The modern world debases. That is its specialty."[11] Péguy and the revolutionaries, traditionalists, Catholics, and mystical idealists expressed a kind of crude neo-romantic repudiation of modernism. In the background of their criticism lingered an idealized version of traditional French culture, with its roots in a cosmological world-view.

This anti-modernism and anti-rationalism was connected to a critique of "individualism and intellectualism." Individualism, the anti-liberals contended, extinguishes the vital traditions which are the unifying and sustaining sources of French culture. By espousing the ideology of individualism, the intellectuals contribute to the "destruction of French culture" and the perpetuation of a condition of chronic disorder. The primacy of the individual, the anti-liberals said, must be replaced by the unquestioned supremacy of the family, neighborhood, church, and nation; intellectualism must be curbed so as to conform to Catholic dogma and French tradition. Thus, the attack on the French Republic signaled a far-reaching assault on the very idea of liberalism.[12] It was this broad-gauged social, political, and cultural critique that represents the more profound meaning of the crisis of liberalism.

It was in the context of Durkheim's perception of the full social and cultural meaning of the crisis of liberalism that his sociology originated and must be understood. Of course, the crisis was social, political, and cultural—not intellectual. However, Durkheim recognized that intellectual doctrines and theories project societal ideals and, as sources of legitimation, effect the political and cultural life of society. This was true, Durkheim thought, particularly of the doctrines of the economists and socialists as well as the sociology of Comte and Spencer, whose formal theories were coupled respectively to conservative and Lockean liberal ideological presuppositions. Durkheim believed that these disparate intellectual doctrines and theories embodied presuppositions and social ideals that perpetuated the social, political, and cultural polarization of the Third Republic. It was crucial, Durkheim thought, to discredit the legitimating function of their ideas by criticizing and reconstructing social theory. Durkheim's analytical debates, in other words, with Comte, Spencer, the socialists, and the economists must be read, in part, as conflicts of world-view and politics. In his effort to safeguard the Republic, Durkheim repudiated all three ideological orthodoxies which underlie these theories: conservatism, liberalism, and revolution. Durkheim sought a doctrine that would unify the social forces and intellectual principles of liberalism and revolution. The presuppositions of Durkheim's social theory lie in an indigenous democratic tradition of French social thought founded upon the fusion of liberal and revolutionary ideas.

Durkheim's social theory cannot be reconstructed simply through textual examination, or by situating him in a sociopolitical context, or by detailing particular influences—say, Comte, or Saint-Simon, or Marx. One needs to know the general intellectual standpoint from which Durkheim polemicized against economism, socialism, or Comte, Spencer, and

Kant. One must inquire, therefore, into the tradition within which Durkheim theorized.

The intellectual milieu of eighteenth-century France can roughly be characterized as consisting of three basic intellectual orientations: conservatism, liberalism, and revolution. All three orthodoxies extended into the nineteenth century with their premises relatively intact. For example, liberal principles are found prominently in the classical economists, in bourgeois historians like Guizot, and in certain strains of Social Darwinism. Revolutionary orthodoxy is maintained in the social thought of Blanqui, Proudhon, and anarcho-syndicalism. However, in contrast to the narrow orthodoxies of the eighteenth century, we find efforts in the nineteenth century to fuse liberal and revolutionary orientations. On the "liberal-democratic" side—for example, in Condorcet, Tocqueville, Saint-Simon, Lamartine, Michelet, Renouvier, the solidarism of Fouillée and Leon Bourgeois, and Durkheimian sociology—we can detect a fusion of liberal themes (individualism, pluralism, political centralization, industrial progress) and revolutionary ideas (social equality, social solidarity, decentralized community control, socialized property). On the "social-democratic" side—for example, in Blanc, Malon, Jaurès, and Millerand—we find a similar effort to bring together liberalism and revolution, with the main difference being the latter group's insistence upon the abolition of private property.

The most striking feature of the French democratic tradition is its commitment to social justice as the supreme value and ideological center of social theory. According to the French democrats, freedom from external coercion is only one aspect of liberty. Without the equalization of the external conditions of social, political, and economic life and the implementation of norms of commutative and distributive justice, individual freedom is merely formal and one-sided for the majority of the population. This ideological shift in French democratic doctrine had significant analytical consequences.

By connecting freedom to conditions of social equality, democratic social theory shifted its conceptual point of reference from the self-sufficient individual of Lockean liberalism to those ideal and material conditions of the social and cultural structure which promote or obstruct social justice. Moreover, whereas Lockean liberalism tended to operate with an instrumentalist schema of action and order—viewing the market and the coercive state as the paradigmatic social forces—the liberal and social democrats exhibited an equal concern for shared, consensually based collective beliefs and values. The latter also interpreted social structure in more voluntarist terms, and consequently one finds a deep current of idealism in their social theory. This idealism was expressed not only in highlighting the idealist dimension of society—Rousseau's "general will," Proudhon's "collective reason," Durkheim's "collective representations"—but in their interpretation of the revolution as a moral transformation instituting a civil religion centered upon the "Principles of 1789."

This common social and moral idealism was the ideological basis of the political alliance between the bourgeoisie and the socialists during the Third Republic. Durkheim believed that only on the basis of this alliance could liberalism and the Republic survive in France. Why would the democratic tradition be able to serve as a cohesive force of French liberalism? Durkheim thought that the democratic tradition integrated the three central principles of French culture: the idea of a moral community, individualism, and social justice. It was Durkheim's chief aim to give the democratic ideology an intellectual form that could achieve this ideological synthesis and penetrate into the collective consciousness of French society and politics.

7. Democracy and Sociology

Durkheim's Synthesis of Liberalism and Revolution

DURKHEIM'S SOCIOLOGY MAY be appropriately understood as a response to the underlying problem of the Third French Republic: the crisis of liberalism. In his sociological studies and his few political essays, Durkheim tried to account for the recurring failure of French liberalism by pointing to such factors as class polarization, the traditionalism of agrarian France, and moral disorder. In addition to these broad structural and cultural factors, Durkheim alluded to the poverty of liberal thought as a key reason for the failure of French liberalism. This reflects Durkheim's belief that the social and political failure of liberalism was in part due to, and reflected in, the conceptual shortcomings of its doctrine. Theoretical debate and critique, in Durkheim's view, were inseparably linked to political practice and social change. Durkheim's theoretical critique and reconstruction of liberalism had a practical or normative impulse and political aim: to provide a sound ideological foundation and ideal for a French liberal order. In this chapter, I focus upon the formal and ideological aspects of Durkheim's critique and revision of the liberal tradition.

Liberalism: Ideology and Science

Durkheim singled out for criticism two distinct strains of the liberal tradition. The first is derived from the contractarianism of Hobbes and Locke and is to be found in classical political economy, utilitarianism, and the sociology of Spencer. Durkheim frequently referred to this liberal current as utilitarian or egoistic individualism, which I have called English or Lockean liberalism. The second current of liberal thought, which Durkheim called moral individualism, was identified with Kant and the neo-critical idealism of Renouvier, Boutroux, and Hamelin. What these two very different strains of liberalism shared was a commitment to the idea of the self-sufficient individual as the starting point and ultimate value of their social, political, and moral theory. Naturally, Durkheim was sensitive to the profound differences between egoistic and moral individualism. He noted, for example, that egoistic individualism tended towards a materialist metaphysic, a naturalistic pleasure-pain psychology, an instrumentalist view of social action, and a notion of happiness as the highest moral and social end. On the other hand, moral individualism embraced an idealist metaphysic or a spiritualized view of nature, asserted a normative conception of social action, and posited freedom and human dignity as the highest moral view. At a substantive level, Durkheim's sociology sought to synthesize these two strains of liberalism. Thus, Durkheim's concept of morality combined the egoistic element of desire or happiness with the idealist stress upon duty; similarly, the instrumentalist and contractarian theory of society was given an idealist or noncontractarian basis in Durkheim's view of society.

At the methodological level, Durkheim repudiated both egoistic and moral individualism. His methodological critique was quite clear and direct: the liberal tradition is rooted in a basically *a priori*, deductive, and subjective methodology. Regarding moral individualism, he noted that by placing the individual, viewed essentially as a creator of values, outside the concept of nature and efficient causality, the neo-critical idealists salvaged a metaphysic of freedom, but only at the cost of a purely subjective or intuitionist methodology. Although the hostility towards science was presumably not shared by English liberalism, the economists nevertheless succumbed to the same deductive and subjective methodology as the idealists.[1] This shared deductive methodology is highlighted, Durkheim contended, in their analysis of moral phenomena. In the Introduction to *The Division of Labor in Society* (henceforth simply *Division*), Durkheim argued:

> The procedure of one, as well as the other, is the following: they start from the concept of man, deducing the ideal from what seems to them suitable to a being who is thus defined; and having set up this ideal, they derive from it the supreme rule of conduct, the moral law. The differences distinguishing the doctrines rest uniquely in the fact that man is not everywhere conceived in the same manner. With some, he is made a creature of pure will; elsewhere place is given to the sensibilities. . . . But if the inspiration varies, the method is everywhere the same. All talk abstractly of the existing reality.[2]

Regarding this deductive methodology, Durkheim concluded: "With such a method, it is impossible to reach a truly objective conclusion."[3]

Naturally, the deductive methodology is not original or unique to liberalism. Deductionism allows for a wide range of ideological and analytical positions. One can, for example, begin from God, consciousness, humanity, reason, ego, or personality, and deduce from any of them the most varied conclusions and principles. The singularity of liberalism lies in its initial premise: the idea of a separate and independent individual.

> They start from the abstract concept of the individual in himself and from it develop the contents. Given the notion of an absolutely autonomous individual, depending only on himself, without historical antecedents, without a social milieu, how should he conduct himself either in his economic relations or

in his moral life? Such is the question which they pose themselves and which they seek to resolve by reasoning.[4]

Durkheim objected to liberal social thought on the grounds that its initial premise—the absolutely autonomous individual—cannot be empirically verified or historically substantiated. "They see in it," Durkheim said, "one of those very simple, very clear notions which the scholar posits and does not demonstrate, whose accuracy everyone can easily verify by introspection and without further procedure. That is to say that it can have only a very subjective value."[5] Far from assuming a logically axiomatic status, the liberal premise was viewed by Durkheim as a "matter of faith"—as a subjective value rooted in determinant sociocultural conditions. By conflating its moral commitment to individualism with a methodological premise for developing a social, political, or moral theory, liberalism, like its ideological opponents, conservatism and radicalism, remains at the level of ideological analysis. "All of them," Durkheim said by way of criticism, "in effect, reduce social science to a simple ideological analysis."[6]

Because it had adopted a deductive methodology which, according to Durkheim, is invariably rooted in subjective bias, liberalism was unable to provide a reasoned defense of its ideas and values. In the end, liberalism appeared as an article of faith whose legitimacy was subject to the same ideological critique as the conservative, revolutionary, or positivist orthodoxy. This was unacceptable to Durkheim, who believed that liberalism, if it was going to acquire legitimacy, must assume a logically compelling character. "We must," he declared, "eliminate these deductions that are generally used only to resemble an argument, and that justify, after the resolution, preconceived sentiments and personal sentiments."[7] To free liberalism from its ideological status, Durkheim thought it was necessary to evolve a social theory that would not be founded upon an *a priori* deductive or subjectivist methodological foundation. Sociology, he believed, could achieve this breakthrough to a nonideological social theory.

In the deductively grounded liberal social theories, Durkheim noted a retreat from the analysis of the particularity and plurality of sociohistorical reality. Instead of examining social facts in their specificity and diversity, liberal social theory concerned itself with ideas about social facts, was preoccupied with ill-defined abstractions—individualism, progress, evolution—and remained satisfied with evolving practical maxims and universal formulas of social order and change. Durkheim wrote: "Instead of observing, describing, and comparing things, we are content to focus our consciousness upon, to analyze, and to combine our ideas. Instead of a science concerned with realities, we produce no more than an ideological analysis."[8] To move from an ideological to an objective social science, Durkheim counseled a return to concrete empirical reality; a science aimed at discovering "the laws of reality" or the "real relations among things." Durkheim's programmatic statement regarding a nonideological social theory is, of course, contained in *The Rules of a Sociological Method.*

The exact argument and the validity of Durkheim's methodology of the social sciences will not concern us. I believe, however, that Durkheim can be faulted for his objectivistic self-understanding of social theory. In any event, I want to raise a different sort of question: given that Durkheim believed a nonideological social science possible, why did he single out sociology as the chosen discipline? After all, Comte's sociology, as Durkheim reiterated frequently, was guilty of similar methodological flaws: intuitionist reasoning, and unacceptable uniformitarian and evolutionary assumptions. Durkheim's turn to sociology is intelligible on two accounts. First, the dominant social sciences—economics and political science—were so firmly entrenched in the deductive tradition, and so intimately joined to Lockean liberal premises, that such a conceptual shift as Durkheim proposed would be strongly resisted. Moreover, where Durkheim saw such a conceptual reorientation occurring—for example, in the German Historical School—it was evident that economics was passing into a more general social science bearing remarkable similarities to Comte's sociology.[9] Second, though Comte's positivism was seriously flawed, Durkheim felt that Comte had formulated two ideas that were crucial to a genuine social science: first, the notion of society as a conceptual totality, consisting of interrelated parts and irreducible to the psychology of individuals; and, second, the idea of social development. To be sure, Durkheim repudiated Comte's unilinear evolutionism but preserved Comte's notion of the continuity of institutional and societal development.[10] Comte's sociology, in Durkheim's view, signaled the beginnings of a return to the analysis of "things" or social facts.

Durkheim perceived in sociology the possibility of a non-ideological social theory. Yet, a problem remained: Comte's sociology had a pervasively anti-liberal bias. Although Durkheim could have attempted to ground sociology in the English tradition associated with Spencer, he was repelled by its dominant Lockean liberalism. In taking up the cause of sociology, Durkheim was forced to dissociate it from both the conservatism of Comte and the Lockean liberalism of Spencer.

Comte, Spencer, and Durkheim

To become a vital intellectual and moral force in French liberal culture, sociology had to renounce its Comtean and Spencerian legacy. This is so, Durkheim thought, because even though Comte and Spencer had made great strides towards formulating the paradigmatic features of sociology, their social theory was wedded to the respective principles of philosophical conservatism and Lockean liberalism. It is precisely in the context of his polemic with Comte and Spencer that Durkheim situates himself in relation to an indigenous democratic tradition.

By referring to Comte as a conservative, I do not mean to suggest that his sociology bears no trace of Enlightenment liberalism. In his commitment to scientific rationalism and

an historical and progressive conception of social development, Comte's sociology has a decidedly modern and liberal
coloring. Yet, Comte shared with the traditionalists, Bonald
and Maistre, a deep and far-reaching critique of the Enlightenment idea of a secular and liberal society. In unison with
the traditionalists, Comte argued against liberty, equality,
democracy, and secularism as illusions of an abstract reason.
Comte's return to the "realities" turns into a pronounced conservatism, as illustrated in his unqualified endorsement of
hierarchy and authoritarianism, obedience and social conformity, and in his call for a new religion complete with priests
and cosmology.

Comte's ideological conservatism was built into the most
essential analytical premises and perspectives of his sociology.
This is clearly evident in Comte's view of social order. Durkheim himself noted two currents in Comte's thought regarding the problem of social order: first, the instrumentalist view
that only the coercive power of the state could secure social
stability against the ever-present structural tendencies towards fragmentation; second, the conservative notion that
social order presupposed order in the cognitive and moral
sphere. What the conservatives asserted was not simply the
necessity of collective beliefs and values, but a full-blown
cosmological world-view. A cosmological world-view such as
Christianity, refers to the idea of an objective order structured
into the world. This order is fixed in essentials, and hierarchy
is its organizing principle. As is evident, the cosmological
world-view is the antinomy of the secular world-view and is
intrinsically hostile to modern values, such as individualism,
democracy, critical rationalism, and pluralism.

Comte agreed with the traditionalists that a cosmological
world-view was a precondition of social order. However, in
contrast to the traditionalists, he felt that Christianity was
dissonant with the emerging scientific and industrial civilization. Moreover, Comte did not share the intense repulsion
for industrialism that characterized the traditionalists. Comte
believed that in an industrial order only science could furnish

a system of order comparable to Christianity. Comte's notion of positivism was meant to be the functional equivalent of Christianity. Considered as a whole, Comte's *Positive Philosophy* and *Positive Polity* constitute a system of worldly order, informed by the cosmic principles of fixity, teleology, and hierarchy.

Durkheim was highly critical of Comte's view of social order, with its obvious ties to conservative values. By positing a cosmological world-view as a necessary basis of social order, Comte failed to grasp the differing modes of solidarity characteristic of traditional and modern society. In *Division*, Durkheim argued that the passage from traditional to modern social types meant the decline of the world viewed as a cosmic order and the appearance of a more pronounced secular and utilitarian structure in modern society. The failure of conservatism to understand the new forms of solidarity inherent in modern society reflected the fact that it ultimately denied the uniquely secular basis of the modern world. "What characterizes industrial societies," Durkheim wrote by way of criticizing the conservative world-view, "is that, freed of every theological idea, they rest on purely secular foundations."[11] Secularism, in Durkheim's view, meant a decisive cognitive shift towards the natural and human sources of action, order, and change. Secularism implied a basically immanent, rationalist, and utilitarian world-view.[12] "There is," Durkheim claimed, "no longer anything about it [the world] that is not temporal and human."[13] In a secular order, collective beliefs and values are not extinguished but transformed: they are attached to very concrete human needs and interests and are not exempt from rational discussion and criticism. Durkheim pointed to the configuration of sentiments and practices associated with ideas such as individualism, democracy, socialism, and progress as examples of modern "religious" belief. Durkheim's central claim, then, was that under modern conditions, religion or collective belief no longer assumes the form of a cosmological system. "The most recent religions," Durkheim wrote in 1908, "are not cosmologies, but are disciplined morals."[14] By distinguishing secular from cosmic world-views, Durkheim was able to incorporate the insight of conservatism—the idea of a moral order founded upon collective beliefs—without taking over its anti-modern values and perspective.

Whereas Comte's sociology was built upon a conservative presuppositional infrastructure, Spencer's embodied assumptions from within the mainstream of English liberalism. In general, Spencer's social theory was, in Durkheim's view, of immense historical significance.[15] At a time when sociology in France languished and appeared to be on the decline, Spencer sustained and reinvigorated the Comtean legacy.[16] Durkheim consistently praised Spencer for his analytical accomplishments: grounding society more rigorously as a "natural" entity; specifying social types and the diversity of social development; and orienting sociology to particular problems of an empirical nature. Durkheim objected to aspects of Spencer's organicism and to any simpleminded extension of the biological paradigm to sociology.[17] In addition, Durkheim considered Spencer's search for a synthetic philosophy highly premature and an impediment to the progress of social science. Even more significantly, Durkheim criticized Spencer's sociology for its sustained attachment to the ideology of English liberalism.

Spencer was a product of Victorian England, and unlike some of his predecessors and contemporaries—Carlyle, J. S. Mill, Coleridge, and H. S. Maine, who drew from the alternative traditions in France and Germany—Spencer never abandoned or substantially modified the chief tenets of English liberalism. The animating principle of Spencer's sociology is the idea of the individual, conceived of as a self-interested, calculating being who strives to free himself or herself from all historical and structural restraints in order to achieve a self-regulating but dynamic equilibrium. In perfect accord with the tradition of English liberalism, from Locke to the economists and the philosophical radicals, Spencer viewed the commercial society—the society of voluntary exchanges and contracts— as the quintessence of rationality and the end point of historical development.

In his first major work, Durkheim's critique of Spencer was aimed precisely at the most basic premises of Spencer's sociology. Durkheim agreed with Spencer that the most fundamental problem of sociology is to understand the rise of modern individualism and to conceptualize the general relation between the individual and society. However, Durkheim observed that the presuppositions and conclusions of his own sociology are vastly different from those of Spencer's sociology. In a highly illuminating passage, Durkheim pointed to this presuppositional difference:

> With him, we have said that the place of the individual in society ... becomes greater with civilization. But this incontestable fact is presented to us under an aspect totally different from that of English philosophy, so that, ultimately, our conclusions are opposed to his more than they are in agreement.[18]

Durkheim identified the premises of Spencer's sociology with those of "English philosophy" or what I call Lockean liberalism. In the course of the *Division*, Durkheim proceeded to develop an all-out attack on its specific doctrines: the idea of the self-interested, self-sufficient individual, the contractarian theory of commercial society, the minimalist state-conception, and so on. Durkheim, in other words, attempted to ally his idea of sociology with a different set of presuppositions which, as he noted, yield a view of the meaning of individualism and modern society opposed to that of Spencer. Thus, although Durkheim took over the great insight of Spencer—the rise of individualism—he repudiated the Lockean presuppositions of Spencer's sociology.

The Democratic Tradition and the Ideological Meaning of Durkheim's Sociology

In Durkheim's view, the sociology of Comte and Spencer gave expression to and helped sustain the social forces of conservatism and Lockean liberalism. Durkheim believed, moreover, that by aligning itself with these two ideologies, sociology unintentionally served as a catalyst in the crisis of liberalism. Durkheim's critique of Comte and Spencer implied a practical aim: by realigning sociology with alternative ideological presuppositions, Durkheim sought to furnish an intellectual defense of the Third Republic. I have already alluded to this presuppositional ideological complex as a native French democratic tradition. I want to show that this democratic tradition formed the ideological foundation of Durkheim's sociology.

As I have already mentioned, French democracy is characterized by its insistence upon the intrinsic connection between liberty and equality. Moreover, the idea of freedom and the relation between the individual and society is reinterpreted in a way that has far-reaching consequences for social theory. The principal figure, who stands at the beginning of this tradition, is Jean-Jacques Rousseau.

Rousseau was above all else a democrat. From his early "Discourses" to the magisterial *Social Contract*, the message is the same: genuine freedom and social progress presuppose social equality and participatory democracy. Rousseau's writings constitute a series of philosophical, sociological, and political meditations on the social, moral, and human costs of inequality and the conditions necessary to enact a democratic social order. Towards this end, Rousseau reexamined the meaning of freedom and the relation between the individual and society. In the English tradition, freedom meant the release of the natural individual from artificial social constraints; there is an inherent antagonism and conceptual polarization between the individual and society. By contrast, Rousseau, and those within the tradition of liberal and social democracy which proceeded from Rousseau, considered liberty as the positive development of individuality, which, of necessity, involved social regulation and constraint. Of Rousseau's idea of freedom, Durkheim wrote in perfect accord:

> Thus, freedom as conceived by Rousseau, results from a kind of necessity. Man is free only when a superior force compels his recognition, provided, however, that he accepts this supe-

riority and that his submission is not won by lies and artifice. He is free if he is held in check.[19]

In the above formulation, freedom presupposes a social and moral framework of rules and regulations which, however, must be self-imposed or based on consensus.[20] Rousseau identified this moral framework of action with the concept of society or "general will" in Rousseau's terms. In doing so, Rousseau prepared the way for reconceptualizing the relation between the individual and society as one of interpenetration, not polarity.[21]

In the above model, the very meaning of society undergoes a significant change vis-à-vis English liberalism. As a moral order or complex of collective beliefs and values, society is viewed as a distinct yet positive force promoting individualism. Again, Durkheim finds in Rousseau a basis for his own theory of society.

> In place of the individual personality of each contracting party, this act of association creates a moral and collective body composed of as many members as the assembly contains voters, and receiving from this act its unity, its common identity, its life and its will.[22]

Durkheim considered Rousseau's view of society to be "far superior to that of such recent theorists as Spencer. . . ."[23]

Rousseau revised the meaning of freedom and the analytical relation between the individual and society. In addition, Rousseau projected into the center of French social thought a holistic and idealist conception of society which was connected to an ideological concern for moral individualism, social justice, and solidarity. Rousseau's democratic reorientation of social thought bore a rich and varied legacy in France. In the nineteenth century, there emerged a liberal and socialist tradition which, though differing on many particulars, was unified in its commitment to the following ideas: the identification of freedom with moral autonomy; the commitment to social equality and justice as the condition of autonomy and social solidarity; the notion that economic progress does not automatically translate into moral progress[24]; a moral and idealist view of society which asserts the need for some form of unifying moral order or civil religion; the notion of the state as an active moral force in promoting autonomy; a stress upon the moral, political, and social importance of intermediary associations between the individual and the state; and, finally, a sympathetic attitude towards a nonrevolutionary, nonstatist socialism. I believe that Durkheim was an heir to this democratic tradition.

Durkheim, it is true, never explicitly identified himself with this tradition, but then, as we know, Durkheim preferred to remain aloof from narrowly defined ideological and political parties. Durkheim's immersion in this intellectual tradition is evidenced by his writings on Rousseau, his extensive study of the French revolutionary tradition from the egalitarians through Proudhon, his early absorption of Renouvier and Boutroux, his lasting friendship with Jaurés, and the fact that many of Durkheim's collaborators and intellectual "advisers," such as Bouglé and Lucien Herr, were steeped in the French democratic tradition. It is impossible not to notice the vital presence of the egalitarians as well as Condorcet and Tocqueville in Durkheim's positive assessment of the spread of equality and justice; or the impact of Rousseau or Michelet in Durkheim's idea of Republicanism as the core of a modern civil religion; or the Proudhonian emphasis upon decentralization and autonomous, democratically organized voluntary associations; or the moral idealism of Renouvier in Durkheim's conception of the inherent worth and dignity of the human personality. The ideas of the liberal and social democratic tradition permeated the social and intellectual milieu of the Third Republic, and Durkheim found in them an alternative to English liberalism as well as to French philosophical conservatism.

The central ideological impulse of the democratic tradition is its social, moral, and political commitment to social justice. In turn, this leads to an attempt to restate the meaning of individualism and freedom in a way that can be harmonized with social solidarity and equality. This same ideological commitment to justice is at the center of Durkheim's sociology.

Durkheim did not endorse the philosophes' attempt to ground liberty or equality as a natural right. On the other hand, Durkheim criticized the conservatives, who viewed the ideology of justice as just another of those vague abstractions of the eighteenth century. "A sentiment so general," Durkheim declared, "cannot be a pure illusion, but must express, in confused fashion, some aspect of reality."[25] Justice, Durkheim contended, is an imperative structured into the sociocultural conditions of modern society. "The task of the most advanced societies is, then, a work of justice."[26]

The rise of modern society entailed the breakdown of the relatively static, group-centered, and hierarchical structure of traditional society. In its place emerged a dynamic, highly differentiated, individual-centered social structure. In the cultural sphere, the sanctification of tradition, order, hierarchy, and the vast moral casuistry that defined and regulated the totality of collective life gave way to a moral and symbolic cultural system that stripped the world of its transcendent character.[27] Its centerpiece was the sanctity of the individual personality. Thus, both structural and cultural forces combined to produce the notion of the individual as the elementary principle and sustaining basis of worldly order. Although Durkheim repudiated the attempt by modern theorists to base a theory of knowledge, politics, morality, and society on individualistic premises, he underscored the significance of the individual in the modern world.[28] Durkheim believed that individualism was a powerful collective belief which, in fact, did express sociocultural conditions. Regardless of the reality of individualism, Durkheim observed that people act as if each separate individual is the sole bearer of worldly order and meaning. From this secular and individualistic perspective, the only legitimate basis of social institutions is to serve as vehicles for the full development of personality.

The "cult of personality," as Durkheim called the collective belief in individualism, is connected to the moral ideal of distributive justice. The development of individuality presupposes that the distribution of wealth, status, and power reflects individual aptitudes and achievements. Social inequalities must express natural inequalities, not those founded upon artificial constraints and mechanisms.[29] The ideal of distributive justice, therefore, implied the attenuation of original inequalities or, as Durkheim said, equality in the external conditions of social, political, and economic competition. Where this condition of external equality is lacking, and where the spontaneous fit between individual aptitude and social function is disrupted, the entire societal community will undergo profound structural and cultural dislocations.

Durkheim argued that social solidarity in traditional society was based upon an all-embracing religio-cosmological order. So long as an intense collective life was maintained, inequalities were "not only tolerable but natural." In the modern, individual-centered society, however, solidarity presupposes the social and moral attachment of the individual to a function, and the interdependency of functions. If the individual feels that his or her individuality is being repressed, those sentiments and norms which bind individuals to social functions will not develop. Lacking such an underlying moral order legitimating contractual relations, the social order is thrown into a state of perpetual conflict and moral turmoil. Durkheim concluded that only by eliminating the conditions of external inequality is solidarity or moral community possible:

> In organized societies, it is indispensable that the division of labour be more and more in harmony with this ideal of spontaneity [the ideal of distributed justice] that we have just defined. If they bend all their efforts, and must so bend them, to doing away with external inequalities as far as possible, that is not only because it is a worthy undertaking, but because their very existence is involved in the problem. For they can maintain themselves only if all the parts of which they are

formed are solidary, and solidarity is possible only under this condition. Hence, it can be seen that this work of justice will become ever more complete, as the organized type develops.[30]

Although Durkheim observed a definite trend towards social equality in the sphere of politics, science, and administration, he was acutely aware of the factors obstructing the equalization of social relations. In particular, he singled out private property, from which evolves an antagonistic class structure, as the material basis of external inequalities. Since private property leads to a condition of rich and poor at birth, and unequal advantage for one class without any necessary corresponding natural or social superiority, there is built into the contractual and social relations between classes a condition of external force, constraint, and conflict. What must be noted in Durkheim's conception of class division and conflict is the decidedly moral and idealist dimension: the members of the disadvantaged class rebel against private property not simply to augment their own wealth but because they are motivated by the ideals of justice and individualism. Class conflict proceeds not so much from a clash of economic interests as from the contradiction between the moral postulate, demanding that each person receive according to his or her capacities and achievements, and the institution of private property, which creates a condition of original inequalities irrespective of individual merit. Though Durkheim may focus upon the idealist aspects of class conflict, he does not overlook its basis in property relations. "The antagonism is not entirely due to the rapidity of these changes, but, in good part, to the still very great inequality of external conditions of the struggle. On this factor, time has no influence."[31] Since class conflict has its material basis in private property, Durkheim attacks the legal-institutional form of private property, i.e., inheritance. "It is obvious that inheritance, by creating inequalities among men at birth, that are unrelated to merit or service, invalidates the whole contractual system at its very roots."[32] Durkheim recommended a "recasting of the morals of property" so that "the property of the individuals should be the counterpart of the services they have rendered in the society."[33] Durkheim assimilated the revolutionary critique of private property. In opposition to English liberalism, Durkheim formulated a doctrine that was responsive to the needs and critical disposition of the working classes, yet in accord with the tradition of moral idealism among the democratic middle class. By legitimating the revolutionary demand for social equality, Durkheim was attempting to do what Lockean liberalism had failed to do for over a century: to forge an alliance between the middle classes and working classes, between liberalism—with its traditional concern for individual liberty—and revolution, with its egalitarian and democratic orientation.

In the doctrine of social justice, Durkheim found a rallying point around which the disparate forces of French society could unite. Durkheim argued that given the structural conditions of social differentiation and the individualistic and secular culture, the equalization and democratization of social conditions had assumed the character of a precondition of individualism and social solidarity. In opposition to Lockean liberalism, Durkheim contended that the rise of individualism is not inconsistent with the expansion of social forces, including the state, an organized labor movement, and professional associations. Durkheim claimed that moral regulation is the precondition of individual freedom. Individual liberty, he declared, is not a natural attribute of human existence but is a condition acquired through the individual's internalization of a framework of moral order which allows the subordination and control of natural forces.[34]

Though Durkheim saw a liberating aspect to social control, he vigorously opposed the conservative demand to revive tradition, custom, or the old moral order.[35] "It is not enough that there be rules," he reasoned, "they must be just and for that it is necessary for the conditions of competition to be equal."[36] With the conservatives, Durkheim advanced a positive assessment of social control through a binding moral order. However, he believed that social control requires a moral order that is consonant with the secular, individualistic, egalitarian, and rationalistic culture of the modern world:

> If, moreover, we remember that the collective conscience is becoming more and more a cult of the individual, we shall see that what characterizes the morality of organized societies, is that there is something more human, therefore more rational, about them. It does not direct our activities to ends which do not immediately concern us; it does not make us servants of ideal powers of nature other than our own, which follow their directions without occupying themselves with the interests of men. . . . The rules which constitute it do not have a constraining force which snuffs out free thought; but, because they are rather made for us, and, in a sense, by us, we are free. We wish to understand them; we do not fear to change them.[37]

The practical intention of Durkheim's sociology is clear: to legitimate the "Principles of 1789" as the moral basis of the Third French Republic. Durkheim projected a synthesis of the liberal and revolutionary traditions, according to which the idea of individualism and moral community were mutually reinforcing principles and the precondition of both was social justice. Durkheim's reconstructed liberalism was paralleled by his analytical shift to holism, social idealism, the interpenetration of the individual and society, and social solidarity.[38] In both his ideological and analytical departures from English liberalism, Durkheim's social theory originates in and continues the democratic tradition of French social thought.

8. The Individual and Society
The Problem of Collective Life

CONTRARY TO POSITIVISM, I have maintained the double character of social theory: as ideology and as analytic. By attributing an ideological component to social theory, I am arguing for a position which takes seriously the affectively rooted, morally resonant interpretations of social reality that inform social theory. In my view, these interpretations should become a sustained focus or topic of theoretical debate and critique. They must not be perceived as merely obstructions to objectivity or residues of a pre-scientific stage of social theory. These interpretations of social reality are as much a part of the practice of social science as are empirical research or analytical model-building. They form, as it were, a framework of presuppositions within which the concepts and problems of empirical and analytical research assume a meaningful relation to everyday life. This does not mean that we can reduce empirical or analytical research to mere superstructural rationalizations of an ideological infrastructure. The questions, problems, and truth-claims of empirical and analytical social theory have a peculiar integrity and logically compelling character that must be accounted for and dealt with on their own terms.

Durkheim's critique of classical political economy and the sociology of Comte and Spencer testify to the ideological character of social theory. Durkheim noted the analytical achievements of Comte and Spencer, but insisted that their sociology was wedded to the ideological presuppositions characteristic of French conservatism and English liberalism, respectively. Durkheim's critique, as we have seen, was aimed precisely at this ideological level as a formative factor in the development of their social theory. Durkheim, of course, declared his sociology to be without presuppositions. We cannot accept Durkheim's claim to presuppositionlessness. In fact, we have argued that Durkheim's sociology was a response to the crisis of liberalism as it was manifested in the Third French Republic. Durkheim's sociology had decidedly practical aims: to resolve the crisis by projecting the moral sanctity of the principles of 1789, and to forge an ideological alliance between the forces of liberalism and revolution. The presuppositions informing Durkheim's concepts and perspectives are derived from the French democratic tradition. In this final section, I want to shift the discussion from the ideological to the analytical level of Durkheim's sociology.

There are fairly evident ways in which Durkheim's ideological commitments structured his sociology. The concern with social justice, for example, shifted empirical and analytical interests from the motives of the individual to the structural and cultural factors inhibiting and fostering social equality. Also, by repudiating the egoistic individualism of English liberalism, with its polarization of the individual and society, the democratic tradition had developed a positive view of society, emphasizing the liberating aspects of social and moral control. Durkheim's democratic premises encouraged the conceptualization of problems of solidarity, moral order, and cultural change. Finally, the social idealism of the democratic tradition—its concern with ideational reality, moral community, and civil religion—provided Durkheim with a striking alternative to the materialist and instrumentalist models of English liberalism and European socialism.

Naturally, these are very general but significant ways in which Durkheim's presuppositions penetrated into his analytical sociology. We cannot, however, decompose Durkheim's analytical sociology into its separate ideological components. In the end, we must turn to these analytical issues themselves; in particular, the problem of collective life. Because Durkheim addressed analytical issues in the context of an ongoing theoretical debate, we will need to refer to this theoretical context.

Instrumentalism: English and French Rationalism

Modern Western rationalism begins with, and appears to repeatedly return to, the dualistic philosophy of Descartes. In the French and English rationalist traditions, there is a pronounced tendency towards a materialist resolution to the Cartesian mind-body problem. The universe is viewed as a natural order reducible to matter in motion. As a part of nature, human beings partake of the same materialist constitution, with the one qualification that a certain propensity for sensitivity or thought—unique only in its level of development—inheres in our organic being. From the standpoint of materialism, human action is conceived in a thoroughly instrumentalist way: as conduct impelled by natural drives and adapted to the ever-changing urgencies of the external environment. In this instrumentalist model, "society" resides in those ephemeral but recurring junctures of contact and collision between internally propelled individuals. To the extent that some kind of collective and authoritative structure beyond the individual forms part of the texture of social reality, it is identified with the constraining force of state power. Thus, even the one mode of collective existence posited—the coercive state—is subject to the same instrumentalist logic. This model of the individual and society is central, Durkheim argued, to the diverse theoretical traditions which he subsumed under the ideological rubric of English liberalism.

Saint-Simon was among the first in the post-Enlighten-ment rationalist tradition to criticize the instrumentalist an-alytic for not articulating unifying societal ends which could provide a more enriched and morally substantial idea of col-lective life. Yet, notwithstanding the writings of his final years, Saint-Simon's social theory falls entirely within the logic of instrumentalism. Saint-Simon proposed that the idea of "industrialism" serve as a common doctrinal basis of mod-ern society. However, industrialism is little different from the productivist principle of the economists or the moral utili-tarianism of the philosophical radicals—each of which pre-supposes the calculating, instrumental rationality of economic technique as a model of social action. Moreover, Durkheim noted that socialism, by admitting only material interests, is but the logical extension of industrialism.[1] "If societies have only economic interests, then economic life is necessarily a social thing. . . . For that reason, economic life should be sub-jected to collective and organized control. This is the eco-nomic principle of socialism."[2] Because socialism is, as it were, merely the logical outcome of the liberal principle of industrialism, it, too, is subject to the same instrumentalism. "Since nothing exists in the world except industrial interests, the only goal this collective administration can pursue will be to make the production of wealth as fructifying as possible, so that everyone can receive the most. . . . That is socialist morality."[3] In both liberalism and socialism, collective life is simply the totality of the instrumental actions of separate individuals conjoined to the equally instrumental action of a coercive state.

A major current of rationalism in France and England acceded to a materialist metaphysic, which entered into social theory as an instrumentalist conception of the individual and society. In effect, as Durkheim noted, the instrumentalist logic of economic technique served as a paradigm of human action and social structure. Durkheim vigorously opposed materi-alism and its associated instrumentalist analytic. Durkheim sought to overcome the insufficiency of instrumentalism by combining it with a noninstrumentalist model of social action. In this regard, the German tradition provided Durkheim with a strictly idealist paradigm of social theory. Though Durkheim was aware of the equally one-sided nature of German idealism, this tradition was of immense significance, as it provided a clear alternative to materialism and instrumentalism. German idealism also reinforced the holistic and idealist bent of the French democratic tradition.

German Idealism: The Voluntarist Alternative

In the German context, Kant was at once the bearer and destroyer of Western rationalism. In his positive view of the role of *a priori* reason and in his methodical pursuit of knowledge, Kant extended the Western rationalist tradition. However, since he renounced the project of a complete system of knowledge by positing a world unknowable in itself, Kant turned against the dogmatic claims of rationalism. Nevertheless, by stressing the active role of mind in the origins of knowledge and moral law, Kant opened the door for a uniquely German form of rationalism. Post-Kantian German philosophy can be read as a return to a thoroughgoing rationalism by expanding Kant's incipient idealism into a full-blown objective idealism. This required the withdrawal of any independent logical status to the Kantian "thing in itself." Kant's philosophy already contained a conceptual opening: by combining Kant's "transcendental unity of apperception" with the active subject of Kant's moral will—as, for example, in Fichte's "Absolute Self" or Hegel's "Geist"—an ideal subject was conceptualized as the logical ground of experience. Material existence was understood as a crystalized residue of mind or some underlying ideal reality.

German idealism, Durkheim thought, was antithetical to the materialist current of French and English rationalism. The vast epistemological and ontological differences between

German and Anglo-French rationalism were paralleled at the social theoretical level. Durkheim pointed to the disparity between the holism, organicism, moral individualism, and statism of German idealism and the atomism, egoistic individualism, and anti-statism of French and English materialism. At a general analytical level, the idealists articulated a voluntarism that again contrasted sharply with the instrumentalist tendency of French and English rationalism. In idealism, we, as human beings, are basically creators of the world as an ideal reality composed of symbols, meanings, and values. Social action proceeds from the internal or subjective orientation to this complex symbolic reality. In this voluntarist model of action, the context of shared symbols and meanings is what constitutes social reality. Society is a uniquely collective, idealist, and moral order. The paradigm of action and social structure in the voluntarist model is cultural or aesthetic creation.

The idealist premises of German rationalism were structured into the social thought of the German Historical School. From an historical perspective, the Historical School is important because it articulated philosophical idealism in an empirically grounded, idealist social theory. This was accomplished, first, by expanding the concept of morality to include law and religion—thus viewing these two major social facts in noninstrumental and idealist terms.[4] Second, the Historical School sought to uncover the moral or idealist underpinnings of economic action. In both instances, the Historical School developed an idealist interpretation of social reality, which was supported by empirical and historical research. As his early essays indicate, Durkheim was impressed by the developments in the German idealist tradition.[5] Nevertheless, he voiced two principal objections to idealist social theory. First, though the Historical School viewed society as an ideal collective entity, there was a pronounced tendency to perceive modern collective life as exhausted and to look to the state as the only remnant of a morally vital collective life. This is connected to a second major defect of their sociological idealism: their failure to seriously consider the integrative functions linked to the utilitarian structure of modern social life.

Durkheim's writings reveal the influence of idealist social theory. In the *Division*, for example, Durkheim takes over the historicist concern for the idealist underpinnings of collective order. However, Durkheim's sustained commitment to French and English rationalism is present both in his view that collective life is a component of modern civil society and in his view that a source of collective life derives from the utilitarian sphere of the division of labor. Durkheim appears to hold a synthetic approach to the problem of collective life. In fact, as I have argued, this multidimensional analytic accords with the more encompassing world-view which Durkheim shared with the French democratic tradition.

The Durkheimian Synthesis of Idealism and Materialism

Between 1893 and 1902, Durkheim developed a model of society that combined the materialist or instrumentalist logic and the idealist or voluntarist logic. The *Division* posed the problem and laid out the framework within which Durkheim theorized, at least until 1902. At issue was the explanation of how collective life is possible; that is, the problem of solidarity (order) and anomie (meaning) in a secular and individual-centered social structure. Durkheim formulated the problem as follows. In traditional society, the elementary units of social structure, clan, caste, horde, or familial-political system were essentially similar in structure and function. In the cultural sphere, there was one inclusive belief system which defined the contents of individual consciousness. Because each individual participated in a common material and symbolic milieu, collective life was orderly and dominated human affairs. In modern society, the processes of sociocultural differentiation produce a condition in which the basic structural units—in this case, occupational groupings—are vastly dissimilar. This structural differentiation is paralleled by a plurality of belief systems. Given this condition of structural or morphological differentiation and cultural or symbolic pluralization, how is societal coherence and a unified collective life possible? By 1902, Durkheim had, in fact, proposed a resolution to the problem of collective life.

Considering the social context of the early 1890s, characterized by the ever-present threat of conservatism and the still dominant humanistic idealism which Durkheim rebelled against as a student, it is not surprising to find in Durkheim's early writings a strong materialist and instrumentalist bias. In his Latin thesis on Montesquieu, Durkheim simply restated the instrumentalist logic by arguing that collective life proceeds from the interdependency of functionally dissimilar occupations and institutional spheres: "It results from the division of labour, which makes the citizens and the social orders dependent upon each other."[6] Of course, Durkheim's notion of the division of labor just restates in sociological terms the economists' concept of a market, or Hegel's similarly instrumental "system of needs": in each case, it is the given needs of the individual or institution which compel a relation of mutual dependency and equilibrium. In this instrumentalist model, collective life is, in the end, contingent upon the solution of technical problems of social and economic management. Accordingly, or so Durkheim thought, there is a latent authoritarianism built into this model, which, as in the Hobbesian paradigm, subverts its individualistic and libertarian premises.[7]

In the *Division*, published in 1893, we find the same instrumentalism with, however, the beginnings of a voluntarist logic. Although Durkheim does not depart from the "interdependency argument," he develops two arguments which already preview the idealist and voluntarist component. In the first place, he points to the sentiments and beliefs which, in turn, form the binding power of functional interdependency. However, in the *Division* this idealism is undeveloped.[8] In the second place, Durkheim refers to the "Principles of

1789" as the core of a new secular morality, but at this point he denies them the status of a unifying basis of collective life. It is curious to note that, as we have seen in the previous chapter, Durkheim's ideological understanding of modern society already gave a central place to the role of ideas and moral beliefs. Yet, it was not until he composed *Suicide* (1897), "Individualism and the Intellectuals" (1898), *Professional Ethics and Civic Morals* (1900), and his 1902 preface to the *Division* that Durkheim managed to satisfactorily articulate the voluntarist logic and integrate it with the instrumentalism of the previous years.

After 1893, Durkheim elaborated the voluntarist logic in a more consistent and integral manner. He conceived of the rules and regulations underlying functional interdependence as part of a distinct occupational moral life. Of these decentralized and multiple centers of collective life, Durkheim wrote:

> It is impossible for men to live together, associating in industry, without acquiring a sentiment of the whole formed by their union, without attaching themselves to that whole, preoccupying themselves with its interests, and taking account of it in their conduct. This attachment has in it something surpassing the individual. This subordination of particular interests to the general interest is, indeed, the source of all moral activity. As this sentiment grows more precise and determined, applying itself to the most ordinary and the most important circumstances of life, it is translated into definite formulae, and thus a body of moral rules is in the process of establishment.[9]

Though Durkheim believed that occupational groups would form a rich and varied moral support for the individual, he was aware of the need to account for the link between these diverse and particular centers of moral life and a unifying belief system. Thus, Durkheim identified the complex of sentiments and ideas revolving around the sacredness of the personality as a basis for a national or civic morality.

This turn to idealism did not signal a repudiation of his

earlier instrumentalism. Durkheim continued to assert the interdependency argument and, in general, maintained a multidimensional theory of society—as morphological structure and symbolic representation. In *Suicide*, for example, he argued:

> Given a people composed of a certain number of individuals arranged in a certain way, we obtain a definite total of collective ideas and practises which remain constant as long as the conditions on which they depend are themselves the same. To be sure, the nature of the collective existence necessarily varies depending on whether its composite parts are more or less numerous, arranged on this or that plan, and so its ways of thinking and acting change; but the latter may be changed only by changing the collective existence itself and this cannot be done without modifying its anatomical constitution.[10]

By 1902, Durkheim advanced a multilayered model of society. The ever-widening and inclusive circles of collective life—family, occupation, and nation—were paralleled by and founded upon the increasing generalization of moral beliefs: domestic ethics, professional ethics, and civic morals. In the instrumentalist concept of functional interdependency, Durkheim found a means by which to link structural differentiation to societal coherence. Similarly, though Durkheim pointed to the moral particularism and polymorphism inherent in occupational differentiation, he observed that these diverse occupational groupings partake of certain common sentiments, values, and beliefs. "As labour is divided," Durkheim reasoned, "law and morality assume a different form in each special function, though still resting everywhere on the same general principles. Besides the rights and duties common to all men, there are others depending on qualities peculiar to each occupation."[11] These "rights and duties common to all men" are the core of a civic morality and entail a common moral order. Thus, Durkheim furnished a bridge between moral diversity and unity, paralleling the link between occupational differentiation and societal unity.

Durkheim was fascinated by the dialectic of multiplicity and unity or the problem of accounting for sociocultural unity in a condition of structural and cultural differentiation. Prior to and including the *Division*, Durkheim operated with a principally instrumentalist logic by positing functional interdependency as the basis for social order. However, this instrumentalism ran counter to Durkheim's ideological commitments, which already pointed to a more voluntarist logic. In his writings between 1895 and 1902, Durkheim treated the same dialectic of multiplicity and unity, but with greater sensitivity to the idealist moment. First, Durkheim pointed to the occupational milieu as a moral environment, composed of unified sentiments, values, and beliefs. Second, Durkheim observed a set of common beliefs which functioned as a civic morality. Durkheim argued that the moral order articulated at the national level underlies the diverse occupational moralities and thus constitutes a pattern of moral unity. In *Suicide* and some of his other writings during this period, Durkheim fused instrumentalism and voluntarism into a very powerful analytical model of modern collective life. This analytical fusion, moreover, was in harmony with his dualistic conception of human beings both as organisms impelled by natural drives and as socially created personalities oriented towards meanings and values; it was also consistent with his dualistic conception of society as morphology and symbol. More generally, this view accorded with the more encompassing dualistic and liberal world view that Durkheim had adopted from the Enlightenment.

A Final Word on the "Late" Durkheim and the Problem of Idealism

Ever since Talcott Parsons's *Structure of Social Action*, a question has been raised regarding a presumed shift in Durkheim's thought from the earlier materialism or dualistic world view to an idealistic perspective characteristic of his later writings.

This is not without some irony, as Durkheim was forever defending himself against charges of materialism.[12] My own view denies any fundamental theoretical break between the early and late Durkheim. Of course, Durkheim revised certain themes and positions. For example, he reconceptualized the process of physical and moral density as a process of collective effervescence. In addition, he progressively attached a greater importance to collective ideas and values in his analysis of social solidarity. Nevertheless, in the end, Durkheim's position remained that of a dualistic world-view and a multi-dimensional social theory.

In the context of this brief discussion, idealism refers to a view of mind—conceived either in individual or collective terms—as the origin, foundation, and ultimate determinate of reality. Within a sociological framework, idealism would mean that normative factors—moral ideals, religious beliefs, legal norms—are primary in understanding and explaining social action, order, and change. As I mentioned previously, there was a very powerful current of idealism in nineteenth-century France, associated with Renouvier, Lachelier, Boutroux, and Hamelin. These neo-critical idealists fused Kant's transcendental and moral idealism with the spiritual, humanistic idealism of French culture. Durkheim had very intimate ties to French idealism: he had thoroughly absorbed the works of Renouvier; Boutroux was his dissertation adviser; and Hamelin was his close friend. There is no doubt that Durkheim was positively impressed by their moral idealism and their profoundly spiritual understanding of the modern world. Nevertheless, he was highly critical of the antiscientific strain of idealism and opposed the attempt to save human freedom by evolving a wholly idealist, dialectical, and teleological system of knowledge. Durkheim adopted the idealist assumption of the irreducible nature of moral and cultural phenomena, but with two qualifications. First, he conceived of cultural reality as part of "nature," i.e., as subject to the rationalistic methods of positive science. Second, he pointed to the material substratum of ideational or cultural forms. Regarding individual mental life, Durkheim wrote: "Nothing could be more absurd than to elevate psychic life into a sort of absolute, derived from nothing and unattached to the rest of the universe. It is obvious that the condition of the brain affects all the intellectual phenomena and is the immediate cause of some of them (pure sensations)."[13] Durkheim drew a parallel between individual consciousness and collective consciousness:

> When we said elsewhere that social facts are in a sense independent of individuals and exterior to individual minds, we only affirmed of the social world what we have just established for the psychic world. Society has for its substratum the mass of associated individuals. The system which they form by uniting together, and which varies according to their geographical disposition and the nature and number of their channels of communication, is the base from which social life is raised.[14]

In the above formulation, Durkheim opposed philosophical and sociological idealism and affirmed a basically dualistic metaphysic: individual and collective consciousness is founded upon a material substratum, which, in addition, has a determinant role in ordering experience.[15]

The argument for Durkheim's idealism seems to be most cogent in reference to two of his later works, *The Evolution of Educational Thought* (1905) and *The Elementary Forms of the Religious Life* (1912). In terms of an idealist intepretation of Durkheim, the former text may be read as his attempt to rewrite the thematic content of the *Division*— the rise of rationalism, individualism, and secularism—from an idealist perspective.[16] In fact, under the pretext of a rather conventional intellectual history of educational thought, Durkheim composed a kind of historical—phenomenological analysis of Western rationalism, detailing the trajectory of Occidental consciousness from Hellenism to modern France. Indeed, it is an extraordinary text, which appears to proceed in a purely idealist and dialectical manner.

In considering the origins, nature, and development of the University of Paris, Durkheim proposed the following methodology:

> What was the educational ideal of which it [the University of Paris] was the concrete expression? In order to ascertain the correct answer, the best method is to trace the genesis of the institution, investigating how it came to be formed, what caused it to come into existence, and what the moral forces were whose consequence it was. By examining the constitution of the original seed out of which it grew, by scrutinizing the various elements of which it was made up and seeing how they were assembled and combined, we shall be able to specify the animating spirit which determined the orientation of the institution.[17]

Institutions, Durkheim seemed to argue, as normative orders, originate from definite moral forces, and evolve according to a specific animating spirit. At the core of Durkheim's dialectical idealism is a presumably idealist or normative model of society and social change: society consists of collective beliefs and values sedimented into institutional patterns and originating during those infrequent periods of intellectual and moral revitalization.

What, then, are we to make of this apparent turn to sociological, if not philosophical, idealism? In the first instance, it is undeniable that Durkheim emphasized the normative component of society to a degree nowhere to be found in the analytical aspects of the *Division* or earlier. Yet, it is equally undeniable that Durkheim continued to insist upon the determinant role of material factors, which, as we have seen, is linked to an instrumentalist logic. Regarding the transformations in educational thought and practice during the Renaissance, Durkheim declared: "Thus the sixteenth century is a period of educational and moral crisis. Changes of economic and social organization had rendered a new kind of education necessary."[18] Durkheim proceeded to detail the impact on education from the rise of the bourgeoisie, new forms of wealth, the link between knowledge and commerce, and so on. These changes in economic and social structure not only formed the broad external milieu of educational institutions, but the ideals and practices of education were informed by the utilitarian considerations generated by these material changes:

> A moment came, sooner here, later elsewhere, when moral and religious considerations were not the only ones which people took into account; when economic, administrative and political interests took on too much importance for it to be possible to go on treating them as insignificant matters which the schoolmaster need not bother himself about. There came a moment when what might be called the purely secular and moral needs of society were felt too intensely for people not to realize the necessity of equipping children in advance with the means of satisfying them one day. Thus a new criterion became established in relation to which the educational value of different types of knowledge was henceforth measured. Henceforward they were judged not only against the yardstick of the highest moral goals which it is possible for men to pursue, but also in terms of the vital needs of society and the conditions which are essential for its effective functioning.[19]

Towards the close of this text, Durkheim reiterates in a broad programmatic statement his own commitment to a social theory that integrates materialism and idealism:

> Moreover, if consciousness is our most distinguishing feature, it can exist only with an organic substratum upon which it is dependent; and it is essential for pupils to be able to understand this dependency. It is essential then for them to understand this organism with which the moral life is so thoroughly intermingled. But consciousness is related not only to the domain of the organism: it is also linked . . . to the whole of its cosmic environment. In particular, the way in which human beings group themselves on the surface of the earth, the configurations that are created by these groupings, or to be more

precise the form and structure of human societies, their density, their extent, the commercial activity which takes place between them and consequently the level of their civilization.[20]

We may agree that in this remarkable text Durkheim often employed a strictly idealist rhetoric which, in fact, betrays an idealist disposition; yet, just when we think that Durkheim has rendered social theory idealist, we find strong statements and lines of argumentation reaffirming a multidimensional social theory.

If we turn to the *Elementary Forms*, we find the same dualistic conceptual structure and thus the same multidimensional social theory. Durkheim reiterated the parallelism between the organism and individual consciousness and morphology and collective consciousness: "It is true that we take it as evident that social life depends upon its material foundation and bears its mark, just as the mental life of an individual depends upon his nervous system and in fact his whole organism."[21] Rather than proceeding further into the details of the *Elementary Forms*, I want instead to conclude this brief section by stating, in the simplest possible way, my understanding of the most basic elements of Durkheim's sociological image of the individual and society.[22]

To begin with, there is Durkheim's conception of humans as double beings: as organism and personality. From the fact of our organic constitution, Durkheim argued that we have elementary needs, drives, and perceptions which are experienced as uniquely private. This is the irreducible "individualistic" component of human nature, strictly speaking. As a part of organic nature, humans are subject to a natural determinism shared by other animal species. This means that a constant interchange must be maintained with external nature. In Durkheim's view, economic conduct is governed by utilitarian interests and consists of adaptive instrumental behavior. In other words, economic conduct is a kind of extension of the Hobbesian state of nature, characterized by egoistic orientations and intense competition for survival and dominance. As a sphere of society, the economy is the preeminently profane side of worldly life, characterized by Durkheim as preoccupied with functional needs and interests.

On the other hand, human beings are viewed as personalities. By the term "personality," Durkheim was referring to the fact that the individual has a socially conferred identity. Durkheim argued that physical proximity and mutual neediness engender social interaction, which, if sufficiently constant and intense, will give rise to common sentiments, beliefs, and values. In fact, Durkheim contended that the supreme societal ideals are generated in those periods when social interaction is, as it were, hypertense. Of course, this cultural realm of symbols and meanings is stamped by the underlying morphological structure, i.e., the number and arrangement of the population, its means of communication, the geographical setting, etc. This ideal or symbolic sphere of collective life is sedimented into relatively stable patterns of institutional life which, in the life cycle of the individual, mediate the formation of the personality. The personality is that component of the psychic life of individuals which binds them to one another to form a moral community.

There is, then, the idealist component of Durkheim's idea of personality, which contrasts sharply with the materialist and deterministic sense given to our organic side. This points to further oppositions: the personality is social in origin and orientation, while the organism is entirely self-related or individualistic; the personality is directed to expressive and symbolic concerns, while the organism is governed by utilitarian or adaptive considerations. This split at the individual level is manifest at the societal level, the opposition running through all of Durkheim's writings between strictly economic affairs—as individualistic, material, and utilitarian—and the cultural life of society, characterized by its social, ideal, and normative nature. The dualistic structure of Durkheim's thought is undeniable.[23]

Durkheim does, however, note points of intersection between these two levels of individual and societal life. In fact, throughout his writings there is the continual attempt to bring these two analytical levels of personal and societal reality into some form of satisfactory synthesis. Thus, Durkheim argued that, at an anthropological level, without the moral constraint exercised by the personality, the individual tends towards a pathological condition of excessive egoism or anomie. This, of course, was Durkheim's point in *Suicide*, which he analyzed under the rubric of egoistic and anomic suicide. At the societal level, the same dynamic operates: without the normative regulation of the economy, the society tends towards a condition of class conflict and moral dislocation. On the other hand, Durkheim argued that if the normative control over the needs and perceptions of the individual is too extensive, individuation will be stifled. Again, Durkheim made this point in his discussion of mechanical solidarity and altruistic suicide. Durkheim's attempted synthesis was not simply an effort to unite two distinct analytical traditions but had a more profound intellectual impulse: to project an image of the individual and society that would fuse and transcend the materialist and idealist dichotomy.

Durkheim's world-view is liberal in its presuppositions and structure. Durkheim repudiated all forms of absolutist metaphysics on account of their assumption of the unity and close-ended nature of reality. Like the philosophes, Durkheim believed that intellectual closure lends itself to dogmatism and authoritarianism. By contrast, Durkheim observed that the plasticity or protean quality of human experience and the plurality of world-views and social systems argue in support of a fundamentally immanent, open-ended, and nondogmatic interpretations of reality.[24] The recognition of the singularity and diversity of experience and the plurality of belief systems does not entail the demise of rationalism:

> Still today, we must remain Cartesians in the sense that we must fashion rationalists, that is to say men who are concerned with clarity of thought; but they must be rationalists of a new kind who know that things, whether human or physical, are

irreducibly complex and who are yet able to look unfalteringly into the face of this complexity. . . . But we must give up mistaking simple conceptual combinations for reality as a whole; we must feel more vividly the infinite richness of reality, we must understand that we can only succeed in thinking about it slowly, progressively and always imperfectly.[25]

Linked to his critique of intellectual closure, Durkheim criticized the romantic and revolutionary quest for the "end of history." In these modes of social criticism, Durkheim perceived an unwillingness to countenance the contingency and pluralism of modern life. From this perspective, we can clearly perceive the deep liberalism of Durkheim's thought. In the final instance, it was Durkheim's aim to give liberalism a doctrinal form by which it could sustain itself as an intellectual, moral, and political force in the face of the ever-present currents of illiberalism.

Summary of Part Three

DURKHEIM'S SOCIOLOGY EMERGED within a sociohistorical context in which the French liberal order was struggling to achieve stability in the face of severe attacks from an array of social, political, and cultural forces. As Durkheim perceived the situation, the Third Republic was balanced precariously between anarchy and authoritarianism. In addition, the very idea of liberalism was being assailed by the vociferous spokesmen for anti-modernism, irrationalism, and utopianism. What the Republic needed, Durkheim thought, was a liberal doctrine capable of uniting the progressive social and political forces. Because he believed that the predominant mode of liberalism, i.e., English liberalism, had lost political and intellectual currency, Durkheim looked to a native French democratic tradition as the basis for reconstructing liberalism as a viable doctrinal basis for the Republic. In democratic liberalism, Durkheim found an ideology that combined the individualism, pluralism, and secular-modernism of liberalism with the egalitarianism, communitarianism, and critical rationalism of the revolutionary tradition. Durkheim believed that democratic liberalism could serve as a link between the bourgeoisie and the radicals by uniting them around a national ideology of individualism and justice. By reexamining the meaning of individualism and equality, the relation between the individual and society, and the moral foundations of a secular order, Durkheim's sociology attempted to justify a democratic policy as the precondition of a liberal France.

In referring to the sociohistorical context and practical motivations behind Durkheim's sociology, I am not suggesting that his sociology is reducible to ideological analysis. My point is that the theoretical debates he engaged in—for example, with the classical economists, the socialists, or Comte— were understood by Durkheim as a part of a more encompassing dialogue on the most pressing intellectual, moral, and political questions of the day. Durkheim perceived, for instance, that the instrumentalist analytic of English liberalism was coupled to a substantive view of the nature of the individual, morality, and society that had consequences for social and political practice. Durkheim's attempt to furnish a satisfactory analytical alternative, through a synthesis of instrumentalism and voluntarism, was integral to formulating his own substantive and practically motivated world-view. In this regard, we can see that Durkheim had not fully thought through the implications of his critique of theoretical traditions and his understanding of theory in general. Though he pointed to the presuppositional and practical levels of Comte's or Spencer's sociology, he continued to assert an objectivistic self-understanding regarding his own sociology. In other words, while Durkheim's critique of the theoretical traditions pointed to an understanding of the ideological and practically consequential level of theorizing, he suppressed the presuppositional level in his own sociology.

Durkheim's world-view is dualistic. It is not, then, mere coincidence that one finds a series of polar concepts—individual/social, profane/sacred, etc.—at the center of his conceptual framework. In point of fact, Durkheim's claim to presuppositionlessness simply manifests the dualism between fact and value, and illustrates Durkheim's difficulty in achieving a satisfactory synthetic world-view and social theory. It should, finally, be remarked that though Durkheim's dualisms may be unsatisfactory—and judging from the secondary literature, seem to engender a tendency towards a one-dimensional resolution to either materialism or idealism—Durkheim was able to construct a liberal and democratic doctrine of immense attraction and importance, especially considered in light of the illiberalism of the post-Durkheimian era.

Part Four
Weber

Introduction to Part Four

DURKHEIM AND WEBER perceived the period between 1890 and World War I as a critical historical juncture in the development of modern liberalism. In both France and Germany, the forces of illiberalism—traditional conservatism, vulgar neo-Romanticism, as well as revolutionary socialism, anarchism, and syndicalism—advanced a multifaceted assault upon the political and sociocultural foundations of liberal civilization.[1] In addition, the internal structural changes in the direction of monopoly capitalism, bureaucratization, political authoritarianism, and militarism signaled the seemingly imminent eclipse of the individualistic and pluralistic premises of a liberal social order. The classical liberal doctrine which identified commercialism with republicanism and scientific-technological advance with the progress of reason and freedom could hardly withstand these structural and cultural countermovements. In fact, there was a marked decline of social and political support for classical liberal ideology.[2]

The social thought of Durkheim and Weber originated from this double perception: on the one hand, the structural and cultural retreat from liberalism, and, on the other, the ideological obsolescence of classical liberalism. The historical significance of their thought lies, in part, in its sustained commitment to rationalism and moral autonomy.[3] Even more fundamental, however, is the fact that both Durkheim and Weber sought to reformulate liberalism in light of the structural and cultural changes in European societies. This entailed a rethinking of elementary assumptions regarding human nature, society, and history as well as reformulating ideological principles and political strategy.

The effort by Durkheim and Weber to modernize liberalism directed them to the European revolutionary traditions. In these revolutionary countermovements, Durkheim and Weber found a powerful critique of the intellectual shortcomings of classical liberalism. Moreover, the revolutionary tradition had pointed to the source of the defects of liberalism and bourgeois society, namely the failure to recognize the legitimate rights and demands of the working classes. Durkheim and Weber sought a social and intellectual realignment beween the liberal and revolutionary traditions. Only a more cooperative stance by liberals towards the revolutionary tradition could reinvigorate liberalism as a social, political, and moral force in the contemporary European order.

In France, Durkheim had recourse to a vital native tradition of democratic thought. Though Germany lacked an indigenous democratic tradition analogous to those associated with the "Principles of 1789," the radical democrats of 1848, or the Communards of 1870, the revival of Kantianism functioned as a powerful intellectual vehicle for liberal democracy in Germany between 1890 and 1914.[4]

Neo-Kantianism was a broad cultural movement fueled by the academic philosophy of the Marburg school (Hermann Cohen and Paul Natorp) and the Baden or Southwest Kantians (Heinrich Rickert and Wilhelm Windelband). At one level, neo-Kantianism was an intellectual critique of the currents of positivism, naturalism, and materialism which followed in the aftermath of the decline of German idealism. Though neo-Kantianism involved a resurgence of epistemological idealism, it repudiated the objective idealism of Hegelianism as well as the religiously resonant, collectivist historicism of the Rankeans. In opposition to the deterministic currents of materialism and collectivist idealism, the neo-Kantians affirmed the autonomy of individuals. Moreover, by giving Kant's categorical imperative a social interpretation, the neo-Kantians assumed a critical posture towards all institutions, cultural forms, and traditions that suppressed autonomy. Thus, neo-Kantianism became the critique of social domination which, in the eyes of many democrats, provided the ethical and idealist underpinnings of a progressive liberal-socialist movement.[5]

Weber identified strongly with the neo-Kantian movement. In his mature epistemological standpoint, Weber's ideas reproduce those of Heinrich Rickert.[6] His ethical ideas generally parallel those of Friedrich Lange and Hermann Cohen, both of whom Weber had read and followed closely in intellectual and practical matters. Speaking more generally, in his commitment to a critical and formal rationalism, moral individualism, and liberal-democratic values, Weber, here also, remained within the neo-Kantian fold. In addition to neo-Kantianism, we need to note three other sources of democratic sentiment with which Weber was closely affiliated. The first source to be mentioned is the revisionist Marxism of Bernstein and the reformist, essentially democratic orientation of the Social Democrats. In general, as Marianne Weber commented, Weber saw in Marxian revolutionary ideology the articulation of democratic ideals.[7] Second, there was the Protestant social reform movement, especially as it was personified in Friedrich Naumann.[8] "The renovation of German liberalism," wrote Naumann in accord with his close friend Weber, "can only occur if the bourgeois-liberal elements recognize that the workers must form the basis of future liberal organization. . . ."[9] The third source of liberal-democratic sentiment is left-wing historicism, with its roots in the cultural individualism and social pluralistic ideal of Herder and Humboldt. Georg Iggers has recently suggested that the historicist critique of natural law had a conservative and liberal wing. Among the liberals, historicism functioned effectively as a defense of the democratic values found in the rationalist natural law tradition.[10] Weber, then, drew from each of these democratic currents in his effort to articulate a broadly based, politically astute, and intellectually sound liberal doctrine that could withstand the onslaught of illiberal forces.[11]

Though Durkheim and Weber confronted a set of circumstances which they perceived in essentially similar terms—as a crisis of liberalism—they were situated within very different intellectual traditions. Consequently, it is not surprising to find substantial divergence between them with regard to elementary epistemological, methodological, and sociological questions.[12] More to the point, despite similar ideological motivations and analytical and thematic concerns, their respective points of view reflect the historic differences between France and Germany. Any attempt to recover the contextual meaning of Weber's social thought must begin from the following dual focus: a consideration of Prussian domination in Germany and the challenge of Marxian socialism.

9. Prussian Hegemony and the Failure of German Liberalism

Weber's Early Materialism

BETWEEN 1892 AND 1905, Weber composed a series of essays and speeches which, from an ideological perspective, address the same concern: the failure of German liberalism. Moreover, as Weber identified the failure of German liberalism with the relative absence of bourgeois class-consciousness, these essays investigate the social, political, and cultural factors obstructing the rise of a self-conscious middle class in Germany.

At a strictly analytical level, it is noteworthy that Weber's several essays between 1892 and 1894, dealing with the social and economic conditions in eastern Germany, reveal an unmistakably materialist orientation. I believe this early materialism is intelligible on three accounts. First, we must take into consideration the strong influence of Marxist writings.[1] Second, Weber's main aim in these essays is to examine the changing economic foundations of Prussian political and cultural hegemony. Third, behind these early essays is a political motivation: to discredit the Prussian Junker class by means of a materialist critique. By employing a materialist analysis, Weber argued that recent historical developments point to the inevitable triumph of industrial capitalism and the bourgeoisie as the future bearers of Germany's social and national progress. In Weber's materialist scenario, the Junkers are viewed as an historically obsolete, economically declining, and politically dangerous class with essentially no significant role to play in Germany's future.[2] As we will see, between 1904 and 1905 Weber's political concerns shift from a denunciation of the Junkers to an active attempt to politicize the German bourgeoisie. Weber's analytic undergoes a parallel movement towards a systematic idealism to balance his early materialism.

In the 1870s, Germany was unified under the controlling authority of Prussia. This meant the political and cultural dominance of the Prussian Junker class. The Junkers were originally a landed aristocracy—not, however, in the mold of the English gentry or the southwestern German aristocrats, who lived off the rents of the small but independent landholdings of the peasants. Due to unique historical circumstances in eastern Germany, the Junkers appropriated the peasants' land and were actively engaged in the economic affairs of the estate.[3] The social conditions of eastern Germany were characterized by extremely large landed estates, organized along the lines of a feudal-manor economy. The relationship between the Junker and the peasant laborer was patriarchal. Weber observed a decisively positive consequence of this situation: the Junker class was sufficiently independent of economic exigencies so as to live a politically active life and adopt a national-political standpoint.

Since the Junkers' economic livelihood was directly tied to the productive side of the estate, the development of industrial and commercial capitalism was a major challenge to their existence. The survival of the Junkers hinged on their adaptive capacity and their ability to fend off the encroaching bourgeois carriers of industrialism who were seeking land and status. The Junkers thus became capitalists, but not without far-reaching consequences: the feudal-manor economy was transformed into a modern commercial enterprise, and the patriarchal community of the estate became an impersonal relation between two hostile classes. This marked the dissolution of the economic basis of the political and cultural hegemony of the Prussian Junkers. Weber noted the apparent paradox of Prussian political success and economic adaptability as illustrated in the policies of Bismarck: "Under his rule his own creation, the nation, to which he gave its unity, slowly and inevitably changed in its economic structure, to the point where it became a different kind of people, requiring other institutions. . . ."[4] Nevertheless, despite the decline of the economic foundation of the Junker class, it maintained a position of political and cultural leadership in Germany. As late as 1917, Weber could still write: "Prussia holds the hegemony and is always the decisive factor in German politics."[5]

Weber's perception of the extent of Prussian domination is revealed in the following passage, which I reproduce in full:

> The class of the rural landowners of Germany, consisting particularly of nobelmen residing in the region east of the Elbe, are the political rulers of the leading German state. The Prussian House of Lords represents this class, and the right of election by classes also gives them a determining position in the Prussian House of Representatives. These Junkers imprint their character upon the officer corps, as well as upon the Prussian officials and upon German diplomacy, which is almost exclusively in the hands of noblemen. The German student adopts their style of life in the fraternities in the universities. The civilian "officer of the reserve"—a growing part of all the more highly educated Germans belong to this rank—also bears their imprint. Their political sympathies and antipathies explain many of the most important presuppositions of German foreign policies. Their obstructionism impedes the progress of the laboring-class; the manufacturers alone would never be sufficiently strong to oppose the workingmen under the democratic rights of electing representatives to the German Reichstag. The Junkers are the props of a protectionism which industry alone would never have been able to accomplish. They

support orthodoxy in the state church. . . . Whatever survivals
of authoritarian conditions surprise him [the American visitor
to Germany] . . . result directly or indirectly from the influence
of these upper classes. . . .[6]

The influence of the Prussian Junkers, in Weber's view, embraced university students, the educational and administrative elite, military officers, and the church hierarchy, and
extended into the inner circle of national political leaders. As
their economic traditionalism, aristocratic cultural values,
political authoritarianism, and militarism indicated, the
ideological character of the Junkers was highly conservative.

The Prussian Junkers, according to Weber, were the back-
bone of German conservatism. There were, however, two additional loci of German conservatism. First, Weber singled
out the church, particularly Lutheranism, with its essentially
patriarchal, anti-capitalist attitude. Like the Catholic church,
the Lutheran church supported "the peasant with his conservative conduct of life, against the dominion of urban rationalistic culture."[7] Second, Weber spoke of the German
educational and cultural elite as reinforcing traditional conservative values. Given the critical importance Weber attached to this cultural elite—a point which will be elaborated
in the next chapter—I want to excerpt Weber's analysis at
length:

As soon as intellectual and esthetic education has become a
profession, its representatives are bound by an inner affinity
to all the carriers of ancient social culture. . . . They look dis-
trustfully upon the abolition of traditional conditions of the
community and upon the annihilation of all the innumerable
ethical and esthetic values which cling to them. They doubt
if the dominion of capital would give better, more lasting guarantees to personal liberty and to the development of intellectual, esthetic, and social culture which they represent, than
the aristocracy of the past has given. They want to be ruled
only by persons whose social culture they consider equivalent
to their own; therefore they prefer the dominion of the economically independent aristocracy to the dominion of the

professional politician. Thus it happens nowadays in the civilized countries—a peculiar and in more than one respect serious fact—that the representatives of the highest interests of culture turn their eyes back, stand with deep antipathy opposed to the inevitable development of capitalism, and refuse to cooperate in the rearing of the structure of the future.[8]

Weber was describing what Fritz Ringer has called the "orthodox mandarins": those strata among the educational elite, rooted in the values and culture of traditional Germany, who opposed social, political, economic, and cultural modernization.[9] In this regard, the traditionalists among the educational elite had a strong affinity with the Lutheran church and the Prussian Junkers. These three social strata, Weber observed, were interdependent and formed the social structural basis of Prussian hegemony.

Despite the fact that these three social strata sought to maintain Germany on the path of traditionalism, the appearance of industrial capitalism, monocratic bureaucracy, and modern science meant the penetration of modernism into the fabric of German society. Weber tended to view the German social structure as an uneasy balance of traditional feudalism and modern industrialism.[10] The two components of Germany were, in Weber's judgment, contradictory, and the future of Germany depended upon whether the forces of feudalism or industrialism would prevail.[11] Though all the historical signposts pointed to modernism, the situation in Germany continued to be dominated by the forces of traditionalism. In the face of this seemingly unique historical condition, Weber raised the following question: how do we account for the fact that only in Germany was the rise of industrial capitalism, monocratic bureaucracy, and modern science not linked to the development of a class-conscious bourgeoisie, i.e., a bourgeois class aware of its own interests and values, and which seeks to realize them through a political struggle against the representatives of traditional conservatism?

In Germany, there was, to be sure, a middle class which had achieved sufficient self-consciousness to elaborate a liberal program.[12] Yet, Weber maintained that the spirit and practice of German liberalism never disengaged itself from the ideological hegemony of Prussian conservatism. Thus, Weber noted that industrial capitalism in Germany was not founded upon the independent rationality of individuals operating through a competitive market system. Quite the contrary, it was the controlling power of the state, with its policy of state enterprises, protectionism, and cartelization, which functioned as the steering mechanism of economic progress. Similarly, the emergence of the modern monocratic bureaucracy represented a mere instrument for the achievement of formalized order and efficient policy implementation. However, in Germany the bureaucracy assumed the dimensions of an ethical class pursuing national interests. Finally, as Weber surveyed the social and historical sciences in Germany, he discovered that, conjoined to the empirical and secular premises of modern science, was the traditionalist pursuit of meaning, synthesis, and world-view. Weber surmised that the ideas and practices of the German bourgeoisie were still subject to Prussian hegemony.

10. The Prospects for Liberal Democracy

Weber's Turn to Idealism

In his early essays, Weber surveyed German and Western history from an essentially materialist standpoint. The primary agency of historical change, industrial capitalism, seemed inevitably to point to the bourgeoisie as the builders of a liberal society. The failure of German liberalism led Weber to pose the following question: what factors in the internal historical evolution of Germany account for the failure of the bourgeoisie to impose their own liberal program on the political and cultural life of Germany? Furthermore, as a self-conscious bourgeois and an advocate of liberal-democratic institutions and values, Weber raised a related question: what were the prospects for liberal democracy in Germany?[1]

In his Freiburg address of 1895, Weber singled out the political factor as decisive in understanding the failure and prospects of German liberalism. Weber pointed to the "political immaturity" of the bourgeoisie and reasoned that the "source of its immaturity lies in its unpolitical past. . . ."[2] In this context, Weber asked whether perhaps the proletariat, as heir to liberal ideals, could serve as the bearer of democratic change and cultural modernism. Because the German working classes lacked not only political maturity but also the kind of economic education that accompanies organized class struggle, Weber discounted their immediate political significance. Weber's attitude towards the German working classes was quite ambivalent. He recognized their legitimate rights and needs; he advocated universal suffrage, extensive social reform, and the right to organize into unions and political parties.[3] However, he repudiated the identification of working classes with the millenial hopes of sociocultural regeneration.[4] Furthermore, he thought that the dogmatic revolutionary posture of the Social Democrats only served to strengthen the forces of conservatism.[5]

The dilemma of German liberalism, Weber concluded, revolved around the political immaturity of the bourgeoisie. We must carefully examine this argument: what did Weber mean by political immaturity, and what, in his view, could be done to expedite the work of political education? At the outset, we must note that Weber rejected the argument that economic or capitalist development in itself would generate a class-conscious bourgeoisie.[6] As Weber saw the issue, the question of political maturity had to be examined on its own terms; it was irreducible to economic development. In what follows, I want to suggest that the notion of political maturity had two interrelated meanings. On the one hand, it referred to a tradition of active political participation in the struggle for and wielding of power, and, on the other hand, it referred to the existence of an active political will.

Given the dual meaning of political maturity, the problem of the political immaturity of the bourgeoisie translated into a specifically institutional and cultural issue. Concerning the former meaning, the issue was quite simply the absence of institutional arrangements in Wilhelmian Germany which functioned as vehicles for political education. Historically, this reflected the political dominance of the authoritarian and military traditions of Prussia as well as the lack of organization and a broad social base for liberal politics. By and large, Weber reasoned, liberals were content with the pseudo-constitutionalism and token parliamentary institutions of Wilhelmian Germany. They were satisfied, in other words, with Prussian hegemony, which presumably served as a safeguard against the politicized and organized working classes.

This fear of the masses—evident in the liberal support for Bismarck's anti-socialist laws and in liberal opposition to universal suffrage—explains in large part the reluctance of the bourgeoisie to press their demands for a genuine parliament. On the other hand, Weber believed that the revolutionary posture of the Social Democrats strengthened the resistance of the conservatives in the face of the demands for liberal reform. Accordingly, Weber's political standpoint had a double aspect: first, he advocated a genuine parliament, paralleled by well-organized political parties, as the institutional preconditions for political training and the acquisition of an independent power base; second, insofar as German liberal parties lacked a broad social base and unified party organization, Weber considered it essential to form at least temporary liberal-socialist alliances. Though Weber recognized that the interests of the middle classes and working classes diverge sharply on certain points, he felt that if liberalism integrated the democratic thrust of the Social Democrats, this common ideological conviction could create a working sociopolitical base. The question was whether the liberals could penetrate through the ideological rigidity of the Erfurt Program to recognize in the Social Democrats an essentially reformist and democratic movement. The English-style socialism of the German revisionists had raised the hopes of left liberals that a common social and ideological front was a realistic possibility. The most notable attempt to link liberalism and socialism was perhaps Naumann's National Social Party.

But Naumann's National Social Party was a dismal failure, as were all other efforts to align liberalism and socialism at a national political level.[7] In part, this reflected the refusal of mainstream German liberalism to rally behind a democratic program.[8] Just as significant, however, was the triumph of the revolutionary Marxist doctrine as the official ideology of the Social Democrats. With the ideological hardening of Social Democracy and the rise of a radical wing of Social Democrats—Karl Liebknecht, Rosa Luxemburg, Franz Mehring—Weber's political strategy moved increasingly away from the quest for a new social and ideological alignment. In his political writings after 1906, Weber was much more preoccupied with the formal side of the institutional problem, i.e., the nature of and prospects for parliamentary government.

Though the historical political dominance of Prussian conservatism, combined with a narrow and fragmented liberal sociopolitical base, is crucial in understanding the failure of German liberalism, such structural factors cannot account for the pronounced complacency of the German bourgeoisie. Even before the politicization of the working classes and the formidable presence of the Social Democrats, German liberals were content with an essentially subordinate and politically ineffectual role. They supported Bismarck even when it was apparent that he would no longer make the concessions to liberal reform that presumably were a precondition of the liberal alliance with Prussian conservatism. In the years following German unification, which was a consequence of the diplomatic and military prowess of Prussianism, the German liberal reform movement virtually came to a halt. Even the reform-minded *Verein für Sozialpolitik*, under the leadership of Schmoller and Wagner, hardly disguised its anti-liberal bias. By the 1890s, liberalism was under attack and everywhere on the decline; the National Liberals virtually blended with Prussian conservatism, and what was left of the liberal reform movement was fragmented into a multiplicity of ineffectual coalition parties.[9]

Why, Weber asked, did the German bourgeoisie retreat from the politics of liberal reform at the moment when Bismarck turned against the liberal alliance? And why did the German bourgeoisie assume a basically unpolitical standpoint in the wake of German unification and the growing resurgence of anti-liberal sentiment? Weber observed this lack of political will:

> After the unity of the nation had been achieved in this way and political "satisfaction" was assured, the growing tribe of German bourgeoisie, intoxicated with success and thirsty for peace, was overcome by a peculiarly "unhistorical" and unpolitical mood. German history seemed at an end.[10]

Instead of viewing national unification as the starting point for liberal reform or the assertion of themselves as a national-political hegemonic agency, the German bourgeoisie recoiled from political struggle and wished to replace national and world-power political interests with ethical concepts of politics. This "peculiarly unhistorical and unpolitical mood" of the German bourgeoisie was not only a consequence of structural conditions. It was, Weber suggested, a cultural problem rooted in the unique religious and intellectual traditions of Germany.

Though Weber never underestimated the social structural patterns underlying a weak and complacent German bourgeoisie, by the early 1900s he was aware of the need to analyze its cultural sources. Moreover, given the emergence of political activism during this period and some faintly hopeful signs of a liberal-socialist alliance, it is not surprising to find that Weber's political motivations centered upon raising the class-consciousness of the bourgeoisie. In light of Weber's general ideological orientation, which led him to uncover the ideal or cultural sources of the "unhistorical and unpolitical mood" of the bourgeoisie, and in light of his political motivation for fostering an "historical and political mood," it is not coincidental that Weber's principal research project was concerned with "the manner in which ideas become effective forces in history."[11] Naturally, I am referring to *The Protestant Ethic and the Spirit of Capitalism*. However, whereas the *Protestant Ethic* treated religious ideas, Weber's several methodological essays also dealt with the role of ideas in history, i.e., the role of the German intellectual tradition in shaping the scientific, political, and cultural consciousness among Weber's contemporaries. In what follows, I discuss some of the general features of the German cultural milieu that, in Weber's view, obstructed the politicization of the bourgeoisie.

The Protestant Ethic: Religious
Sources of Bourgeois Heteronomy

The conclusions Weber reached as a result of his early essays had already disposed him to a pessimistic outlook. Weber was convinced that neither economic nor political factors were propitious for mobilizing German liberals. Moreover, in the contemporary situation, Germany was without a class to represent its national interests in the arena of world politics. At one level, Weber's strong nationalist convictions stemmed from his perception that national social and cultural development was inexorably linked to the power-political struggle for dominance on a global scale. Weber viewed the traditional liberal politics of "progress, happiness, and peace" as fundamentally misconceived and dangerous. A contemporary liberal program, Weber thought, had to incorporate elements of a *Realpolitik*.[12] In his desire to comprehend the failure of German liberalism and stimulate its practice, Weber turned to the analysis of the cultural realm. Somewhere in the recesses of the cultural life of the nation, Weber mused, there may be a suppressed political will waiting to be tapped and ignited. Perhaps a piercing intellectual jolt would unleash the stored-up critical energies of German liberalism. The jolt, of course, was *The Protestant Ethic*.

The Protestant Ethic contains multiple levels of meaning. No doubt this reflects the several layers of intentionality and argumentation informing it. Viewed in relation to the diverse contemporary intellectual traditions—German idealism, Marxism, evolutionism, and classical economics—*The Protestant Ethic* is a contribution to the debates around the problems of idealism versus materialism and normative versus instrumental action. At a more concrete thematic level, it is addressed to questions about the origins and meaning of modern capitalist culture, the question of rationality, and the relation between rationalism, irrationalism, and modernity. Within Weber's own intellectual development, *The Protestant Ethic* marked the beginning of a Weberian sociology and world-view. In effect, *The Protestant Ethic* led Weber to pose a whole set of conceptual, analytical, and thematic questions which are, in a sense, meaningful only in their internal setting and line of investigation. It is this which permits us to conceive of Weber's sociology as, in part, a progressive process of self-contained reflection upon persisting analytical and thematic problems.

Nevertheless, *The Protestant Ethic* was embedded in distinct ideological and political motivations. Similarly, Weber's comparative sociological studies were linked to ideological considerations through their thematic concerns with capitalism, rationalism, and modernity. The analytic and thematic structure of Weber's sociology is the topic of the next chapter. Presently, I want to examine the ideological dimensions of *The Protestant Ethic*.

In *The Protestant Ethic*, Weber investigated a causal relation between Puritanism and the psychological and cultural presuppositions, or "spirit," of modern capitalist culture. Weber studied the origins and nature of those character traits and the type of worldly orientation which distinguishes rational-bourgeois capitalism from traditionalistic conduct. The character traits and worldly orientation which Weber contrasted with traditionalism, he called "inner-worldly asceticism." The attempt by the individual to thoroughly master and systematize all aspects of the environment, including the emotional or irrational dimensions of human nature, is a principle feature of worldly-ascetic action. This tends to produce a personality type which in its secular form is identical to the modern bourgeois, i.e., a self-reliant, methodical, calculating, internally motivated individual.

The connection between the Protestant Reformation and

the rise of modern capitalism and the modern bourgeois personality type was not, however, an intrinsic or necessary one. Though Weber pointed to the positive relation between the Reformation and modern capitalist culture in Calvinism, Pietism, Methodism, and Baptism, he contrasted these variants of worldly ascetic Protestantism with the Lutheran Protestantism dominant in Germany. In Weber's analysis, Lutheranism is the antithesis of the worldly ascetic variants of Protestantism. The Lutheran church not only retains the traditionalism of the Catholic church, but, in its sanctification of the worldly orders, it accords the highest value to passive worldly adjustment, obedience to existing authority, and indifference towards worldly aims and routines. Weber wrote:

> The objective historical order of things in which the individual has been placed by God becomes for Luther more and more a direct manifestation of divine will. . . . The individual should remain once and for all in the station and calling in which God had placed him and should restrain his worldly activity within the limits imposed by his established station in life. . . .
>
> Thus for Luther the concept of the calling remained traditionalistic. His calling is something which man has to accept as a divine ordinance, to which he must adapt himself. . . ; obedience to authority and the acceptance of things as they were, were preached.[13]

Generally speaking, Weber viewed Lutheranism as a type of mystical-world religion which cultivates a naive emotionalism and is rooted in a traditionalistic practical orientation.[14]

The doctrinal difference between the otherworldly mysticism of Lutheranism and the innerworldly asceticism of Puritanism is immense: "In the puritan concept of the calling the emphasis is placed on this methodical character of worldly asceticism, not as with Lutheranism on the acceptance of the lot which God has irretrievably assigned to man."[15] From this doctrinal difference follow very significant practical consequences: the Lutheran accepts the world as it is and is calmly resigned to whatever vocation he or she is appointed. The Puritan, on the other hand, confronts the world without illusions and superstitions, with the intention of shaping the natural and social milieu in accordance with transcendent moral ideals.

In differentiating the doctrinal and practical meaning of Lutheranism from Puritanism, Weber was, it should be noted, contrasting the type of bourgeois individual characteristic of Germany with the type which prevails in other Western societies. The individual rooted in Lutheran traditions is an "other-directed" type of personality who responds to the environment in an emotional, disconnected manner and is infused with an attitude of dependency and resignation. By contrast, the individual nurtured within Puritan traditions is an "inner-directed" type of personality, sober, self-assertive, and actively engaged in worldly affairs. In the context in which Weber composed *The Protestant Ethic*, this contrast would not have been missed by the essentially bourgeois public to which it was addressed. In fact, Weber juxtaposed the "Lutheran personality" type and the Puritan individual precisely in order to stimulate the critical self-reflection of the German bourgeoisie by confronting them with a model of an independent bourgeois individual.

In *The Protestant Ethic*, Weber had arrived at the conclusion that the Lutheran ethos of passivity and world resignation had penetrated to the core of German bourgeois culture and psychology.[16] Weber hoped to disturb that ethos of complacency which had settled into the character of the German bourgeoisie. The dissociation of the bourgeoisie from Prussian conservatism was a precondition for their politicization and the activation of the German liberal movement. In *The Protestant Ethic*, Weber took an initial step in that direction by personifying, as it were, the ideal of bourgeois class-consciousness in the form of the Puritan individual.

The German Ideology: Intellectual
Sources of Bourgeois Heteronomy

As Weber worked on *The Protestant Ethic*, he was simultaneously composing a series of methodological essays on the epistemological status of the social sciences. It has been customary to treat the methodological essays separately from Weber's general intellectual development.[17] In fact, Weber's methodological essays have generated a virtual mountain of secondary literature, hardly any of which attempts to relate the essays to Weber's substantive social research or overall world-view.[18] In opposition to this tendency in Weber-scholarship, I want to claim that these essays detail Weber's critical encounter with the "German ideology," i.e., the tradition of German *Wissenschaft* associated with German Romanticism, idealism, and historicism.[19] Furthermore, in a manner akin to Marx's *The German Ideology*, these essays served Weber as a vehicle of general philosophical and sociological self-clarification.[20] Paralleling the logico-epistemological critique of collectivist historicism, objective idealism, and the naturalistic theories of social evolutionism, Marxism, and economism, Weber advanced a politically motivated critique of the most fundamental operative premises of the German intellectual tradition. Weber linked the German ideology with a worldly orientation that works against the formation of a self-conscious, independent liberal movement. The critique of the German ideology was, therefore, the other side of the critique of the German Lutheran religious tradition.

In opposition to naturalistic and idealist models of social science, Weber underscored the significance of "value-ideas" for social scientific practice. In Weber's view, science consists of an "analytic apparatus"—a set of problems oriented toward a specific subject-matter and founded upon a shared methodology—and "unreflectively utilized standpoints," or what Weber elsewhere called "viewpoints." These viewpoints function as a constitutive and directive cognitive element in scientific practice. The viewpoint carves out a segment of real-

ity as the object of scientific interest, defines the chief problems of research, and consequently affects the logical structure
of science. Moreover, though Weber believed that science pro-
gresses through cumulative specialized research, he claimed
that the fundamental transformations in science stem from
changes in the underlying viewpoint. A shift in viewpoint
stimulates a corresponding alteration in the analytic apparatus: new areas of reality are open to scientific interest, new
problems emerge, and the logical form of science undergoes
revision.[21]

From this perspective, Weber conceived of the raging
methodological controversy among his contemporaries as
symbolic of a more inclusive cultural transformation.[22] In this
regard, Weber was critical of this methodological outpouring
to the extent that its participants detached the epistemological problems of science from the more profound problems of
culture. More specifically, Weber repudiated the assumption
that scientific progress proceeds from the resolution of purely
methodological problems:

> Only by laying bare and solving *substantive problems* can sci-
> ences be established and their methods developed. On the other
> hand, purely epistemological and methodological reflections
> have never played the crucial role in such developments. Such
> discussions can become important for the enterprise of science
> only when as a result of considerable shift of the "viewpoint"
> from which a datum becomes the object of analysis, the idea
> emerges that the new "viewpoint" also requires a revision of
> the logical forms in which the "enterprise" has theretofore
> operated, and when, accordingly, uncertainty about the nature
> of one's own work arises. This situation is unambiguously the
> case at present.[23]

Weber reasoned that, in the contemporary situation, changes
in culture and world-view had stimulated questions concerning the logical form of science, and, consequently, critical
methodological reflection was a legitimate activity of the scientist and logician. However, since the analytical apparatus

of science cannot be completely divorced from general view-points, a logico-epistemological critique must be connected to a cultural critique of the value-related ideas and assumptions that are structured into scientific research.

Weber believed that insofar as intellectual traditions are built into scientific research, science has a practically consequential aspect. This is so because the attitudes and orientations associated with the operative intellectual traditions become a part of the very nature of science itself. Furthermore, to the extent that science shapes the cultural life of the society, it necessarily cultivates and legitimates certain national orientations and character types which, in turn, affect the political outlook and practice of its citizens. Indeed, since science was becoming the virtual monopoly of the bourgeoisie, the effect of science on political and cultural consciousness would be a principal factor in the "political maturity" of the bourgeoisie.

Of all Weber's methodological essays, it is in his essays on Roscher and Knies that we clearly observe the logico-epistemological critique unfold into a general cultural critique of the German ideology. At first glance, it appears that Weber was concerned solely with general problems in the methodology of the social sciences. On the basis of Rickert's epistemological ideas, Weber proposed to analyze and critique the methodological view of Roscher and Knies.[24] Thus, in his Knies essay, Weber declared: "My purpose is not to provide a portrait of Knies, but rather to provide a sketch of these [logical] problems, problems which inevitably arise in our discipline."[25] Weber warned us, however, against interpreting these essays as mere pretexts for discussing logical problems: "This first section will surely produce the impression that I am using Knies only as a 'pretext' for the discussion of these scholarly problems."[26] Though Weber was certainly interested in logical analysis, he made it very clear that questions of logic, if pursued rigorously, lead to the analysis and critique of those assumptions or intellectual traditions which form the deepest presuppositional level of science: "I shall attempt to show how he [Knies] came to terms with these [logical] problems and how—given his assumptions, assumptions which many still share—he had to come to terms with them."[27] Weber's intention was to show that Roscher and Knies were committed to certain peculiar assumptions about human nature, society, history, and the world order—assumptions identified with what I call the German ideology—and that these assumptions shaped their logical analysis in a manner detrimental to the progress of science. Furthermore, Weber claimed that these assumptions continued to serve as a vital part of contemporary German *Wissenschaft* and thus retained a formative role in shaping the cultural and political life of Germany. To repeat, my thesis is that Weber's logical critique of Roscher and Knies was linked to a politically motivated cultural critique of the German ideology.

The German intellectual tradition may be conveniently divided into two branches.[28] First, there are individualistic, strongly liberal currents found, for example, in the Kantian notion of moral autonomy, in the cultural individualism of Herder and Humboldt for whom sociocultural pluralism was a condition of freedom and individual development, and in the liberal Protestantism of Schleiermacher. Though these liberal currents were largely suppressed after the liberation of Germany, they were ever-present and were revived by the neo-Kantians, the Protestant social reform movement, and the liberal historicists of Weber's generation. However, as Troeltsch correctly observed, the German ideology reflects a post-Kantian intellectual reorientation.[29] Under the impact of Napoleon's occupation, the German intellectuals turned from the individualism and cosmopolitanism of the French Enlightenment to a collectivist and nationalist standpoint, which had deep roots in German religious and intellectual history.[30] What I call the German ideology refers to this collectivist German intellectual tradition.

The history of the German ideology may be traced, on the one hand, from the later writings of Fichte through the right-wing Hegelian contemporaries of Marx, and, on the other, from the later Humboldt through the immensely influential Rankean school of history.[31] In the realm of social theory, the collectivist orientation was represented by the Historical School of Jurisprudence and the Historical School of Economics, of which Roscher and Knies were the principal founders. The German ideology, of course, had its rivals: for example, German idealism was opposed by the materialists, positivists, and the subjectivist philosophies of Schopenhauer and Nietzsche: the Rankeans were opposed by the surging advocates of economic and cultural history, including among them Weber's teachers Levin Goldschmidt and August Meitzen; and the Historical School of Economics suffered assaults by economic liberals and socialists. Yet, in many of the leading universities, it was the bearers of the German ideology, such powerful figures as Schmoller, Wagner, Georg von Below, Felix Rachfahl, and Eduard von Hartmann, who retained ideological hegemony in the educational system. No doubt this reflected, in part, the compatibility between the German ideologists and the Prussian ruling elite. In fact, as we have seen, Weber had observed a symbiotic relation between Prussian political hegemony and the German academic elite, based upon their common defense of the social structure and values of the traditional order. From a political perspective, Weber viewed the German ideology as the idiom by means of which the carriers of traditionalism articulated and defended their political and cultural hegemony.

In the writings of Roscher and Knies, Weber perceived that the assumptions of the German ideology formed the intellectual underpinnings of historical economics. Naturally, there were important differences among the idealist and historicist currents of the German ideology. Nevertheless, certain common ideas are shared by all the German ideologists. To begin with, there are the twin ideas of the "organic" and "individual" structure of reality.[32] According to this view, reality is composed of a multiplicity of "individuals," each having its own nature and internal dynamic of development. These "individuals" are unique and indivisible units of reality.

They must be intuitively grasped as a whole and therefore cannot be analytically decomposed into their component parts. The German ideologists single out the personality, the *Volk* (or cultural community), and humanity as distinct or independent "individuals."

Weber suggested that this metaphysic underlies the social science of Roscher and Knies. Roscher and Knies view the personality as a real entity or "substance" identifiable with a natural substratum. The personality, in their view, has its own nature, internal unity, and principle of harmonious development. Of their idea of personality, Weber wrote:

> As Knies sees it, the essence of "personality" is, above all, to be an "entity." In the hands of Knies, however, this "entity" is immediately transformed into the idea of a naturalistically and organically conceived "homogeneity." The latter is in turn interpreted as "free of" (objective) inner "contradictions."[33]

For Roscher and Knies, the personality consists of a fixed number of primeval instincts—self-preservation, perfection, altruism—which, if not interfered with, will unfold in a manner producing harmony within and between individuals.[34] Because the personality is an "organic" entity, "a scientific *analysis* of the individual is *impossible.*"[35] For Roscher and Knies, the specific dignity of the social sciences derives from the fact that their object, humankind, is free of the predictability and calculability characteristic of natural events.

The personality is just one mode of "individuality." In the social theory of Roscher and Knies, the primary agent of action and change is not the personality but the collective action of the *Volk*. Like the personality, the *Volk* is also an "individual." The *Volk* is a natural entity, internally unified, self-developing, and resistant to scientific analysis. Regarding this curious concept, Weber wrote:

> For Knies, "Volk" are bearers of homogeneous "instinctual forces." Single cultural phenomena which develop historically and are empirically identifiable do not constitute the components of the "total character." On the contrary, the "total char-

acter" is the *ontological* ground of the individual cultural phenomena. This "total character" is not a composite. On the contrary, it is *the* entity which provides the ground for all its single elements. . . . Knies makes no attempt to analyze the nature of this mysterious power. It is analogous to the "life force" of "vitalism." Like the Roscherian "horizon," it is absolutely the ultimate causal agent that can be identified in the analysis of historical phenomena.[36]

From the organic perspective of Roscher and Knies, the different realms of culture—science, art, religion, etc.—are not independent spheres amenable to scientific conceptualization and analysis; rather they are domains or emanations of the agency of the *Volk*, which, as an organic entity, can only be intuited in its "total character."[37]

"Finally," Weber argued, "there is an ultimate organic relation above the 'organisms' of the individual *Volk:* that of humanity."[38] This brings us to Roscher and Knies's theory of history. Because the evolution of humanity is viewed as an organic relation, history cannot be represented as the multiple evolution of particular historical societies. "On the contrary, it is to be conceived as a total evolution in which each *Volk* plays the role which history assigns to it. *It follows* that this role is *unique.*"[39] History, like the personality and *Volk*, is an "individual" with its own characteristic organic unity.

Given this theory of the organic and "individual" nature of reality, a problem arises: how do the different types of individual entities—personality, *Volk*, humanity—maintain an overall unity or solidarity between these independent levels? If, as this theory proposes, each personality is an independent entity whose development proceeds solely from its inner nature, how do these monadlike personalities cooperate and form enduring integrated patterns of community? In principle, the personality and the *Volk* are separate, irreducible modes of individual existence. Therefore, the behavior of the personality cannot be explained by referring to the logic of the *Volk*. Moreover, it would be a violation of the freedom of the personality, i.e., of its unpredictable nature, to superimpose upon it the patterned regularity of the cultural community of the *Volk*. In any event, this would not account for the organic unity between different and autonomous *Volk*. Roscher and Knies do not lack a resolution to this problem: following the tradition of the German ideology, they posit an underlying metaphysical reality or predetermined harmony as the basis of order. In the work of Roscher, for example, "the ultimate and maximally abstract laws of events—the 'most general' laws in the Hegelian sense—*constitute* 'ideas of God.' Natural laws are his decrees."[40] In the end, Roscher, like his teacher Ranke, adopted a "fundamentally religious view of the world. . . ." Weber concluded: "In this respect, Roscher . . . was thoroughly unmodern."[41]

As I stated at the beginning of this section, Weber's essay on Roscher and Knies had a double purpose. On the one hand, Weber wanted to demonstrate that the viewpoint adopted by Roscher and Knies, what I call the German ideology, shapes the logical form of their social science. Weber tried to show the negative consequences of the German ideological tradition for the advancement of the empirical social sciences. He focused his logical critique on the combination of emanationist and naturalistic logic found in the methodology of the Historical School of Economics. In this regard, Weber was following the general neo-Kantian program of criticizing the legacy of Hegelian panlogism and scientific naturalism.

Weber's aim, however, was not only to relate the German ideology to general logical problems in the social sciences. He was equally interested in connecting the German ideology with the political failure of German liberalism. From this perspective, the German ideological tradition furnished the elementary cognitive and normative materials of the German cultural milieu. The German public derived a good part of its images of self, society, history, and world-order from the stock of intellectual material provided by the German ideology. Through the agencies of the family and educational and other secondary institutions, the German ideology instilled in the German citizen a set of attitudes or worldly orientations which, in the end, produced something akin to a national character type.

What kind of politically relevant orientation did the German ideology produce? The idea that reality consists of individualized organic entities places a cognitive premium upon the intuitive grasp of the whole, not the empirical analysis of the concrete aspects of phenomena. This undermines a sober, calculating, and "objective" view of political realities. By stressing, moreover, the inner unity and harmonious structure of reality, the German ideology devalues the orientation to conflict and struggle which Weber considered an essential element of politics. This tendency to avoid concrete empirical analysis, to overlook the conflictual nature of reality, was part of a strong undercurrent of other-worldliness in the German ideology. As in certain mystical-world religions, the highest value was placed upon the orientation to a transcendent reality beyond the senses and analytical understanding. This other-worldliness gives the individual a basically emotional and idealist disposition which, in effect, detaches the individual from everyday routines and responsibilities. In opposition to an active, inner-worldly orientation, the German ideology fashioned an attitude of indifference to, and devaluation of, worldly affairs. Finally, the collectivist assumptions of the German ideology fostered a sense of passivity and dependency which, combined with the notion of the metaphysical ordering of reality, generated a pervasive ethos of resignation and fatalism.

To the extent that political maturity means the capacity to confront world realities as a struggle and conflict of interests and ideals, the German ideology exhibited an attitude of definite political immaturity. Like the Lutheran religious tradition, the German ideology lacked the inner-worldly, aggressively individualistic, and sober orientation that characterized other western European societies. Both the German intellectual and religious traditions displayed a traditionalist attitude which bolstered Prussian hegemony. Hence, Weber could point to the German ideology and Lutheranism as the cultural sources of the political immaturity of the German bourgeoisie.

The Search for an Alternative to the German Ideology: Weber's Turn to the Western Liberal Tradition

Weber's critique of the German ideology revealed his deepest intellectual commitments. This is so because his opposition to the German ideology, on both epistemological and sociopolitical grounds, challenged him to articulate an alternative viewpoint. Moreover, given Weber's broad ideological motivation to revitalize German liberalism, he found it necessary to provide the bourgeoisie with elements of a world-view that embodied a politically active orientation. Accordingly, Weber drew from the religious and intellectual traditions of the "West," particularly the activist side of Protestantism and the liberal currents of the Enlightenment.

Weber's intellectual posture was virtually in direct opposition to that of the German ideology. Regarding the idea of the personality, he repudiated its reification by the German ideology. Personality, Weber argued, signifies "a concept which entails a constant and intrinsic relation to certain ultimate values and 'meanings' of life, 'values' and 'meanings' which are forged into purposes and thereby translated into rational-teleological action."[42] To the extent that personality means translating moral commitments into purposeful rational action, the predictability and calculability of action is a precondition of human freedom. It is humankind's capacity to take a deliberate attitude towards the world, lend it significance, and act purposefully which is the characteristic meaning of personality.

Weber's concept of personality is highly rationalistic, revealing strong traces of Enlightenment and Kantian influence. However, I want to point to an equally decisive Puritan dimension revealed in Weber's notion of personality. In

"Science as a Vocation," Weber wrote: "In the field of science only he who is devoted *solely* to the work at hand has 'personality'; and this holds not only for the field of science."[43] It is not enough, Weber argued, to be oriented to values and meanings; personality presupposes that these values and meanings be translated into callings and tasks to which the individual devotes one's life. "The crucial trait here is the inner devotion to the task."[44]

The idea of inner devotion refers to what Weber elsewhere called passion, enthusiasm, or the Dionysian element of action. Weber's disdain for Chinese civilization and bureaucratic civilizations in general derived from his perception that bureaucracy is accompanied by the decline of passion.[45] "Both the Puritan and the Confucian were 'sober men.' But the rational sobriety of the Puritan was founded in a mighty enthusiasm which the Confucian lacked completely."[46] On the other hand, Weber's high regard for aspects of Indian and Slavic culture reflects their apparently positive valuation of heightened enthusiasm. However, it was only the Puritan who combines inner devotion with an inner-worldly orientation. "The rejection of the world by Occidental asceticism was insolubly linked to its opposite, namely, its eagerness to dominate the world."[47] Weber's admiration for the Puritan was tempered only by the Puritan's hostility towards sensual culture. Weber looked approvingly, I believe, at the rich sensual life found in certain strands of Indian and Slavic culture. However, he felt that for devotion to assume an inner-worldly orientation, sensuality had to be sublimated into the rational order of everyday life. The Puritan achieved this by sublimating devotion into a vocational ethic—that is, by making functionally specialized occupational tasks a moral obligation. By combining the ideal of moral autonomy with devotion to a worldly calling, Weber's concept of personality incorporated the aggressively individualistic and activistic orientations of the Enlightenment and worldly-ascetic Protestantism.

When we turn to Weber's concept of society and history, we find similar sharp contrasts to the German ideology. Weber replaced the organicism and collectivism of the German ideology with a rationalist and nominalist view of society and history. The idea of society refers, Weber reasoned, to the matrix of reciprocal relations between economy, polity, and culture, conditioned by shared historical traditions. The only historical agents are individuals acting in association and within determinant sociocultural settings. Similarly, Weber repudiated the German idealist tendency to reduce the development of the different spheres of culture to emanations of the *Volkgeist*. In contrast to this view, Weber asserted the need to analyze each cultural sphere in terms of its internal logic and in relation to the encompassing sociocultural context. In this regard, Weber's critique of the German ideology was applicable to orthodox Marxism, which, Weber held, conceives of the different cultural spheres as simply supporting fixtures superimposed upon the economy. By way of criticism, Weber wrote: "It is obvious, however that all those factors (religion, polity, etc.) which are 'accidental' according to the economic interpretation of history follow their own laws in the same sense as the economic factor."[48] The nominalist and rationalist presuppositions of Weber's concept of society and history reveal his roots in the western Enlightenment tradition.

Weber criticized the German ideological tradition for cultivating what amounted to an ethic of worldly adjustment. The individual was to view himself or herself as a vehicle of the natural life-forces residing in the *Volk*. Similarly, the metaphysic of world-order fostered an attitude of world acceptance and resignation. Given the cultural dominance of Lutheranism and the German ideological tradition, it was not surprising that the German bourgeoisie accepted a subordinate role in the cultural and political life of Germany. To revitalize German liberalism, Weber thought that it was necessary to furnish a configuration of cultural symbols and worldly orientations tailored to the independent needs, interests, and ideals of the bourgeoisie. From the Protestant and Enlightenment traditions of "western" Europe, Weber shaped a viewpoint that reflected his own commitment to a liberal polity and secular culture. This is apparent, for example, in his conception of personality, which stresses the element of an active individual will, or self-motivated, goal-directed action. Again, Weber's secularism involved viewing worldly order and meaning as a product of human struggle and conflict. The value was placed upon world mastery, not adjustment to a fixed world-order.

11. Universal History and the Problem of Rationality and Modernity

FROM THE LATER part of the 1890s to the early 1900s, there was a feeling among progressive liberals that the time was ripe for a broad-based social reform movement. Within the *Verein für Sozialpolitik*, the younger generation challenged the leadership of the enlightened conservatism of Schmoller and sought to steer the *Verein* towards a more liberal-democratic posture. The liberal Protestants, led by Naumann, broke from the conservative anti-Semitic Christian Socialism of Adolf Stoecker. In 1896, Naumann launched the National Social Association, a unique blend of social democracy and national *Realpolitik*. It appeared that the broad anti-Catholic and anti-conservative sentiment among liberals could serve as a rallying point for social reform. Moreover, the revisionism of Georg von Vollmar and Eduard Bernstein was enthusiastically embraced by the leading intellectual spokesmen, including Weber, for progressive liberalism. If a united liberal movement could support democratic reform, and if the Social Democrats, as revisionism seemed to promise, could back electoral change, then a liberal-socialist alliance could be the vehicle for shattering Prussian hegemony.

At best, this was an outside possibility, and Weber, though supportive of Naumann, remained somewhat detached and pessimistic regarding its prospects. Yet, the atmosphere of rebellion and perhaps some lingering idealism colored Weber's perspective as well. In the early 1900s, Weber still believed that the politicization of the bourgeoisie was possible and the key to revitalizing German liberalism. However, as all readers of *The Protestant Ethic* know, this is far from a hopeful testament on the fate of liberalism in the modern world.

By the time Weber had written *The Protestant Ethic*, the situation in Germany had begun to change significantly. The 1903 Reichstag elections demonstrated yet again the polarization of German society between the conservatives and the Social Democrats. Not only did the major liberal parties make a poor showing, but Naumann's National Social party went down in crushing defeat. During this period, Weber commented: "The time is still far off when we shall be able to join hands with the urban proletariat for a solution of social problems. I hope that this will come, but for the time being there can be no question of it."[1] The politics of the *Verein* remained conservative, and Weber joined Werner Sombart and Edgar Jaffe as the new editorial board of the *Archiv für Sozialwissenschaften und Sozialpolitik*. Finally, the Social Democrats renounced revisionism and the reformist politics of liberalism. Around this time, we can observe definite changes in Weber's political, ideological, and theoretical perspective.

Weber became increasingly disappointed with the bourgeoisie and critical of the Social Democrats. As the prospects for a liberal-socialist national alliance ended, Weber pinned his hopes for liberal reform on formal changes in the constitution and parliament. By the post–World War I years, Weber's despair over the turn of events led him to revive the Caesarist politics he earlier condemned in his Freiburg address.

From the early 1900s, Weber's ideological perspective widened and became decidedly pessimistic. Whereas his essays between 1892 and 1895 focused exclusively upon Germany, after 1900 Weber turned to an analysis of the prospects and fate of liberalism in America, western Europe, and non-western societies. Moreover, Weber argued that recent economic and political developments pointed to the world-historical decline of liberalism. In a passage that is characteristic of his ideological pessimism, he declared:

> The opportunities for democracy and individualism would look very bad today were we to rely upon the lawful effects of material interests for their development. For the development of material interests points, as distinctly as possible, in the opposite direction: in the American "benevolent feudalism," in the so-called "welfare institutions" in Germany, in the Russian factory constitution..., everywhere the house is ready-made for a new servitude.[2]

In everything Weber wrote, the same theme was sounded: the development of monopoly capitalism and universal bureaucratization was undermining the historic conditions of European liberalism.

Though Weber identified the later phases of capitalist development with a collectivist and static bureaucratic social order, his pessimism was not unconditional and one-dimensional. Given his assertion of the relative autonomy of ideal interests and ideas, Weber avoided conflating socio-historical development with the "development of material interests." Though, Weber says, material interests point to bureaucratic collectivism, it does not necessarily follow that ideal interests are equally determined in that direction. Whether liberalism would survive was, in the end, a question of the "resolute will of a nation" to maintain a vital liberal heritage.[3] Nevertheless, as Weber observed the growing dominance of the "cult of order," he was not hopeful: "We are 'individualists' and partisans of 'democratic' institutions against the stream of material interests."[4]

As Weber's political emphasis centered increasingly upon formal problems of government organization, and as his ideological horizons extended to nonwestern societies, we find a parallel alteration in his historico-sociological outlook. From *The Protestant Ethic* to *The Agrarian Sociology of Ancient Civilizations, Economy and Society,* and *Gesammelte Aufsätze zur Religions Soziologie* (*The Collected Essays in the Sociology of Religion*), Weber's intellectual orientation is truly universal-historical. Weber undertook a comparative historical sociology of civilizations, analyzing their different sociocultural patterns of order and change. On the other hand, whole chunks of *Economy and Society* disclose the formalistic turn in Weber's sociology.[5] In *Economy and Society,* Weber developed a formal analytical framework which set out a program for a specialized discipline of sociology.

The tension between the formal and historical side of Weber's sociology has led some Weber scholars to interpret his *oeuvre* by stressing either the formal sociological orientation or the universal-historical standpoint.[6] In fact, some commentators have suggested that Weber's later sociological perspective, dealing as it does with "generalized rules of action" and "pure forms of association," is antithetical to his earlier historical standpoint.[7] Wolfgang Mommsen has recently criticized this position by pointing to Weber's sustained historical interest in the cultural significance of unique social phenomena:

> He always paid the utmost attention to the historical dimension of all social phenomena, for it was only in this way, in his opinion, that their cultural significance could be ascertained at all. It was not so much the goals of his scholarly work, but rather the approaches which were subjected to substantial change after 1913. Henceforth Weber analyzed social phenomena, which he considered to be of the utmost significance in view of the prospects of liberal bourgeois societies, in the light of a truly universal historical perspective, in a more elevated level and in a much more systematic manner, yet his fundamental concerns were still much the same.[8]

The significant change in Weber's work was not from an historical to a formal sociology; nor did Weber discard his earlier thematic concern with capitalism and liberal-bourgeois society for an exclusively theoretical focus. The main aim of Weber's social theory, Mommsen contends, was, from his early to his late period, to clarify the historical origins, present state, and future prospects of Western liberal civilization.[9] However, after *The Protestant Ethic*, Weber sought to situate modern European civilization in relation to world history and, on the basis of liberal values, furnish a comprehensive framework within which to analyze the origins and fate of Western humanity. Thus, Weber's mature work reveals, on the one hand, his turn to world-historical analysis, and, on the other, the articulation of a compendium of sociological concepts and abstract models of social processes as prerequisites for undertaking his projected universal-historical sociology. In Mommsen's view, then, the historical and formal levels of analyses interpenetrate and cohere around Weber's universal-historical project of determining the characteristic uniqueness of Occidental culture and disclosing its implications for human development and freedom in the modern world.

Leaving aside, for the moment, Mommsen's thematic interpretation of Weber's main aims, we are in full accord with Mommsen's claim that Weber's categorical apparatus is meaningless unless comprehended in relation to its value-presuppositions and universal-historical horizons. It has been demonstrated quite conclusively by Löwith, Mommsen, and Abramowski that Weber's most essential concepts—for example, bureaucracy, the Occidental city, and rational-bourgeois capitalism—were constructed to highlight those aspects of modern culture which reflect his concern with individual autonomy, ethical responsibility, political leadership, and personal meaning.[10] The one-sided and contemporary character of the ideal typical concept was, of course, what Weber's doctrine of value-relatedness (*wertbeziehung*) meant when applied in his epistemology. And, as Mommsen points out, Weber remained faithful to his position throughout his scholarly career.[11] Moreover, Weber was committed to the idea that theoretical frameworks function effectively not as closed systems or timeless, universally valid propositions, but only as historically oriented concepts, models, and causal analyses of long-term historical change.[12]

It is not in Weber's causistry of categories (Kategorien-lehre) nor in a presumably emerging paradigm of social action that one will discover the main aims and structure of Weber's work. To grasp Weber's social theory, we must, first of all, uncover its comparative historical programmatic structure, and, second, retrieve the system-building principles, to use Hans Freyer's phrase, in terms of which Weber's research proceeded and cohered.

The Program of a Comparative Sociology

Weber's social theory can only be understood by specifying its universal-historical horizon and comparative analytical program. After *The Protestant Ethic*, Weber undertook a systematic study of the "major" civilizations: eastern and western Antiquity, Islam, the Orient, and the medieval and modern Occident. Reacting against universal evolutionary schemes of social development, with their Europocentrism and uniformitarian bias, Weber sought a comparative methodology oriented to the causal explanation of sociocultural differences: "The aim [of a comparative study] should be . . . to identify and define the individuality of each development, the characteristics which made the one conclude in a manner so different from that of the other. This done, one can then determine the causes which led to their differences."[13] Weber's conception of the comparative method entails two related aspects.

First, since Weber's interest lay in accounting for divergent paths of social development, it was necessary to abstract the individual elements of social structure and culture that distinguish one civilization from another. This, of course, in-

volves comparing histories to uncover sociocultural uniqueness. As Weber once remarked, the only way to determine the
characteristic uniqueness of the Occidental city is to contrast
it with the city in Islam, Antiquity, and the Orient.[14] And this
specification of historical individuality, Weber insisted, requires the elaboration of typological concepts and models.

Second, the development of clear concepts aimed at de-
lineating sociocultural differences was a preliminary to the
main aim of comparative study: historical explanation. This
was a two-sided procedure. First, the causal significance of
these abstracted elements of social structure and culture had
to be assessed both individually and in combination. Thus,
in *The Protestant Ethic*, Weber tells us that he intended to
causally link Protestantism not only to capitalism but to other
features of modern culture as well. Similarly, Weber related
the Occidental city to the formation of an independent
bourgeoisie, but he also assessed its causal significance for
the rise of a rational theology, economic commercialization,
legal formalism, etc. On the other hand, these individual elements of social structure and culture had also to be causally
explained. Thus, Weber situated Protestantism within the internal religious development of the Judeo-Christian tradition.
Similarly, Weber pointed to certain unique developments in
the religious, military, and political spheres to account for the
rise of the Occidental city. Again, in accounting for the primacy of the patrimonial state in Oriental civilization, Weber
repeatedly stressed the need to construct and regulate water-
ways and canals on a massive geographical scale and to pro-
tect frontier fortifications.[15]

To summarize, Weber's program for a comparative sociology entailed the following formal structure. First, although
Weber would speak now and again of particular historic societies, his focal unit of analysis was civilizations. Second,
Weber's interests lay in explaining the differences between
civilizations. Third, the delineation of sociocultural divergence required systematic civilizational comparisons and the
construction of topological concepts and models. Fourth, hav-

ing articulated the historical singularity of civilizational development, Weber had to assess individual civilizational elements—economy, polity, religion, modes of administration—for their causal significance, and he had to explain each element historically as well. This comparative program underlies his two major works—*Economy and Society* and *The Collected Essays in the Sociology of Religion*—and is the essential Weberian program for sociology.

Weber's effort to elaborate a comparative sociology against universal historical horizons cohered around a set of master problems. Weber's neo-Kantianism led him to repudiate the notion that social science could reproduce history in its essentials or full complexity. Conceptual analysis and historical explanation is always one-sided, Weber thought, by virtue of its embeddedness in the perspectives and problems of the present. It follows that we need to recover the master problems which unify Weber's program for a comparative sociology.

My claim is that we can discern multiple thematic levels in Weber's work. I discuss four master problems, which, proceeding from the more limited and concrete to the more general and abstract, may be enumerated as follows: capitalism, Occidental rationalization, rationality, and modernity. Though these problematics overlap in Weber's work, they are independent interpretive levels. This is the case, I believe, to the extent that these different problematics articulate different aspects of experience. The problem of capitalism, for example, is concerned with the institutional transformation of the Occident. The problem of modernity proceeds from the transformation of a cosmic order into a secular order and focuses upon the problematic nature of meaning and moral commitment in a secular order. Weber's social theory, in my view, is the articulation of the multiple dimensions of contemporary Western experience within a universal historical framework.[16] My discussion of the master problems in Weber's work proceeds by way of a critical commentary on the thematic history of Weber-scholarship.

Capitalism and Rationalization

In the early commentary on Weber, there is an attempt to interpret his ideas as a dialogue with Marx. Not only, it was argued, did Weber's early writings assimilate the Marxist questioning concerning base-superstructure and the focus upon class analysis, but, as Karl Löwith wrote: "The sphere of their investigations is one and the same: the 'capitalist' constitution of modern economy and society."[17] Though Weber and Marx differed significantly on epistemological and ideological issues, both theorists projected capitalism as a totalizing concept embracing the economic, political and cultural meaning of contemporary history.[18] Thus, the problem of human development in a capitalist society was identified as the converging point between Marx and Weber.

The capitalism problem is highlighted in Weber's work as early as his dissertation on the history of trading companies in the Middle Ages (1889) and forms a main theme in his writings on the East Elbian social condition (1892–1895), in *The Protestant Ethic*, in *Economy and Society*, in his comparative studies of religion and society, and in his lectures translated into English under the title *General Economic History*. With regard to the question of the relation between Marx and Weber and the broader issue of the thematic unity of Weber's work, we need to note two aspects of Weber's conceptualization of the problem of capitalism.

First, as Randall Collins has recently argued, Weber's theory of capitalism departs in fundamental ways from that of Marx.[19] Weber includes not only a discussion of the ideal or cultural origins of capitalism, but, in his later model, Weber explored the political, legal, and broad institutional preconditions of capitalism. Whereas Marx tended to collapse the question of the origins of capitalism into the materialist analysis of primitive accumulation, Weber offered a multidimensional model of the historical development of capitalism.[20] On the structural or "materialist" side, as a result of his study of patrimonial bureaucratic societies (Egypt, the Roman Empire, and China), Weber was convinced that modern capitalism could flourish only in a highly differentiated society. As a precondition of institutional differentiation and individuation, Weber pointed to the cultural movements towards fraternization and universalization. The Protestant ethic was, in Weber's view, the culmination of the Judeo-Christian tradition, whose practical significance lay in the complete eradication of the duality between world and religion, conjoined with an ethic of world mastery. Weber's mature analysis of capitalism reveals a rigorous concern with its ideational and institutional development articulated within a long-term historical and comparative perspective.

Although some of Weber's writings on capitalism display a Marxist orientation, his most theoretical model of capitalism, that found in Part I of *Economy and Society*, is a highly formal conceptualization in which rational calculability is its defining feature.[21] This points, I believe, to the second crucial feature of Weber's analysis of capitalism: by the time he began *Economy and Society*, he had generalized his concern with capitalism into a broader analysis of Occidental rationalization. In a programmatic statement introducing *Economy and Society*, Weber wrote: "The basic idea was to study economic development particularly as part of the general rationalization of life."[22] Weber held that Occidental rationalization was not simply an attribute of capitalism, as later Marxists and critical theorists would claim, but a life-pattern characteristic of the separate spheres of economy, law, politics, culture, and administration.[23]

The same commentators who linked Weber to Marx and the capitalism problem recognized the shift in Weber's writings to the more general problem of Occidental rationalization. Siegfried Landshut, who in the late 1920s developed a very influential interpretation of Weber, argued that the problem of rationalization proceeds intrinsically from the capitalism problem.[24] In Landshut's view, Weber derived his concept of Occidental rationality from the instrumental rationality intrinsic to modern capitalism. "Calculability," Landshut reasoned, "is for Weber the unique feature of modern occidental culture."[25] Occidental rationalization signifies, in Landshut's view, a general ethos of impersonality and rational methodical calculation permeating every sphere of modern society. Following Landshut, Hans Freyer wrote that one great theme unifies Weber's historical sociology: "the irresistible rationalization of all spheres of cultural life."[26] Finally, following the interpretations of Landshut and Freyer, Löwith claimed: "Weber analyses capitalism in terms of universal and inevitable rationalization."[27]

In the early German commentary on Weber, the rationalization problem is given a basically historico-philosophical meaning. Rationalization is interpreted in relation to the German idealist tradition and refers to the objectification of a world of institutions and culture and its inevitable loss of meaning and suppression of individuality.[28] Thus, in this reading of Weber, the underlying theme of *The Protestant Ethic* is the mechanization of spirit as exemplified in the movement from the idealism, charisma, and voluntarism of Puritanism to the materialism and routinization of everyday life in the "iron cage" of capitalism. This same dialectic of idealism, objectification, and loss of the subject underpins Weber's analysis of the ironic relation between socialism's categorical imperative to eradicate human domination and its actual effect of intensifying authoritarian bureaucratic control, and between the unitary religio-spiritual world view of Protestantism and its consequent projection of a fragmented secular world emptied of meaning and lacking a transcendent moral order. In certain formulations of this dialectic, Weber seemed to subscribe to a one-dimensional cultural pessimism. For example, in words recalling Simmel's "Tragedy of Culture" theme, Weber wrote: "Ultimately, it is an everyday occurrence that associations which have originated from great world-images turn into 'mechanisms,' which become disengaged from these world-images. This appears simply as the general 'tragedy' of every attempt to realize ideas in reality."[29] How-

ever, as Löwith and Abramowski observe, in its projection of
a rationally calculable, disenchanted world of pluralized
value spheres, the rationalization process carries with it aspects of personal freedom, responsibility, and inner meaning.[30]

The rationalization problem, it is argued, is Weber's attempt to recast the Marxian problematic of alienation in idealist language (as the perpetual conflict between substantive
or value rationality and formal or instrumental rationality),
bereft of its utopianism. The rationalization and alienation
themes pose the same historico-philosophical problem: the
dialectic of freedom and domination, or, in Weber's terms, the
"paradox of man and fate."[31]

There are two fundamental problems with the German
interpretation of the rationalization problem. First, it conflates several distinct layers of philosophical, historical, and
sociological meaning. While it is true that the "paradox of
rationalization" is a part of the thematic structure of *The
Protestant Ethic*, this historico-philosophical thesis must be
differentiated from other historical, sociological, and epistemological arguments—for example, the causal significance of
ideas in history, the adequacy of ideal typical concepts, analytical problems regarding base-superstructure, interests
and ideas, and instrumental versus normative action. Second,
the rationalization problem, as interpreted by early German
commentary, falters in the face of large portions of Weber's
work—much of which is not focused upon the Occident and
does not proceed from the rationalization problem.[32]

In American Weber-scholarship, the rationalization problem also serves as an encompassing interpretive framework.
However, whereas the Germans situate Weber in the mainstream of German idealism and conceptualize rationalization
as an historico-philosophical problem, in American commentary Weber is placed in the western Enlightenment tradition
and rationalization is identified with the empirico-historical
process of modernization. Parsons, for example, views the
rationalization process as the centerpiece of Weber's evolutionary theory of the differential development of societies.

Bendix, though critical of Parsons's evolutionary and idealist interpretation of rationalization, preserves its identification with an empirical process of Western modernization. By identifying the rationalization problem with the modernization framework of the western Enlightenment, those features of Weber's thought are highlighted that resonate with the empirical and liberal American tradition.[33]

The rationalization problem, as Bendix understands it, involved Weber's attempt to account for the unique sociohistorical development of the Occident. Bendix suggests that, considering Weber's major works, we find a methodical and deliberate articulation of an empirically grounded rationalization problem. Bendix argues as follows:

> His [Weber's] essay on Judaism is only the starting point of an explanation that occupied him for the rest of his life. His studies of ancient civilization, his sociology of law and of the types of domination, his essay on the city and his lectures on general economic history—all are continuations of the sociology of religion. While the study of religion [Ancient Judaism] explains the initial differentiation of ethical rationalism in the West, as well as analyzes one of its late developments in *The Protestant Ethic*, these continuations are addressed in large part to the questions of how the basic assumptions of that rationalism had become the dominant value or orientation of the Western world. A major part of Weber's answer is contained in his political sociology. . . . These studies supplement the initial essay on *The Protestant Ethic* by showing that this religious development of the Reformation was one late element in the century-long emergence of certain unique features of Western civilization.[34]

Bendix's contention is that each of Weber's major works is organized around the theme of Occidental rationalization. Moreover, each essay reveals only one phase in the rationalization process. The 1905 edition of *The Protestant Ethic* is the end point of Occidental rationalization. The starting point is *Ancient Judaism*, written and published more than a decade later. The intermediate stages—the processes by which ethical rationalism becomes the dominant value orientation in the West—form Part II of *Economy and Society,* composed between 1911 and 1913. The full articulation of the rationalization process was never completed by Weber. There is the missing volume on Christianity as well as numerous other historical gaps—for example, the "material" origins of the Reformation. Moreover, Weber never defined his work as the decoding of an encompassing Occidental rationalization process.

Bendix's work is important because he has interpreted the rationalization problem in empirical and historical terms, relying heavily upon textual analysis. Recently, however, Friedrich Tenbruck has raised serious questions aimed precisely at undermining the textual basis of Bendix's interpretation.[35]

Tenbruck points to the problem of the time-sequence of Weber's texts. Bendix confuses publication dates with composition dates, Tenbruck says. Bendix's claim, for example, that *The Protestant Ethic* was intended to conclude the Occidental rationalization process relies on the 1920 edition. The original 1905 edition contains no reference to a rationalization process culminating in the disenchantment of the world, as Bendix believes. Again, Bendix maintains that after completing *The Protestant Ethic,* Weber turned to his comparative religious studies in order to fix the point of origins and then finally sketched the mediating stages of political and economic developments in Part II of *Economy and Society.* The problem is that Part II of *Economy and Society* was written prior to Weber's comparative religious studies, although it was published later.[36] How could Weber specify all the intervening stages of Occidental rationalization prior to determining and writing down the point of origin? There are other problems with Bendix's interpretation as well. There is no textual evidence, for example, to suggest that Weber conceived *The Protestant Ethic* as a part of a comprehensive rationalization process. In fact, in several different places, Weber tells us that he abandoned his original plan to examine the relation between Protestantism and modern culture in order to "write down some comparative studies of the general historical relationship of religion and society."[37] Finally, Bendix's interpretation shares the same flaw as the German version of the rationalization problem: the 1905 edition of *The Protestant Ethic*, whole sections of *Economy and Society*, and the studies of China and India are not oriented to the rationalization problem. It appears that the rationalization problem is not the most general and inclusive point of thematic unity in Weber's work.

The Problem of Rationality

A point of contention between Tenbruck and Bendix is the significance of Weber's studies of China and India. Bendix argues that these studies are "control tests" used by Weber as part of a grand historical experimental design aimed at assessing the causal significance of worldly ascetic rationalism in the Occident.[38] Tenbruck proposes a more general interpretation of Weber's comparative studies: "The debate stands much more around the general question of how rationality is produced in the interplay of ideas and interests."[39] Tenbruck—and here we need also to mention the work of Benjamin Nelson—broadens the rationalization problem into the universal historical problem of rationality.

Nelson states that Weber's "Author's Introduction" to *The Collected Essays in the Sociology of Religion* (1920) reveals his main aims as a theoretician. First, "the 'Author's Introduction' helps us to see that his discussion of the foundations of capitalism . . . were ancillary to a wider interest in the distinctive structures and scope . . . of rationalism and rationalization in the Orient and Occident."[40] Second, in order to study the different crystalizations of rationalism in the Orient and Occident, Weber committed himself to what he called a universal-historical perspective.[41] Third, as the main theoretical axis for interpreting rationalization in the Orient and

Occident, Weber analyzed the processes of fraternization and universalization, i.e., the breakdown of dualisms and all sociocultural particularisms to allow for wider social communities and more general cultural forms (modern science, formal law, universal norms). Nelson contends that Weber intended to establish a "new sociological analytic" which involved truly universal-historical horizons and a comparative historical orientation. Though Nelson refers to the universal-historical nature and comparative intentions of Weber's sociology, he does not discuss Weber's analysis of rationality.

Tenbruck offers a bolder thesis: "His [Weber's] pressing interest in occidental rationalization was the starting point and a continuing focus of his life-work. Yet, only a small portion of his *oeuvre* was oriented to occidental development, while the whole of his work, including the methodology, lives by the question: what is rationality?"[42] Tenbruck shifts the polemical context of Weber's sociology from a narrowly conceived dialogue with Marxism, idealism, and positivism regarding materialism versus idealism, problems of base-superstructure, and individual and society, to the more general debate around the question of rationality and the relation between religion and rationality.

Conventional wisdom in the nineteenth century was divided between the following two positions. One school of thought held that religion is a false cognitive interpretation of the world. In place of grasping the world "out there," religion fabricates an unreal world. In this view, religion and rationality are placed in an antithetical relation, with religion referring to a flight from reality and rationality. Against this viewpoint were the evolutionists, who maintained that religion is a forerunner to rationality. Religion anticipates rationality in that it projects the beginning, however inadequate, of a cognitive mastery of the external world. From this perspective, the advance of reason, measured by the cognitive systematization of the empirical world, depends upon the replacement of religion by science. "Both schools," writes Tenbruck, noting their similar conceptions of reason, "as-

sessed rationality [and religion as well] according to its cognitive grasp of the world, and so, ultimately, according to a
model of science."[43]

According to Tenbruck, Weber departed from conventional wisdom in two ways. First, Weber argued that religion
does not proceed from the cognitive interest in mapping outer
reality. Rather, religion develops as a response to the perception of evil and offers an account of it in the form of a theodicy.
This inner compulsion to rationalize suffering and evil drives
religion to articulate beliefs that oppose the world. Second,
this tension between "religion" and "world" generates a process of internal religious development. Tenbruck points to a
"double pressure of rationality" intrinsic to religion. Religious views of the world are compelled to make sense of all
aspects of existence which are perceived as unfathomable. As
a consequence, religious world-views contribute an ever more
unified and comprehensive explanation of worldly suffering
and evil. The upshot of this process, Tenbruck argues, is that
"under such pressure . . . the specific ends and ways to salvation . . . are being progressively conceptualized into explicit
and dominant perspectives of reality, in order to provide a
systematic theodicy of the world as a whole and, at the same
time, a complete rationalization of practical conduct."[44] Rationality develops, then, not as a "natural" outcome of man's
rational interests or some imputed cognitive impulse to master reality; rather, rationality, in the sense of an inclusive
world-view implying a methodical patterning of conduct,
originates and develops in history primarily as an outcome
of the process of religious rationalizaton.[45]

According to Tenbruck, Weber held that it was only in the
Occident that the process of religious rationalization reached
its fullest development, as measured by the elimination of
magic and the formation of a unitary ethical personality.[46]
Hinduism, Confucianism, and the various heterodox religions
of the Orient remained immersed in magic and lacked the
idea of an ethical personality.[47] This was so, Weber thought,
because the carriers of orthodoxy suppressed ethical

prophecy—the chief motive force in religious rationalization.[48] As a result, religious rationalization in the Orient was short-circuited and tended to reinforce Oriental traditionalism.

In the Occident, however, Weber discovered a religious developmental process linking Judaism, medieval Catholicism, and Protestantism. Notwithstanding crucial doctrinal and practical differences, Western religious evolution departed from Oriental religiosity by forging the notion of a personal creator-God and coupling this to the idea of humans as worldly instruments of God. Thus, salvation was predicated upon matters of conscience and ethical conduct, not on magic or mystical experience. In contrast to the ethic of world adjustment or flight and its link to traditionalism, Occidental religious development elaborated codes of theoretical and practical rationalism centered upon world mastery through calculated, methodical control and organization. Judaism initiated the Occidental religious rationalization process which culminated in the disenchanted cosmos of Protestantism. Protestantism, in turn, further unleashed the forces of modernization: capitalism, the nation-state, and science.

In Occidental religious rationalization, Tenbruck finds the core Weberian insight: "Certain ideas under the compulsion of an inner logic develop their rational consequences and thereby effect universal-historical processes."[49] Weber's insight was that ideas as world-views have an inner logic that channels interests and directs the main lines of development of entire civilizations. That, Tenbruck says, is the meaning of Weber's cryptic statement: "Not ideas, but material and ideal interests, directly govern men's conduct. Yet very frequently the world-images that have been created by 'ideas' have, like switchmen, determined the tracks along which action has been pushed by the dynamic of interests."[50]

Tenbruck is correct to note that in his late works Weber elaborated an idealist dialectic. Weber maintained that religious ideas "contain a law of development and a compelling force entirely their own."[51] Presumably, Weber arrived at this thesis as a result of his analysis of the Occidental religious rationalization process: "That great historic process in the development of religions, the elimination of magic from the world which had begun with the old Hebrew prophets and ... came here [in Protestantism] to its logical conclusion."[52] Tenbruck's argument, however, needs to be qualified in two respects. First, though Weber imputes an inner logic to ideas, he insists that their diffusion and historical impact are contingent upon the coalescence of collectivities to serve as their carriers. Moreover, these social groupings, according to Weber, represent particular material and ideal interests which effect the extent and direction of intellectual rationalization. Since he does not specify the social and interest-bound context of ideational evolution, one is left with a spiritualist interpretation of Weber. Tenbruck's idealist distillation of Weber is further reflected in his thesis that for Weber religious rationalization is the ultimate determinant of social development.[53] The rationalization of political, economic, and social interests are, as Tenbruck reads Weber, effective only if conjoined to religious rationalization. Tenbruck reduces rationalization to religious rationalization, and this is inconsistent with Weber's assertion that each sphere of life—economy, polity, military, administration, science, religion, art—contains its own inner dynamic and *sui generis* modes of rationalization. No one sphere can be singled out as the bearer of social development without undermining the multidimensional character of Weber's theory of rationalization processes.[54] Besides religious rationalization, there are, Weber argues:

> rationalization of economic life, of technique, of scientific research, of military training, of law and administration. Furthermore, each one of these fields may be rationalized in terms of very different ultimate values and ends, and what is rational from one viewpoint may well be irrational from another. Hence rationalizations of the most varied character have existed in various departments of life and in all areas of culture. To char-

acterize their differences from the viewpoint of cultural history, it is necessary to know what departments are rationalized, and in what direction.[55]

In several programmatic declarations in his later works, it becomes apparent that Weber's main aim was to establish the seemingly simple thesis of the *multiple meanings of rationalism by arguing for the historicity of reason.* As early as the 1905 edition of *The Protestant Ethic*, Weber held:

> In fact, one may—and this simple proposition which is often forgotten, should be placed at the beginning of every study which essays to deal with rationalism—rationalize life from fundamentally different basic points of view and in very different directions. Rationalism is an historical concept which covers a whole world of different things.[56]

There are two points that need to be highlighted. First, these programmatic statements make it clear that Weber's substantive research must be interpreted as an analysis of rationalization processes, conceived in multidimensional terms and within a comparative and universal historical framework. This implies, as an interpretive task, the reconstruction of the various types of rationalization processes. To avoid excessive formalism this reconstruction must preserve the rich comparative historical and civilizational analysis within which rationalization processes are embedded. Second, the program of analyzing rationalization processes must be connected to Weber's thesis regarding the historical character of rationality. I want to pursue this latter theme in some detail, particularly as it links up to Weber's analysis of modernity.

Much to his credit, Tenbruck perceives that Weber's analysis of rationalization processes coheres around the theme of the historical constitution of reason. Weber, Tenbruck rightly insists, repudiated the long-standing notion that rationality is implanted in human nature and is unitary in structure. Instead, Weber held that rationality must be conceived in historical terms—as a product of the interplay of interests and ideas, and therefore multidimensional.

Moreover, and here we need to extend and deepen Tenbruck's analysis, Weber perceived that built into the naturalistic and unitary view of rationality was the idea of an ethically structured world. For example, the Enlightenment, it is true, identified rationality with the cognitive mastery of the phenomenal world, and regarded science as the highest form of rationality. However, the philosophes also identified science with a normative commitment to enlightenment, autonomy, and progress. In fact, the rationality of science proceeded from its link to this value constellation. To take another illustration, the Greeks defined rationality, in formal terms, as conformity to the immanent purpose (*telos*) of an entity. However, within Greek thought rationality was associated with substantive values: self-sufficiency, beauty, perfection, moderation. In the Middle Ages, rationality meant essentially self-adjustment to the ideal pattern of the cosmos, conceived in static, hierarchic, and telic terms. In each case, the idea of rationality is embedded within a moral or cosmological framework.

Weber's critique of the "monistic" idea of rationality and his alternative historical and multidimensional conception of it rests upon a set of presuppositions about the nature of reality. Proceeding from the most general to the most specific presuppositions, we begin with Weber's idea of the *inherent meaninglessness and chaotic character* of noumenal reality. Weber adopts a "postcosmological" or secular view of reality, in terms of which meaning and order are not part of the structural anatomy of the cosmos but enactments of human beings. Two consequences follow from Weber's secular standpoint. First, lacking a transcendent anchor beyond the flux of meaningless experience—for example, the notion of a transcendent divinity or the idea of a teleological natural order—the idea of a secular order entails an *immanent* standpoint towards experience. Second, given the assumption of the conditional or historical character of cognition and evaluation, all frameworks of worldly order and meaning are perspectival, i.e., one-sided perceptions of meaning and order. Therefore, Weber concludes, confronted with a *pluralistic* universe of perceptions and meanings as they are manifested in ever-changing perspectives, our assessments of rationality can only be relative to our perspective. As Weber remarked by way of illustrating his perspectival conception of rationality: "A thing is never irrational in itself, but only from a particular rational point of view."[57]

To recapitulate, Weber's analysis of rationalization processes points to a more general argument regarding the historical nature of rationality. This thesis, in turn, presupposes a secular world-view, in terms of which order and meaning are viewed as human projections. The other side to secularism is a perspectivist theory of rationality. My contention, then, is twofold. First, though Weber's study of rationalization processes is the main aim of his comparative sociology, its underlying thesis concerning the historical and multidimensional nature of rationality presupposes a secular view of the universe. Second, and this is the claim that I detail in the following pages, secularism not only serves as a presupposition of Weber's analysis of rationalism and rationalization processes, but, in addition, assumes an independent thematic importance to the extent that Weber's articulation of secularism led him to pose the problem of modernity.

The problem of modernity may be put in the form of a relatively simple question: what are the unique conditions of social life in the modern world, and how do they differ from the conditions of social existence in the pre-modern world? Posed in this general way, it is obvious that Weber's substantive research was directed to the problem of modernity.[58] However, this broad characterization of the problem of modernity does not allow us to adequately distinguish it from Weber's analysis of rationalization processes. Though Weber's analysis of modernity often occurred in the context of his research into rationalization processes, in several of his late essays—particularly the "Introduction" and "Theoretical Interlude" to *The Collected Essays in the Sociology of Religion* and the lectures on science and politics as a vocation—Weber's historico-sociological study of rationalization processes passes into a phenomenological discussion on questions of self, meaning, and world in modern times.[59] In what follows, we examine three dimensions to the problem of modernity. First, the origins of the question of modernity. Second, the idea of disenchantment and intellectualization as the core of Weber's concept of modernity. Third, Weber's attitude towards modernity.

Modernity and the Problem of Meaning

What is there in the form of life of contemporary Europe that gives rise to the question of modernity? Before we can address this question, we need to note Weber's idea of the human "metaphysical need for a meaningful cosmos."[60] The need for meaning derives from the experience of "senselessness." By senselessness Weber has in mind such human events as innocent suffering, death, and the element of randomness in the distribution of weath, power, and status. Weber further argues that, historically speaking, religion has functioned to satisfy the human need for meaning: "All religions have demanded as a specific presupposition that the course of the world be somehow meaningful."[61] Humans, Weber contends, need to make sense of those occurrences which appear unfathomable; religion elaborates theodicies and provides us with interpretations of life. The defining characteristic of modernity, Weber says, is the eclipse of a religio-cosmological world-view by a secular (scientific-mathematical) one.[62] The secular world-view—what Weber sometimes calls the "cosmos of natural causality"—is antithetical to the religious postulate of a meaningful cosmos. "In principle the empirical as well as the mathematically oriented view of the world develops refutations of every intellectual approach which in any way asks for a 'meaning' of inner-worldly occurrences."[63] Since Weber takes the human experience of senselessness as a universal, the need for meaning persists in the modern world. The question arises: as science cannot speak to the demands for a meaningful cosmos, and religion has lost its cognitive dominance, how are we to accomplish the legitimation of seemingly random patterns of worldly fortune, senseless suffering, and death? The modern individual, Weber concludes, faces a distinctive existential dilemma unknown in its intensity and clarity to previous historical periods: the problem of meaning. Why has modernity become a problem for social theory? Weber's reply is that the form of life in the modern world is problematic at the level of meaning. The problem of meaning, in other words, gives rise to the question of modernity.

What, according to Weber, is the nature of the modern world? Streamlining Weber's argument to its essentials, the idea of modernity is analyzed in terms of the twin processes of disenchantment and intellectualization. A disenchanted world refers to the elimination of magic from our conception of the universe. Weber analyzed disenchantment in terms of the Occidental religious rationalization process. Disenchantment is only one phase in Western secularization. The crucial stage is the passage from disenchantment to a fully articulated scientific world-view, which projects an autonomous world disengaged from religio-cosmological premises. Disenchantment and the empirical-mathematical scientific worldview are components of the general process of intellectualization. The intellectualization of modern culture signifies replacement of the ethico-religious presuppositions of civilization by formal-rational ones. The dominance of monocratic bureaucracy, formal law, rational capitalism, and legal-rational authority reflects the pervasive intellectualization of modern culture. As impersonal, rationally calculable norms and rules replace substantively rational or religio-ethical conditions of social life, humankind is disabused of the idea of the inherent meaningfulness and orderliness of the universe. As the contents of life are emptied of objective meaning and order, the conferral of meaning and order on human affairs is viewed as a subjective act, entailing a built-in contingency that evokes the problem of meaning in modern culture. The nature of this contingency will be explored in the context of unfolding Weber's attitude toward modernity.

To ascertain Weber's attitude toward modernity, we need to recall his previous statement concerning the opposition between the religio-cosmological and the secular world-views. These two antithetical world-views, Weber argued, correspond to two contrasting life orientations: the "religious" and "secular" orientations.[64] Weber analyzed modernity from both these ideal typical points of view.

Frequently, interpretations of Weber fail to notice that Weber analyzes modernity from both these ideal typical standpoints. As a result, Weber's discussion of the "critique of modernity" represented by the "religious attitude" has been identified with his own personal standpoint. Accordingly, Weber is viewed as an integral figure in the turn-of-the-century anti-modernism and cultural pessimism characteristic of the vulgar idealism of Lagarde and Langbehn, the German Youth Movement, and the orthodox mandarins.[65] This misreading of Weber is nowhere more evident than in his articulation of the so-called thesis of the "meaninglessness of modern culture," developed in the "Theoretical Interlude" and in "Science as a Vocation." This thesis states that insofar as culture is viewed as susceptible to infinite refinement and perfection, the progress of culture cannot serve as a value conferring meaning on human existence. This is so only under the supposition that meaning entails the "completion" and "fulfillment" of some life-task as conceived in terms of the idea of a fixed and finite world-order. Given the dynamic character of modern culture, this is no longer possible.[66] The thesis of the meaninglessness of modern culture represents the religious attitude. "The purely inner-worldly perfection of self of a man of culture, hence the ultimate value to which 'culture' has seemed to be reducible, is meaningless for religious thought."[67]

The question, of course, is whether the religious standpoint is Weber's? To answer this, we must examine his analysis of religion in the modern world. Weber maintained that as culture is intellectualized, it is increasingly devalued by religion. Modern religions are emptied of worldly content and are disposed to other-worldly and mystical religiosity.[68] It becomes difficult, Weber argued, to sustain genuine religious feelings in the face of pervasive intellectualization. "The specific intellectual and mystical attempts at salvation in the face of these tensions," Weber wrote, "succumb in the end to the world dominion of unbrotherliness."[69] Or "in the midst of a culture that is rationally organized for a vocational workaday life, there is hardly any room for the cultivation of a cosmic brotherliness."[70]

The striving for and maintenance of genuine religiosity in the modern intellectualized culture, Weber thought, are all but impossible except for the religious virtuoso. Without the true experience of the sacred, and lacking the everyday practice of benevolence and brotherliness, genuine religiosity tends to degenerate into an artificial, forced religiosity. In "Science as a Vocation," Weber considered the deterioration of genuine religiosity. He pointed to the "pretended" religiosity of "some modern intellectuals" who substitute "all sorts of psychic experiences" for "the dignity of mystic holiness."[71] Weber admonished those in the academic community who attempted to construct "new religions without a new and genuine prophecy."[72] The result, Weber said, is failure: "Academic prophecy, finally, will create only fanatical sects but never a genuine community."[73] Weber was equally scornful of youth who chase after the idols of "personality" and "experience": "What is hard for modern man, and especially for the younger generation, is to measure up to *workaday* existence. The ubiquitous chase for 'experience' stems from this weakness; for it is weakness not to be able to countenance the stern seriousness of our fateful times."[74] In the end, Weber believed that this pretended religiosity, like the youthful search for experience, is a deception masking a general flight from modernity.

Weber once described himself as "religiously unmusical." I believe Weber meant that he was unable to experience genuine religiosity. Neither prophet nor priest, Weber did not hold a self-image as a religious virtuoso. Instead, Weber consistently portrayed himself as a worldly man assuming a secular attitude towards modern culture. This becomes evident in his discussion of modern science.

Weber's discussion of science presupposes the opposition between science and religion. Modern science is an irreligious power. "That science today is irreligious no one will doubt in his innermost being."[75] It follows that the direction of religious commitment in the modern world is away from "the rationalism and intellectualism of science."[76] The religious attitude devalues the strict empiricist ideal of modern science. For Tolstoy, who exemplifies the religious attitude toward modern culture, the inability of modern science to disclose the significance of life renders it meaningless. The religious critique of science, Weber noted, is widespread not only among the lay public but also flourishes in the academic community. Weber, as is well known, was a tireless critic of scientists who attempt to represent the meaning of life in the name of science. For Weber, the attempt to develop a world view from science—so characteristic of Marxism, academic socialism, Comte's positivism, Spencer's social evolutionism, and the German Historical School—signaled the resistance of social scientists to a strictly secular perspective on science.

A genuine secular perspective on science assumes the renunciation of the religious claim to be able to disclose an objectively meaningful world. "The fate of an epoch which has eaten of the tree of knowledge," wrote Weber as early as 1904, "is that it must know that we cannot learn the *meaning* of the world from the results of its analysis."[77] From a secular perspective, science must attend to research—the development of causal and interpretive knowledge—not to the construction of world-views. Is science, then, without any deeper human significance than its potential for control over the forces of nature and society? Although modern science is no longer linked to transcendent values (science as the path to God, true nature, true art), modern science is not legitimated on technocratic grounds alone. Weber believed that science can be a "moral force" by uncovering the ultimate values directing individual conduct, thereby promoting self-awareness and a "sense of responsibility."[78] Weber thought this clarifying function of science was particularly important in the face of the dominance of seemingly autonomous forms of social life—bureaucracy, capitalism—which tend to deny to the individual both "agency" and moral responsibility. The suppression of the individual was reflected, moreover, in the predominance of methodological holism and naturalism in the human sciences—for example, in Marxism, positivism, organic social theories, evolutionism, and the German idealist tradition. Weber's ongoing battle against the varieties of holism and naturalistic modes of social science was connected to their suppression of individual freedom and moral responsibility. Thus, Weber maintained that to the extent that science could recover the origin and movement of social life in the purposeful actions of individuals, it could highlight the aspect of freedom and moral responsibility that is as much a part of modernity as the heteronomy of the iron cage.

Science cannot, however, lay bare the objective meaning and value of life. It is precisely the inability of science to divulge a meaningful cosmos that, as we have already argued, gives rise to the problem of meaning in modernity. Here, however, we want to be exceedingly careful in interpreting Weber. I want to insist that Weber's perspective on modernity is strikingly different from the cultural pessimism of the antimodernists (for example, Lagarde and Langbehn, the Stefan Georg cult, the Nietzsche cults, and German Expressionism) and from the existentialist metaphysical anguish of an absurd world.[79]

Cultural pessimism has deep roots in German culture and is a backlash movement by a traditional elite against modernization.[80] To grasp its critique of modernity, it is necessary to comprehend the rudiments of its ideology. Cultural pessimism presupposes a unitary world-view in which there is one set of valid beliefs, values, and meanings. Moreover, this unitary configuration of beliefs and values are embedded in the social institutions and cultural life of the people which gives to the nation its identity and character as an organic social whole. It is precisely the cognitive, normative, and societal unity that is defined as the necessary condition of freedom (in the sense of personal development that is harmonious internally, with outer nature, and society) and meaning (in the sense of a moral order that secures personal identity and social solidarity). The educated elite have a unique and privileged role as interpreters of the unitary world-view and thus serve as the guardians of the societal community and national identity. As a process of differentiation entailing the loss of cognitive, normative, and societal unity, modernity signifies the decline of freedom and meaning. Thus, cultural pessimists often described modernity as a spiritual totality that is fully mechanized or petrified. It follows that insofar as modernity is spiritually exhausted only a complete civilizational transformation could achieve the rebirth of freedom and meaning.

Cultural pessimism is a unique world-view including the following three aspects. First, the idea that freedom and meaning presuppose a unitary world-view which, as it informs subjective and objective Geist, creates an organic social whole. Second, the view that modernity destroys unity and organic totality and therefore undermines freedom and meaning. Third, because of the complete spiritual exhaustion of modernity, the regeneration of freedom and meaning necessitates a wholistic civilizational reconstruction that returns to the unitary/organic model.

Weber was not a cultural pessimist. In several of his writings, particularly his early methodological essays, *The Protestant Ethic*, and "Science as a Vocation," he argued that the unitary world-view is characteristic of pre-modern societies. In the Christian-feudal and early Protestant epochs, for example, the operative cognitive and normative categories were fused into a synthetic view of the world as a cosmos. In contrast to all such "organic periods," the modern era breaks down the unitary world-view. This does not signify, however, that the modern world is devoid of freedom and meaning or that the individual is thrown into a state of metaphysical anguish.[81] Weber's position is that in modernity the conditions and nature of freedom and meaning are transformed, not extinguished.

In place of the unitary world-view of pre-modern epochs, the modern world entails the differentiation and formalization of cognitive spheres. Weber points to the differentiation of the spheres of truth or science, beauty or aesthetics, and goodness or morality. "We realize again today that something can be sacred not only in spite of its not being beautiful, but rather because and in so far as it is not beautiful. . . . And since Nietzsche, we realize that something can be beautiful, not only in spite of the aspect in which it is not good, but rather in that very aspect. . . . It is commonplace to observe that something may be true although it is not beautiful and not holy and not good.[82] Weber holds that the postulate of the unity of the ethical cosmos is replaced by value pluralism in modernity. In fact, he argues that the notion of an ethically unified cosmos is an illusion. Behind the projected ethical unity there have always been heterogeneous and conflicting institutional and value orders. "Our [modern] civilization destines us to realize more clearly these [institutional and value] struggles again, after our eyes have been blinded for a thousand years—blinded by the allegedly or presumably exclusive orientation, the grandiose moral fervor of Christian ethics."[83] In this regard, Weber suggests that the modern epoch, with its manifest value pluralism, resembles the Graeco-Roman civilization. However, unlike the personal gods of the Greek and Roman Pantheon, the gods of the modern age are secular and impersonal values and are not integrated, as they were in antiquity, within a religio-cosmological system.[84] It was this secular condition of value pluralism and conflict paralleling the institutional and cognitive differentiation that Weber assumed as the point of departure in analyzing the problem of freedom and meaning in modernity.

Briefly, I want to state what I take to be Weber's perspective on freedom and meaning in modernity. In pre-modern societies, values and meaning are experienced as a quasi-natural organic ethic.[85] In the modern secular, differentiated, and pluralistic order, meaning is a personal relation to values which are translated into worldly purposes and pursued in the different institutional spheres. The notion that values have to be pursued in an institutional context in order to be a source of personal meaning reflects Weber's view of modernity as a secularized Protestant culture. In the Protestant era, the individual was religiously enjoined to participate in institutional spheres. Accordingly, this personal and worldly activity, because of its connection to religious symbolism, had a transcendent meaning. With the secularization of Protestantism, we can no longer assign a transcendent meaning to institutional action. Yet—and this is the Protestant legacy that continues to haunt us—vocational specialization continues to be viewed as the sphere where personality is formed and proved, values are projected and realized, and personal achievement and worth is measured. This is what Weber meant when he wrote towards the end of *The Protestant Ethic:* "Limitation to specialized work, with a renunciation of the Faustian universality of man which it involves, is a condition of any valuable [wertvollen] work in the modern world."[86] We find parallel arguments linking the conditions of personal meaning to specialized institutional action in Weber's remarks on the politician, scientist, and bureaucrat—each of whom seeks to realize personal values in their respective institutional spheres.

With the dissolution of the unitary world-view and the breakdown of an organic social order, values and meaning lose both their absolutist and quasi-natural character; values and meaning become a personal achievement and burden. It is precisely this loss of a transcendent rooting which previously secured the objectivity of values that leads to the problematic because contingent nature of values in modernity. This renunciation of transcendent faith coupled to the inability of science to furnish values and meanings yields a condition of the loss of moral certitude. In the Puritan—with his or her loss of the certainty of salvation—Weber perceived an anticipation of the modern dilemma. The Puritan, of course, was still a pre-modern because of his or her transcendent faith. The modern age finds its "natural" moral ambience in the polarity of our personal capacity to create values and meaning and our inability to secure certainty.

Weber's remarks on the place of values in modern life are not without a certain pathos. Like Goethe's Faust, Weber knew that the modern age meant the renunciation of "an age of full and beautiful humanity, which can no more be repeated in the course of our cultural development than can the flower of the Athenian culture of antiquity."[87] Moreover, Weber believed that personal fulfillment in modernity involves such an heroic effort of passionate devotion to values and worldly action that it would exclude large portions of the population, most of whom would pass their lives in a narrow utilitarianism.[88] Nevertheless, modernization was a two-sided process, Weber insisted. What we lose in moral certitude, we gain in personal freedom and responsibility.

Weber's perspective on freedom in modernity—like his analysis of values—avoids both the one-dimensional negativism of cultural pessimism and the millennialism tied to the idea of progress. In opposition to the critics of modernity, Weber believed that the other side to the loss of transcendent faith was the expansion of personal freedom—in the sense of personal choice and responsibility.[89] Without recourse to an absolutist metaphysic, the modern individual is compelled to personally choose and legitimate values. Similarly, Weber felt that the replacement of an organic social order by a differentiated one extended the realm of individual freedom.[90] In a differentiated order, the tensions and conflicts between institutional spheres and competing powers enhance freedom of movement by protecting the individual from absolute control by any one institutional sphere or power. Karl Löwith has pointed to multiple role-playing, a necessary condition in a differentiated order, as a central aspect of Weber's notion of freedom. "Man's individuality lies in fully participating in separate roles . . . not in standing outside of modern special-ized existence. . . . This kind of individuality enables the in-dividual to faithfully attend to the particularity of the given situation without a total commitment (and the suppression of personality). . . . This individualism . . . may not be capable of breaking through the hardened framework of institutional affiliation and dependence, but it can break this cage for him as a person."[91] Finally, Weber argued that differentiation would be accompanied by the profusion of voluntary asso-ciations, for example, political parties, religious, artistic, and literary sects, which would offset some of the reifying tend-encies of bureaucratization and capitalism. We have not hith-erto grasped that Weber did not describe modern society as a mass society composed of atomized individuals over-whelmed by authoritarian bureaucratic structures. Rather, he insisted that between the individual and the state—in so-called civil society—there were a multiplicity of voluntary associations which played a major role in preserving voca-tional values and spiritual ideals and in the formation of the personality of the individual.[92] In his remarks on voluntary associations at the German Sociological Meetings, Weber stated directly: "In comparison to men in other societies, modern man is a *vereinmensch* [a man formed by the many voluntary associations he belongs to]."[93]

Weber's analysis of freedom, like that of value, reflects an historicist perspective. Weber was convinced that the expan-sion of freedom he perceived in modernity was tied up with a unique historical configuration of events and processes. "The historical origin of modern freedom has had certain unique preconditions which will never repeat themselves. . . . First, the overseas expansion. . . . Second, the uniqueness of the economic and social structure of the early capitalist epoch in western Europe. Third, the conquest of life by science. . . . Finally, certain concepts of ideal values, which grew out of a world of definite religious ideas, have stamped the external peculiarity and cultural values of modern man. . . ."[94] Moreover, it is a commonplace that, in Weber's view, these material and ideal conditions were being undermined by the development of advanced capitalism, bureaucratization, and the replacement of vocational ideals and spiritual values by a hedonistic utilitarianism. We need not repeat all those well-known passages exhibiting Weber's dark thoughts about the coming of a new servitude.

Just as we have seen that his analysis of values cannot be equated with cultural pessimism, neither can we identify his perspective on freedom with a one-dimensional pessimism. We must not forget that Weber's descriptions of the dark side of modernity were only developmental possibilities (directed particularly to Germany). In order to achieve a balanced view, these historical tendencies must be seen in relation to offsetting modern conditions, for example, individualistic and democratic traditions and their institutionalization as legally guaranteed civil and political rights, parliamentary institutions and the rule of law, the formation of strong trade unions, the spread of voluntary associations, the continued institutional differentiation between family, economy, universities, and state, and the separation of the private and public realms. My aim is not to downplay the depth of Weber's anxiety about modernity. Rather, I merely wish to urge that whatever despair Weber may have felt about the prospects of freedom and meaning in modernity, his sustained analysis of modernity—rather than occasional rhetorical flourishes—represents a much more nuanced and complex view of modernity than is usually presented.

Summary of Part Four

BETWEEN 1890 AND 1920, liberalism failed to gain political and cultural dominance in Germany. Despite the rise of modern capitalism, bureaucracy, and science, which in other European societies was accompanied by a class-conscious bourgeoisie, the German middle classes lacked an independent and assertive disposition. The ineffectual and subordinate political role of the German bourgeoisie was reinforced by their fear of an organized working class espousing the ideology of revolutionary socialism. The consequence was that, from the 1890s, the sociopolitical polarization of Germany bolstered Prussian hegemony.

The prospects of a liberal Germany hinged, in Weber's opinion, on the possibilities of a liberal-socialist alliance. To be a viable social and political ideology, liberalism had to incorporate the democratic thrust of the Social Democrats. This meant that the bourgeoisie had to free themselves from the dominion of Prussian conservatism. On the other hand, the Social Democrats had to relinquish their revolutionary rhetoric and throw into relief their decidedly democratic and reformist orientation. In both cases, the prospects of a liberal Germany were countered by deeply rooted historical forces. Weber's investigations into the political and cultural origins of the German bourgeoisie unveiled a pronounced traditionalism. The bourgeoisie adopted many of the elements of the Prussian conservative ideology and sought to imitate the life-style of the landed aristocracy. On the other hand, the dog-matic Marxism adopted by the Erfurt Program steered the working classes towards sociocultural and political isolation. By the early 1900s, it was evident that Germany was not ready for a liberal-socialist alliance on a national level. Progressive liberals remained divided and lacked both a broad social base and an organized party machine. The Social Democrats moved unmistakably to the left and criticized the idealism and reformism of liberal democrats.

The period between 1900 and 1905, which saw the revi-talization of progressive liberalism and its demise, was the crucial stage in Weber's intellectual development. Prior to his mental breakdown in 1897, Weber remained within the fold of National Liberalism, even to the extent of advocating an imperialistic *Realpolitik*. After 1900, Weber broke from the National Liberals, resigned from the conservative Pan-German Union, and adopted a more English and democratic-styled liberalism. At a general ideological level, the essay on Roscher and Knies marked Weber's complete dissociation from collectivist historicism and his commitment to a neo-Kantian epistemology and ethics. It is true that during the 1890s, Weber's rebellion against the older members of the *Verein* led him away from a narrow historicism. Yet, in these essays Weber's epistemology is unclear, fusing elements of Marxism with a narrow economic-historiographic approach. In addition, there is a positivist bias in these early writings, particularly in his 1896 essay on the decline of ancient civi-lization.[1] After 1900, Weber criticized historicism, Marxism, and the new economic history (for example, that of Eduard Meyer) from his newly adopted neo-Kantian standpoint. From a strictly analytical perspective, *The Protestant Ethic* reveals Weber's turn to idealism and the beginning of his materialist-idealist synthesis. The argument has been made, in this re-gard, that Weber's earlier essays already give evidence of a materialist-idealist synthesis.[2] Weber's references to the psychological desire for freedom among the farm laborers are taken as an idealist explanation of their migration from eastern Germany. My point is that this idealist explanation is *not* systematically interwoven into Weber's early essays or elaborated into a sociological analytic.[3] *The Protestant Ethic* began this process, but it was not until he composed his studies in religion and society that Weber achieved a theory of material and ideal interests and the relation of ideas to interests. Finally, this formal analytical theory was worked out in the context of an historico-sociological inquiry into the problems of capitalism, Occidental rationalization, rationality, and modernity.

In the face of attacks on liberalism from traditional conservatism and revolutionary socialism, i.e., from collectivist, irrationalist, and authoritarian ideologies, Weber maintained his commitment to moral individualism, critical rationalism, and a pluralistic social order. Though there was no doubt that liberalism was everywhere on the decline, Weber was far from joining in the chorus of the "decline of the West." Weber retained a conviction that the liberal heritage was still vital to Western societies, even if temporarily suppressed. In the end, Weber sought to give liberalism a formulation which would sustain its political and ethical values while resonating with contemporary realities.[4]

General Conclusion

THE CRITICAL JUNCTURE in the history of modernity is the eighteenth century.[1] Though the revolutions in science, religion, and the mechanical arts of the preceding centuries effectively destroyed the Aristotelian and medieval cosmos, it was the philosophes who translated scientific and this-worldly active rationalism into a secular world-view.[2] Modern social theory emerged in the context of the triumph of secular rationalism in the eighteenth century. It is therefore essential to ascertain how secular rationalism was built into the presuppositions and program of Enlightenment social theory.

Historians of social theory have advanced a fairly stereotyped interpretation of the Enlightenment and the main lines of development of European social theory. The philosophes' commitment to *a priori* rationalism, methodological individualism, and analytical instrumentalism, simultaneously yielded the premises and classical formulations of Anglo-American social science and impeded the elaboration of the classical tradition of European social theory. It was in the aftermath of the industrial and French revolutions, i.e., in the post-Enlightenment period, that the fundamental analytical presuppositions—empiricism, historicism, objectivity, holism, and voluntarism—and themes—community, alienation, sacred, and authority—of European social theory originated. European social theory, so the argument runs, finds its analytical and conceptual beginnings in the social thought of the counter-Enlightenment.

In this reading of the history of social theory, there are two lines of continuity between the Enlightenment and the European tradition. First, the modernist and liberal values of the Enlightenment were preserved in classical European social theory. Second, unlike the mainstream sociological tradition, Marx inherited the extreme ideological manifestations of the Enlightenment and its analytical core. Thus, the history of European social theory is reconstructed as two intersecting yet separate and opposing lines of development represented by Marxism and sociology.

My work advances a two-sided critique of this historical interpretation. First, I point to certain methodological problems in this historical schema. There is an almost total neglect of the historical mediations between the originating and developing contexts of European social theory. Nisbet, for example, develops in great detail the apparent parallelism between the presuppositions of French conservative social thought and Durkheimian sociology. Yet, nowhere does he trace the concrete historic connections between philosophical conservatism and Durkheim's sociology. These same historical works fail to develop discriminating concepts of the Enlightenment and the counter-Enlightenment. Zeitlin, for example, seeks to trace Marx's social theory to the Enlightenment. However, Zeitlin does not inquire into which analytical and ideological aspects of the Enlightenment Marx inherited. Nisbet lumps all the Enlightenment critics together as philosophical conservatives. Accordingly, he is unable to grasp the profound differences between the conservative, romantic, and revolutionary critics of the Enlightenment. I have sought to remedy these methodological shortcomings by developing more complex and discriminating concepts of the broad intellectual traditions within which modern social theory developed. In addition, I have specified the way in which these macrotraditions were diversified in the various national contexts and served as intellectual milieus linking the early history of modern social theory to its development throughout the nineteenth century in Germany and France.

The second part of my critique centers upon the substantive interpretation of the Enlightenment and its relation to the classical European tradition. My contention is that the orthodox interpretation of the Enlightenment mirrors the distorted view of the philosophes projected by the counter-Enlightenment.[3] It follows that our interpretation of the relation between the Enlightenment and classical social theory will be misleading. From the later part of the nineteenth century, there began an effort to reexamine the Enlightenment and its place in modern intellectual history. In the works of Dilthey, Meinecke, Cassirer, Gay, and Ernest Becker, we are presented with an alternative conception of the Enlightenment.[4] In Part One, I have detailed the essentials of this revisionist view of the Enlightenment. My aim has been to incorporate this revisionist historiography of the Enlightenment into a reinterpretation of the development of European social theory.

This is not the place to repeat the text of my argument. Two points must suffice. First, the analytical legacy of the Enlightenment cannot be narrowly identified with the contractarian assumptions that characterized nineteenth-century Anglo-American social science. In the Enlightenment science of man, we find alternative theoretical assumptions. Montesquieu and the French philosophes, and Hume and the Scottish philosophes, reacted against the premises and program of social contract theory. In their criticism of contractarianism and the holistic idealist tradition of Catholicism, the Enlightenment science of man articulated the presuppositions and broad programmatic aims of classical European social theory.

Between the Enlightenment science of man and its full elaboration by the classical European tradition stands the counter-Enlightenment. The importance of the counter-Enlightenment is threefold. First, the counter-Enlightenment thinkers served as carriers and elaborators of the program of the Enlightenment science of man. Second, the counter-Enlightenment extended the analytical critique of social contract theory begun in the Enlightenment. Third, from the standpoint of a communitarian ideology, the counter-Enlightenment formulated the problems of alienation and social order for modern social theory.

Classical European social theory continued the project of the Enlightenment science of man and represents a major turning point in systematic social theory. Marx and classical sociology did what the philosophes and the counter-Enlightenment failed to do—namely, elaborate a full theoretical research program complete with exemplary studies (Marx's *Capital*, Durkheim's *Suicide*, Weber's *Protestant Ethic*), which could rival the contractarian tradition with its elegant economic theories of society.[5]

To fully comprehend the origins and development of social theory, it is necessary to view it as embedded in an encompassing ideological milieu. The practical and normative motivations of social theory are disclosed in the configuration of moral, political, and metaphysical assumptions comprising the ideological dimension.

From its inception, Enlightenment social theory was implicated in the practical struggle for a liberal order. Informing the philosophes' analytical critique of contractarian and Catholic tradition was a broad ideological assault aimed at the dogmatic, authoritarian, and closed disposition of all metaphysical systems, of which rationalism and Christianity were featured examples. Within the context of the eighteenth century, it was the English social and political specification of liberal ideology, with its ideal of a market society, that achieved dominance. The interesting feature of European liberalism is that it was unable to forge a stable social and ideological consensus. Bourgeois society failed to integrate the traditional landed aristocracy, the cultural elite, and the mass of laborers—all of whom were poised in opposition to it.

By the 1840s, at a time when industrialism was in high

gear, liberalism had sunk to new lows in its effort to defend bourgeois interests. Liberal economic and political theory had relieved itself both of its scientific pretensions and its universal claims and blatantly appeared as an ideology of class domination. Moreover, the liberal parties in France and Germany capitulated to the anti-democratic policies of conservative regimes. Meanwhile, standing in continued opposition to liberalism and bourgeois society were the conservatives, romantics, and revolutionaries—all of whom projected, at times, an anti-liberal and anti-modernist posture. Although Marx was reared in the liberal tradition, his perception of the social decline of bourgeois society, coupled to heightened revolutionary criticism and practice, led him to abandon liberalism. However, in contrast to the conservatives, romantics, and French revolutionaries, for whom liberal and modern civilization was irredeemably petrified and therefore required a complete civilizational transformation, Marx sought to preserve the core of liberalism and modernity in the supersession of bourgeois society by communism.[6]

The rise of a powerful socialist movement in the later part of the nineteenth century, combined with the surging forces of conservative and romantic reactionary criticism, kept liberalism defensive and insecure. This instability was intensified by the incapacity of liberal social thought to comprehend the developments of contemporary society or to secure widespread social support. European societies were changing, and the survival of a liberal civilization required a reconstruction of the presuppositions, ideals, and social theory of liberalism. Though Durkheim and Weber rejected the Marxian or revolutionary resolution to the dilemma of liberalism, they maintained that a revitalized liberalism had to draw from the revolutionary critique of liberal orthodoxy. The prospects of liberal civilization, Durkheim and Weber clearly understood, depended upon the formation of a new social and ideological alliance between the progressive middle classes and the working classes, between liberalism and revolution.

The paradox of nineteenth-century liberalism was that

although it functioned as an ideology of class domination, its universal ideals entailed a democratic polity and society that underscored the limitations of bourgeois society. In other words, to the extent that liberalism retained its ideological vitality, it projected a post-bourgeois society. Insofar as liberalism functioned as a class-bound ideology, it lost much of its legitimating power and accelerated social polarization. Instead of liberals surmounting this dilemma by elaborating a democratic program, we find that throughout the nineteenth century, liberals supported the forces of traditional conservatism. Marx, Durkheim, and Weber sought a resolution to the liberal dilemma. Marx believed that bourgeois society was already being transformed into a socialist order that would realize the individualistic and democratic values of liberalism. Durkheim and Weber alluded to the susceptibility of a revolutionary movement to deteriorate into a static bureaucratic order. They looked to renovate liberalism by reworking its premises, reconceiving its analysis of history and modern society, and linking liberalism to a democratic practice. It may, of course, be argued that their specific attempts at reconstruction and transcendence are flawed. Marx's historical materialism ultimately suppresses the idealist aspect, and his politics yields too much to the elitist, instrumental French tradition. Durkheim's analytical holism was excessive and perhaps violated a voluntarist theory of institutions and consistent democratic politics. Weber, perhaps more than Marx or Durkheim, managed a satisfactory synthesis of materialism and idealism, individualism and holism; yet, his liberalism is compromised by his early militant nationalism and residues of the aristocratic *Bildung* tradition. Nevertheless, what needs to be emphatically underlined is that Marx and classical sociology arose in the context of the failure of European liberalism and sought to preserve its progressive core by reconstruction and transcendence.

The dilemma of liberalism is still with us and is now a world-historical condition. Though we face different circumstances and problems, the general configuration of social and ideological forces continues to threaten the survival of a rational and humane society in ways inconceivable to Marx, Durkheim, and Weber. It is urgent that the two great traditions of social theory, Marxism and sociology, which are presently polarized, recover their original impulse to synthesize liberalism and revolution and unite as advocates of a rational society.

Appendix
Beyond Presentism and Historicism

Understanding the History of Sociology

THE NEW HISTORY and philosophy of science associated with the names of Paul Feyerabend, Thomas Kuhn, Imre Lakatos, and Stephen Toulmin has revolutionized our image of the nature and growth of science. Instead of viewing science as a wholly rational enterprise, moved by criticism and unfolding in a progressive manner, Kuhn, for example, underscores the nonrational aspects of science and the historical discontinuities in its development. The work of the new history and philosophy of science, especially Kuhn's *Structure of Scientific Revolutions*, has effected a major reorientation in the historiography of the natural and social sciences. In place of the "Whiggish" or "presentist" histories which reconstruct scientific growth as a continuous cumulative progression of knowledge leading to the present, the new historiography, which assumes discontinuity in scientific change, proposes an historicist study of the past aimed at recovering the movement of science "from within."[1] In the recent work of John Dunn, Robert Alun Jones, J. D. Y. Peel, George Stocking, and most notably Quentin Skinner, the idea of an historicist historiography of the social sciences has been fully articulated.[2] This Appendix offers a critical assessment of the "new historicism" and suggests an alternative historiographic model to both presentism and historicism.

Presentism

The question of how to study the social scientific past cannot be separated from the question of the nature of social science and its development. Presentism and historicism must be understood both as methodologies for the study of the history of social science and as theories of science. As historicism emerges as a critique of presentism, we need to outline presentism.

Presentism assumes a continuity in subject-matter and problems between past and present social scientists. For example, Parsons's claims that the work of classical and contemporary sociologists proceeds from the very same problem of social order—the "utilitarian dilemma" of the contractarians—illustrates the presentist idea of continuity.[3] In the social sciences, the presentist assumption of continuity is frequently linked to a cumulation model of science.[4] As social scientists are oriented to the same subject-matter and problems, the gradual improvement of research methods and conceptual clarification yields cumulative scientific progress. To the extent that the actual history of social science is perceived as discordant with the cumulation model, ad hoc explanations are offered. Thus, Merton points to the polarization between theory and research as the main obstacle to cumulation; while Randall Collins argues that the survival of romantic, aesthetic, and ideological notions of social science impedes scientific cumulation.[5] Finally, presentism shows strong affinities with a positivist idea of science.

The methodological principles of presentism follow from its implicit theory of science. First, the continuity between the past and present means that the problems and doctrines of the present may serve as the criteria for organizing, interpreting, and judging past ideas. Second, to the extent that the continuity between past and present is translated into a cumulation model, the past resolves itself into a simple division between those false ideas that have been refuted and those true ideas that have been subsequently incorporated into contemporary systematic knowledge. The history of social science may therefore be reconstructed by piecing together the increments of valid knowledge as if they led in a linear manner to the current state of knowledge.[6] Third, from the identification of science with empirically verified and logically axiomatic statements, it follows that a history of social science must disentangle ideological residues from valid scientific knowledge. A presentist historiography reconstructs the history of science as a progressive movement towards the present, marked by occasional detours and brilliant anticipations, but in the main consisting of piecemeal contributions to current systematic knowledge.

Historicism

Our discussion of historicism begins with its critique of presentism and proceeds to outline its alternative methodological program for a history of social science. George Stocking has stated the critique of presentism succinctly:

> The Whig historian reduces the mediating process by which the totality of an historical past produces the totality of its consequent future to a search for the origins of certain present phenomena. He seeks out in the past phenomena which seem to resemble those of concern in the present, and then moves forward in time by tracing lineages up to the present in simple sequential movement. When this abridging procedure is charged with a normative commitment to the phenomena whose

origins are sought, the linear movement is "progress". . . . The result is whiggish history. Because it is informed by a normative commitment, its characteristic interpretive mode is judgement rather than understanding. . . . Because it wrenches the individual historical phenomenon from the complex network of its contemporary context in order to see it in abstracted relationship to analogues in the present, it is prone to anachronistic misinterpretation.[7]

Historicism has two major objections to a presentist historiography. First, insofar as its aim is to legitimate current scientific standards and practices, presentism represents an evaluative or ideological attitude towards the past.[8] Second, by searching in the past for the origins of, anticipations of, and contributions to current systematic knowledge, presentism ends up advancing historically absurd interpretations.[9] For example, past texts are organized and systematized to present a coherent position on some current doctrine or topic whose terms of discussion were unavailable to past authors. The historical absurdity of this procedure is heightened when the past author is praised or criticized for anticipating or not anticipating the full articulation of the doctrine and its present terms of discourse. The historicist critique amounts to the claim that presentism is not a genuinely historical approach to science, but a form of mythology or ideology.[10]

Within the context of this discussion, historicism may be defined as the attempt "to understand the science of a given period in its own terms."[11] Peel urges that a genuine historicist historiography "must be history 'as it really happened.' "[12] And Jones "stresses an understanding of the total sociohistorical context within which sociological theories have emerged—i.e., to understand the past, completely as possible, in its own terms."[13] Understanding the past in its own terms means recognizing that the conditions and therefore the questions and answers of science vary historically.[14] The changing nature of science is particularly true in the social sciences, where the constant movement of social existence yields new subject-matter and redirects scientific interest. In contrast to presentism, historicism assumes discontinuity between the past and the present as a result of changing problems and subject-matter. Expressing the doctrine of the historical discontinuity in the development of sociology, Peel maintains:

> In fact, however, each new emerging social context, in all its uniqueness, enlarges sociology's subject and provides not only a new subject-matter but new occasions for theorizing. So there is an important sense in which Marx and Dahrendorf, Spencer and Parsons, Weber and Bendix are neither competitors nor associates in theory-building. Very often the theories of the classical sociologists are neither true nor false in the light of the purposes which led *us* to theorize; because they are in large measure the attempts to grapple with a different reality, the answers to different problems, the upshot of different purposes.[15]

The historicist doctrine of discontinuity is connected to an essentially "empiricist" image of science. Science is a response to particular problems raised by the concrete concerns of the given sociohistorical context; and as the social conditions change, so do the problems and aims of science.

On the basis of its "empiricist" and discontinuous model of science, the new historicism recommends a methodology aimed at reconstructing the particular and changing features of social science. However, historicism needs to be distinguished from another historically oriented approach, "contextualism," which seeks to explain ideational development by referring to the sociohistorical setting as its determinant.[16] In its Marxian and sociology of knowledge version, contextualism invokes antecedent "material" factors—for example, class position—as full explanations of ideational or textual meaning.[17] Historicists maintain that although ideas need to be situated in their actual sociohistorical context, the text contains a line of questioning and argumentation which must be independently considered in order to ascertain its meaning.[18] Contextualism, with its proneness to an epiphenomenalist view of ideas, violates the integrity of the text. Asserting the integrity of the text, however, does not entail assuming its complete autonomy, as the New Critics and some structuralists hold. The new historicists seek to avoid both the epiphenomenalism of contextualism and the idealism of textualism by arguing that to specify the historical meaning of a text or idea complex, we need to recover the author's intention.[19] The author's intention refers to what the author intended to do in writing the text—for example, to criticize or support the existing state of affairs.[20] To determine the author's intention, it is necessary to have extensive knowledge of the existing state of affairs, particularly the available linguistic conventions, existing social arrangements, and idioms of discourse, in relation to which the meaning of the terms and arguments of the text can be fixed. The context, viewed as a field of meanings within which textual discourse acquires its specific sense, functions, in addition, to limit possible textual meanings and therefore is the ultimate arbiter among competing interpretations.

The new historicism is an attempt to formulate a genuinely historical study of social science. The past is to be understood "as it actually happened." To avoid the psychologistic and intuitive approach of nineteenth-century historicism, the new historicism proposes an intentionalist theory of textual meaning along with a "logic of validation" to supersede the present babel of interpretations.[21] Although the new historicism shares with its predecessor the aim to redescribe the past in its own terms, our contemporary historicists uphold the presentist claim that the overall direction of historical research is largely a function of current standards and practices.[22]

A Critique of Historicism

The historicist program is a much needed corrective to presentism. To the extent that historicism counsels us to take note of the particular and changing features of social science, it is a giant step towards a genuine history of social science.

However, the new historicism holds an unacceptable model of interpretation and an equally objectionable theory of science. In the following pages, I state this twofold criticism and proceed to outline an alternative proposal for a historiography of the social sciences.

We turn first to the difficult problem of interpreting past texts. The historicists argue for an intentionalist theory of textual meaning. The intentionalist thesis states that to decode the meaning of the text, the interpreter must recover the author's intention, i.e., what the author intended to do in writing the text. Intentionalism does not entail a retreat from the text and context into an exclusive focus upon biographical details or the search for "motives" that caused the text. Quite the contrary, in order to recover the author's intention, it is necessary to situate the statements of the text in relation to their broader linguistic context so as to determine their "illocutionary force"—i.e., what the author was doing in issuing a particular statement. Thus, the intentionalist theory of interpretation moves back and forth between biography, text, and context in order to recover the author's intention. Against the intentionalist theory of interpretation, we offer three criticisms.

First, the intentionalist thesis assumes that the author's statements of intentionality fully and accurately comprehend the range of authorial intention and the significance of the text. In light of psychoanalysis, however, we cannot assume that the author has such privileged access to his or her own intentions. Recently, Quentin Skinner—the main architect of the intentionalist theory—has qualified his position in this regard.[23] He now maintains that in certain cases the author's stated intentions must be disregarded. Although Skinner doesn't believe that this concession undermines the intentionalist thesis—since authorial intention continues to serve as the core of textual meaning—nevertheless, by acknowledging unintended meanings we are led to a much stronger claim for interpreting the text independently of the author's intention.

The assertion of elements of textual autonomy is our second criticism of the intentionalist theory. Reacting against the theories of intentionalism and contextualism, French structuralism and hermeneutical theory have claimed at least the partial semantic autonomy of the text. Ricoeur, for example, maintains that written discourse, in contrast to oral speech, requires the differentiation of textual meaning from authorial intention: "With written discourse, the author's intention and the meaning of the text cease to coincide. . . . Not that we can conceive of a text without an author; the tie between the speaker and the discourse is not abolished, but disintended and complicated. . . . The text's career escapes the finite horizon lived by its author. What the text says now matters more than what the author meant to say."[24] In a similar vein, Gadamer writes: "The text is part of the whole of the tradition. . . . The real meaning of a text, as it speaks to the interpreter, does not depend upon the contingency of the author and whom he originally wrote for. It is partly determined also by the historical situation of the interpreter and hence by the totality of the objective course of history."[25] Nonintentionalist theories of interpretation illustrate the need to differentiate textual meaning from authorial intention by referring to the phenomenon of "unintended meanings"— what the author said is not what the author intended to say.[26] It is important to note that in his recent writings, Skinner has once again modified his intentionalist theory. Skinner now distinguishes between "heteronomous texts" and "autonomous texts."[27] Similarly, whereas Skinner once held that the main aim of interpretation is the recovery of the author's intention, he now suggests that this is just one among the many tasks of textual interpretation.[28] Whether Skinner's qualifications save his overall theory of interpretation or indicate its failure need not be decided, since, in my view, there is another more fatal flaw in his interpretive theory.

My third criticism is aimed at the objectivism of intentionalism and the historicist approach in general. Intentionalism maintains that although past texts are conditioned by the author's intention and the sociohistorical context, the present interpretation of the past is somehow free of such determination. Historicists of course acknowledge the effectiveness of the present in the initial selection of historical materials. However, they assume that, inspired by the positivist spirit of selflessness, the interpreter can exercise sufficient methodological self-control to prevent the intrusion of present interests and attitudes into the objective reconstruction of the past. The other side to objectivism is a rather simpleminded copy model of interpretation.

Starting in the period between the two world wars, objectivism—the idea that it is possible to furnish a nonperspectivist or objective description of the world—has been subject to a massive critique.[29] The application of the critique of objectivism to a theory of interpretation has been achieved, above all, by Hans-Georg Gadamer.[30] Gadamer argues that interpretation is less a reenacting of the past or a subjection of the past to the present than a dialogue between the past and present. Substituting a phenomenological perspective for a realistic metaphysic, Gadamer says that the text is not a "thing in itself" with a fixed meaning to be recovered by suppressing the present. Instead, Gadamer reasons that the interpreter is always historically situated and conditioned by "traditions" or "prejudgements" which structure the interpreter's perception of the past. The text is constituted and exists as an object of knowledge only in relation to the present context and standpoint of the interpreter, i.e., in relation to the questions the interpreter asks and the assumptions the interpreter makes about the author, work, and context. To avoid reducing the text to a mere projection of the present, Gadamer states that the text itself poses questions and responds to the interpreter's questioning insofar as the interpreter is open to the claims of the text. The truth of the text is revealed in the communicative process between the interpreter and the text. Moreover, the aim of interpretation is not to recover authorial intention but to reach an agreement about the topic discussed in the text. The nature of interpretation conforms less to a methodology of validation than to a dialogue.

The second part of my critique of historicism centers upon

its theory of science—in particular, its doctrine of historical discontinuity and its related "empiricist" idea of science. The doctrine of historical discontinuity states, to repeat, that in the social sciences the subject-matter and problems of the past are different from those of the present. This is so because "society," the subject-matter and source of problems in the social sciences, is continually changing. The historicist maintains that each generation of social scientists faces a unique subject-matter and set of problems that reflect the particular sociohistorical constitution of society. Thus, in light of "the final uniqueness of each instance of sociology," Peel urges us to recognize "that theories are the product of particular purposes and a particular subject-matter."[31] The "empiricism" of historicism is in evidence in its assumption that the subject-matter, problems, and ideas of social science arise from and remain embedded in their particular sociohistorical conditions. Expressing this "empiricism," Skinner writes: "Any statement . . . is inescapably the embodiment of a particular intention, in a particular occasion, addressed to the solution of a particular problem, and thus specific to its situation in a way that it can only be naive to try to transcend. . . . There are only individual answers to individual questions, with as many different answers as there are questions."[32] Historicism denies a general level of social science, i.e., that there are universal problems intrinsic to the nature of social science and that it is possible to articulate universally valid answers.

There are two arguments which could be advanced against the "empiricism" of historicism. Confining myself to indicating their broad contours, the first states that unless one is prepared to deny the legitimacy of the claim of social science to develop systematic knowledge, the existence of general problems and generalized explanations of human behavior must be admitted.[33] Without pursuing this further, I simply note that the recent work of Jeffrey Alexander, Anthony Giddens, and Roland Robertson argues forcefully for a general level of social science consisting of "theoretical logics," "central problems," and "major axes of sociological analysis."[34]

Pointing to general problems and a general level of social science appears to contradict Skinner's claim that every statement or text has only a particular meaning corresponding to the particular intentions of the author, its orientation to particular problems, and its addressing a particular audience. Without denying that texts embody particular meanings due to their specific context, problem-orientation, and author's intention, I would argue, nevertheless, that Skinner is wrong in thinking that particularized meanings cover the full range of textual meaning. Although they are the embodiment of a particular intention, statements or texts contain presuppositions and intellectual claims of a general nature. Thus, although the statements of *Capital* must be understood in relation to Marx's intention to criticize the economists and the political economy of capitalism, the discourse of *Capital* makes general claims about history, human nature, the nature of science, the relation between the individual and social structure, and so on. Texts consist of statements and discourse which proceed at different levels of abstraction. Moreover, some texts, especially so-called classic texts—for example, Marx's *The German Ideology*, Tönnies's *Community and Society*, or Weber's *Economy and Society*—though limited by the particular idiom historically available, nevertheless deliberately deal with problems, articulate concepts, and pursue a line of analysis whose interest and validity transcend their context.[35] As one analyzes a text at the highest level of generality, the text assumes increasing autonomy from authorial intention and its originating context. To the extent that there is a level of textual meaning that refers to truly general problems and systemic knowledge, it then becomes urgent to reconsider the historicist doctrine of historical discontinuity.

Unlike the new historicists, the historicists of the late eighteenth and the nineteenth centuries (Burke, Herder, Humboldt, Müller, Ranke, Savigny) held that the other side to historical discontinuity is the continuity between past and present. Despite changing sociohistorical conditions, successive generations were viewed as inextricably linked through tradition—a heritage of common institutions and shared cultural commitments. Recently, in an attempt to revitalize the idea of tradition, Gadamer and Edward Shils have argued that insofar as tradition underscores the context-bound character of experience, its embeddedness in and continuity with the past, it is indispensable for a theory of history.[36] If we accept, as I believe we must, the notion of tradition linking the past and present, then our view of the historical development of social science needs to be modified accordingly. Specifically, we would need to be aware that frequently the particularity of idioms in which problems are posed and subject-matter is defined conceals general interests and a continuity in questioning and argumentation with predecessors. I believe this dialectic of particularity and generality or discontinuity and continuity can be illustrated rather simply.

Studying, let's say, the problem of capitalism in Marx and Weber, we would certainly need to attend to the fact that Marx faced a different historical configuration of capitalism than did Weber. Moreover, the historicist could rightly observe that the particular social and intellectual context within which the problem of capitalism was posed varied between Marx and Weber. No doubt one could discern in Marx intentions and a line of argumentation different from Weber's. Accordingly, a study of the problem of capitalism in Marx and Weber would necessitate specifying their different views of capitalism in light of their divergent contexts and intentions.

However, there are two arguments that point with equal necessity to the continuity between Marx and Weber. First, as Anthony Giddens, Dieter Lindenlaub, and Karl Löwith have persuasively argued, to the extent that Marx conceptualized the problem of capitalism in general historical, analytical, and ideological terms—for example, as a totalizing concept within which to grasp the movement of modern history, as an analytical argument regarding the priority of "materialist" conditions in explaining social action and order, and as a question of individual freedom and development in a capitalist society—there are evident points of continuity with Weber.[37] An additional basis of the continuity between Marx and Weber derives from the similarity in their experience of capitalism. The continuity in their experience of capitalism reflects, despite historical changes, continuity in the basic institutional structure of capitalism and continuity in the perspectives in terms of which Marx and Weber interpreted their experience of capitalism. Moreover, to the extent that Marx and Weber pose the problem of capitalism in general historical, analytical, and ideological terms, and to the extent that their experience of capitalism remains representative of ours, their analysis of capitalism retains a contemporary significance. Alan Dawe has recently commented on the idea of the representative nature of historical experience. The continuity of experience, writes Dawe:

> links the world we live in today with the reflections on the worlds in which they lived. . . . For while not ignoring historical particularity, what makes their work live on is the continuing relevance of their concerns to our experience. When Weber speaks to us of his bureaucratic nightmare of a world, he is also speaking to us in our world. . . . Through the *creative* power of their thought . . . they reveal the historical and human continuity which makes their experience *representative* of ours. The point is always the link with experience. . . . As long as they continue to speak to *our* experience, to *our* lives and times, they live on.[38]

Although the continuity of experience links their world to ours, there are two additional factors which actually account for the contemporary character of so-called classic works. First, classic works remain contemporary insofar as they contain ideological and analytical presuppositions and substantive insights that have a contemporary resonance. No doubt this would partially explain the contemporary relevance of Marx, Durkheim, and Weber, in contrast to the largely historical status of a Comte, Hobhouse, or Sumner. A second explanation of the contemporary status of classics points to the formation and institutionalization of schools or traditions whose inspiration and perhaps exemplary works are derived from the classics.[39] There is little doubt that the establishment of a school or tradition of social theory by Marx or Durkheim, and the failure of, say, Simmel or Tönnies to do so, is a crucial variable in explaining their differential impact on contemporary sociology. Naturally, these two factors explaining the contemporary relevance of classic works are related, though they are also distinct. This is so because the successful creation and institutionalization of schools or traditions entail, besides a powerful theory, other nonintellectual considerations, such as the personal charisma of the group leader, a favorable academic and national milieu, the right appointments, a receptive and supportive extra-academic public, and so on.[40]

To summarize, my critique of historicism is twofold. First, I argue against its intentionalist theory of textual meaning and interpretation. Historicism identifies textual meaning with the particular intention of the author and assumes a copy model of interpretation. I contend that an intentionalist theory of interpretation suppresses levels of textual meaning that in certain ways transcend authorial intention and context. Moreover, I argue that interpretation conforms less to a copy model than to a model of dialogue. Second, historicism takes over an empiricist and discontinuous model of scientific change. The former, I maintain, contradicts the rationalist premises of modern science, and in opposition to the latter, I specify the logical and historical bases of a theory of continuity in social scientific development. By way of some concluding remarks, I offer below a model of the historiography of social science that integrates aspects of presentism and historicism while avoiding their defects.

The Theory and History of Social Science

It has been my general contention that the type of historiography of social science that one advances follows more or less directly from one's view of the nature and growth of social science. Every historiography of social science, in other words, presupposes a theory of science. Specifically, I argue that both presentism and historicism hold unacceptable models of social science and therefore cannot serve as a sound methodological basis for a history of social science. Presentism rightly underscores the intellectual continuity beween the past and present, but it misrepresents the nature of historical development in the social sciences by assimilating it to an increasingly less plausible model of cumulative growth. Reacting to the gross violation of the historical record resulting from the Whiggish attempt to fit history into an inappropriate scientific model, historicism calls for a return to history "as it really happened." However, historicism builds into its allegiance to the historical record a false theory of historical discontinuity, which is translated into a simple-minded empiricist theory of science. Historicism's chief error in this regard is to assume that intellectual continuity in the social sciences automatically implies a cumulative model of scientific growth and therefore a commitment to a presentist historiography. In the course of outlining a model of social science, I articulate a conception of the historical development of social science that specifies levels of continuity and discontinuity and therefore will better serve us in studying the social scientific past.

In the diverse movements of the new philosophy of science, phenomenological and hermeneutical philosophy, ordinary language analysis, and critical theory, we find elaborations of what I call a postpositivist theory of science.[41] Despite very significant differences among postpositivist articulations, the unifying idea is a multileveled conception of science. Without denying an empirical and logical dimension, postpositivist theorists point to nonempirical, nonlogical spheres or presuppositions—for example, Gadamer's "prejudgements" (*Vorurteilsstruktur*), Gouldner's "background assumptions," Holton's "themata," Kuhn's "paradigms," Pepper's "world hypotheses," or Polanyi's "tacit dimension." Simplifying matters enormously, we may speak of science as a two-tiered structure consisting of an "analytical" realm of hypotheses, empirical statements, logical rules, theoretical postulates, models, and explanations, and an "ideological" realm of reality-defining assumptions and epistemological presuppositions.

On the basis of a postpositivist conception of science, we can outline a model of social scientific change, confining ourselves solely to developmental patterns proceeding from the "internal" structure of science. Our most important revision in viewing the historical development of social science follows from the inclusion of the ideological realm into our idea of science. In the process of developing explanations of human behavior, social science projects images of self, society, and world, and builds into its theoretical Gestalt assumptions of a moral, political, and metaphysical nature. By virtue of its ideological realm, social science furnishes material for personal identity, cognitive and moral order, and political belief. Functioning, in part, as an affectively charged world-view, social scientific theories shape the conceptions of order, meaning, and identity that inform daily life. The ideological dimension of social science and its embeddedness in everyday life are the basis, I contend, of the noncumulative and nonrevolutionary nature of social scientific change. Briefly, the reason seems to be that ideological commitments at the most elementary affective, moral, and cognitive levels are resistant to evidentiary and logical criticism. While this accounts for the noncumulative character of social science, its nonrevolutionary nature follows from the argument that as social scientific ideas become part of our taken-for-granted world and are therefore affectively charged and supported by practical interests, everyday life will function as a conservative force perpetuating social scientific traditions, or at least opposing revolutionary ideational changes. Hence, the ideological dimension of social science is the main source of its static, nondevelopmental character.

To this analysis, however, we need to add that the ideological configuration of social science is sufficiently general to permit changes in the analytical realm. Thus, while the ideological presuppositions of Marxism have remained more or less stable, its analytical component has assumed diverse formulations. From this we conclude that while the ideological realm of social science tends towards constancy and stability, the analytical realm is susceptible to variation and change, including, at the more empirical and middle-range theoretical levels, cumulative progress. It is precisely this two-tiered structure of social science that accounts for our contemporary perception of social science as static and noncumulative, yet also developmental and cumulative, and that links the history of social science respectively to the historiographic principles of the humanities and the sciences.

Assuming a multileveled conception of social science, I have proposed a more differentiated model of the developmental logic of social scientific change. Corresponding to its multiple levels are different processes of change, disclosing continuity and discontinuity between the past and present as well as aspects of cumulation and noncumulation. A history of social science that recognizes the multileveled nature of social science would have to attend to the differential developmental patterns of the ideological and analytical realms. Finally, in contrast to presentism and historicism, both of which render the past virtually meaningless for the present, in my view our history preserves a contemporary theoretical importance in two respects. First, as Merton and Stocking argue, the past remains theoretically relevant to the extent that its ideas have not been incorporated into current systematic knowledge or its questions and problems remain significant but unanswered.[42] Second, insofar as the ideological and analytical ideas of past works speak to present interests or are elaborated into schools, paradigms, or traditions that extend into the present, the study of the social scientific past will have contemporary intellectual significance. If we speak of, or write about, the classical tradition, we do so because its ideas have so penetrated our discipline that they remain an indispensable point of departure for contemporary sociological analysis.[43]

Notes

Preface

1. Karl Löwith, "Max Weber und Karl Marx," *Archiv für Sozial-wissenschaft und Sozialpolitik*, 67 (1932): 53.

2. Among historians and social theorists, the efforts of Anthony Giddens to critically reassess the relation between Marxian social theory and sociology are outstanding. See, in particular, Anthony Giddens, *Capitalism and Modern Social Theory* (Cambridge, England: Cambridge University Press, 1971).

3. Daniel Rossides, *The History and Nature of Sociological Theory* (Boston: Houghton Mifflin, 1978), p. 3.

4. Alvin Gouldner, *The Coming Crisis of Western Sociology* (New York: Avon Books, 1971), p. 116.

Introduction

1. Geoffrey Hawthorn, *Enlightenment and Despair: A History of Sociology* (Cambridge, England: Cambridge University Press, 1976), p. 1.

2. Raymond Aron, *Main Currents in Sociological Thought* (New York: Anchor Books, 1968), vol. 1, p. 1.

3. See Stephen Collini, "Sociology and Idealism in Britain, 1880–1920," *Archives Européennes de Sociologie*, 19 (1978).

4. Many historical works have as their main aim the reorientation of contemporary social theory. The strategy is to find in the early

history of social theory a standard for present theory, which is defined as a betrayal of that original ideal. It seems fair to say that most historical works originate from discontent with present social theory. For example, Jonathan Turner and Leonard Beeghley openly acknowledge that they wrote their historical work essentially to criticize and reorient present-day theory: "As we will come to see, some of sociology's early masters had a vision of what theory in science *should be* which was superior not just to that of their contemporaries, but also to that which prevails in modern sociology. An implicit theme, therefore, of this book is that modern sociology has often lost the vision of its early masters. . . . To delve into the emergence of sociological theory is thus to seek redirection and reinspiration from those who saw that a theory of the social universe must ultimately seek the basic theoretical principles guiding the operation of this universe." Turner and Beeghley, *The Emergence of Sociological Theory* (Homewood, Ill.: Dorsey Press, 1981), p. 13. From a very different perspective, Ernest Becker's historical studies originate from his perception that the original project of social science, a unified and normative science of man, has been suppressed. Becker's aim is to recover the "lost science of man" as a contemporary project by ascribing to the intentions and project of the "founding fathers" a normative status. See Becker, *The Lost Science of Man* (New York: George Braziller, 1971) and *The Structure of Evil: An Essay on the Unification of the Science of Man* (New York: Free Press, 1968).

5. The postpositivist interpretation of science is less the articulation of one thinker or a unified school of thought than the outcome of the efforts of separate and often unrelated intellectual groupings. Simplifying matters enormously, we may single out three such groupings of postpositivist thought. First, the new history and philosophy of science represented, most notably, by Paul Feyerabend, *Against Method* (London: New Left Books, 1975); Mary Hesse, *Models and Analogies in Science* (London: Sheed & Ward, 1963); Norwood Hanson, *Patterns of Discovery* (Cambridge, England: Cambridge University Press, 1958); Gerald Holton, *Thematic Origins of Scientific Thought* (Cambridge, Mass.: Harvard University Press, 1973); Thomas Kuhn, *The Structure of Scientific Revolutions* (Princeton, N.J.: Princeton University Press, 1970); Imre Lakatos, *The Methodology of Scien-*

tific Research Programmes, ed. John Worrall and Gregory Currie (Cambridge, England: Cambridge University Press, 1978); Michael Polanyi, *Personal Knowledge* (New York: Harper & Row, 1964); Dudley Shapere, "Notes Toward a Post-Positivist Interpretation of Science," in *The Legacy of Logical Positivism*, ed. Peter Achinstein and Stephen Barker (Baltimore: Johns Hopkins University Press, 1969); and Stephen Toulmin, *Human Understanding* (Oxford: Clarendon Press, 1972). An extremely valuable discussion of the contemporary status of postpositivist philosophy of science is to be found in *The Structure of Scientific Theories*, ed. with a Critical Introduction and an Afterword by Frederick Suppe (Urbana: University of Illinois Press, 1977). As a second group of postpositivists, I would include the critical theory of Jürgen Habermas, *Knowledge and Human Interests* (Boston: Beacon Press, 1972); Karl-Otto Apel, *Towards a Transformation of Philosophy* (London: Routledge and Kegan Paul, 1980); and Albrecht Wellmer, *The Critical Theory of Society* (New York: Herder & Herder, 1971). Finally, I would identify as postpositivist the interpretive or hermeneutical theory of science associated with the diverse movements of phenomenology, hermeneutics, and ordinary language philosophy. In all three groupings, but especially the last, there are theorists whose critique of positivism goes beyond postpositivism and ends in anti-science. However, that is not the aim of postpositivism. Its aim, I believe, is to articulate a multi-leveled conception of science which would incorporate aspects of the more general and potent concept of reason inherent in the Western philosophical tradition. In other words, postpositivists seek to integrate classical and positivist theory.

6. Jeffrey Alexander, *Theoretical Logic in Sociology* (Berkeley and Los Angeles: University of California Press, 1982), vol. 1.

7. Turner and Beeghley, *Emergence of Sociological Theory*.

8. Ibid., chap. 1.

9. For an argument which stresses ideology as an impediment to an explanatory social science, see Randall Collins, *Conflict Sociology* (New York: Academic Press, 1975); and Collins with Michael Makowsky, *The Discovery of Society* (New York: Random House, 1978), p. 242.

10. Donald Martindale, for example, writes: "Sociology is part of

that great evolution of thought in Western civilization which passes from religion through philosophy to science." Martindale, *The Nature and Types of Sociological Theory* (Boston: Houghton Mifflin, 1966), p. 4.

11. I believe the following passage reveals Mannheim's reductionist account of social theory: "Men living in groups do not merely coexist physically as discrete individuals. They do not confront objects of the world from the abstract levels of a contemplating mind as such. . . . On the contrary, they act with and against one another in diversely organized groups, and while doing so they think with and against one another. These persons, bound together into groups, strive in accordance with the character and position of the groups to which they belong to change the surrounding world of nature and society or attempt to maintain it in a given condition. It is the direction of this will to change or maintain . . . which produces the guiding thread for the emergence of their problems, their concepts, and their forms of thought." Karl Mannheim, *Ideology and Utopia* (New York: Harcourt, Brace & World, 1936), pp. 3–4. The reduction of thought to the desire to maintain or change nature and society is applied to social theory in Mannheim's essay "Conservative Thought," in *Essays on Sociology and Social Psychology*, ed. Paul Kecskemeti (New York: Oxford University Press, 1953); also see *Ideology and Utopia*, pp. 269–270.

12. Irving Zeitlin, *Ideology and the Development of Sociological Theory* (Englewood Cliffs, N.J.: Prentice-Hall, 1968), p. vii.

13. Rossides, *The History and Nature of Sociological Theory*, p. 1.

14. Göran Therborn, *Science, Class, and Society: On the Formation of Sociology and Historical Materialism* (London: New Left Books, 1976), pp. 143–144.

15. Robert Nisbet, *The Sociological Tradition* (New York: Basic Books, 1966), pp. 18–20.

16. Ibid., pp. 5–6.

17. Cf. Talcott Parsons's review of Nisbet's *The Sociological Tradition* in *American Sociological Review*, 32 (1967): 640–643.

18. Gouldner, *Crisis of Western Sociology*, p. 29.

19. Gouldner affirms the autonomy of analytical theory in principle. For example, he writes: "That the ideological implications and social consequences of an intellectual system do not determine

its validity, for theory does indeed have a measure of autonomy, is not in the least denied here." Ibid., p. 13. Moreover, Gouldner explicitly denies that he is making a logical argument, i.e., a statement on the necessary structure of social theory: "Whether social theories *unavoidably* require and must rest *logically* on some background assumptions is a question that simply does not concern me here" (p. 31). However, despite Gouldner's disclaimers, he actually does make logical claims, as when he asserts, for example, "Like it or not, and know it or not, sociologists will organize their researches in terms of their prior assumptions; the character of sociology will depend upon them and will change when they change" (p. 28). Similarly, though Gouldner denies reductionist intentions, his analysis of the role of nonrational factors (background assumptions, personal sentiments, political ideology) as the source of postulations (p. 29), as determining facts (pp. 41–42), as directing research and theory construction (pp. 21, 29), and as the basis of scientific change and the very success of a theory (p. 34) leaves no room for the analytical determination of theory.

20. Hawthorn, *Enlightenment and Despair*, chap. 1; Becker, Structure of Evil, pp. 5–6.

21. See Talcott Parsons, *The Structure of Social Action* (New York: Free Press, 1968) and "Economics and Sociology: Marshall in Relation to the Thought of His Times," *Quarterly Journal of Economics*, 46 (1931–1932).

22. See Becker, *Structure of Evil;* Hawthorn, *Enlightenment and Despair;* and S. N. Eisenstadt with M. Curelaru, *The Form of Sociology* (New York: Wiley, 1976).

23. Robert Bierstedt, "Sociological Thought in the Eighteenth Century," in *A History of Sociological Analysis*, ed. Tom Bottomore and Robert Nisbet (New York: Basic Books, 1978), p. 23.

24. Martindale, *Nature and Types of Sociological Theory*, p. 35.

25. Cf. Parsons, *Structure of Social Action;* and Nisbet, *Sociological Tradition*.

26. See Nisbet, *Sociological Tradition;* Zeitlin, *Ideology and the Development of Sociological Theory;* Albion Small, *The Origins of Sociology* (Chicago: University of Chicago Press, 1924); and Robert Spaemann, *Der Ursprung der Soziologie aus dem Geist der Restauration* (Munich: Kosel-Verlag, 1959).

27. Nisbet, *Sociological Tradition*, pp. 17–18.

28. See ibid., p. viii; and Zeitlin, *Ideology and the Development of Sociological Theory*, p. viii.

29. On the tendency of the philosophes to move away from natural law, compare the statement by Peter Gay: "But far from being disciples of any natural law doctrine, the philosophes were providing a bridge to nineteenth-century utilitarianism and historicism." Gay, *The Party of Humanity* (New York: Norton, 1963), pp. 200–201. Regarding the idea that the Enlightenment broke from contract theory, see Werner Sombart, "Anfänge der Soziologie," in *Hauptprobleme der Soziologie*, ed. Melchior Palyi (New York: Arno Press, 1975). Sombart's argument differs from mine in that he contends that the initial break with contract theory occurred among the first-generation English philosophes, for example, Bernard Mandeville and William Petty. Moreover, Sombart holds that the main line of development of social science proceeds through the Scottish, not the French, philosophes. Sombart's hostility to France prevented him from perceiving that it was the French social theorists, especially Montesquieu, Voltaire, and Turgot, along with Hume, who originated the idea of modern social science. Cf. J. B. Bury, *The Idea of Progress* (New York: Dover, 1955), pp. 144–158.

30. The strong version of this thesis of the polarization of Marxism and sociology is what is presented in the body of the text. A weaker version may, on the one hand, simply point to more continuities and similarities while not challenging the polarization thesis. On the other hand, a weak version of this polarization thesis confines Marxism to the prehistory of a scientific social theory. Marx becomes just one more forerunner locked into a speculative-synthetic conception of social science. This argument polarizes Marxism and classical sociology by assigning the former a merely historical status in contrast to the latter's contemporary theoretical significance. This is the interpretation offered by, among others, Martindale, *Nature and Types of Sociological Theory;* Pitirim Sorokin, *Contemporary Sociological Theories* (New York: Harper & Row, 1964).

31. See, for example, Max Horkheimer, "Traditional and Critical Theory," in *Critical Theory* (New York: Seabury Press, 1972).

32. See, for example, Therborn, *Science, Class, and Society;* also see

Alvin Gouldner's critique of Therborn in *The Two Marxisms* (New York: Seabury Press, 1980), pp. 374–380.

33. See, for example, Jürgen Habermas, "Kritische and Konservative Aufgaben der Soziologie," in *Theorie und Praxis* (Neuwied: Luchterhand, 1967).

34. See, for example, Karl Korsch, *Three Essays on Marxism* (New York: Monthly Review Press, 1972), pp. 11–15; Jerzy Szacki, *A History of Sociological Thought* (Westport, Conn.: Greenwood Press, 1979), p. 147; and Therborn, *Science, Class and Society*, p. 40.

35. Consider, for example, the following statement by Zolton Tar: "In nineteenth-century Western European societies, two sociological orientations emerged independently of each other as theoretical responses to the socio-historical developments after the French Revolution. They were Comte's positivist sociology and the social theory of Marx and Engels. The line of development of the former orientation can be followed up to Talcott Parsons and contemporary Western academic sociology, and the latter from Marx and Engels to modern Marxist social sciences both in the East and West." Zolton Tar, *The Frankfurt School* (New York: Wiley, 1977), p. 41.

36. For an analysis which reconstructs the historical development of Marxism and sociology as two separate movements, reflecting underlying class and ideological and analytical differences, see Herbert Marcuse, *Reason and Revolution: Hegel and the Rise of Social Theory* (Boston: Beacon Press, 1968), pp. 323–388.

37. Modifying, yet subscribing to this position, Gouldner writes: "A major structural characteristic of Western Sociology develops after the emergence of Marxism; following this, Western Sociology is divided into two camps, each with its own continuous intellectual tradition and distinctive intellectual paradigms, and each greatly insulated from or mutually contemptuous of the other. After the sprawling genius of Saint-Simon, Western Sociology underwent a kind of "binary fission" into two sociologies, each differentiated from the other both theoretically and institutionally, and each the reverse or mirror image of the other. One was Comte's program for a 'pure' sociology, which, in time, became Academic Sociology, the university sociology of the middle class. . . . The other was the sociology of Karl Marx or

Marxism, the party sociology of intellectuals oriented toward the proletariat. . . ." Gouldner, *Crisis of Western Sociology,* p. 111.

38. See Löwith, "Weber und Marx," p. 53.

39. Tom Bottomore shows that, in fact, Marxists often had a quite ambivalent attitude to sociology. On the one hand, Marxists have continually borrowed ideas and methods from sociology and even projected Marxism as a sociological system. On the other hand, Marxists have sought to distance themselves from sociology and, accordingly, have stressed their essential differences and separate identity. See Tom Bottomore, *Marxist Sociology* (New York: Holmes & Meier, 1975).

40. See, in particular, Habermas, *Knowledge and Human Interests;* and Wellmer, *Critical Theory of Society.*

41. See Jean Baudrillard, *The Mirror of Production* (St. Louis: Telos Press, 1975); Jean-Joseph Goux, *Économie et Symbolique: Marx, Freud* (Paris: Seuil, 1973); and Gilles Deleuze and Felix Guattari, *L'Anti-Oedipe: Capitalisme et Schizophrénie* (Paris: Éditions du Minuit, 1972), vol. 1.

42. By far the best work on the relation between Marx and classical sociology is Giddens, *Capitalism and Modern Social Theory.*

43. See Sidney Hook, "The Enlightenment and Marxism," *Journal of the History of Ideas,* 29 (1968). In fact, Marx's rather uncritical identification of industrialism (and the accompanying pattern of instrumental domination of nature) with social progress has been recently criticized by radical ecologists. See, in particular, Murray Bookchin, *Post-Scarcity Anarchism* (San Francisco: Ramparts Press, 1971) and *Toward an Ecological Society* (New York: Black Rose Books, 1982).

44. Marx, Durkheim, and Weber were, of course, aware of the different outcomes of liberalism on the Continent, in England, and in America. In fact, I will argue in the subsequent chapters that it was their perception of this divergence, coupled with liberalism's failure on the Continent, that was the decisive practical event in their theorizing. Of all the classical theorists to deal with the problem of the divergence in liberal development, it was perhaps Tocqueville who posed the problem and analyzed it in the most detail—without, however, a concomitant theoretical reckoning. See Alexis de Tocqueville, *Democracy in America*

(New York: Schocken, 1970) and *The Old Regime and the French Revolution* (New York: Doubleday, 1955).

45. Cf. Leo Strauss, *Liberalism, Ancient and Modern* (New York: Basic Books, 1968).

46. Bruno Snell, *The Discovery of the Mind* (New York: Harper & Row, 1960); Eric Havelock, *Preface to Plato* (New York: Grosset & Dunlap, 1971); Colin Morris, *The Discovery of the Individual: 1050–1200* (New York: Harper & Row, 1972); and Isaiah Berlin, *Four Essays on Liberty* (New York: Oxford University Press, 1970), p. 129.

47. See Leonard Krieger, *The German Idea of Freedom* (Boston: Beacon Press, 1959); and Colin Loader, "German Historicism and Its Crisis," *Journal of Modern History,* 48 (1976). For a general discussion of the idea of individualism and its diverse formulations, see Steven Lukes, *Individualism* (New York: Harper & Row, 1973).

48. On the liberal tradition, see David Sidorsky, "Introduction," in *The Liberal Tradition in European Thought* (New York: Capricorn Books, 1971); Guido de Ruggiero, *The History of European Liberalism* (Boston: Beacon Press, 1966); F. A. Hayek, *The Constitution of Liberty* (Chicago: University of Chicago Press, 1960); Leo Strauss, *Liberalism, Ancient and Modern* and *Natural Rights and History* (Chicago: University of Chicago Press, 1953); and Berlin, *Four Essays on Liberty.*

49. Harold Lasky has underscored this tension between the universalistic claims of liberalism and its particularistic nature due to its link to the bourgeois defense of private property. See Lasky, *The Rise of European Liberalism* (New York: Unwin Books, 1962), pp. 14–15, 139–145.

50. See Reinhard Bendix, *Nation-Building and Citizenship* (Berkeley and Los Angeles: University of California Press, 1964).

51. On "late" Enlightenment utopianism, see Frank Manuel, *The Prophets of Paris* (New York: Harper & Row, 1962).

PART ONE: The Origins of European Social Theory
Chapter 1

1. Given the context and intent of my discussion, it is, I believe,

legitimate to single out only those ideas held in common by the philosophes, i.e., the underlying configuration of Enlightenment social thought. Treating the Enlightenment as a unified social and cultural movement reflects a long-established tradition in Enlightenment scholarship. Recently, Peter Gay, for example, speaks of the philosophes as a family, although a "stormy one," and notes that the philosophes thought of themselves in similar terms. See Peter Gay, ed. *The Enlightenment, vol. 1. The Rise of Modern Paganism* (New York: Norton, 1977), pp. 3–37; also see J. H. Brumfitt, *The French Enlightenment* (Cambridge, Mass.: Schenkman, 1972), pp. 9–26. For a useful survey of the different forms Enlightenment social thought assumed in various national contexts, see Robert Bierstedt, "Sociological Thought in the Eighteenth Century," in *A History of Sociological Analysis*, ed. Tom Bottomore and Robert Nisbet (New York: Basic Books, 1978).

2. Baron de Montesquieu, *The Spirit of the Laws* (New York: Hafner Press, 1975), p. 3.

3. François Marie Arouet de Voltaire, *The Philosophy of History* (New York: Citadel Press, 1965), p. 27.

4. Ibid., p. 30.

5. David Hume, *Essential Works*, ed. Ralph Cohen (New York: Bantam Books, 1965), p. 195.

6. Ibid., p. 207.

7. Voltaire, *Works* (New York: E. R. Dumont, 1901), vol. 11, p. 177.

8. Hume, *Essential Works*, p. 196.

9. Regarding the profound influence of Montesquieu on the Scottish Enlightenment in general, see Anand C. Chitnis, *The Scottish Enlightenment* (Totowa, N.J.: Rowman and Littlefield, 1976), p. 95.

10. Quoted in David Kettler, *The Social and Political Thought of Adam Ferguson* (Columbus: Ohio State University Press, 1965), p. 195.

11. Hume, *Essential Works*, p. 466.

12. Ibid., p. 467.

13. Peter Gay, ed., *The Enlightenment: A Comprehensive Anthology* (New York: Simon and Schuster, 1973), p. 551.

14. Marquis de Condorcet, *Sketch for a Historical Picture of the Progress of the Human Mind* (New York: Noonday Press, 1955), p. 112.

15. Montesquieu, *Laws*, pp. 6–7.

16. Quoted in Isabel F. Knight, *The Geometric Spirit: The Abbé de Condillac and the French Enlightenment* (New Haven: Yale University Press, 1968), p. 293.

17. Thomas Hobbes, *Leviathan*, ed. Michael Oakeshott (New York: Collier-Macmillan, 1971), p. 20.

18. Jean-Jacques Rousseau, *The Social Contract and Discourses*, ed. G. D. H. Cole (New York: Dutton, 1973), p. 45. There is some controversy surrounding the exact meaning of this phrase. It has been argued that the "facts" Rousseau refers to are the facts of the Bible; thus, Rousseau can be read as rejecting the biblical account of the origins of humans. However, if we read the passage following the above quotation, it is clear that Rousseau is rejecting historical facts as well. "The investigations we may enter into . . . must not be considered as historical truths, but only as mere conditional and hypothetical reasonings. . . ."

19. Gay, *Enlightenment Anthology*, p. 550.

20. Ibid.

21. Voltaire, for instance, in his *Essay on the Manners and Spirit of Nations*, writes: "I should like to discover the nature of human society at that time, how people lived within their families, what arts were cultivated, rather than repeat so many misfortunes and combats. . . ." Quoted in George Havens, *The Age of Ideas* (New York: Free Press, 1955), p. 198.

22. Voltaire, "History," in Denis Diderot, *The Encyclopedia: Selections*, ed. Stephen Gendzier (New York: Harper & Row, 1967), p. 125. I am not arguing that historiography in the eighteenth century was empiricist. My point is that the tradition of a "fact-critical" historiography was well established during this period, and that this empirical concern for facts became a part of the epistemological program of the Enlightenment.

23. Quoted in Raymond Aron, *Main Currents in Sociological Thought* (New York: Anchor Books, 1968), vol. 1, p. 16.

24. David Hume, *On Human Nature and the Understanding*, ed. Anthony Flew (New York: Collier Books, 1962), p. 175.

25. Ibid., p. 174.

26. Regarding the failure of seventeenth-century thought to adequately mediate between the particular event and a pattern of universal history, see Peter Hanns Reill, *The German Enlightenment and the Rise of Historicism* (Berkeley and Los Angeles: University of California Press, 1975), p. 29.

27. Montesquieu, *Laws*, p. lxvii.

28. Condorcet, *Sketch*, p. 104.

29. Anne Robert Jacques Turgot, "On Universal History," in *Turgot: On Progress, Sociology, and Economics*, ed. Ronald Meek (Cambridge, England: Cambridge University Press, 1973), p. 64.

30. D'Alembert, Jean le Rond, *Preliminary Discourse to the Encyclopedia of Diderot* (Indianapolis: Bobbs-Merrill, 1963), pp. 35–36. At the thematic level, Enlightenment historical consciousness is not reducible to a unilinear doctrine of social progress. More characteristic is a basically "dualistic" and cyclical viewpoint according to which, in any given historical period, either reason or superstition holds dominance, but only for a short duration. Compare the following statement by d'Alembert: "Barbarism lasts for centuries; it seems that it is our natural element; reason and good taste are only passing." Ibid., p. 103. Or to quote Montesquieu, "Almost all the nations of the world travel this circle: to begin with, they are barbarous; they become conquerors and well-ordered nations; this order permits them to grow, and they become refined; refinement enfeebles them, and they return to barbarism." Quoted in Henry Vyverberg, *Historical Pessimism in the French Enlightenment* (Cambridge, Mass.: Harvard University Press, 1958), p. 155. Similarly, Voltaire affirms that "an age of barbarism follows an age of refinement." Quoted in Vyverberg, *Historical Pessimism*, p. 181. Finally, Hume writes: "When the arts and sciences came to perfection in any state, from that moment they naturally or rather necessarily decline, and seldom or never revive in that nation where they formerly flourished." Hume, *Essential Works*, p. 439. To the extent that the philosophes were committed to some ideological notion of progress, they were, in any event, aware of the costs or negative consequences of progress, i.e., specialization and fragmentation of the personality, the decline of the aesthetic sensibilities, the loss of certainty, etc. On the dualistic and cyclical historical

viewpoint of the Enlightenment, see Gay, *The Enlightenment*, vol. 1, pp. 32–38. On the strains of historical pessimism, see the above-cited study by Henry Vyverberg.

31. Hume, *Essential Works*, p. 105.

32. For an historical analysis that grasps the twofold orientation of Enlightenment social theory but is unable to fully appreciate the complexity of the science of man, see Geoffrey Hawthorn, *Enlightenment and Despair: A History of Sociology* (Cambridge, England: Cambridge University Press, 1976).

33. Hume, *On Human Nature and the Understanding*, p. 272.

34. Quoted in Ernst Cassirer, *The Philosophy of the Enlightenment* (Princeton, N.J.: Princeton University Press, 1951), p. 219.

35. See Hume, *Essential Works*, pp. 106–107; also see Montesquieu, *Laws*, p. lxvii.

36. Hume, *Essential Works*, p. 495.

37. Voltaire, *Works*, vol. 11, p. 181.

38. Concerning the philosophes' positive view of the nonlogical side of human nature and, more generally, their view of the relation between reason and the passions, see Lester Crocker, *Age of Crisis* (Baltimore: Johns Hopkins University Press, 1959), chap. 9.

39. Quoted in Peter Gay, *The Enlightenment*, vol. 2, p. 191.

40. Denis Diderot, *Early Philosophical Works*, ed. Margaret Jourdain (Chicago: University of Illinois Library, 1916), p. 27.

41. Gay, *Enlightenment Anthology*, p. 374.

42. Ibid., p. 663.

43. On the question of reconciling the naturalistic and materialistic disposition of the philosophes with moral autonomy, see Crocker, *Age of Crisis*.

44. Montesquieu, *Laws*, p. 3.

45. Quoted in Keith M. Baker, *Condorcet* (Chicago: University of Chicago Press, 1975), p. 444.

46. Quoted in Crocker, *Age of Crisis*, p. 375.

47. Even Diderot, who sometimes flirted with a vitalistic materialism, in the end embraced a dualistic view of human nature: "Is it certain that physical pleasure and pain, perhaps the only principles of action in the animal, are also the only principles

of the actions of man? Isn't the distinction between the physical and moral as solid as that between an animal that feels and an animal that reasons?" Quoted in Crocker, *Age of Crisis*, p. 359.

48. The theoretical premises of this discussion have been elaborated in detail by Jeffrey Alexander, *Theoretical Logic in Sociology* (Berkeley and Los Angeles: University of California Press, 1982), vol. 1; also see Jürgen Habermas, *Theory and Practice* (Boston: Beacon Press, 1973).

49. Montesquieu, *Laws*, p. 293.

50. Hume, *Essential Works*, p. 507; Voltaire, *The Age of Louis XIV* (New York: Everyman's Library, 1969), p. 4.

51. J. H. Brumfitt, *Voltaire, Historian* (New York: Oxford University Press, 1970), pp. 124–125.

52. Talcott Parsons, *The Structure of Social Action* (New York: Free Press, 1968), vol. 1. Recently, Charles Camic has attacked Parsons by arguing that, in fact, the utilitarian theorists were quite sensitive to the nonlogical and collective aspects of social life. Camic's argument points, quite correctly, to the more balanced and multidimensional view of social action and order held by the utilitarians. However, Camic misses the central point of Parsons's claim—namely, that this more comprehensive philosophical image of social life was *not* incorporated into the analytical premises of economic theory. See Charles Camic, "The Utilitarians Revisited," *American Journal of Sociology*, 81 (1976).

53. For an argument along these lines, see Gay, *Enlightenment Anthology*, p. 17, and *The Party of Humanity* (New York: Norton, 1963), p. 289.

54. Immanuel Kant, *Critique of Pure Reason* (New York: St. Martin's Press, 1965), p. 9. Also see Denis Diderot, *Rameau's Nephew and Other Works*, ed. Jacques Barzun and Ralph H. Bowen (New York: Bobbs-Merrill, 1964), p. 298.

55. I have attempted to extend and deepen the analysis by Peter Gay. In one passage, Gay writes: "The philosophes had two enemies: the institutions of Christianity and the idea of hierarchy." Gay, *Party of Humanity*, p. 124. My point is that the critique of Christianity and the idea of hierarchy were part of a more comprehensive critique of all modes of closure, dogmatism, and absolutism; in a word, all forms of illiberalism.

56. Hume, *On Human Nature and the Understanding*, pp. 27–28.

57. Cf. Cassirer, *Philosophy of the Enlightenment*, pp. 13–14; and Charles Frankel, *The Faith of Reason* (New York: Octagon Books, 1969).

58. On the limits of reason and the Enlightenment critique of metaphysics, see Gay, *The Enlightenment*, vol. 1, pp. 143–145.

59. See, for example, D'Alembert, *Preliminary Discourse*, p. 112.

60. Voltaire writes: "It is undeniably a terrible reproach that the Christian church should have been perpetually torn with strife, and that blood should have been shed for so many centuries by men who proclaimed the god of peace. Paganism knew no such fury. . . . The spirit of dogma bred the madness of religious wars in the minds of men." Voltaire, *Age of Louis XIV*, p. 394.

61. On the philosophes' opposition to dogmatic religion, yet advocacy of some form of natural religion, see Ira O. Wade, *The Structure and Form of the French Enlightenment* (Princeton, N.J.: Princeton University Press, 1977), vol. 2, p. 413.

62. See Kant, *Critique of Pure Reason*, pp. 28–32.

63. D'Alembert, *Preliminary Discourse*, p. 26.

64. Gay, *Enlightenment Anthology*, p. 285.

65. Compare the discussion by Charles Taylor, *Hegel* (Cambridge, England: Cambridge University Press, 1975).

66. Regarding the general transformation from cosmos to secularism, see Alexandre Koyré, *From the Closed World to the Infinite Universe* (Baltimore: Johns Hopkins University Press, 1957). For an analysis of the role of the Enlightenment in the articulation of a secular order, see Crocker, *Age of Crisis*, pp. 4–56; and *Ethical Thought in the French Enlightenment* (Baltimore: Johns Hopkins University Press, 1963).

Chapter 2

1. I borrow the term "counter-Enlightenment" from the enormously learned essay by Isaiah Berlin, "The Counter-Enlightenment," in *Against the Current* (New York: Viking Press, 1980).

2. Robert Nisbet writes: "The conservatives at the beginning of the

nineteenth century form an Anti-Enlightenment. There is not a work, not a major idea indeed, in the conservative renaissance that does not seek to refute ideas of the philosophes." Nisbet, *The Sociological Tradition* (New York: Basic Books, 1966), p. 12. Also see Karl Mannheim, "Conservative Thought," in *From Karl Mannheim*, ed. Kurt Wolff (New York: Oxford University Press, 1971). The classic statement still remains Ernst Troeltsch's "The Ideas of Natural Law and Humanity in Western Politics," in Otto Giercke, *Natural Law and the Theory of Society: 1500–1800*, ed. Ernest Barker (Boston: Beacon Press, 1957).

3. Ernst Cassirer, *The Problem of Historical Knowledge: Philosophy, Science, and History Since Hegel* (New Haven: Yale University Press, 1974), p. 224.

4. Jack Lively, "Introduction," in Joseph de Maistre, *Works* (New York: Schocken Books, 1971), p. 32.

5. Peter Gay, *The Enlightenment*, vol. 2, p. 381. Hans-Georg Gadamer demonstrates the underlying epistemological continuities between the Enlightenment and Romantic historical consciousness. See Gadamer, *Truth and Method*, pp. 246–253.

6. Adam Ferguson, *An Essay on the History of Civil Society*, 2nd ed. (London: Printed for A. Millar and T. Caddell, 1768), p. 97.

7. Voltaire, *Works*, vol. 24, p. 9.

8. Johann Gottfried von Herder, "Yet Another Philosophy of History," in *J. G. Herder on Social and Political Culture*, ed. F. M. Barnard (Cambridge, England: Cambridge University Press, 1969), p. 181.

9. Montesquieu, *Laws*, p. lxvii.

10. Quoted in Gay, *The Enlightenment*, vol. 2, p. 382.

11. Hume, *Essential Works*, p. 458.

12. See George Iggers, *The German Conception of History* (Middletown, Conn.: Wesleyan University Press, 1968).

13. See, for example, Friedrich Meinecke, *Cosmopolitanism and the National State* (Princeton, N.J.: Princeton University Press, 1970).

14. Quoted in F. C. Green, *Rousseau and the Idea of Progress* (Oxford: Clarendon Press, 1950), p. 4.

15. Arguments which dissent from viewing Hegel as a conservative

have been made by Herbert Marcuse in *Reason and Revolution* (Boston: Beacon Press, 1968), and by Charles Taylor in *Hegel.* The analyses by Jürgen Habermas in *Theory and Practice* and Joachim Ritter in *Hegel and the French Revolution* (Cambridge, Mass.: MIT Press, 1982) effectively refute the interpretation of Hegel as a political conservative.

16. Robert Nisbet, *The Sociological Tradition*, p. 13.

17. Joseph de Maistre, *Works*, ed. Jack Lively (New York: Schocken Books, 1971), p. 108.

18. Cf. Albert Salomon, *The Tyranny of Progress: Reflections on the Origins of Sociology;* Robert Spaemann, *Der Ursprung der Soziologie aus dem Geist der Restauration;* Herbert Marcuse, *Reason and Revolution;* Irving Zeitlin, *Ideology and the Development of Sociological Theory* (Englewood Cliffs, N.J.: Prentice-Hall, 1968); and Nisbet, *The Sociological Tradition.*

19. Criticisms of the conservative thesis are to be found as well in Anthony Giddens, "Classical Social Theory and the Origins of Modern Sociology," *American Journal of Sociology*, 81 (1976). Also see Gianfranco Poggi, "The Chronic Trauma: The Great Transformation, Restoration Thought and the Sociological Tradition," *British Journal of Sociology*, 19 (1968).

20. See Lewis Coser, *Masters of Sociological Thought*, 2nd ed. (New York: Harcourt Brace Jovanovich, 1977), p. 151.

21. See Anthony Giddens, "Four Myths in the History of Social Thought," in *Studies in Social and Political Theory* (New York: Basic Books, 1977), p. 215.

22. Lewis Coser, "Durkheim's Conservatism and Its Implications for His Sociological Theory," in Emile Durkheim et al., *Essays on Sociology and Philosophy*, ed. Kurt Wolff (New York: Harper & Row, 1960). For a similar interpretation regarding the whole of sociology, see Jürgen Habermas, "Kritishe und Konservative Aufgaben der Soziologie," in *Theorie und Praxis* (Neuwied: Luchterhand, 1967); also see Hermann Strasser, *The Normative Structure of Sociology: Conservative and Emancipatory Themes in Social Thought* (London: Routledge & Kegan Paul, 1976).

23. Writing about the resurgence of conservatism in Germany between 1890 and World War I, Fritz Stern remarks: "They attacked the progress of modernity—the growing liberalism and

secularism. They enumerated the discontents of Germany's industrial civilization and warned against the loss of faith, of unity, of 'values.' All were foes of commerce and cities as well—heroic vitalists who denigrated reason and routine." In Stern's view, the first decades of the twentieth century in Germany and France witnessed a virtual "conservative revolution"—whose major spokesmen, however, were outside mainstream academia. See Fritz Stern, *The Politics of Cultural Despair* (Berkeley and Los Angeles: University of California Press, 1961), pp. xl, xvi.

24. See Arthur Lovejoy's essays on Romanticism published in his *Essays in the History of Ideas* (Baltimore: Johns Hopkins University Press, 1948).

25. For analyses that stress, perhaps too much, this modernist current of Romanticism, see Alvin W. Gouldner, "Romanticism and Classicism: Deep Structures in Social Science," in *For Sociology* (New York: Basic Books, 1973); Morse Peckham, *The Triumph of Romanticism* (Columbia: University of South Carolina Press, 1971); and R. A. Foakes, *The Romantic Assertion* (London: Methuen, 1958).

26. Cf. Mannheim, "Conservative Thought"; and Klaus Epstein, *The Genesis of German Conservatism* (Princeton, N.J.: Princeton University Press, 1966).

27. On the two sides of Romanticism, and the triumph of collectivism in the later phases, see Fritz Lübbe, *Die Wendung vom Individualismus zur Sozialen Gemeinschaft im Romantischen Roman* (Berlin: Junker u. Dunnhaupt, 1931). The same argument is made by Friedrich Meinecke in *Cosmopolitanism and the National State.* Both these studies suffer, however, in that they underemphasize the tension between these two sides of Romanticism and do not see that they are less chronological phases than concurrent trends of romantic thought.

28. See, for example, Johann Gottlieb Fichte, *Science of Knowledge* (New York: Appleton-Century-Crofts, 1970), p. 26: also see F. W. J. Schelling, *System of Transcendental Idealism* (Charlottesville: University of Virginia Press, 1978).

29. Fichte, *Science of Knowledge*, p. 37.

30. Quoted in M. H. Abrams, *Natural Supernaturalism* (New York: Norton, 1971), p. 28.

31. By far the best historical inquiry into the relation of romanticism and German sociology is the superb work by Fritz Ringer, *The Decline of the German Mandarins* (Cambridge, Mass.: Harvard University Press, 1969).

32. Hans Freyer, "Die Romantiker," in *Gründer der Soziologie*, ed. Fritz Karl Mann (Jena: G. Fischer, 1932), pp. 94–95.

33. Helmut Schelsky, *Ortbestimmung der Deutschen Soziologie* (Düsseldorf: E. Diederich, 1959), p. 12.

34. Arthur Mitzman's arguments can be found in the following works: "Anti-Progress: A Study in the Romantic Roots of German Sociology," *Social Research*, 33 (1966); *The Iron Cage* (New York: Grosset & Dunlap, 1969); and *Sociology and Estrangement* (New York: Knopf, 1973).

35. See Mitzman, *Sociology and Estrangement*, pp. 26, 31–32.

36. See Georg Iggers, *The German Conception of History*, pp. 127, 240; Walter Rohlfing, "Fortschrittsglaube in Wilhelminischen Deutschland" (Ph.D. diss., University of Göttingen, 1955).

37. What Max Weber admired in Stefan George was the "seriousness," "devotion," and artistic subtlety of his poetry; he was repelled by the cultish anti-modernism of George and his disciples. Marianne Weber puts this well: "He was highly impressed by its [George's poetry's] great artistry, but he could not find in it the *religious* prophethood that the disciples ascribed to their master—just as he rejected any sort of cult created about a contemporary and any elevation of a human being to the position of an authority on *all* of existence as 'deification of a living creature.' Also, the poet's negative attitude towards the formative forces of modern culture struck him as alien and unfruitful, though Weber was keenly aware of what was wrong with this culture." Max Weber himself was to write: "I suppose that in decisive points Stephan George and his pupils in the final analysis serve 'other gods' than I, no matter how highly I may esteem their art and their intentions." Marianne Weber, *Max Weber, A Biography* (New York: Wiley, 1975), pp. 457, 459.

38. Max Weber, "Religious Rejections of the World and Their Directions," in *From Max Weber*, ed. Hans Gerth and C. Wright Mills (New York: Oxford University Press, 1946), pp. 353–355; henceforth cited as *From Max Weber*. I develop the relation of

Weber to romanticism and modernity in chapters 10 and 11. For an historical argument that parallels mine in linking Weber to modernism and liberalism, see Ringer, *Decline of the German Mandarins*, pp. 132–133, 170–171, 213–214.

39. See Maurice Mandelbaum, *History, Man, and Reason: A Study in Nineteenth-Century Thought* (Baltimore: Johns Hopkins University Press, 1974); and Michael Ermarth, *Wilhelm Dilthey* (Chicago: University of Chicago Press, 1978), pp. 37–90.

40. Irving Babbitt, *Rousseau and Romanticism* (Boston: Houghton Mifflin, 1919).

41. See Lucio Colletti, *From Rousseau to Lenin* (New York: Monthly Review Press, 1972).

42. Lester Crocker, *Rousseau's Social Contract* (Cleveland: Case Western University Press, 1968).

43. Stephen Ellenburg, *Rousseau's Political Philosophy* (Ithaca, N.Y.: Cornell University Press, 1976).

44. On Rousseau's doctrine of progress, see the very fine essay by F. C. Green, *Rousseau and the Idea of Progress*.

45. Quoted in C. H. Driver, "Morelly and Mably," in *The Social and Political Ideas of Some Great French Thinkers of the Age of Reason*, ed. F. J. C. Hearnshaw (New York: Barnes & Noble, 1950), p. 239.

46. Quoted in Émile Durkheim, *Socialism*, ed. Alvin W. Gouldner (New York: Collier Books, 1962), p. 82.

47. Ibid., p. 86.

48. Kingsley Martin, *The Rise of French Liberal Thought* (New York: New York University Press, 1954), p. 242.

49. Driver, "Morelly and Mably," p. 226.

50. Ibid., p. 243.

51. G. D. H. Cole, *Socialist Thought: The Forerunners, 1789–1850* (New York: St. Martin's Press, 1962), pp. 11–12.

52. J. L. Talmon, *The Rise of Totalitarian Democracy* (Boston: Beacon Press, 1952), p. 17.

53. Martin, *The Rise of French Liberal Thought*, p. 242.

54. Ibid., p. 249.

55. Durkheim's argument is to be found in *Socialism*, pp. 80–105.

56. See R. B. Rose, *Gracchus Babeuf: The First Revolutionary Communist* (Stanford, Calif.: Stanford University Press, 1978).

57. John Anthony Scott, ed., *The Defense of Gracchus Babeuf* (New York: Schocken Books, 1967), p. 91.

58. Ibid., p. 57.

59. Ibid., p. 92.

60. Quoted in Talmon, *Totalitarian Democracy*, p. 184.

61. Scott, *The Defense of Gracchus Babeuf*, p. 94.

62. Ibid., p. 105.

63. See Irving Zeitlin, *Ideology and the Development of Sociological Theory;* and Gören Therborn, *Science, Class, and Society* (London: New Left Books, 1976).

64. Cf. Talmon, *Totalitarian Democracy*, p. 60.

65. See Eugene Weber, *Peasants into Frenchmen: The Modernization of Rural France, 1870–1914* (Stanford, Calif.: Stanford University Press, 1976); R. D. Anderson, *France, 1870–1914: Politics and Society* (London: Routledge & Kegan Paul, 1977).

66. Cf. George Lichtheim, *The Origins of Socialism* (New York: Praeger, 1969), p. 88.

67. Within the French revolutionary tradition, only Blanqui appears to have incorporated secular presuppositions into his social theory and critique of bourgeois society. See Alan B. Spitzer, *The Revolutionary Theories of Louis Blanqui* (New York: Columbia University Press, 1957).

Summary of Part One

1. There are several good monographs on British social thought. The following should be consulted: Philip Abrams, ed., *The Origins of British Sociology, 1848–1914* (Chicago: University of Chicago Press, 1968); W. G. Runciman, *Sociology in Its Place* (Cambridge, England: Cambridge University Press, 1970), chap. 1; Geoffrey Hawthorn, Enlightenment and Despair; J. W. Burrow, *Evolution and Society* (Cambridge, England: Cambridge University Press, 1966); and Stefan Collini, "Sociology and Idealism in Britain, 1880–1920," *Archives Européennes de Sociologie*, 19 (1978). Regarding the analytical development of English

social theory, the best treatment, in my view, remains Talcott Parsons, *The Structure of Social Action.*

PART TWO: Marx
Introduction

1. On the relevant biographical facts, see David McLellan, *Karl Marx: His Life and Thought* (New York: Harper & Row, 1977); Fritz Raddatz, *Karl Marx: A Political Biography* (Boston: Little, Brown, 1979); and Isaiah Berlin, *Karl Marx* (New York: Oxford University Press, 1968).

2. Raddatz, *Karl Marx*, pp. 6, 22.

3. See Karl Marx and Friedrich Engels, *Collected Works*, 17 vols. to date (New York: International Publishers, 1980), vol. 1; henceforth cited simply as *Collected Works.*

4. Ibid., p. 18. The translation has been modified. Henceforth, when I modify translations, I will cite the German edition as well: Marx and Engels, *Werke* (Berlin: Dietz Verlag, 1956–1967), supplementary volume, part 1, p. 8.

5. Marx attended Savigny's classes at Berlin and was personally introduced to Saint-Simon not only by his father and Baron von Westphalen but also by his Berlin teacher Eduard Gans. Mention should also be made of Marx's close relation to the historian Karl Köppen, of whom not enough is known. On the relation between Saint-Simon and Marx, see Georges Gurvitch, "La Sociologie du jeune Marx," in *La Vocation actuelle de la sociologie* (Paris: Presses Universitaires de France, 1950).

6. David McLellan has shown the extent to which Marx borrowed from the ideas of the other Young Hegelians. See McLellan's *The Young Hegelians and Karl Marx* (New York: Praeger, 1969).

7. *Collected Works*, vol. 1, p. 28; *Werke*, suppl. vol., part 1, p. 260.

8. *Collected Works*, vol. 1, p. 85; *Werke*, suppl. vol., part 1, p. 326.

9. See McLellan, *The Young Hegelians*, p. 8.

10. Regarding Marx's intellectual outlook between 1841 and 1842, Richard Hunt concludes: "All in all, Marx used his journalism to affirm the principles of German and European liberalism in a version now expressly democratic and *covertly* republican." Richard N. Hunt, *The Political Ideas of Marx and Engels: Marxism*

and Totalitarian Democracy, 1818–1850 (Pittsburgh: University of Pittsburgh Press, 1974), p. 39.

11. On the crucial relation between Feuerbach's critique of Hegel and the development of Marx's revolutionary standpoint, see Shlomo Avineri, *The Social and Political Thought of Karl Marx* (Cambridge, England: Cambridge University Press, 1971).

12. Quoted in McLellan, *Karl Marx*, p. 64.

13. For instances of Marx's idealism during this period, see *Collected Works*, vol. 3, pp. 137, 144.

14. Marx' materialism, of course, must not be understood in a metaphysical way, as, for example, one finds it in Engels's *Dialectics of Nature* (New York: International Universities Press, 1940). For an elucidation of the meaning of Marx's *historical* materialism, see Robert C. Tucker, *Philosophy and Myth in Karl Marx* (Cambridge, England: Cambridge University Press, 1965), pp. 177–186. For an attempt to obviate a strictly naturalistic interpretation of historical materialism by providing a transcendental reading of Marx, see Jürgen Habermas, *Knowledge and Human Interests* (Boston: Beacon Press, 1972), chap. 2.

15. Regarding Marx's perception of bourgeois society as turning against its liberal principles, see *Collected Works*, vol. 5, p. 439; vol. 6, p. 490.

Chapter 3

1. Cf. Leszek Kolakowski, *Main Currents of Marxism* (Oxford: Clarendon Press, 1978), vol. 1, p. 410.

2. *Collected Works*, vol. 5, pp. 195–196.

3. Ibid., vol. 4, p. 126.

4. Ibid., vol. 5, p. 3.

5. Ibid., vol. 3, pp. 332–333.

6. Ibid., p. 332.

7. Ibid., vol. 4, p. 192.

8. Ibid., p. 139.

9. Ibid., vol. 3, p. 336.

10. Ibid., p. 299; *Werke*, suppl. vol., part 1, p. 539.

11. Throughout Marx's writings one can find various programmatic statements of this dialectical conception of social theory. See, for example, *Collected Works*, vol. 5, p. 53; and Karl Marx, *Theories of Surplus Value* (Moscow: Progress Publishers, 1975), vol. 1, p. 285. Recently, a number of interpretations of Marx have appeared which point to Marx's tendency to reduce, at a metatheoretical level, the idealist moment to a strictly materialist anthropology and epistemology. See, for example, Jürgen Habermas, *Knowledge and Human Interests;* Albrecht Wellmer, *The Critical Theory of Society* (New York: Herder & Herder, 1971); and Trent Schroyer, *The Critique of Domination* (Boston: Beacon Press, 1975). Jeffrey Alexander, in a *tour de force* effort, has attempted to take this argument one step further, claiming that though Marx's early writings and some of his political and historical essays follow a multidimensional logic, his systematic theory of society, from *The German Ideology* on, proceeds in terms of the primacy of instrumental action, i.e., individual action is explained in terms of constraining "external" conditions. See Alexander, *Theoretical Logic in Sociology*. Without gainsaying the reductionist current in Marx—in fact, I explore ideological dimensions of this tension in Chapter 5—I believe a multidimensional logic is built into the premises of Marx's critique of capitalism. By identifying his analysis of capitalism as a critique, Marx makes it known that under implicit consideration is the dialectic of consciousness or normative action. The critique of capitalism, as is well known, had two sides. First, it was a critique of the "objective" conditions of modern society conceived of as a capitalist society. Marx analyzed the mechanisms of societal reproduction in terms of socioeconomic production. On the other hand, the critique simultaneously had as its object the science of political economy. Classical economics was the object of critique because, in its ideological aspects, it expressed and legitimated the moral beliefs which functioned as the normative basis of capitalism. Marx's critique presupposed the efficacy of ideas and moral conceptions in the patterning of capitalist social relations. Practically speaking, the aim of the critique was to delegitimize the "bourgeois ideology" and infuse into the culture of capitalism a critical spirit that would find a "natural" carrier in the working classes. Marx's critique was therefore twofold. First, it was a critique of the

"objective" conditions of capitalism; second, it was a critique
of the ideational or normative basis of capitalism. It is the in-
separability of these two aspects of Marx's critique of capitalism
that gives his substantive social theory its dialectical character.
Without grasping the critique of consciousness that Marx built
into his analysis of capitalism, one is left with a quasi-positivist
and reductionist social theory. In a sense, this line of reasoning
does not refute Alexander's claim, since his argument is that
Marx's reductionism is at the level of his explanation of social
action and order, not at a philosophical, anthropological, or in-
tentional level. For an attempt to interpret the tension between
determinism and voluntarism in Marx without suppressing it
or reducing it to mechanical determinism, see Alvin Gouldner,
The Two Marxisms (New York: Seabury Press, 1980).

12. *Collected Works*, vol. 3, p. 75; *Werke*, vol. 1, p. 279.

13. This theme is developed explicitly in Marx's early writings, particularly in *A Critique of Hegel's Doctrine of the State* and "On
the Jewish Question." Both essays are found in *Collected Works*,
vol. 3.

14. Karl Marx, *Grundrisse* (New York: Vintage Books, 1974), p. 325.

15. Karl Marx, *Capital*, (New York: International Publishers, 1973),
vol. 1, p. 488.

16. Ibid., p. 487.

17. Ibid.

18. *Collected Works*, vol. 3, p. 296; *Werke*, suppl. vol., part 1, p. 536.

19. Karl Löwith, *Meaning in History* (Chicago: University of Chicago
Press, 1949); Robert Tucker, *Philosophy and Myth in Karl Marx;*
M. H. Abrams, *Natural Supernaturalism* (New York: Norton,
1971); and Eric Voegelin, *From Enlightenment to Revolution*
(Durham, N.C.: Duke University Press, 1975). For arguments
which highlight Marx's integration of Romanticism into a modernist framework, see Paul Breines, "Marxism, Romanticism,
and the Case of Georg Lukàcs," *Studies in Romanticism*, 16
(1977): 475–476; Gouldner, "Romanticism and Classicism: Deep
Structures in Social Science," in *For Sociology;* and Michael
Löwy, "Marxism and Revolutionary Romanticism," *Telos*, 49
(1981). Jürgen Habermas has argued convincingly that Marx

takes over the idealist presupposition or ideal of society as a unified moral order which serves as a standard against which to criticize bourgeois society. However, Marx avoids idealism by arguing that this ideal is anticipated in the conflict-ridden conditions of bourgeois society. Moreover, Marx rejects the idealist premise of an absolute subject guaranteeing, in the end, the reconciliation of all conflicts. For Marx, the subject of history is the human species forming itself through its practical activity. Thus, transcendence is necessarily contingent upon the conditions of existence and the formation of the will to transcendence. See Jürgen Habermas, *Theory and Practice* (Boston: Beacon Press, 1972), pp. 217–218.

20. See Abrams, *Natural Supernaturalism.*

21. Compare the following statement by Leszek Kolakowski: "It appears in fact that the theory in question, together with the paradigmatic image of a lost paradise, is an unchanging feature of man's speculation about himself, assuming different forms in different cultures but equally capable of finding expression within a religious or a radically anti-religious framework." Kolakowski, *Main Currents of Marxism*, vol. 1, p. 39.

22. *Collected Works*, vol. 3, p. 80; *Werke*, vol. 1, p. 284.

23. *Collected Works*, vol. 3, p. 80.

24. Ibid., p.81; *Werke*, vol. 1, p. 285.

25. *Collected Works*, vol. 3, p. 164; *Werke*, vol. 1, p. 366.

26. For an argument which maintains that Marx was primarily an individualist in his theorizing, see Louis Dumont, *From Mandeville to Marx* (Chicago: University of Chicago Press, 1977), pp. 137, 167. Dumont's argument is complex, but I believe that he conflates Marx's ideological commitment to individualism with analytical individualism. On the problematics of analytical individualism and holism in Marx, see Alexander, *Theoretical Logic in Sociology*, vol. 2.

27. Cf. *Collected Works*, vol. 3, p. 299; vol. 5, p. 475.

28. Ibid., vol. 5, p. 86.

29. Ibid., vol. 6, p. 170.

30. Ibid., vol. 5, p. 78.

31. Ibid., vol. 3, p. 299.

32. Marx, *Grundrisse*, p. 496.

33. Ibid., p. 83.

34. Ibid., p. 84.

35. Ibid., p. 156.

36. Ibid., p. 84.

37. For a penetrating analysis of Marx's general view of social reality and, in particular, his treatment of the problem of social order, see Gianfranco Poggi, *Images of Society* (Stanford: Stanford University Press, 1972).

38. *Collected Works*, vol. 6, p. 487; *Werke*, vol. 4, p. 465.

39. Marx, *Grundrisse*, p. 410.

40. Cf. Shlomo Avineri, *Social and Political Thought of Karl Marx*, pp. 162–174.

41. Karl Marx, *Surveys from Exile*, ed. David Fernbach (New York: Vintage Books, 1974) pp. 299–300.

42. Marx, *Grundrisse*, p. 162.

Chapter 4

1. Aristotle's critique of *chrematistic* is instructive for both its clarity and its limitations. Commerce, Aristotle reasoned, asserts the accumulation of monetary wealth as the highest goal of all activity. For all those engaged in commerce, "the whole idea of their lives is that they ought to increase their money without limit." *The Basic Works of Aristotle*, ed. Richard McKeon (New York: Random House, 1941) p. 1139. Towards this end, Aristotle said, "men turn every quality or art into a means of getting wealth; this they conceive to be the end and to the promotion of the end they think all things must contribute" (p. 1140). Aristotle concluded, "in this art of wealth-getting there is no limit to the end, which is riches of the spurious kind" (p. 1139). Aristotle, in words anticipating Marx's own critique, attacks commerce for transforming all aspects of nature into mere means for the accumulation of wealth. By converting natural and human factors into instrumentalities, commerce damages our rich inner life; commerce destroys the unity between the individual, nature, and community. In its historical context, Aristotle's critique of commerce was intended to support the

preexisting order of the *Oikos* and *Polis*. Aristotle's critique of commerce is, in other words, predicated upon the idea of a relatively fixed and self-sufficient order of the cosmos. Hence, its limitation: Aristotle was unable to conceive of the possibility of combining economic progress and individualism with social solidarity. A good deal of Aristotle's critique, which of course can be found in Plato and other Greek literary figures, entered into the mainstream of Western culture and reappeared particularly forcefully in the French revolutionary tradition and Romanticism.

2. This is the argument clearly implied by Avineri. For a critique of Avineri's position, see Dick Howard, *The Development of the Marxian Dialectic* (Carbondale: Southern Illinois University Press, 1972). There is, however, a sense in which Marx continued to work within the premises of German idealism. Marx's critique remained transcendental in the Kantian sense. In Kant's critique of reason, critique was identified with the epistemological effort aimed at uncovering the conditions of possible experience or knowing. Within Kant's idealist framework, the constitutive activity of the subject was limited to its synthetic form-giving categorical functions. Critique unmasked the false claims of reason to go beyond this form-giving activity. Fichte expanded the role of the subject to the complete constitution of experience— thereby reasserting the primacy of the ontological moment as a necessary step in arriving at a consistent idealism. In Hegel, critique took a further step: its task was to account for the historical self-generation of the subject who constitutes the world. Marx sought to replace an idealist conception of the process of subject-object constitution with the "materialist" notion of labor or practical-critical activity. Nevertheless, Marx's theorizing follows the mode of transcendental inquiry. See Habermas, *Knowledge and Human Interests*, chaps. 2 and 3.

3. George Lichtheim, *The Origins of Socialism*, (New York: Praeger, 1969), p. 179; also see Sidney Hook, *From Hegel to Marx* (New York: Reynal & Hitchcock, 1936), p. 204.

4. Regarding Hess's indebtedness to French egalitarianism, see Hampden J. Jackson, *Marx, Proudhon, and European Socialism* (New York: Collier Books, 1962), p. 39; on Hess's impact on Marx, see McLellan, *The Young Hegelians and Karl Marx*, p. 142.

5. Weitling's influence on Marx has been downplayed on the basis

of Marx's rather abrupt and angry repudiation of Weitling's politics during the early days of the Communist Correspondence Committee in Brussels. However, during his early intellectual development, Marx held Weitling in the highest regard, as is illustrated by the following statement: "As for the educational level or capacity for education of the German workers in general, I call to mind *Weitling's* brilliant writings, which as regards theory are often superior even to those of *Proudhon. . . .*" *Collected Works*, vol. 3, p. 202.

6. See George Lichtheim, *Origins of Socialism*, pp. 171, 179; Hampden Jackson, *Marx, Proudhon*, pp. 44, 50; and Lewis Coser, *Masters of Sociological Thought*, (New York: Harcourt Brace Jovanovich, 1977). p. 61.

7. J. L. Talmon, *Political Messianism: The Romantic Phase* (New York: Praeger, 1960), p. 21.

8. See Karl R. Popper, *The Open Society and Its Enemies* (Princeton, N.J.: Princeton University Press, 1971).

9. Compare, for instance, the following declaration by Michael Harrington: "The commitment to democracy dominates Marx's whole life; it can be found in *The Communist Manifesto* and, above all, in *Das Kapital*, and not just in the early writings." Michael Harrington, *Socialism* (New York: Bantam Books, 1977), p. 49.

10. "Marx was the first socialist figure to come to an acceptance of the socialist idea *through* the battle for the consistent extension of democratic control from below. He was the first figure in the socialist movement who, in a personal sense, came through the bourgeois-democratic movement; *through* it to its farthest bounds, and then out by its farthest end. In this sense, he was the first to fuse the struggle for consistent political democracy with the struggle for a socialist transformation. But, it may be asked, wasn't it the case that, in his course from bourgeois democracy to communism, Marx relinquished his early naive notions about political democracy? Not in Marx's view." Hal Draper, *Karl Marx's Theory of Revolution* (New York: Monthly Review Press, 1977), vol. 1, p. 59.

11. This point has been made quite well by Adam Ulam. Despite Marx's "list of indictments against liberal society, Marx was

carried a long way toward acceptance of its values and ethics. . . . The main accusation against liberalism is not the unreality of its values . . . but the hypocrisy inherent in their being combined with the bourgeois system of property. . . . His quarrel with bourgeois society is that through its institution of property it denies to him the realization of his essentially bourgeois and liberal values." Adam Ulam, *The Unfinished Revolution* (New York: Random House, 1960), pp. 100–101.

12. Avineri draws this contrast between the French revolutionaries and Marx as follows: "The Socialists and Proudhonists . . . were all more than sceptical about political liberalism. This scepticism, turned into radical and uncritical hatred, sometimes brought them into direct or indirect alliance with the aristocracy and the autocracy of the Ancient Regime against the common enemy—the bourgeoisie and political liberalism. Marx, with all his critique of bourgeois liberalism, always supports political liberalism against the traditional Right. . . . For Marx socialism grows out of the contradictions inherent in bourgeois society and political liberalism." Avineri, *Social and Political Thought of Karl Marx*, pp. 182–183.

13. Reacting to Marx's position that the workers must form alliances with the bourgeoisie and prepare themselves for a protracted revolutionary struggle, Andreas Gottschalk, a spokesman for the artisan members of the Communist League, all but accused Marx of being a bourgeois democrat. "You have never been serious about the emancipation of the repressed. The misery of the worker, the hunger of the poor has for you only a scientific, a doctrinaire interest. . . . You do not believe in the permanence of the revolution." Quoted in P. H. Noyes, *Organization and Revolution: Working-Class Associations in the German Revolution of 1848–1849* (Princeton, N.J.: Princeton University Press, 1966), p. 287.

14. *Collected Works*, vol. 5, p. 49.

15. Ibid., vol. 3, pp. 142–143.

16. In the "Afterward to the Second German Edition" of *Capital*, Marx provides what I believe is his clearest definition of the Hegelian perspective. "In its rational form it [the dialectic] is a scandal and abomination to bourgeoisdom and its doctrinaire professors, because it includes in its comprehension an affir-

mative recognition of the existing state of things, at the same time also, the recognition of the negation of that state, of its inevitable breaking up; because it regards every historically developed social form as in fluid movement, and therefore takes into account its transient nature not less than its momentary existence; because it lets nothing impose upon it, and is in its essence critical and revolutionary." Marx, *Capital*, vol. 1, p. 20.

17. *Collected Works*, vol. 3, p. 199.

18. Ibid., vol. 6, pp. 319–320.

19. Marx, *Capital*, vol. 1, p. 503.

20. Karl Marx, "Critique of the Gotha Program," *The First International and After*, ed. David Fernbach (New York: Vintage Books, 1974), p. 346.

21. See Bertell Ollman, "Towards Class Consciousness in the Working Class," *Politics and Society*, 3 (1972).

22. *Collected Works*, vol. 3, p. 313.

23. Ibid., vol. 6, p. 231.

24. Ibid., p. 497.

25. Marx, *The First International and After*, p. 375.

26. Cf. Hunt, *Political Ideas of Marx and Engels*, pp. 147–175; Boris Nicolaievsky, "Toward a History of 'The Communist League,' 1847–1852," *International Review of Social History*, 1 (1956).

27. *Collected Works*, vol. 11, p. 446.

28. Quoted in Hunt, *Political Ideas of Marx and Engels*, p. 265.

29. Marx, *The First International and After*, p. 271.

30. Ibid., p. 299.

31. Ibid., p. 83.

32. Hal Draper writes: "Indeed, in a general way, Marx's socialism as a political program may be most quickly defined . . . as *the complete democratization of society*, not merely of political forms." Draper, *Karl Marx's Theory of Revolution*, vol. 1, p. 282.

33. *Collected Works*, vol. 6, p. 504.

34. Ibid., p. 102.

35. Quoted in Hunt, *Political Ideas of Marx and Engels*, p. 136.

36. Marx, *The First International and After*, pp. 209–211.

37. *Collected Works*, vol. 3, p. 206.

38. Ibid., vol. 3, p. 182.

39. Ibid., p. 206.

40. Ibid., vol. 5, p. 53.

41. Harrington, *Socialism*, p. 62.

42. Lichtheim, *Origins of Socialism*, p. 203.

43. Marx, *The First International and After*, p. 253.

44. Ibid., p. 395.

45. Ibid., p. 324.

46. Ibid., p. 373.

47. Regarding the extent of revolutionary upheaval during this period, see Oscar Hammen, *The Red '48ers* (New York: Scribner's, 1969), pp. 149, 185.

48. Karl Marx, "Address of the Central Committee to the Communist League," *The Revolutions of 1848*, ed. David Fernbach (New York: Vintage Books, 1974), p. 324.

49. Ibid., p. 325.

50. Ibid., p. 324.

51. There is, as one might expect, a great deal of debate on the concept of the dictatorship of the proletariat. There is sufficient secondary literature on this concept to support a thoroughly democratic interpretation of this idea as well. Cf. Hal Draper, "Marx and the Dictatorship of the Proletariat," in *Études de Marxologie*, ed. Maximelien Rubel (Paris: Institut de Science Économique Appliquée, 1962); and Hunt, *Political Ideas of Marx and Engels*, pp. 284–336. The argument made by these authors, to simplify things immensely, is that for Marx the dictatorship of the proletariat signified essentially temporary class rule by the working class. Marx's basically democratic version of this idea contrasts with the Blanquist notion of authoritarian rule by vanguard minority.

52. Quoted in Bertram D. Wolfe, *Marxism* (New York: Dial Press, 1965), p. 157.

53. *Collected Works*, vol. 10, pp. 319–320.

54. Quoted in Nicolaievsky, "Toward a History of 'The Communist League,' 1847–1852," p. 249.

55. Harrington, *Socialism*, p. 49.

56. Avineri, *Social and Political Thought of Karl Marx*, p. 196.

57. Quoted in Wolfe, *Marxism*, p. 196.

58. *Collected Works*, vol. 6, p. 519.

59. Ibid., vol. 7, pp. 505–506.

60. Hunt, *Political Ideas of Marx and Engels*, p. 201.

61. *Collected Works*, vol. 6, p. 212.

62. Ibid., p. 519.

Chapter 5

1. See Kolakowski, *Main Currents of Marxism*, vol. 1, pp. 220–221; Berlin, *Karl Marx*, pp. 14–15.

2. *Collected Works*, vol. 3, p. 295; vol. 6, p. 514.

3. Ibid., vol. 3, pp. 224, 295, 300.

4. Quoted in Herbert Marcuse, *Reason and Revolution: Hegel and the Rise of Social Theory* (Boston: Beacon Press, 1968), p. 338.

5. *Collected Works*, vol. 6, p. 510.

6. Ibid., vol. 6, pp. 516–517; *The First International and After*, pp. 298–299.

7. *Collected Works*, vol. 3, p. 270; *Werke*, suppl. vol., part 1, p. 510.

8. *Capital*, vol. 1, p. 14.

9. *Collected Works*, vol. 3, p. 271; *Werke*, suppl. vol., part 1, p. 510.

10. Karl Marx and Friedrich Engels, *Selected Correspondence, 1846–1895* (New York: International Publishers, 1942), p. 57.

11. *Capital*, vol. 1, p. 8.

12. See chap. 2, "The Metaphysics of Political Economy," of *Poverty of Philosophy* in *Collected Works*, vol. 6.

13. Among the numerous expositions of Marx's theory of capitalist development, I would suggest the following for their lucid character: Paul Sweezy, *The Theory of Capitalist Development* (New York: Monthly Review Press, 1968); Karl Korsch, *Karl Marx* (New York: Russell & Russell, 1963); Ernest Mandel, *The Formation of the Economic Thought of Karl Marx* (New York: Monthly Review Press, 1971); and Anthony Giddens, *Capitalism*

and Modern Social Theory (Cambridge, England: Cambridge University Press, 1971).

14. *Collected Works,* vol. 3, p. 231.

15. Ibid., pp. 271–272.

16. Ibid., p. 280.

17. Quoted in Avineri, *Social and Political Thought of Karl Marx,* p. 60. For a more extensive analysis of these issues in Marx's early writings, see Bertell Ollman, *Alienation;* Istvan Mészáros, *Marx's Theory of Alienation* (London: Merlin Press, 1970); Nicholas Lobkowics, *Theory and Practice: History of a Concept from Aristotle to Marx* (Notre Dame, Ind.: University of Notre Dame Press, 1972); Franz von Magnis, *Normative Voraussetzungen im Denken des Jungen Marx, 1843–1848* (Munich: Karl Alber Frieburg, 1975); and Joachim Israel, *Alienation: From Marx to Modern Sociology* (Atlantic Highlands, N.J.: Humanities Press, 1979).

18. *Capital,* vol. 1, p. 16.

19. Cf. Trent Schroyer, *The Critique of Domination,* pp. 32–33.

20. Cf. Wolfe, *Marxism,* pp. 327–329.

21. Marx, *The First International and After,* p. 81.

22. Ibid., p. 82.

23. Marx, *Grundrisse,* pp. 704–706.

24. For an extensive analysis of this text, see Albrecht Wellmer, *Critical Theory of Society,* pp. 107–114.

25. *Capital,* vol. 3, p. 437.

26. Ibid., p. 440.

27. Ibid.

28. Marx, *Grundrisse,* p. 832.

29. *Capital,* vol. 1, p. 592.

30. Regarding the problem of integrating Enlightenment and romantic themes in German thought, see Charles Taylor, *Hegel* (Cambridge, England: Cambridge University Press, 1975), pp. 3–51.

31. See Lucio Colletti's essay, "Marxism: Science or Revolution?" in *From Rousseau to Lenin: Studies in Ideology and Society* (New York: Monthly Review Press, 1972); also see Gouldner, *The Two*

Marxisms. Another key essay is Jürgen Habermas's "Between Philosophy and Science: Marxism as Critique," in *Theory and Practice.*

32. Cf. Herbert Marcuse, *Eros and Civilization* (Boston: Beacon Press, 1966); Shierry Weber, "Aesthetic Experience and Self-Reflection as Emancipatory Processes," in *Critical Theory,* ed. John O'Neill (New York: Seabury Press, 1976). Charles Taylor provides an exemplary discussion of the German context and systematics of this problem of synthesizing autonomy and expressivism. See Taylor, *Hegel.*

33. *Collected Works,* vol. 3, pp. 276–277; *Werke,* suppl. vol., part 1, p. 517.

34. Cf. the discussion by Tucker, *Philosophy and Myth in Karl Marx,* pp. 150–164.

35. An interesting interpretation of Marx against the horizon of the ancients is Hannah Arendt's *The Human Condition* (Chicago: University of Chicago Press, 1971).

36. Marx, *Grundrisse,* p. 712.

37. Ibid., p. 611.

38. *Capital,* vol. 3, p. 820.

39. It seems to me that it was precisely this reversal that Hannah Arendt failed to see in her critique of Marx. Thus, she did not notice that, in certain significant ways, Marx returned to the conceptualizing of the spheres of necessity and freedom of the ancients.

40. Marx, *Grundrisse,* p. 712.

41. Ibid., p. 693.

Summary of Part Two

1. This position can be traced back to the classical sociological critique of Marx, as well as to the critique of Marx sounded by the revisionism of Bernstein. For recent criticisms of Marx along these lines, see Jürgen Habermas, "Between Philosophy and Science: Marxism as Critique," in *Theory and Practice;* and Norman Birnbaum, "The Crisis in Marxist Sociology," in *Towards a Critical Sociology* (New York: Oxford University Press, 1971).

2. Popper, *The Open Society and Its Enemies;* Talmon, *Political Messianism;* Lewis Feuer, *Ideology and the Ideologists* (New York: Harper & Row, 1975); and Ernst Bloch, *On Karl Marx* (New York: Herder & Herder, 1971).

3. Lukàcs, *History and Class Consciousness* (Cambridge, Mass.: MIT Press, 1973), p. 1.

PART THREE: Durkheim
Introduction

1. Karl Marx and Friedrich Engels, *Selected Correspondence: 1846–1895* (New York: International Publishers, 1942), p. 313.

2. See, for example, Karl Korsch, *Three Essays on Marxism* (New York: Monthly Review Press, 1972), pp. 11–12.

3. Irving Zeitlin, *Ideology and the Development of Sociological Theory* (Englewood Cliffs, N.J.: Prentice-Hall, 1968), p. 235.

4. See Steven Lukes, Émile Durkheim (New York: Penguin Books, 1977), p. 321; Lewis Coser, *Masters of Sociological Thought* (New York: Harcourt Brace Jovanovich, 1977), p. 172.

5. Quoted in Lukes, *Émile Durkheim*, p. 321.

6. Jeffrey Alexander has explored the convergence of Marxism and Durkheim's *Division of Labor in Society* at the level of analytical presuppositions in *Theoretical Logic in Sociology* (Berkeley and Los Angeles: University of California Press, 1982), vol. 2. Also Mark Traugott has shown that a certain reading of Durkheim's morphological analysis of society reveals remarkable parallels with the Marxist tradition. See Traugott, "Introducton," in Durkheim's *On Institutional Analysis* (Chicago: University of Chicago Press, 1978).

7. See Talcott Parsons, *The Structure of Social Action* (New York: Free Press, 1968), vol. 1; Harry Alpert, *Émile Durkheim and His Sociology* (New York: Atheneum, 1961); and Robert Nisbet, *The Sociology of Émile Durkheim* (New York: Oxford University Press, 1974).

8. Anthony Giddens, *Émile Durkheim* (New York: Viking Press, 1978), p. 21.

9. See Durkheim, *The Elementary Forms of the Religious Life* (New York: Free Press, 1965), p. 471; also see Durkheim's review of

Antonio Labriola, in which he maintained: "As for ourselves, we arrived at this proposition [regarding the material origins of consciousness] before we became acquainted with Marx, to whose influence we have in no way been subjected." Durkheim, *On Institutional Analysis*, p. 127.

10. See Durkheim, *On Institutional Analysis*, pp. 129, 137.

11. Compare the statement of Edward Tiryakian: "The major inspirational source and chief theoretician of the French left in the nineteenth century was Pierre-Joseph Proudhon, not Marx, who was to remain relatively insignificant in French socialist circles until the formation of the Communist party and its takeover of the labor movement and *L'Humanité*." See Edward Tiryakian, "Émile Durkheim," in *A History of Sociological Analysis*, ed. Tom Bottomore and Robert Nisbet (New York: Basic Books, 1978), p. 192.

12. See George Lichtheim, *Marxism in Modern France* (New York: Columbia University Press, 1966), pp. 14–15, 19–21; on the French labor movement, see Bernard H. Moss, *The Origins of the French Labor Movement, 1830–1914* (Berkeley and Los Angeles: University of California Press, 1976).

13. Dominick LaCapra, *Émile Durkheim: Sociologist and Philosopher* (Ithaca, N.Y.: Cornell University Press, 1972), p. 22.

14. Anthony Giddens has provided an excellent analysis of the relation between Marxism and Weber and Durkheim in *Capitalism and Modern Social Theory* (Cambridge, England: Cambridge University Press, 1971), pp. 185–204.

15. Quoted in Robert L. Hoffman, *Revolutionary Justice: The Social and Political Theory of P. J. Proudhon* (Urbana: University of Illinois Press, 1972), pp. 226–227.

16. Ibid., p. 108.

17. Ibid., pp. 257–258.

18. Ibid., p. 257.

19. Alpert, *Durkheim and His Sociology*, pp. 26–27.

20. Lukes, *Émile Durkheim*, p. 55–56.

21. Alpert, *Durkheim and His Sociology*, pp. 25–26.

22. Aron writes: "A sociology justifying rationalist individualism but also preaching respect for collective norms—such, it seems

336 NOTES FOR PAGES 153–157

to me, is Durkheim's ideal." Raymond Aron, *Main Currents in Sociological Thought* (New York: Anchor Books, 1968), vol. 2, p. 113.

Chapter 6

1. George Lichtheim, *A Short History of Socialism* (New York: Praeger, 1970), p. 28; George Sabine, *A History of Political Theory* (New York: Holt, Rinehart & Winston, 1965), p. 561; Preserved Smith, *A History of Modern Culture* (New York: Collier Books, 1962), vol. 2, p. 311.

2. See Guido de Ruggiero, *The History of European Liberalism* (Boston: Beacon Press, 1966), pp. 169–172.

3. Quoted in Roger Soltau, *French Political Thought in the Nineteenth Century* (New Haven: Yale University Press, 1931), p. 39.

4. See Gouldner's historical interpretation of Comte's sociology in *The Coming Crisis of Western Sociology* (New York: Avon Books, 1971).

5. See Eugene Weber, *Peasants into Frenchmen: The Modernization of Rural France, 1880–1914* (Stanford: Stanford University Press, 1976), pp. 41, 118–119, 241, 308–309.

6. See René Rémond, *The Right Wing in France* (Philadelphia: University of Pennsylvania Press, 1966).

7. On the French Right during the Third Republic, see LaCapra, *Émile Durkheim*, pp. 38, 56–57.

8. Durkheim, *On Morality and Society*, ed. Robert Bellah (Chicago: University of Chicago Press, 1973), p. 56; also see the excellent historical analysis of the French republicans by R. D. Anderson, *France, 1870–1914: Politics and Society* (London: Routledge & Kegan Paul, 1977), pp. 88–102.

9. Cf. Coser, *Masters of Sociological Thought*, p. 161; and Lukes, *Émile Durkheim*, p. 75.

10. Durkheim, *Suicide* (New York: Free Press, 1951), p. 370.

11. Quoted in Perry M. Sturgess, "Social Theory and Political Ideology: Célestin Bouglé and the Durkheimian School" (Ph.D. diss., City University of New York, 1978), p. 401.

12. See Michael Curtis, *Three Against the Third Republic: Sorel, Barrès, and Maurras* (Princeton, N.J.: Princeton University Press, 1959).

Chapter 7

1. See, for example, Durkheim, *On Institutional Analysis*, p. 49.
2. Durkheim, *The Division of Labor in Society*, p. 421.
3. Ibid.
4. Durkheim, *On Morality and Society*, pp. 37–38.
5. Ibid., pp. 38–39.
6. Ibid., p. 39.
7. Durkheim, *Division*, p. 45.
8. Durkheim, *The Rules of Sociological Method* (New York: Free Press, 1966), pp. 14–15.
9. See, for example, Durkheim, *Textes* (Paris: Les Éditions de Minuit, 1975), vol. 1, pp. 148–158.
10. Regarding Durkheim's critique of Comte's unilinear evolutionism, see ibid., pp. 68–70, 122–129.
11. Durkheim, *Socialism*, ed. Alvin Gouldner (New York: Collier Books, 1962), p. 204.
12. Ibid., p. 151.
13. *Division*, p. 182.
14. *Textes*, vol. 2, p. 144.
15. Recently, there has been some debate regarding the nature and scope of Spencer's influence upon Durkheim. One commentator has gone so far as to assert that "the major components of Durkheim's sociology . . . were constructed in substantial opposition to Spencer." See Robert Alun Jones, "Durkheim's Response to Spencer: An Essay Toward Historicism in the Historiography of Sociology," *Sociological Quarterly*, 15 (1974): 344. In response to Jones, Robert Perrin has argued that despite Durkheim's criticisms of Spencer, there are many profound points of continuity and convergence in their sociology. Robert Perrin, "Durkheim's Misrepresentation of Spencer: A Reply to Jones' 'Durkheim's Response to Spencer,' " *Sociological Quarterly*, 16 (1975). Jones clearly overstates his case, while Perrin fails to see that Durkheim did theorize from within a different tradition, implying, as Durkheim himself stated, quite opposite presuppositions.
16. See *On Morality and Society*, p. 11.
17. See *On Institutional Analysis*, p. 111.

18. *Division*, p. 193.

19. Durkheim, *Montesquieu and Rousseau: Forerunners of Sociology* (Ann Arbor: University of Michigan Press, 1965), p. 88.

20. Cf. Durkheim, *Moral Education* (New York: Free Press, 1973), p. 50.

21. Cf. Parsons's argument regarding the influence of Rousseau on Durkheim. See Talcott Parsons, "The Life and Work of Émile Durkheim," in Durkheim's *Sociology and Philosophy* (New York: Free Press, 1974).

22. *Montesquieu and Rousseau*, p. 99.

23. Ibid., p. 83.

24. Echoing Rousseau, Durkheim argued: "The progress of industry and that of morality do not necessarily coincide." *Textes*, vol. 1, p. 270.

25. *Division*, p. 379.

26. Ibid., p. 384.

27. Ibid., p. 380.

28. Nisbet couldn't be further off the mark when he writes: "Durkheim rejected individualism on every possible ground. He found it insupportable as a principle of social solidarity, as an ethic or moral value, as a cornerstone of the social order. . . ." Nisbet, *Sociology of Émile Durkheim*, p. 16.

29. Durkheim recognized that the principles of distributive and commutative justice rest upon the same moral sentiment: "the sympathy that man has for man." This moral sentiment, Durkheim argued, points to the arbitrariness of inequalities based upon merit. "But where human sympathy is concerned, even these inequalities can not be justified. For it is man as a human being that we love or should love and regard, not man as a scholar or genius or as an able man of business. . . . Essentially, are not these inequalities of merit fortuitous too?" Durkheim, *Professional Ethics and Civil Morals* (London: Routledge & Kegan Paul, 1957), p. 219. Durkheim was alluding here to a future stage in moral development in which all inequalities, whether based upon birth or merit, are modes of egoism that are inconsistent with the general human sentiment of sympathy. Durkheim called this new moral principle "charity" and suggested that it

corresponds to a post-scarcity socioeconomic system in which distribution could be based upon need, not utility.

30. Durkheim, *Division*, pp. 380–381, and *De la division du travail social* (Paris: Presses Universitaires de France, 1960), p. 374. Where, as in this case, I include a reference to the French edition, the translation has been modified.

31. Durkheim, *Division*, p. 367.

32. Durkheim, *Professional Ethics and Civil Morals*, p. 213.

33. Ibid., p. 214.

34. Durkheim, *Division*, p. 387.

35. Durkheim, *Suicide*, p. 384.

36. Ibid., p. 249.

37. Durkheim, *Division*, pp. 407–408; *De la division du travail social*, pp. 403–404.

38. For arguments paralleling my own, see Joseph Neyer, "Individualism and Socialism in Durkheim," and Melvin Richter, "Durkheim's Politics and Political Theory," in Durkheim, *Essays on Sociology and Philosophy*, ed. Kurt Wolff (New York: Harper & Row, 1960).

Chapter 8

1. Durkheim, *Socialism*, p. 181.

2. Ibid., p. 236.

3. Ibid.; also see Durkheim, *Suicide*, p. 255.

4. Durkheim, *Textes*, vol. 1, pp. 276–278.

5. The influence of German thought on Durkheim is an issue far from settled. The trend has been to situate Durkheim within the internal development of French intellectual history. This is clearly the position taken by Parsons and Lukes. See Parsons, *Structure of Social Action*, vol. 1, p. 307; and Lukes, *Émile Durkheim*, p. 90. Although I, too, situate Durkheim within the democratic tradition of French thought, I believe that the impact of German thought, particularly Kant and the historical economists, was considerable. However, there are two factors which make it difficult to gauge the extent of the German influence. First, many of the central ideas of German thought can be found

in the French tradition. The impact of Kant, for example, was mediated by the neo-critical French idealists, who added, as it were, a distinctively French sense to Kant. Second, as Theodor Adorno noted in his "Introduction" to the German translation of Durkheim's *Sociology and Philosophy,* Durkheim is "lax beim Zitieren seiner Quellen" (Durkheim neglects to cite his sources). Given the national tensions between Germany and France, Durkheim may have been reluctant to acknowledge the extent of the German influence on his thought.

6. Durkheim, *Montesquieu and Rousseau,* p. 34.

7. See, for example, Durkheim's comments on Spencer in *Division,* pp. 193–194. Durkheim noted a similar tendency in Kant: see Durkheim, *On Morality and Society,* p. 47.

8. For an analysis of the instrumentalism of Durkheim's *Division,* see Gianfranco Poggi, *Images of Society* (Stanford, Calif.: Stanford University Press, 1972), pp. 169–189; and Alexander, *Theoretical Logic in Sociology,* vol. 2.

9. Durkheim, *Division,* pp. 14–15.

10. Durkheim, *Suicide,* p. 387.

11. Ibid., p. 380.

12. See Bouglé's "Preface to the Original Edition" of Durkheim's *Sociology and Philosophy,* pp. xxxvii–xli.

13. Durkheim, *Sociology and Philosophy,* pp. 23–24.

14. Ibid., p. 24.

15. Cf. the discussion by Robert Bellah in his "Introduction" to Durkheim's *On Morality and Society,* pp. xix–xxi; also see Mark Traugott's "Introduction" to Durkheim, *On Institutional Analysis.*

16. See the suggestive remarks of Jeffrey Alexander, "Indispensable Durkheim: An Alternative Historical Method to 'Division of Labor,' " *Contemporary Sociology,* 9 (1980); Alexander develops this argument in detail in his *Theoretical Logic,* vol. 2.

17. Durkheim, *The Evolution of Educational Thought* (London: Routledge & Kegan Paul, 1977), p. 75.

18. Ibid., p. 225.

19. Ibid., pp. 284–285.

20. Ibid., p. 339.

21. Durkheim, *Elementary Forms of the Religious Life*, p. 471.

22. See the excellent discussion of Durkheim's theory of society by Edward Tiryakian, "Émile Durkheim," in *A History of Sociological Analysis*, pp. 214–225.

23. Cf. Parsons, *Structure of Social Action*, vol. 1, p. 443.

24. See, for example, Durkheim, *Evolution of Educational Thought*, pp. 320–348.

25. Ibid., p. 348.

PART FOUR: Weber
Introduction

1. On the resurgence of illiberalism during this period, see Fritz Stern, *The Politics of Cultural Despair: A Study of the Rise of the Germanic Ideology* (Berkeley and Los Angeles: University of California Press, 1961) and *The Failure of Illiberalism: Essays on the Political Culture of Modern Germany* (New York: Knopf, 1972); also George L. Mosse, *The Crisis of German Ideology: Intellectual Origins of the Third Reich* (New York: Grosset & Dunlap, 1964).

2. George Lichtheim, *Marxism* (New York: Praeger, 1961).

3. See H. Stuart Hughes, *Consciousness and Society: The Reorientation of European Social Thought, 1890–1930* (New York: Knopf, 1958); and Talcott Parsons, *The Structure of Social Action* (New York: Free Press, 1968), vol. 2.

4. On the ideological significance of neo-Kantianism, see Thomas E. Willey, *Back to Kant: The Revival of Kantianism in German Social and Historical Thought, 1860–1914* (Detroit: Wayne State University Press, 1978); Lichtheim, *Marxism;* Andrew Arato, "The Neo-Idealist Defense of Subjectivity," *Telos*, 21 (1974); and Hans-Ludwig Ollig, *Der Neukantianismus* (Stuttgart: Metzler, 1979).

5. Thomas Willey, *Back to Kant*, p. 9; and Georg Iggers, *The German Conception of History* (Middletown, Conn.: Wesleyan University Press, 1978), p. 128.

6. See, for example, Thomas Burger, *Max Weber's Theory of Concept Formation* (Durham, N.C.: Duke University Press, 1976).

7. Marianne Weber, *Max Weber: A Biography* (New York: Wiley, 1975), p. 319.

8. See William O. Shanahan, "Friedrich Naumann: A Mirror of Wilhelmian Germany," *The Review of Politics*, 13 (1951). Also, on the broader relationship of Protestantism and liberalism, see Walter Nigg, *Geschichte des Religiosen Liberalismus* (Zurich and Leipzig: Max Neihaus, 1937).

9. Quoted in James J. Sheehan, *The Career of Lujo Brentano: A Study of Liberalism and Social Reform in Imperial Germany* (Chicago: University of Chicago Press, 1966), p. 146.

10. Georg Iggers writes: "Nevertheless, the rejection of natural law doctrine was not accompanied in Germany by an equally radical rejection of the ethical and political values associated with the natural law tradition. If by liberalism is meant the affirmation of the notion of the absolute value of the human personality, of human dignity and worth, and the affirmation of the right of individual persons to develop fully their potentialities, then many thinkers of the historicist orientation stood in the liberal tradition, as they did in their demands for constitutional government, due process, individual liberties, and representative institutions. German liberal thought saw in historicism a better theoretical foundation for a theory of liberty than in natural law." Georg Iggers, *The German Conception of History*, p. 272.

11. Paul Honigsheim, for example, writes the following of Weber's intellectual orientation: "At this time Weber formulated his own philosophy, which was a synthesis of Protestant religiosity, neo-Kantian epistemology and ethics, and left-wing, socially-minded liberalism." Paul Honigsheim, "Max Weber: His Religious and Ethical Background and Development," *Church History*, 19 (1950): 22. In addition, Georg Iggers has argued that Weber, along with others, had definite roots in the Western liberal and democratic traditions: "In brief, just as earlier [German] liberal historians had shared Western political ideals, Weber, Troeltsch, and Meinecke, along with philosophers Hermann Cohen and Paul Natorp, supported democratic and even moderately socialist concepts similar to those prevalent in Western countries." Iggers, *The German Conception of History*, p. 128.

12. In response to Parsons's "convergence thesis," a number of interpretations of the historical and systematic development of sociology have stressed the differences between Durkheim and Weber. Reinhard Bendix, for example, speaks of "Two Socio-

logical Traditions," and more recent critics of Parsons have attempted to elaborate in great detail the systematic divergences between Durkheim and Weber. In light of the similar motivations and thematic concerns which I have indicated, it would be a mistake to overemphasize their differences. Although it is true that the social and intellectual context of their sociology produced differences regarding the details of their epistemology and sociology, Parsons was not unaware of this. It appears to me that while Parsons may have gone astray in his argument, the critics of Parsons have not, in the main, addressed Parsons at the level of discourse represented in *The Structure of Social Action*. See Reinhard Bendix, "Two Sociological Traditions," in *Scholarship and Partisanship: Essays on Max Weber* (Berkeley and Los Angeles: University of California Press, 1971). Also see the recent critics of Parsons: Jere Cohen, Lawrence E. Hazelrigg, and Whitney Pope, "On the Divergence of Weber and Durkheim," *American Sociological Review*, 40 (1975). For criticisms of Parsons that address him at the level of discourse represented in *The Structure of Social Action*, see R. Stephen Warner, "Toward a Redefinition of Action Theory," *American Journal of Sociology*, 83 (1978); and Jeffrey Alexander, "Formal and Substantive Voluntarism in the Work of Talcott Parsons," *American Sociological Review*, 43 (1978).

Chapter 9

1. The evidence pointing to the Marxist influence on Weber is substantial. Dieter Lindenlaub, *Richtungskämpfe im Verein für Sozialpolitik* (Wiesbaden: Franz Steiner, 1967) argues that the younger members of the *Verein*, particularly Tönnies, Sombart, and Weber, initiated an intensive discussion of Marx during the early 1890s. A point of critical contention between the older members (Schmoller and Wagner) and younger members, indicates Lindenlaub, centered upon the latter's positive appropriation of Marxism. Lindenlaub provides further documentation that the interest in Marx on the part of the younger *Verein* members differed from that of such economic critics of Marx as Böhm-Bawerk. For Weber and the others, it was the Marxist notion of capitalism (viewed as a totalizing concept within which modern history could be grasped), not the technical economic analysis,

that proved attractive. Contemporaries of Weber, moreover, situated Weber fully within the Marxist tradition. "The works of Weber and Sombart," wrote Naumann, "have renewed Marxist questioning a half century later and with new means." Troeltsch grouped the writings of Weber with the economic historical works of the Marxists. See Lindenlaub, *Richtungskämpfe*, p. 281; and Ernst Troeltsch, *Der Historismus und seine Probleme* (Tübingen: J. C. B. Mohr, 1922), pp. 368–369. Through the writings of Albert Salomon ("Max Weber's Political Ideas," *Social Research*, 2 [1930], Hans Gerth and C. Wright Mills ("Introduction" in *From Max Weber* [New York: Oxford University Press, 1946]), and numerous others, the claim highlighting the importance of Marx in Weber's intellectual development has become a commonplace in Weber scholarship. For strong statements of this thesis, see Irving Zeitlin, *Ideology and the Development of Sociological Theory* (Englewood Cliffs, N.J.: Prentice-Hall, 1968); Coser, *Masters of Sociological Theory* (New York: Harcourt Brace Jovanovich, 1977), p. 228; Alvin W. Gouldner, *The Coming Crisis of Western Sociology* (New York: Avon Books, 1971), p. 121; and Julius Loewenstein, *Marx Against Marxism* (London: Routledge & Kegan Paul, 1980), chap. 15. For a more nuanced interpretation of the Marxist impact on Weber (but one which continues to insist on the primacy of this relationship for Weber's intellectual development), see Anthony Giddens, *Capitalism and Modern Social Theory* (Cambridge, England: Cambridge University Press, 1971), pp. 185–195, and "Marx, Weber, and the Development of Capitalism," *Sociology*, 14 (1970). Those who hold to the thesis that Weber carried on a lifelong dialogue with Marxism further divide into two groups. There are those who maintain that Weber's sociology was a reaction against Marx and represents the bourgeois antithesis to Marxism. This is the position taken by, among others, Parsons, in "Capitalism in Recent German Literature," *Journal of Political Economy*, 37 (1929); and Wolfgang Mommsen, in "Max Weber als Kritiker des Marxismus," *Zeitschrift für Soziologie*, 3 (1974). On the other hand, there are those who maintain that Weber developed a positive critique of Marx and that his sociology must be read as a supplement or completion of Marxism. See Joseph Schumpeter, *Capitalism, Socialism, and Democracy* (New York: Harper & Row, 1942); George Lichtheim, *Marxism;* and Karl Löwith, "Entzauberung des Welt durch Wissenschaft," *Merkur*, 5 (1964). Turning to Weber's early writings, the thesis of the Marxist impact on Weber finds substantial textual support. In several essays between 1893 and 1896, Weber appears to have fully appropriated the Marxist conception of capitalism as the framework for interpreting social change. The extent to which Weber assimilated Marxism is revealed in his 1896 essay on "The Social Causes of the Decline of Ancient Civilization." One short passage will suffice to illustrate Weber's absorption of Marxism: "It is clear, therefore, that the disintegration of the Roman Empire was the inevitable political consequence of a basic economic development: the gradual disappearance of commerce and the expansion of a barter economy. Essentially this disintegration simply meant that the monetarized administrative system and political superstructure of the Empire disappeared, for they were no longer adapted to the infrastructure of a natural economy." Quoted in Weber, *The Agrarian Sociology of Ancient Civilizations* (London: New Left Books, 1976), p. 408. An attempt to demonstrate that this work proceeds within a Marxism framework is argued by Jonathan Weiner, "Max Weber's Marxism: Theory and Method in *The Agrarian Sociology of Ancient Civilizations*," *Theory and Society*, 11 (May 1982). In calling attention to the Marxist influence on Weber, I do not wish to subscribe to the thesis that Weber's sociology is either a negative or positive critique of Marxism. It is clear—and this will be elaborated in Chapter 11—that despite his positive perception of Marxism, Weber's analysis of universal history and the problems of rationalism, rationalization processes, and modernity form an independent analytical project irreducible to Marxian analysis and quite outside its theoretical parameters. However—and this is the point which needs to be emphasized here—at a time when Weber sought an alternative to both German idealism and English economism, Marxism served him as a suitable vehicle through which to articulate his own theoretical synthesis. Recently, Guenther Roth ("The Historical Relationship Between Weber and Marxism," in *Scholarship and Partisanship: Essays on Max Weber*) has suggested that Weber's early materialism derives less from Marx than from the surging currents of economic historiography, which emerged as a reaction to the idealist tradition of German historicism. This argument is made cogent by the fact that Weber's two teachers, Levin Goldschmidt and August Meitzen, were among the pioneers of the new economic history. Nevertheless, it is the distinctively Marxian materialist orientation that one finds in the early Weber. Until we have something approaching a systematic historical study of the full intellectual and social context of Weber's early writings, these issues will remain in part in the domain of ideological analysis and political maneuver.

2. See Weber's 1895 "Freiburg Address" in *Gesammelte Politische Schriften*, ed. Johannes Winckelmann (Tübingen: Mahr, 1971); selections from the "Address" can be found in Weber, *Selections in Translation*, ed. Walter Runciman (Cambridge, England: Cambridge University Press, 1978), pp. 263–264.

3. Weber argues that in southwest Germany the level of agrarian economic development was much higher than in the east. In the southwest the population was denser, there were more towns, and there was communication and economic exchange between regions, which translated into better economic conditions. As a consequence, the peasants were able to pay taxes and rents sufficient to maintain the landed aristocracy. In the east, however, the peasants lacked a developed economic awareness, and only by appropriating the lands could the landed aristocracy maintain an adequate life-style. See Weber's "Capitalism and Rural Society in Germany," in *From Max Weber: Essays in Sociology* (New York: Oxford University Press, 1946), pp. 377–381.

4. Weber, *Selections in Translation*, pp. 263–264.

5. *From Max Weber*, p. 394.

6. Ibid., p. 373.

7. Ibid., p. 370.

8. Ibid., pp. 371–372.

9. Fritz Ringer, *The Decline of the German Mandarins* (Cambridge, Mass.: Harvard University Press, 1969).

10. For more contemporary sociological assessments of this feature of Germany, see Talcott Parsons, "Social Structure and Democracy in Pre-Nazi Germany," in *Essays in Sociological Theory* (New York: Free Press, 1954); and Ralf Dahrendorf, *Society and Democracy in Germany* (New York: Anchor Books, 1967).

11. See Sheehan, *The Career of Lujo Brentano*, p. 133.

12. On the history of German liberalism, see James J. Sheehan, *German Liberalism in the Nineteenth Century* (Chicago: University of Chicago Press, 1978).

Chapter 10

1. Weber repeatedly identified himself both as a bourgeois, as in the Freiburg Address, and as a democrat. See, for example, *From Max Weber*, pp. 71, 370.

2. Weber, *Selections in Translation*, p. 265.

3. See, for example, the essay by T. S. Simey, "Max Weber: Man of Affairs or Theoretical Sociologist?" *Sociological Review*, 14 (1966).

4. See the fascinating discussion between Weber and Sombart on the relation between technology and culture, which took place in Frankfurt at the first German Sociological Meeting. Weber's lecture is reprinted in Max Weber, *Gesammelte Aufsätze zur Sociologie und Sozialpolitik*, ed. Marianne Weber (Tübingen: Mohr, 1924).

5. *From Max Weber*, p. 372.

6. Weber, *Selections in Translation*, p. 265.

7. On the failure of German liberals to effect a decisive realignment, see Guenther Roth, *The Social Democrats in Imperial Germany* (New York: Arno Press, 1977).

8. Thomas Willey writes: "The liberal movement in Germany remained essentially anti-democratic to the end of the century. . . ." Willey, *Back to Kant*, p. 16. On the sustained resistance to working-class politics, see Hojo Holborn, *A History of Modern Germany, 1840–1945* (New York: Knopf, 1973).

9. Sheehan, *German Liberalism*.

10. Weber, *Selections in Translation*, p. 264.

11. Max Weber, *The Protestant Ethic and the Spirit of Capitalism* (New York: Free Press, 1958), p. 90.

12. It may perhaps be argued that my interpretation of Weber is severely compromised by his nationalism. A number of commentators, Wolfgang Mommsen and Raymond Aron being the most notable, have argued that the power-political interests of the nation-state were the supreme value for Weber. This *Macht-*

politik led Weber to legitimate imperialism as a component of liberal ideology. This perspective attributes to Weber a cynical view of democratization: Weber's advocacy of universal civil and political rights and representative institutions are viewed as simply necessary conditions of domestic stability and an aggressive foreign policy. However, even proponents of this interpretation admit that, after 1900, Weber dropped the militaristic and imperialistic side of his nationalism and became a fierce critic of *Machtpolitik:* "There is no more pernicious distortion of political power," Weber wrote, "than the worship of power for itself. The pure Machtpolitik ... may provide a powerful effect, but his work has no meaning and leads nowhere." Quoted in Robert Beetham, *Max Weber and the Theory of Politics* (London: Allen & Unwin, 1974), p. 137. Moreover, the above view of Weber is further weakened by the fact that it devalues Weber's abiding commitment to individual autonomy and social justice. Weber's struggle for universal suffrage and parliamentary government was not cynical but reflects Weber's sustained concern for freedom, moral autonomy, and the "dignity of the personality." See Anthony Giddens, *Politics and Sociology in the Thought of Max Weber* (London: MacMillan Press, 1972), pp. 55–56; and Beetham, *Max Weber and the Theory of Politics*, p. 113. The whole range of opinions in the debate concerning Weber's political ideology is represented in the 1964 Heidelberg conference on Max Weber. See Otto Stammer, ed., *Max Weber and Sociology Today* (New York: Harper & Row, 1971). It appears to me that Weber sought a balance between the demands of national power politics, which inexorably followed from the worldwide competition of nations for markets, political advantage, and cultural dominion, and the legitimate claims by the underprivileged for justice, autonomy, and dignity.

13. Weber, *The Protestant Ethic*, pp. 85–86.

14. Ibid., pp. 112–114.

15. Ibid., p. 162.

16. This was a view that appears to have been fairly common among liberal Protestants. See, for example, Shanahan, "Friedrich Naumann," p. 285.

17. See, for example, Reinhard Bendix, *Max Weber: An Intellectual Portrait* (New York: Doubleday, 1962); and Günter Abramowski, *Das Geschichtsbild Max Webers* (Stuttgart: Ernst Klett, 1966).

18. The exception here is the penetrating essay by H. H. Brunn, *Science, Values and Politics in Max Weber's Methodology* (Copenhagen: Munksgaard, 1972).

19. There have been numerous attempts to define the meaning of the German ideology. Among those which I have drawn from, I should like to mention the following: Ernst Troeltsch, "The Ideas of Natural Law and Humanity in World Politics" in Giercke, *Natural Law and The Theory of Society, 1500–1800* (Cambridge, England: Cambridge University Press, 1934); Georg Iggers, *The German Conception of History;* Fritz Ringer, *Decline of the German Mandarins;* Leonard Krieger, *The German Idea of Freedom* (Boston: Beacon Press, 1959); and Ralf Dahrendorf, *Society and Democracy in Germany.*

20. In passing, we should note that the other major thinker whose ideas developed as a self-conscious reaction to the German ideology is, of course, Friedrich Nietzsche. There is still much debate surrounding the Weber-Nietzsche relation. See Eugene Fleishman, "De Weber à Nietzsche," *Archives Européennes de Sociologie,* 2 (1965). Also Guenther Roth, "Weber's Generational Rebellion and Maturation," in *Scholarship and Partisanship,* pp. 22–25.

21. Max Weber, *The Methodology of the Social Sciences,* (New York: Free Press, 1949), p. 112.

22. On the methodological controversies, see the fine introductory essays by Guy Oakes in Max Weber's *Critique of Stammler* (New York: Free Press, 1977) and *Roscher and Knies* (New York: Free Press, 1975).

23. Weber, *Methodology,* p. 116.

24. Weber, *Roscher and Knies,* p. 213.

25. Ibid., p. 237.

26. Ibid.; altered translation.

27. Ibid.

28. For an analysis of the two currents within the German ideological tradition, see Colin Loader, "German Historicism and Its Crisis," *Journal of Modern History,* 48 (1976).

29. Troeltsch, "The Ideas of Natural Law."

30. See, for example, Krieger, *The German Idea of Freedom;* and Friedrich Meinecke, *Cosmopolitanism and the National State*

(Princeton, N.J.: Princeton University Press, 1970). Also see Lewis White Beck, *Early German Philosophy* (Cambridge, Mass.: Harvard University Press, 1969).

31. See, for example, Georg Iggers, *The German Conception of History*.

32. A good general summary is provided by Hans Freyer, "Die Romantiker," in *Gründer der Soziologie*, ed. Fritz Karl Mann (Jena: G. Fischer, 1932).

33. Weber, *Roscher and Knies*, p. 199.

34. Ibid., p. 200.

35. Ibid., p. 201.

36. Ibid., p. 204.

37. Weber traces this view back to Savigny and the Historical School of Jurisprudence, on the one hand, and to Fichte, on the other. See Weber, *Roscher and Knies*, pp. 60–61.

38. Ibid., p. 205.

39. Ibid.

40. Ibid., p. 71.

41. Ibid., p. 210.

42. Ibid., p. 192.

43. Max Weber, "Science as a Vocation," in *From Max Weber*, p. 137.

44. Ibid.

45. See Weber's The Religion of China: Confucianism and Taoism (New York: Free Press, 1951), p. 233. In this regard, compare Nietzsche's attitude towards the decline of passion, in *The Gay Science* (New York: Vintage Books, 1974), p. 112.

46. Weber, *The Religion of China*, p. 248.

47. Ibid.

48. Weber, *Methodology*, p. 70.

Chapter 11

1. Quoted in T. S. Simey, "Max Weber: Man of Affairs or Theoretical Sociologist?," p. 308. In a letter to Brentano, Weber wrote: "Wretched results of the Reichstag elections: Strengthening of the agrarian *right*, the possibility that the reactionaries will form a majority together with the Center Party against the National

Liberals and the entire left: The only ray of hope: Naumann and the *possibility* that in [the] future the social Democrats will abandon their braggadocio and pursue practical politics. But will they?" Quoted in Marianne Weber, *Max Weber*, p. 400.

2. Quoted in *From Max Weber*, p. 71. On Weber's pronounced mood of pessimism during these years, see David Beetham, *Max Weber and the Theory of Modern Politics*.

3. Quoted in *From Max Weber*, p. 71.

4. Ibid.

5. See, for example, Friedrich Tenbruck, "Formal Sociology," in *Georg Simmel*, ed. Kurt Wolff (Columbus: Ohio State University Press, 1959).

6. See the discussion by Hans Freyer, *Soziologie als Wirklichkeits- wissenschaft* (Berlin: B. G. Teubner, 1930), p. 147.

7. The whole issue of the relation between the formal and historical sides of Weber's sociology has been brilliantly discussed by Wolfgang Mommsen, "The Universal Historian and the Social Scientist," in *The Age of Bureaucracy* (Oxford: Basil Blackwell, 1974). Also see the highly informative essay by Guenther Roth, "History and Sociology in the Work of Max Weber," *British Journal of Sociology*, 27 (1976).

8. Mommsen, *Age of Bureaucracy*, p. 11.

9. Ibid., p. 5.

10. See Karl Löwith, "Max Weber und Karl Marx," *Archiv für Sozialwissenschaft und Sozialpolitik*, 67 (1932). Abramowski, *Das Geschichtsbild Max Webers;* and Wolfgang Mommsen, "Max Weber's Political Sociology and His Philosophy of World History," *International Social Science Journal*, 17 (1965).

11. Mommsen, *Age of Bureaucracy*, p. 11.

12. In an illuminating passage, Weber writes: "Sociology proceeds according to considerations of the service it can render through its concepts formation to the historically causal attribution of culturally significant phenomena." Remarking on this passage, Guenther Roth writes: "Weber did not go all the way in reducing sociology to Clio's handmaiden, but the formulation of 'type concepts and general uniformities' in *Economy and Society* was indeed primarily an auxiliary operation for historical analysis proper. Sociology in this sense was part of the 'methodology' of

history, basically a causal analysis." Both quotations from Roth, "History and Sociology," p. 307. In an effort to clarify Weber's views on sociology and history, Roth proceeds to outline three levels of analysis. First, "configurational" analysis, which is mainly a static conceptualization of a broad sociocultural condition—for example, Weber's characterization of Occidental rationalization in the "Author's Introduction" to the *Gesammelte Aufsätze zur Religionssoziologie*. Second, "developmental or secular" theories of long-term causal relationships—for example, the relation between Protestantism and capitalism. Finally, "situational" analysis, which refers to the analysis of contemporary conditions—for example, Weber's many political essays on Russia and Germany.

13. Max Weber, *The Agrarian Sociology of Ancient Civilization*.

14. Weber's full remark runs as follows: "We are absolutely in accord that history should establish what is specific to, say, the medieval city; but this is possible only if we first find what is missing in other cities (ancient, Chinese, Islamic). And so it is with everything else. It is the subsequent task of history to find a causal explanation for these specific traits. . . . Sociology, as I understand it, can perform this very modest preparatory work." Quoted in Roth, "History and Sociology," p. 307.

15. See Bryan S. Turner, *Weber and Islam* (London: Routledge & Kegan Paul, 1974), p. 78.

16. This position is similar to that of Siegfried Landshut, who maintained that Weber's sociology is the "articulated problematic of reality itself." Landshut, *Kritik der Soziologie* (Munich: Duncker & Humboldt, 1929); quoted in Wolfgang Schluchter and Guenther Roth, *Max Weber's Vision of History* (Berkeley and Los Angeles: University of California Press, 1979), p. 13.

17. Löwith, "Weber und Marx," p. 53.

18. See Dieter Lindenlaub, *Richtungskämpfe im Verein für Sozialpolitik*, pp. 293–297.

19. Randall Collins, "Weber's Last Theory of Capitalism: A Systematization," *American Sociological Review*, 45 (1980).

20. Steven Seidman and Michael Gruber, "Capitalism and Individuation in the Sociology of Max Weber," *British Journal of Sociology*, 28 (1977).

21. Cf. the analysis by Anthony Kronman, "Autonomy and Interaction in the Thought of Max Weber" (Ph.D. diss., Yale University, 1972).

22. Quoted in Guenther Roth, "Introduction" to Weber's *Economy and Society*, p. lviii.

23. This of course was the position that Georg Lukàcs sought to establish in his *History and Class Consciousness* (Cambridge, Mass.: MIT Press, 1973). Compare the comments of Trent Schroyer, *The Critique of Domination* (Boston: Beacon Press, 1975), p. 184.

24. Landshut, *Kritik der Soziologie.*

25. Ibid., p. 58.

26. Freyer, *Soziologie*, pp. 156–157.

27. Löwith, "Weber und Marx," p. 62.

28. This dialectic of means-ends reversal is explored in depth in Löwith, "Weber und Marx." Also see Werner Stark, "Max Weber and the Heteronomy of Purpose," *Social Research*, 34 (1967).

29. Weber, *Gesammelte Aufsätze zur Soziologie und Sozialpolitik*, p. 445.

30. See, in particular, Abramowski, *Das Geschichtsbild Max Webers*, pp. 160–185.

31. Max Weber, *The Religion of China: Confucianism and Taoism* (New York: Free Press, 1951), p. 238.

32. See, for example, Tenbruck, "Thematic Unity in the Work of Max Weber," pp. 324–325; and Roth, "History and Sociology," p. 310.

33. Bendix, *Max Weber*, p. xxiv.

34. Ibid., pp. 279–280.

35. Friedrich Tenbruck, "Das Werk Max Webers," *Kölner Zeitschrift für Soziologie*, 27 (1975). A slightly condensed translation of this essay has appeared under the title "The Problem of Thematic Unity in the Works of Max Weber," *British Journal of Sociology*, 31 (1980). My references will be to the English version, although I have modified some of the translations.

36. Tenbruck writes: "The rationalization thesis stands, and so falls, because it is assumed that WEWR [Weber's comparative studies of religion and society published in the *Archiv für Sozialwissen-*

schaft und Sozialpolitik between 1915 and 1919] were written before ES [*Economy and Society*]. . . . If the references used by Bendix are scrutinized with regard to chronology, it is hard to avoid the conclusion that Bendix has erroneously supposed that Weber had written WEWR before ES." Tenbruck, "Thematic Unity in Weber," pp. 324–325. Tenbruck further criticizes Bendix for offering an empiricist and historicist interpretation of the rationalization process: "For Bendix rationalization remains a historically fortuitous occurrence, the result of a series of particular events that consecutively have produced a specific outcome. Between the rationalism of Judaism and the inner-worldly asceticism of Protestantism no process of religious disenchantment is discerned. Instead, the legacy of Judaic rationalism is transposed by purely secular forces to become a prevailing world view. The significance of religious ethics is restricted to the demonstration of 'how some had an accelerating and others a retarding effect upon the rationality of economic life.' " Ibid., p. 326. Tenbruck's article has stimulated a debate in two areas. First, there is the question of the dates of and the relation between ES and WEWR. Second, Tenbruck has raised the question of an historicist versus an evolutionary interpretation of Weber. Regarding the dating problem, Wolfgang Schluchter has sought to serve a major blow to Tenbruck's argument. Schluchter has argued that, according to Weber's own remarks, it appears that the bulk of materials for his comparative studies of religion, including the "Intermediate Reflections" on which Tenbruck relies heavily, was composed earlier than or simultaneously with ES. Further, Schluchter points to Weber's statements that ES and WEWR were intended to appear more or less together, and that WEWR was a supplement to the chapters on religion in ES. See Wolfgang Schluchter, "Excursus: The Selection and Dating of the Works Used," in *Max Weber's Vision of History*, pp. 59–64. Without a detailed biography which relates Weber's life-events to a critical examination of his works, such discussions will remain conjectural, and whatever conclusions are drawn will be highly tentative. However Tenbruck fares on the dating question, his thesis that the late Weber turned towards an evolutionary or developmental history is bound to lead to a fresh examination of Weber's works. Already, the sides are clearly drawn between the evolutionists and the historicists. Schluchter has offered a major interpretation of Weber's theory of rationalization as a developmental or evolutionary history. See Wolf-gang Schluchter, *The Rise of Western Rationalism* (Berkeley and Los Angeles: University of California Press, 1981). On the other side, Randall Collins's recent systematization of Weber's theory of capitalism is a powerful statement of the historicist position. In a way, the contemporary discussion over Weber and, quite obviously, over the aim of social theory mirrors the debate in the 1960s between the Parsonians and the historicists and com-parativists, represented by Bendix, Roth, and Nelson.

37. Weber, *Protestant Ethic*, p. 284.

38. Bendix, *Max Weber*, p. 268. It has become a commonplace of Weber-scholarship to remark that Weber's monographs on China and India were part of a grand experimental-historical design aimed at testing the causal significance of Protestantism for capitalist development. Besides Bendix, see Parsons, *The Structure of Social Action*, p. 540; and Mommsen, *The Age of Bureaucracy*, p. 102. Joseph Levenson and Franz Schurmann, in *China: An Interpretive History* (Berkeley and Los Angeles: Uni-versity of California Press, 1969), state this thesis with elegant simplicity: "Max Weber was anxious to make a negative proof of his famous Protestant-ethic-to-European-capitalism thesis, by showing the quite non-Protestant Confucian ethic as the inhib-itor of otherwise probable capitalism in China" (p. 75). C. K. Yang, in his "Introduction" in Weber's *Religion of China*, states that Weber's "major objective in this volume was to demonstrate that China's failure to develop rational bourgeois capitalism was owing mainly to the absence of a particular kind of religious ethic as the needed motivating force" (p. xiv). While this thesis may resonate with the scientific aspirations of Anglo-American sociology, it does not correspond to the structure of Weber's argument. To work, the argument presupposes that Weber held *all* the essential elements of social structure and culture constant except religious development. But Weber did not do this. In-stead—in his analysis of China, for example—Weber argued that such necessary institutional preconditions of capitalism as for-mal law, autonomous cities, an independent bourgeois class, and the notion of citizenship were absent. In fact, a careful reading of the China monograph reveals that a central claim was that modern capitalism's failure to develop reflects the sustaining power of the patrimonial bureaucracy and the sib. This same

argument regarding the suppression of capitalism by bureaucratic absolutism is found in Weber's analysis of ancient bureaucratic societies, particularly Egypt and the Roman Empire. Weber's comparisons between the Occident and Orient were intended, in addition, to discredit monocausal and unilinear evolutionary theories of history. Finally, Weber contrasted the Occident and Orient not only to highlight Occidental development but to detail the historical individuality of the Occident and Orient as well as to account for their unique development. This interpretation accords with the comparative and differential structure of Weber's universal history and, as we shall see, corresponds to Weber's more general problematic of analyzing rationalism and rationalization processes in different civilizations.

39. Tenbruck, "Thematic Unity in Weber," p. 328.

40. Benjamin Nelson, "Max Weber's 'Author's Introduction': A Master Clue to His Main Aims," *Sociological Inquiry,* 44 (1974): 7.

41. Benjamin Nelson, "On Orient and Occident in Max Weber," *Social Research,* 43 (1976): 115.

42. Tenbruck, "Thematic Unity in Weber," p. 343.

43. Ibid., p. 334.

44. Ibid., p. 335.

45. Ibid., p. 334.

46. Weber, *Religion of China,* p. 226.

47. Weber, *Religion of India,* pp. 335, 342.

48. Weber wrote: "By themselves, the masses, as we shall see, have everywhere remained engulfed in the massive and archaic growth of magic—unless a prophecy that holds out specific promises has swept them into a religious movement of an ethical character." *From Max Weber,* p. 276.

49. Tenbruck, "Thematic Unity in Weber," p. 337. Tenbruck's interpretation shows strong affinities with Talcott Parsons's "Introduction" to Weber's *The Sociology of Religion* (Boston: Beacon Press, 1964). See also Robert N. Bellah, "Religious Evolution," in *Beyond Belief* (New York: Harper & Row, 1970).

50. Quoted in Tenbruck, "Thematic Unity in Weber," p. 335.

51. Weber, *Protestant Ethic,* p. 278.

52. Ibid., p. 105.

53. Cf. the critique of Tenbruck by Stephen Kalberg, "The Search for Thematic Orientations in a Fragmented Oeuvre: The Discussion of Max Weber in Recent German Sociological Literature," *Sociology*, 13 (1979).

54. For recent attempts to reconstruct Weber's multidimensional theory of rationality and rationalization processes, see the following essays: Stephen Kalberg, "Max Weber's Types of Rationality: Cornerstones for the Analysis of Rationalization Processes in History," *American Journal of Sociology*, 85 (1980); Gert Muller, "The Notion of Rationality in the Work of Max Weber," Archives Européennes de Sociologie, 20 (1979); and Ulrike Vogel, "Einige Ueberlegungen zum Begriff der Rationalitat bei Max Weber," *Kölner Zeitschrift für Soziologie und Sozialpsychologie*, 25 (1973).

55. Weber, *Protestant Ethic*, p. 26.

56. Ibid., pp. 77–78.

57. Weber, *Methodology*, p. 81. Weber's metaphysic bears a remarkable similarity to that of Nietzsche. The affinity can be economically and tellingly highlighted by referring to several passages in Nietzsche's *The Gay Science*. First, Nietzsche's post-cosmological world-view: "The total character of the world, however, is in all eternity chaos—in the sense not of a lack of necessity but a lack of order, arrangement, form, beauty, wisdom, and whatever other names there are for our aesthetic anthropomorphisms" (p. 168). From this secular standpoint, Nietzsche describes in the strongest possible terms the perspectival nature of consciousness and the heightened awareness of the contingent, morally problematic nature of the modern experience: "How far the perspective character of existence extends or indeed whether existence has any other character than this; whether existence without interpretation, without 'sense,' does not become 'nonsense'; whether, on the other hand, all existence is not essentially actively engaged in *interpretation*— that cannot be decided even by the most industrious and most scrupulously conscientious analysis and self-examination of the intellect; for in the course of this analysis the human intellect cannot avoid seeing itself in its own perspectives, and *only* in these. We cannot look around our own corner; it is a hopeless

358 NOTES FOR PAGES 256–260

curiosity that wants to know what other kinds of intellects and perspectives there *might* be; for example, whether some beings might be able to experience time backward, or alternately forward and backward (which would involve another direction of life and another concept of cause and effect). But I should think that today we are at least far from the ridiculous immodesty that would be involved in decreeing from our corner that perspectives are permitted only from this corner. Rather has the world become 'infinite' for us all over again, inasmuch as we cannot reject the possibility that *it may include infinite interpretations*" (p. 336). For a contemporary interpretation of the unique character of modernity that continues the line of theorizing of Nietzsche and Weber, see Martin Heidegger, "The Age of the World Picture," in *The Question Concerning Technology, and Other Essays* (New York: Harper and Row, 1977).

58. See Talcott Parsons's "Introduction" in Weber's *The Sociology of Religion*, p. lix.

59. Cf. Schluchter's remarks in Schluchter and Roth, *Max Weber's Vision of History*, pp. 13, 59. Also see Hannah Arendt, *The Human Condition* (Chicago: University of Chicago Press, 1971), p. 227.

60. *From Max Weber*, p. 281.

61. Ibid., p. 353.

62. Ibid., p. 155.

63. Ibid., p. 351.

64. Ibid., pp. 281, 353–356.

65. See Arthur Mitzman, *Sociology and Estrangement* (New York: Knopf, 1973), pp. 26–32; and Fritz Stern, *The Failure of Illiberalism*, p. 20.

66. *From Max Weber*, pp. 339, 356–357.

67. Ibid., p. 356.

68. Ibid., p. 359.

69. Ibid., p. 357.

70. Ibid.

71. Ibid., p. 154.

72. Ibid., p. 155.

73. Ibid.

74. Ibid., p. 149.

75. Ibid., p. 142.

76. Ibid.

77. Weber, *Methodology*, p. 57.

78. *From Max Weber*, p. 152. Cf. Thomas Burger, "Max Weber, Interpretive Sociology, and the Sense of Historical Science: A Positivist Conception of *Verstehen*," *Sociological Quarterly*, 18 (1977).

79. Regarding the various movements of cultural pessimism during this period, see Stern, *The Politics of Cultural Despair;* George Mosse, *Crisis of German Ideology*. On the literary and artistic expressions of cultural pessimism, see Walter Sokol, *The Writer in Extremis: Expressionism in Twentieth-Century German Literature* (New York: McGraw-Hill, 1964) and Frederick Levine, *The Apocalyptic Vision: The Art of Franz Marc as German Expressionism* (New York: Harper and Row, 1979).

80. See Ringer, *Decline of the German Mandarins*.

81. This was the position assumed by Karl Jaspers, for whom Weber is the "existential philosopher incarnate." Quoted in Löwith, "Weber und Marx," p. 60. There are two points I want to insist on. First, according to Weber, the world as experienced by individuals is always a humanly constituted world infused with values and meaning. Second, Weber's problematic was not "human existence" but societies and civilizations viewed historically as differentially constituted. This historical and sociocultural view of human existence separates Weber from modern existentialists.

82. *From Max Weber*, pp. 147–148.

83. Ibid., p. 149.

84. Ibid.

85. Ibid., p. 356.

86. Weber, *The Protestant Ethic*, p. 180.

87. Ibid., p. 181.

88. Weber writes: "Where the fulfillment of the calling cannot directly be related to the highest spiritual and cultural values ... the individual generally abandons the attempt to justify it at all. In the field of its highest development, in the United

States, the pursuit of wealth, stripped of its religious and ethical meaning, tends to become associated with purely mundane passions, which often actually give it the character of sport." *The Protestant Ethic*, p. 182.

89. Cf. Abramowski, *Das Geschichtsbild Max Webers*, chap. 4.

90. Cf. Donald Levine, "Rationality and Freedom: Weber and Beyond," *Sociological Inquiry*, 15 (1981).

91. Löwith, "Weber und Marx," p. 98.

92. Weber, *Gesammelte Aufsätze zur Soziologie und Sozialpolitik*, pp. 444–446.

93. Ibid., p. 442.

94. *From Max Weber*, p. 71.

Summary of Part Four

1. There is evidence suggesting that the currents of materialism and positivism that had penetrated into German culture during the latter part of the nineteenth century had a definite impact on Weber. In one of his adolescent essays—which by our contemporary standards would be a highly mature piece—Weber wrote: "Nations cannot completely abandon the course on which they have set out any more than celestial bodies can leave their orbits—provided that there are no external disturbances. . . ." Marianne Weber remarks that Max Weber's youthful essays are filled with the positivist faith. "He is convinced that such laws [of history] exist, just as they do in nature." Both quotations are taken from Marianne Weber, *Max Weber*, p. 47. In addition, Weber appears to have taken a strong interest in Spinoza, who was then regarded as a materialist and determinist. However, without a detailed historical examination of Weber's early intellectual development, it is impossible to determine what impact, if any, Spinoza had on Weber.

2. Merleau-Ponty has captured and stated Weber's liberalism elegantly: "Weber's liberalism does not demand a political utopia. It does not consider the formal universe of democracy to be an absolute. He admits that all politics is violence—even, in its own fashion, democratic politics. His liberalism is militant, suffering, heroic. He recognizes the rights of his adversaries, refuses to hate them, does not try to avoid confronting them, and in order

to refute them relies only upon their own contradictions and upon the discussions which expose them. He who under the Empire decided against submarine warfare and in favor of a white peace declared himself jointly responsible with the patriot who would kill the first Pole who entered Danzig. He opposed the pacifist left, which made Germany alone responsible for the war and exonerated in advance the foreign occupation, because he thought that these abuses of self-accusation paved the way for a violent nationalism in the future. Still, he testified in favor of the students who were involved in pacifist propaganda. Though he did not believe in the revolution, he made public his esteem for Liebknecht and Rosa Luxemburg." Maurice Merleau-Ponty, "The Crisis of the Understanding," in *The Primacy of Perception* (Evanston, Ill.: Northwestern University Press, 1964), p. 208.

3. See Arthur Mitzman, *The Iron Cage* (New York: Grosset & Dunlap, 1969), pp. 75–80.

4. This idea was proposed to me by Jeffrey Alexander. See, in addition, Alexander's suggestive remarks on the early writings of Weber, in *Theoretical Logic in Sociology* (Berkeley and Los Angeles: University of California Press, 1983), vol. 3.

Conclusion

1. This has recently been stated, somewhat obscurely, by Michel Foucault in *The Order of Things* (New York: Vintage Books, 1973). Notwithstanding Foucault's brilliance, his schema frequently violates the historical record. In particular, Foucault repeats all the well-known myths about the Enlightenment—for example, its dogmatic rationalism, instrumentalism, and materialism. Thus, Foucault ends up identifying Enlightenment social thought with the contractarian tradition of classical economics and finds in the post-Enlightenment era, with its relativism, historicism, evolutionism, and holism, the true beginnings of modern social thought.

2. See Herbert Butterfield, *The Origins of Modern Science: 1300–1800* (New York: Collier Books, 1962), p. 178; and Alfred Cobban, *Burke and the Revolt Against the Eighteenth Century* (London: Allen & Unwin, 1960), p. 30.

3. Regarding the romantic distortion of the Enlightenment, see

Ernst Cassirer, *The Philosophy of the Enlightenment* (Princeton, N.J.: Princeton University Press, 1951), p. 198; and Peter Gay, *The Party of Humanity* (New York: Norton, 1963), pp. 265–271.

4. Wilhelm Dilthey, "Das Achtzehnte Jahrhundert und die Geschichtliche Welt," in *Gesammelte Schriften* (Stuttgart: Teubner, 1957), vol. 3; Friedrich Meinecke, *Historism* (London: Routledge & Kegan Paul, 1972); Cassirer, *Philosophy of the Enlightenment;* Gay, *The Enlightenment;* and Ernest Becker, *The Structure of Evil* (New York: Free Press, 1968).

5. See Imre Lakatos, *The Methodology of Scientific Research Programmes,* ed. John Worrall and Gregory Currie (Cambridge, England: Cambridge University Press, 1978). For an interesting attempt to apply Lakatos's notion of a scientific research program to an analysis of sociology, see Edward Tiryakian, "Émile Durkheim," in *A History of Sociological Analysis,* ed. Bottomore and Nisbet (New York: Basic Books, 1968).

6. On the problem of modernism in critical social theory, see Joel Whitebook, "Saving the Subject: Modernity and the Problem of the Autonomous Individual," *Telos,* 50 (1981–1982).

Appendix

1. Gerard Radnitzky, "Life Cycles of a Scientific Tradition," *Main Currents of Modern Thought,* 32 (1975).

2. John Dunn, "The Identity of the History of Ideas," in *Philosophy, Politics, and Society,* series IV, ed. Peter Laslett, W. C. Runciman, and Quentin Skinner (London: Oxford University Press, 1972); Robert Alun Jones, "On Understanding a Sociological Classic," *American Journal of Sociology,* 83 (1977); J. D. Peel, "History and Sociology," in *Herbert Spencer* (New York: Basic Books, 1971); George Stocking, "On the Limits of 'Presentism' and 'Historicism' in the Historiography of the Behavioral Sciences," *Journal of the History of the Behavioral Sciences,* 1 (1965); and Quentin Skinner, "Meaning and Understanding in the History of Ideas," *History and Theory,* 8 (1969).

3. See the critique of Parson's "presentism" by Charles Camic, "The Utilitarians Revisited," *American Journal of Sociology,* 85 (1979).

4. In the humanities, particularly in the history of philosophy, we find a different version of presentism. The unit of analysis here

is so-called classic works which are assumed to embody timeless truths. Though there is continuity in the problems discussed between early and later classic works, their timeless status precludes cumulative development. Instead, the relation between classic works is that of a dialogue across centuries. It follows that the historian's main aim is to reconstruct the dialogue, thereby preserving and transmitting to the present age the embodied wisdom. It must be emphasized that the major architect of the critique of presentism, Quentin Skinner, works entirely in the field of the history of political philosophy, where we find, moreover, a long tradition of this type of presentist historiography. Skinner's critique was chiefly a reaction to this version of presentism, and in my view its legitimacy is confined to the excesses of this presentist tradition. To be sure, historiography in the social sciences is not entirely free of this type of presentism, as Jones has shown (see Robert Jones, "On Understanding a Sociological Classic"). Nevertheless, there is simply no counterpart in sociology or anthropology, for example, to the idea—found prominently in the historiography of political philosophy—of a unified tradition consisting of Greek, Christian, and early modern classic works. Much of the historiography in the social sciences, in fact, highlights differences and discontinuities within the sociological tradition. In addition, the scientific orientation of the social sciences, with their commitment to change, if not progress, stands opposed to the ahistorical disposition of this type of presentism. Hence, because I do not see that this type of presentism is all that widespread in the social sciences, its critique, though welcome, is less applicable and forceful in relation to their historiography.

5. Robert Merton, *Social Theory and Social Structure* (Glencoe, Ill.: Free Press, 1949); and Randall Collins, *Conflict Sociology* (New York: Academic Press, 1975).

6. See, for example, the remarks of Stanislav Andreski, "Introduction" to Herbert Spencer, *Principles of Sociology* (Hamden, Conn.: Archon Books, 1969).

7. Stocking, "Limits," p. 212.

8. See Robert Alun Jones, "Durkheim's Response to Spencer: An Essay Toward Historicism in the Historiography of Sociology," *Sociological Quarterly,* 15 (1974): 342; and Peel, *Herbert Spencer,* p. 259.

9. See Skinner, "Meaning and Understanding," pp. 7–29.

10. See, for example, Peel, *Herbert Spencer*, p. 259; and Skinner, "Meaning and Understanding," pp. 12–25.

11. George Stocking, "Cultural Darwinism and 'Philosophical Idealism' in E. B. Tylor: A Special Plea for Historicism in the History of Anthropology," *Southwestern Journal of Anthropology*, 21 (1965).

12. Peel, *Herbert Spencer*, p. 264.

13. Jones, "Durkheim's Response to Spencer," p. 355.

14. See Camic, "Utilitarians Revisited," p. 543; Jones, "On Understanding a Sociological Classic," p. 355; and Skinner, "Meaning and Understanding," p. 52.

15. Peel, *Herbert Spencer*, p. 264.

16. See Jones, "On Understanding a Sociological Classic"; and Quentin Skinner, "Meaning and Understanding," p. 42, and "Hermeneutics and the Role of History," *New Literary History*, 7 (1976): 214–216.

17. See, for example, Karl Mannheim, *Ideology and Utopia* (New York: Harcourt, Brace & World, 1936); Georg Lukàcs, *Die Zerstorung der Vernunft* (Neuwied: Luchterhand, 1962).

18. See Jones, "On Understanding a Sociological Classic," pp. 295–296.

19. See Skinner, "Meaning and Understanding," p. 49, "Hermeneutics and the Role of History," p. 214, and *The Foundations of Modern Political Thought* (Cambridge, England: Cambridge University Press, 1978), vol. 1, p. xiii; and Geoffrey Hawthorn, *Enlightenment and Despair* (Cambridge, England: Cambridge University Press, 1976), pp. 6–7.

20. Skinner, "Meaning and Understanding," pp. 45–49, and "Motives, Intentions, and the Interpretation of Texts," *New Literary History*, 3 (1972): 403–404.

21. For a discussion of the link between intentionalism and validation, see E. D. Hirsch, *Validity in Interpretation* (New Haven: Yale University Press, 1967).

22. See, for example, Peel, *Herbert Spencer*, p. 259; Skinner, "Meaning and Understanding," pp. 5–6; and Jones, "On Understanding a Sociological Classic," p. 284. Also see the dissenting opinion

of Camic, "The Utilitarians Revisited," p. 518, and the ensuing Jones–Camic debate in the *American Journal of Sociology*, 86 (1981).

23. Quentin Skinner, "Some Problems in the Analysis of Political Thought and Action," *Political Theory*, 2 (1974): 284.

24. Paul Ricoeur, "The Model of the Text: Meaningful Action Considered as a Text," *Social Research*, 38 (1971): 534.

25. Hans-Georg Gadamer, *Truth and Method* (New York: Seabury Press, 1975), pp. 263–264.

26. See David Hoy, *The Critical Circle* (Berkeley and Los Angeles: University of California Press, 1978).

27. Skinner, "Hermeneutics and the Role of History," pp. 222–228.

28. Skinner, "Motives, Intentions, and the Interpretation of Texts," p. 405.

29. See, for example, Habermas, *Knowledge and Human Interests* (Boston: Beacon Press, 1972); Edmund Husserl, *The Crisis of European Sciences and Transcendental Phenomenology* (Evanston, Ill.: Northwestern University Press, 1970); Stephen Pepper, *World Hypotheses* (Berkeley: University of California Press, 1942); and Ludwig Wittgenstein, *Philosophical Investigations* (New York: Macmillan, 1958).

30. See Gadamer, *Truth and Method;* also see Richard Palmer, *Hermeneutics* (Evanston, Ill.: Northwestern University Press, 1969).

31. Peel, *Herbert Spencer*, pp. 264–265.

32. Skinner, "Meaning and Understanding," p. 50.

33. See Stocking, "Limits," p. 215.

34. Jeffrey Alexander, *Theoretical Logic in Sociology* (Berkeley and Los Angeles: University of California Press, 1982), vol. 1; Anthony Giddens, *Central Problems in Social Theory* (Berkeley and Los Angeles: University of California Press, 1979); and Roland Robertson, "Major Axes in Sociological Analysis," in *Approaches to Sociology*, ed. John Rex (London: Routledge & Kegan Paul, 1974).

35. Cf. Bhikhu Parekh and R. N. Berki, "The History of Political Ideas: A Critique of Quentin Skinner's Methodology," *Journal of the History of Ideas*, 34 (1973): 171.

36. Gadamer, *Truth and Method*, esp. pp. 178–179, 249–253, 311–341; and Edward Shils, *Tradition* (Chicago: University of Chicago Press, 1981).

37. Anthony Giddens, *Capitalism and Modern Social Theory* (Cambridge, England: Cambridge University Press, 1971); Dieter Lindenlaub, *Richtungskämpfe im Verein für Sozialpolitik* (Wiesbaden: Franz Steiner, 1967); and Karl Löwith, "Max Weber und Karl Marx," *Archiv für Sozialwissenschaft und Sozialpolitik*, 67 (1932).

38. Alan Dawe, "Theories of Social Action," in *A History of Sociological Analysis*, ed. Bottomore and Nisbet, p. 366.

39. See Terry Clark, "Émile Durkheim and the French University," in *The Establishment of Empirical Sociology*, ed. Anthony Oberschall (New York: Harper & Row, 1972); Edward Shils, "Tradition, Ecology, and Institution in the History of Sociology," *Daedalus*, 99 (1970); and Edward Tiryakian, "The Significance of Schools in the Development of Sociology," in *Contemporary Issues in Theory and Research*, ed. William Snizek et al. (Westport, Conn.: Greenwood Press, 1979).

40. See Tiryakian, "Significance of Schools."

41. See my discussion in the Introduction, esp. note 5. Also see the following secondary works and anthologies: Anthony Giddens, "Positivism and Its Critics," in *Studies in Social and Political Theory* (New York: Basic Books, 1977); Fred Dallmayr and Thomas McCarthy, eds., *Understanding and Social Inquiry* (Notre Dame, Ind.: University of Notre Dame Press, 1977); Paul Rabinow and William Sullivan, eds., *Interpretive Social Science* (Berkeley and Los Angeles: University of California Press, 1979).

42. Merton, *Social Theory and Social Structure;* and Stocking, "Limits."

43. See R. Stephen Warner, "The Uses of the Classic Tradition," in *Sociological Theory* (Morristown, N.J.: General Learning Press, 1976), pp. 7–8; and Roland Robertson, *Meaning and Change* (New York: New York University Press, 1978), p. 4.

Works Cited

Preface and Introduction

ALEXANDER, JEFFREY. *Theoretical Logic in Sociology.* Vol. 1. Berkeley and Los Angeles: University of California Press, 1982.

APEL, KARL-OTTO. *Towards a Transformation of Philosophy.* London: Routledge & Kegan Paul, 1980.

ARON, RAYMOND. *Main Currents in Sociological Thought.* Vol. 1. New York: Anchor Books, 1968.

BAUDRILLARD, JEAN. *The Mirror of Production.* St. Louis: Telos Press, 1975.

BECKER, ERNEST. *The Lost Science of Man.* New York: George Braziller, 1971.

————. *The Structure of Evil: An Essay of the Unification of the Science of Man.* New York: Free Press, 1968.

BENDIX, REINHARD. *Nation-Building and Citizenship.* Berkeley and Los Angeles: University of California Press, 1964.

BERLIN, ISAIAH. *Four Essays on Liberty.* New York: Oxford University Press, 1970.

BIERSTEDT, ROBERT. "Sociological Thought in the Eighteenth Century." In *A History of Sociological Analysis,* edited by Tom Bottomore and Robert Nisbet. New York: Basic Books, 1978.

BOOKCHIN, MURRAY. *Post-Scarcity Anarchism.* San Francisco: Ramparts Press, 1971.

————. *Toward an Ecological Society.* New York: Black Rose Books, 1982.

BOTTOMORE, TOM. *Marxist Sociology.* New York: Holmes & Meier, 1975.

BURY, J. B. *The Idea of Progress.* New York: Dover, 1955.

COLLINI, STEFAN. "Sociology and Idealism in Britain, 1880–1920." *Archives Européennes de Sociologie,* 19 (1978).

COLLINS, RANDALL. *Conflict Sociology.* New York: Academic Press, 1975.

————, with Michael Makowsky. *The Discovery of Society.* 2nd rev. ed. New York: Random House, 1978.

DELEUZE, GILLES, and FELIX GUATTARI. *L'Anti-Oedipe: Capitalisme et Schizophrénie.* Vol. 1. Paris: Éditions du Minuit, 1972.

EISENSTADT, S. N., with M. CURELARU. *The Form of Sociology.* New York: Wiley, 1976.

FEYERABEND, PAUL. *Against Method.* London: New Left Books, 1975.

GAY, PETER. *The Party of Humanity.* New York: Norton, 1963.

GIDDENS, ANTHONY. *Capitalism and Modern Social Theory.* Cambridge, England: Cambridge University Press, 1971.

GOULDNER, ALVIN W. *The Coming Crisis of Western Sociology.* New York: Avon Books, 1971.

————. *The Two Marxisms.* New York: Seabury Press, 1980.

GOUX, JEAN-JOSEPH. *Économie et Symbolique: Marx, Freud.* Paris: Seuil, 1973.

HABERMAS, JÜRGEN. *Knowledge and Human Interests.* Boston: Beacon Press, 1972.

————. "Kritische und Konservative Aufgaben der Soziologie." In *Theorie und Praxis.* Neuwied: Luchterhand, 1967.

HANSON, NORWOOD. *Patterns of Discovery.* Cambridge, England: University Press, 1958.

HAVELOCK, ERIC. *Preface to Plato.* New York: Grosset & Dunlap, 1971.

HAWTHORN, GEOFFREY. *Enlightenment and Despair: A History of Sociology.* Cambridge, England: Cambridge University Press, 1976.

HAYEK, F. A.   *The Constitution of Liberty*. Chicago: University of Chicago Press, 1960.

HESSE, MARY.   *Models and Analogies in Science*. London: Sheed & Ward, 1963.

HOLTON, GERALD.   *Thematic Origins of Scientific Thought*. Cambridge, Mass.: Harvard University Press, 1973.

HOOK, SIDNEY.   "The Enlightenment and Marxism." *Journal of the History of Ideas*, 29 (1968).

HORKHEIMER, MAX.   "Traditional and Critical Theory." In *Critical Theory*. New York: Seabury Press, 1972.

KORSCH, KARL.   *Three Essays on Marxism*. New York: Monthly Review Press, 1972.

KRIEGER, LEONARD.   *The German Idea of Freedom*. Boston: Beacon Press, 1959.

KUHN, THOMAS.   *The Structure of Scientific Revolutions*. Princeton, N.J.: Princeton University Press, 1970.

LAKATOS, IMRE.   *The Methodology of Scientific Research Programmes*. Edited by John Worral and Gregory Currie. Cambridge, England: Cambridge University Press, 1978.

LASKY, HAROLD.   *The Rise of European Liberalism*. New York: Unwin Books, 1962.

LOADER, COLIN.   "German Historicism and Its Crisis." *Journal of Modern History*, 48 (1976).

LÖWITH, KARL.   "Max Weber und Karl Marx." *Archiv für Sozialwissenschaft und Sozialpolitik*, 67 (1932).

LUKES, STEVEN.   *Individualism*. New York: Harper & Row, 1973.

MANNHEIM, KARL.   "Conservative Thought." In *Essays on Sociology and Social Psychology*, edited by Paul Kecskemeti. New York: Oxford University Press, 1953.

———.   *Ideology and Utopia*. New York: Harcourt, Brace & World, 1936.

MANUEL, FRANK.   *The Prophets of Paris*. New York: Harper & Row, 1962.

MARCUSE, HERBERT.   *Reason and Revolution: Hegel and the Rise of Social Theory*. Boston: Beacon Press, 1968.

MARTINDALE, DONALD. *The Nature and Types of Sociological Theory*. Boston: Houghton Mifflin, 1966.

MORRIS, COLIN. *The Discovery of the Individual: 1050–1200*. New York: Harper & Row, 1972.

NISBET, ROBERT. *The Sociological Tradition*. New York: Basic Books, 1966.

PARSONS, TALCOTT. "Economics and Sociology: Marshall in Relation to the Thought of His Times." *Quarterly Journal of Economics*, 46 (1931–1932).

———. "Review of Robert Nisbet, *The Sociological Tradition.*" *American Sociological Review*, 32 (1967).

———. *The Structure of Social Action*. New York: Free Press, 1968.

POLANYI, MICHAEL. *Personal Knowledge*. New York: Harper & Row, 1964.

ROSSIDES, DANIEL. *The History and Nature of Sociological Theory*. Boston: Houghton Mifflin, 1978.

RUGGIERO, GUIDO DE. *The History of European Liberalism*. Boston: Beacon Press, 1966.

SHAPERE, DUDLEY. "Notes Toward a Post-Positivist Interpretation of Science." In *The Legacy of Logical Positivism*, edited by Peter Achinstein and Stephen Barker. Baltimore: Johns Hopkins University Press, 1969.

SIDORSKY, DAVID, ed. "Introduction." In *The Liberal Tradition in European Thought*. New York: Capricorn Books, 1971.

SMALL, ALBION. *The Origins of Sociology*. Chicago: University of Chicago Press, 1924.

SNELL, BRUNO. *The Discovery of the Mind*. New York: Harper & Row, 1960.

SOMBART, WERNER. "Anfänge der Soziologie." In *Hauptprobleme der Soziologie*, edited by Melchior Palyi. New York: Arno Press, 1975.

SPAEMANN, ROBERT. *Der Urspung der Soziologie aus dem Geist der Restauration*. Munich: Kosel-Verlag, 1959.

STRAUSS, LEO. *Liberalism, Ancient and Modern*. New York: Basic Books, 1968.

———. *Natural Rights and History*. Chicago: University of Chicago Press, 1953.

SUPPE, FREDERICK, ed. *The Structure of Scientific Theories*. Urbana: University of Illinois Press, 1977.

SZACKI, JERZY. *A History of Sociological Thought*. Westport, Conn.: Greenwood Press, 1979.

TAR, ZOLTON. *The Frankfurt School*. New York: Wiley, 1977.

THERBORN, GÖRAN. *Science, Class, and Society: On the Formation of Sociology and Historical Materialism*. London: New Left Books, 1976.

TOCQUEVILLE, ALEXIS DE. *Democracy in America*. New York: Schocken, 1970.

――――. *The Old Regime and the French Revolution*. New York: Doubleday, 1955.

TOULMIN, STEPHEN. *Human Understanding*. Oxford: Clarendon Press, 1972.

TURNER, JONATHAN H., and LEONARD BEEGHLEY. *The Emergence of Sociological Theory*. Homewood, Ill.: Dorsey Press, 1981.

WELLMER, ALBRECHT. *The Critical Theory of Society*. New York: Herder & Herder, 1971.

ZEITLIN, IRVING. *Ideology and the Development of Sociological Theory*. Englewood Cliffs, N.J.: Prentice-Hall, 1968.

PART ONE: The Origins of European Social Theory

ABRAMS, M. H. *Natural Supernaturalism*. New York: Norton, 1971.

ABRAMS, PHILIP, ed. *The Origins of British Sociology, 1848–1914*. Chicago: University of Chicago Press, 1968.

ALEXANDER, JEFFREY. *Theoretical Logic in Sociology*. Vol. 1 Berkeley and Los Angeles: University of California Press, 1982.

ANDERSON, R. D. *France, 1870–1914: Politics and Society*. London: Routledge & Kegan Paul, 1977.

ARON, RAYMOND. *Main Currents in Sociological Thought*. Vols. 1–2. New York: Anchor Books, 1968.

BABBITT, IRVING. *Rousseau and Romanticism*. Boston, Houghton Mifflin, 1919.

BAKER, KEITH M. *Condorcet*. Chicago: University of Chicago Press, 1975.

BERLIN, ISAIAH. "The Counter-Enlightenment." In *Against the Current.* New York: Viking Press, 1980.

BIERSTEDT, ROBERT. "Sociological Thought in the Eighteenth Century." In *A History of Sociological Analysis,* edited by Tom Bottomore and Robert Nisbet. New York: Basic Books, 1978.

BRUMFITT, J. H. *The French Enlightenment.* Cambridge, Mass.: Schenkman, 1972.

———. *Voltaire, Historian.* New York: Oxford University Press, 1970.

BURROW, J. W. *Evolution and Society.* Cambridge, England: Cambridge University Press, 1966.

CAMIC, CHARLES. "The Utilitarians Revisited." *American Journal of Sociology,* 81 (1979).

CASSIRER, ERNST. *The Philosophy of the Enlightenment.* Princeton, N.J.: Princeton University Press, 1951.

———. *The Problem of Historical Knowledge: Philosophy, Science, and History Since Hegel.* New Haven: Yale University Press, 1974.

CHITNIS, ANAND C. *The Scottish Enlightenment.* Totawa, N.J.: Rowman & Littlefield, 1976.

COBBAN, ALFRED. *In Search of Humanity.* New York: George Braziller, 1960.

COLE, G. D. H. *Socialist Thought: The Forerunners, 1789–1850.* New York: St. Martin's Press, 1962.

COLLETTI, LUCIO. *From Rousseau to Lenin: Studies in Ideology and Society.* New York: Monthly Review Press, 1972.

COLLINI, STEFAN. "Sociology and Idealism in Britain, 1880–1920." *Archives Européennes de Sociologie,* 19 (1978).

CONDORCET, MARQUIS DE. *Sketch for a Historical Picture of the Progress of the Human Mind.* New York: Noonday Press, 1955.

COSER, LEWIS. "Durkheim's Conservatism and Its Implications for His Sociological Theory." In Émile Durkheim et al., *Essays on Sociology and Philosophy,* edited by Kurt Wolff. New York: Harper & Row, 1960.

———. *Masters of Sociological Thought.* 2nd ed. New York: Harcourt Brace Jovanovich, 1977.

CROCKER, LESTER. *Age of Crisis.* Baltimore: Johns Hopkins University Press, 1959.

————. *Ethical Thought in the French Enlightenment.* Baltimore: Johns Hopkins University Press, 1963.

————. *Rousseau's Social Contract.* Cleveland: Case Western University Press, 1968.

D'ALEMBERT, JEAN LE ROND. *Preliminary Discourse to the Encyclopedia of Diderot.* Indianapolis: Bobbs-Merrill, 1963.

DIDEROT, DENIS. *Early Philosophical Works.* Edited by Margaret Jourdain. Chicago: University of Illinois Library, 1916.

————. *Rameau's Nephew and Other Works.* Edited by Jacques-Barzun and Ralph H. Bowen. New York: Bobbs-Merrill, 1964.

DRIVER, C. H. "Morelly and Mably." In *The Social and Political Ideas of Some Great French Thinkers of the Age of Reason,* edited by F. J. C. Hearnshaw. New York: Barnes & Noble, 1950.

DURKHEIM, ÉMILE. *Socialism.* Edited by Alvin W. Gouldner. New York: Collier Books, 1962.

ELLENBURG, STEPHEN. *Rousseau's Political Philosophy.* Ithaca, N.Y.: Cornell University Press, 1976.

EPSTEIN, KLAUS. *The Genesis of German Conservatism.* Princeton, N.J.: Princeton University Press, 1966.

ERMARTH, MICHAEL. *Wilhelm Dilthey.* Chicago: University of Chicago Press, 1978.

FERGUSON, ADAM. *An Essay on the History of Civil Society.* 2nd ed. London: Printed for A. Millar and T. Caddell, 1768.

FICHTE, JOHANN GOTTLIEB. *Science of Knowledge.* New York: Appleton-Century-Crofts, 1970.

FOAKES, R. A. *The Romantic Assertion.* London: Methuen, 1958.

FRANKEL, CHARLES. *The Faith of Reason.* New York: Octagon Books, 1969.

FREYER, HANS. "Die Romantiker." In *Gründer der Soziologie,* edited by Fritz Karl Mann. Jena: G. Fischer, 1932.

GADAMER, HANS-GEORG. *Truth and Method.* New York: Seabury Press, 1975.

GAY, PETER. *The Enlightenment: An Interpretation. Vol. 1, The Rise of Modern Paganism. Vol. 2, The Science of Freedom.* New York: Norton, 1977.

————. *The Party of Humanity.* New York: Norton, 1963.

————, ed. *The Enlightenment: A Comprehensive Anthology*. New York: Simon & Schuster, 1973.

GIDDENS, ANTHONY. "Classical Social Theory and the Origins of Modern Sociology." *American Journal of Sociology*, 81 (1976).

————. "Four Myths in the History of Social Thought." In *Studies in Social and Political Theory*. New York: Basic Books, 1977.

GOULDNER, ALVIN W. "Romanticism and Classicism: Deep Structures in Social Science." In *For Sociology*. New York: Basic Books, 1973.

————. *The Two Marxisms*. New York: Seabury Press, 1980.

GREEN, F. C. *Rousseau and the Idea of Progress*. Oxford: Clarendon Press, 1950.

HABERMAS, JÜRGEN. "Kritische und Konservative Aufgaben der Soziologie." In *Theorie und Praxis*. Neuwied: Luchterhand, 1967.

————. *Theory and Practice*. Boston: Beacon Press, 1973.

HAMPSON, NORMAN. *A Cultural History of the Enlightenment*. New York: Pantheon, 1968.

HAVENS, GEORGE. *The Age of Ideas*. New York: Free Press, 1955.

HAWTHORN, GEOFFREY. *Enlightenment and Despair: A History of Sociology*. Cambridge, England: Cambridge University Press, 1976.

HERDER, JOHANN GOTTFRIED VON. "Yet Another Philosophy of History." In *J. G. Herder on Social and Political Culture*, edited by F. M. Bernard. Cambridge, England: Cambridge University Press, 1969.

HOBBES, THOMAS. *Leviathan*. Edited by Michael Oakeshott. New York: Collier-Macmillan, 1971.

HUBERT, RENÉ. *Les Sciences Sociales dans L'Encyclopédie*. Paris: De l'edition de Paris, 1923.

HUME, DAVID. *Essential Works*. Edited by Ralph Cohen. New York: Bantam Books, 1965.

————. *Hume on Human Nature and the Understanding*. Edited by Anthony Flew. New York: Collier Books, 1962.

IGGERS, GEORG. *The German Conception of History*. Middletown, Conn.: Wesleyan University Press, 1968.

KANT, IMMANUEL. *Critique of Pure Reason*. New York: St. Martin's Press, 1965.

KETTLER, DAVID. *The Social and Political Thought of Adam Ferguson.* Columbus: Ohio State University Press, 1965.

KNIGHT, ISABEL F. *The Geometric Spirit: The Abbé de Condillac and the French Enlightenment.* New Haven: Yale University Press, 1968.

KORSCH, KARL. *Three Essays on Marxism.* New York: Monthly Review Press, 1972.

KOYRÉ, ALEXANDRE. *From the Closed World to the Infinite Universe.* Baltimore: Johns Hopkins University Press, 1957.

LICHTHEIM, GEORGE. *The Origins of Socialism.* New York: Praeger, 1969.

LIVELY, JACK. "Introduction." In Joseph de Maistre, *Works.* New York: Schocken Books, 1971.

LOVEJOY, ARTHUR. *Essays in the History of Ideas.* Baltimore: Johns Hopkins University Press, 1948.

LÜBBE, FRITZ. *Die Wendung vom Individualismus zur sozialen Gemeinschaft im Romantischen Roman.* Berlin: Junker U. Dunnhaupt, 1931.

MAISTRE, JOSEPH DE. *Works.* Edited by Jack Lively. New York: Schocken Books, 1971.

MANDELBAUM, MAURICE. *History, Man, and Reason: A Study in Nineteenth-Century Thought.* Baltimore: Johns Hopkins University Press, 1974.

MANNHEIM, KARL. "Conservative Thought." In *From Karl Mannheim,* edited by Kurt Wolff. New York: Oxford University Press, 1971.

MARCUSE, HERBERT. *Reason and Revolution: Hegel and the Rise of Social Theory.* Boston: Beacon Press, 1968.

MARTIN, KINGSLEY. *The Rise of French Liberal Thought.* New York: New York University Press, 1954.

MEINECKE, FRIEDRICH. *Cosmopolitanism and the National State.* Princeton, N.J.: Princeton University Press, 1970.

MITZMAN, ARTHUR. "Anti-Progress: A Study in the Romantic Roots of German Sociology." *Social Research,* 33 (1966).

———. *The Iron Cage.* New York: Grosset & Dunlap, 1969.

———. *Sociology and Estrangement.* New York: Knopf, 1973.

MONTESQUIEU, BARON DE. *The Spirit of the Laws.* New York: Hafner Press, 1975.

NISBET, ROBERT. "Conservatism and Sociology." *American Journal of Sociology*, 58 (1952).

———. *The Sociological Tradition.* New York: Basic Books, 1966.

PARSONS, TALCOTT. *The Structure of Social Action.* Vols. 1–2. New York: Free Press, 1968.

PECKHAM, MORSE. *The Triumph of Romanticism.* Columbia: University of South Carolina Press, 1971.

POGGI, GIANFRANCO. "The Chronic Trauma: The Great Transformation, Restoration Thought and the Sociological Tradition." *British Journal of Sociology*, 19 (1968).

REILL, PETER HANNS. *The German Enlightenment and the Rise of Historicism.* Berkeley and Los Angeles: University of California Press, 1975.

RINGER, FRITZ. *The Decline of the German Mandarins.* Cambridge, Mass.: Harvard University Press, 1969.

RITTER, JOACHIM. *Hegel and the French Revolution.* Cambridge, Mass.: MIT Press, 1982.

ROHLFING, WALTER. "Fortschrittsglaube in Wilhelminischen Deutschland." Ph.D. diss., University of Göttingen, Germany, 1955.

ROSE, R. B. *Gracchus Babeuf: The First Revolutionary Communist.* Stanford, Calif.: Stanford University Press, 1978.

ROUSSEAU, JEAN-JACQUES. *The Social Contract and Discourses.* Ed. G. D. H. Cole. New York: Dutton, 1973.

RUGGIERO, GUIDO DE. *The History of European Liberalism.* Boston: Beacon Press, 1966.

RUNCIMAN, W. G. *Sociology in Its Place.* Cambridge, England: Cambridge University Press, 1970.

SABINE, GEORGE H. *A History of Political Theory.* New York: Holt, Rinehart & Winston, 1965.

SALOMON, ALBERT. *The Tyranny of Progress: Reflections on the Origins of Sociology.* New York: Noonday Press, 1955.

SCHELLING, F. W. J. *System of Transcendental Idealism.* Charlottesville: University of Virginia Press, 1978.

SCHELSKY, HELMUT. *Ortbestimmung der Deutschen Soziologie.* Düsseldorf: E. Diederich, 1959.

SCHLERETH, THOMAS J. *The Cosmopolitan Ideal in Enlightenment Thought.* Notre Dame: University of Notre Dame Press, 1977.

SCOTT, JOHN ANTHONY, ed. *The Defense of Graccius Babeuf.* New York: Schocken Books, 1967.

SMALL, ALBION. *The Origins of Sociology.* Chicago: University of Chicago Press, 1924.

SPAEMANN, ROBERT. *Der Ursprung der Soziologie aus dem Geist der Restauration.* Munich: Kosel-Verlag, 1959.

SPITZER, ALAN B. *The Revolutionary Theories of Louis Blanqui.* New York: Columbia University Press, 1957.

STERN, FRITZ. *The Politics of Cultural Despair.* Berkeley and Los Angeles: University of California Press, 1961.

STRASSER, HERMANN. *The Normative Structure of Sociology: Conservative and Emancipatory Themes in Social Thought.* London: Routledge & Kegan Paul, 1976.

STRAUSS, LEO. *Natural Rights and History.* Chicago: University of Chicago Press, 1953.

TALMON, J. L. *The Rise of Totalitarian Democracy.* Boston: Beacon Press, 1952.

TAYLOR, CHARLES. *Hegel.* Cambridge, England: Cambridge University Press, 1975.

THERBORN, GÖRAN. *Science, Class, and Society: On the Formation of Sociology and Historical Materialism.* London: New Left Books, 1976.

TROELTSCH, ERNST. "The Ideas of Natural Law and Humanity in World Politics." In Otto Giercke, *Natural Law and the Theory of Society: 1500–1800,* edited by Ernest Barker. Boston: Beacon Press, 1957.

TURGOT, ANNE ROBERT JACQUES. "On Universal History." In *Turgot: On Progress, Sociology, and Economics,* edited by Ronald Meek. Cambridge, England: Cambridge University Press, 1973.

VOLTAIRE, FRANÇOIS MARIE AROUET DE. *The Age of Louis XIV.* New York: Everyman's Library, 1969.

———. "History." In Denis Diderot, *The Encyclopedia: Selections,* edited by Stephen Gendzier. New York: Harper & Row, 1967.

———. *The Philosophy of History.* New York: Citadel Press, 1965.

———. *Works.* Vols. 1–42. New York: E. R. Dumont, 1901.

VYVERBERG, HENRY. *Historical Pessimism in the French Enlightenment.* Cambridge, Mass.: Harvard University Press, 1958.

WADE, IRA O. *The Structure and Form of the French Enlightenment.* Vols. 1–2. Princeton, N.J.: Princeton University Press, 1977.

WEBER, EUGENE. *Peasants into Frenchmen: The Modernization of Rural France, 1870–1914.* Stanford, Calif.: Stanford University Press, 1976.

WEBER, MARIANNE. *Max Weber: A Biography.* New York: Wiley, 1975.

WEBER, MAX. "Religious Rejections of the World and Their Directions." In *From Max Weber,* edited by Hans Gerth and C. Wright Mills. New York: Oxford University Press, 1946.

ZEITLIN, IRVING. *Ideology and the Development of Sociological Theory.* Englewood Cliffs, N.J.: Prentice-Hall, 1968.

Part Two: Marx

ABRAMS, M. H. *Natural Supernaturalism: Tradition and Revolution in Romantic Literature.* New York: Norton, 1971.

ALEXANDER, JEFFREY. *Theoretical Logic in Sociology.* Vol. 2. Berkeley and Los Angeles: University of California Press, 1982.

ARENDT, HANNAH. *The Human Condition.* Chicago: University of Chicago Press, 1971.

ARISTOTLE. *The Basic Works of Aristotle.* Edited by Richard McKeon. New York: Random House, 1941.

AVINERI, SHLOMO. *The Social and Political Thought of Karl Marx.* Cambridge, England: Cambridge University Press, 1971.

BERLIN, ISAIAH. *Karl Marx.* New York: Oxford University Press, 1968.

BIRNBAUM, NORMAN. "The Crisis in Marxist Sociology." In *Towards a Critical Sociology.* New York: Oxford University Press, 1971.

BLOCH, ERNST. *On Karl Marx.* New York: Herder & Herder, 1971.

BREINES, PAUL. "Marxism, Romanticism, and the Case of Georg Lukàcs." *Studies in Romanticism,* 16 (1977).

COLLETTI, LUCIO. *From Rousseau to Lenin: Studies in Ideology and Society.* New York: Monthly Review Press, 1972.

COSER, LEWIS. *Masters of Sociological Thought.* 2nd ed. New York: Harcourt Brace Jovanovich, 1977.

DRAPER, HAL. *Karl Marx's Theory of Revolution.* Vols. 1–2. New York: Monthly Review Press, 1977.

———. "Marx and the Dictatorship of the Proletariat." In *Études de Marxologie,* edited by Maximelien Rubel. Paris: Institut de Science Économique Appliquée, 1962.

DUMONT, LOUIS. *From Mandeville to Marx.* Chicago: University of Chicago Press, 1977.

ENGELS, FRIEDRICH. *Dialectics of Nature.* New York: International Publishers, 1940.

FEUER, LEWIS. *Ideology and the Ideologists.* New York: Harper & Row, 1975.

GIDDENS, ANTHONY. *Capitalism and Modern Social Theory.* Cambridge, England: Cambridge University Press, 1971.

GOULDNER, ALVIN W. *The Two Marxisms.* New York: Seabury Press, 1980.

———. *For Sociology.* New York: Basic Books, 1973.

GURVITCH, GEORGES. "La Sociologie du jeune Marx." In *La Vocation actuelle de la sociologie.* Paris: Presses Universitaires de France, 1950.

HABERMAS, JÜRGEN. *Knowledge and Human Interests.* Boston: Beacon Press, 1972.

———. *Theory and Practice.* Boston: Beacon Press, 1973.

HAMMEN, OSCAR. *The Red '48ers.* New York: Scribner's, 1969.

HARRINGTON, MICHAEL. *Socialism.* New York: Bantam Books, 1977.

HOOK, SIDNEY. *From Hegel to Marx.* New York: Reynal & Hitchcock, 1936.

HOWARD, DICK. *The Development of the Marxian Dialectic.* Carbondale: Southern Illinois University Press, 1972.

HUNT, RICHARD N. *The Political Ideas of Marx and Engels: Marxism and Totalitarian Democracy, 1818–1850.* Pittsburgh: University of Pittsburgh Press, 1974.

ISRAEL, JOACHIM. *Alienation: From Marx to Modern Sociology.* Atlantic Highlands, N.J.: Humanities Press, 1979.

JACKSON, HAMPDEN J. *Marx, Proudhon, and European Socialism.* New York: Collier Books, 1962.

KANT, IMMANUEL. *Critique of Judgement.* New York: Hafner, 1972.

KOLAKOWSKI, LESZEK. *Main Currents of Marxism.* Vols. 1–3. Oxford: Clarendon Press, 1978.

KORSCH, KARL. *Karl Marx.* New York: Russell & Russell, 1963.

LICHTHEIM, GEORGE. *The Origins of Socialism.* New York: Praeger, 1969.

LOBKOWICS, NICHOLAS. *Theory and Practice: History of a Concept From Aristotle to Marx.* Notre Dame, Ind.: University of Notre Dame Press, 1972.

LÖWITH, KARL. *Meaning in History.* Chicago: University of Chicago Press, 1949.

LÖWY, MICHAEL. "Marxism and Revolutionary Romanticism." *Telos,* 49 (1981).

LUKÀCS, GEORG. *History and Class Consciousness.* Cambridge, Mass.: MIT Press, 1973.

MCLELLAN, DAVID. *Karl Marx: His Life and Thought.* New York: Harper & Row, 1977.

———. *The Young Hegelians and Karl Marx.* New York: Praeger, 1969.

MAGNIS, FRANZ VON. *Normative Voraussetzungen im Denken des Jungen Marx, 1843–1848.* Munich: Karl Alber Frieburg, 1975.

MANDEL, ERNEST. *The Formation of the Economic Thought of Karl Marx.* New York: Monthly Review Press, 1971.

MARCUSE, HERBERT. *Eros and Civilization.* Boston: Beacon Press, 1966.

———. *Reason and Revolution: Hegel and the Rise of Social Theory.* Boston: Beacon Press, 1968.

MARX, KARL. *Capital.* Vols. 1–3. New York: International Publishers, 1973.

———. *The First International and After.* Edited by David Fernbach. New York: Vintage Books, 1974.

———. *Grundrisse.* Ed. Martin Nicolaus. New York: Vintage Books, 1974.

———. *The Revolutions of 1848.* Ed. David Fernbach. New York: Vintage Books, 1974.

———. *Surveys from Exile.* Ed. David Fernbach. New York: Vintage Books, 1974.

———. *Theories of Surplus Value.* Vols. 1–3. Moscow: Progress Publishers, 1975.

———, and FRIEDRICH ENGELS. *Collected Works.* 17 vols. to date. New York: International Publishers, 1980.

———. *Selected Correspondence, 1846–1895.* New York: International Publishers, 1942.

———. *Werke.* Vols. 1–42 plus supplementary volumes. Berlin: Dietz Verlag, 1956–1967.

MESZÁROS, ISTVAN. *Marx's Theory of Alienation.* London: Merlin Press, 1970.

NICOLAIEVSKY, BORIS. "Toward a History of 'The Communist League,' 1847–1852." *International Review of Social History,* 1 (1956).

NOYES, P. H. *Organization and Revolution: Working-Class Associations in the German Revolution of 1848–1849.* Princeton, N.J.: Princeton University Press, 1966.

OLLMAN, BERTELL. *Alienation: Marx's Conception of Man in Capitalist Society.* Cambridge, England: Cambridge University Press, 1971.

———. "Towards Class Consciousness in the Working Class." *Politics and Society,* 3 (1972).

POGGI, GIANFRANCO. *Images of Society.* Stanford, Calif.: Stanford University Press, 1972.

POPPER, KARL. *The Open Society and Its Enemies.* Vols. 1–2. Princeton, N.J.: Princeton University Press, 1971.

RADDATZ, FRITZ. *Karl Marx: A Political Biography.* Boston: Little, Brown, 1979.

SCHILLER, FRIEDRICH. *On the Aesthetic Education of Man.* New York: Frederick Ungar, 1974.

SCHROYER, TRENT. *The Critique of Domination.* Boston: Beacon Press, 1975.

SWEEZY, PAUL. *The Theory of Capitalist Development.* New York: Monthly Review Press, 1968.

TALMON, J. L. *Political Messianism: The Romantic Phase.* New York: Praeger, 1960.

TAYLOR, CHARLES. *Hegel.* Cambridge, England: Cambridge University Press, 1975.

TUCKER, ROBERT C. *Philosophy and Myth in Karl Marx.* Cambridge, England: Cambridge University Press, 1965.

ULAM, ADAM. *The Unfinished Revolution.* New York: Random House, 1960.

VOEGELIN, ERIC. *From Enlightenment to Revolution.* Durham, N.C.: Duke University Press, 1975.

WEBER, SHIERRY. "Aesthetic Experience and Self-Reflection as Emancipatory Process." In *Critical Theory,* edited by John O'Neill. New York: Seabury Press, 1976.

WELLMER, ALBRECHT. *The Critical Theory of Society.* New York: Herder & Herder, 1971.

WOLFE, BERTRAM D. *Marxism.* New York: Dial Press, 1965.

PART THREE: Durkheim

ADORNO, THEODOR. "Introduction." In Durkheim, *Soziologie und Philosophie.* Frankfurt: Suhrkamp, 1967.

ALEXANDER, JEFFREY. "Indispensable Durkheim: An Alternative Historical Method to 'Division of Labor.'" *Contemporary Sociology,* 9 (1980).

————. *Theoretical Logic in Sociology.* Vol. 2. Berkeley and Los Angeles: University of California Press, 1982.

ALPERT, HARRY. *Émile Durkheim and His Sociology.* New York: Atheneum, 1961.

ANDERSON, R. D. *France, 1870–1914: Politics and Society.* London: Routledge & Kegan Paul, 1977.

ARON, RAYMOND. *Main Currents in Sociological Thought.* Vol. 2. New York: Anchor Books, 1968.

BELLAH, ROBERT N. "Introduction." In Durkheim, *On Morality and Society.* Chicago: University of Chicago Press, 1973.

BOUGLÉ, CÉLESTIN. "Preface to the Original Edition." In Émile Durkheim, *Sociology and Philosophy*. New York: Free Press, 1974.

COSER, LEWIS. *Masters of Sociological Thought*. 2nd ed. New York: Harcourt Brace Jovanovich, 1977.

CURTIS, MICHAEL. *Three Against the Third Republic: Sorel, Barrès, and Maurras*. Princeton, N.J.: Princeton University Press, 1959.

DURKHEIM, ÉMILE. *De la division du travail social*. Paris: Presses Universitaires de France, 1960.

―――. *The Division of Labor in Society*. New York: Free Press, 1933.

―――. *The Elementary Forms of the Religious Life*. New York: Free Press, 1965.

―――. *Essays on Sociology and Philosophy*. Edited by Kurt Wolff. New York: Harper & Row, 1960.

―――. *The Evolution of Educational Thought*. London: Routledge & Kegan Paul, 1977.

―――. *Montesquieu and Rousseau: Forerunners of Sociology*. Ann Arbor: University of Michigan Press, 1965.

―――. *Moral Education*. New York: Free Press, 1973.

―――. *On Institutional Analysis*. Edited by Mark Traugott. Chicago: University of Chicago Press, 1978.

―――. *On Morality and Society*. Edited by Robert Bellah. Chicago: University of Chicago Press, 1973.

―――. *Professional Ethics and Civic Morals*. London: Routledge & Kegan Paul, 1957.

―――. *The Rules of Sociological Method*. New York: Free Press, 1966.

―――. *Socialism*. Ed. Alvin W. Gouldner. New York: Collier Books, 1962.

―――. *Sociology and Philosophy*. New York: Free Press, 1974.

―――. *Suicide*. New York: Free Press, 1951.

―――. *Textes*. Vols. 1–3. Paris: Les Éditions de Minuit, 1975.

GIDDENS, ANTHONY. *Émile Durkheim*. New York: Viking Press, 1978.

―――. *Capitalism and Modern Social Theory*. Cambridge, England: Cambridge University Press, 1971.

GOULDNER, ALVIN W. *The Coming Crisis of Western Sociology.* New York: Avon Books, 1971.

HOFFMAN, ROBERT L. *Revolutionary Justice: The Social and Political Theory of P. J. Proudhon.* Urbana: University of Illinois Press, 1972.

JONES, ROBERT ALUN. "Durkheim's Response to Spencer: An Essay Toward Historicism in the Historiography of Sociography." *Sociological Quarterly,* 15 (1974).

KORSCH, KARL. *Three Essays on Marxism.* New York: Monthly Review Press, 1972.

LACAPRA, DOMINICK. *Émile Durkheim: Sociologist and Philosopher.* Ithaca, N.Y.: Cornell University Press, 1972.

LICHTHEIM, GEORGE. *Marxism in Modern France.* New York: Columbia University Press, 1966.

―――. *A Short History of Socialism.* New York: Praeger, 1970.

LUKES, STEVEN. *Émile Durkheim.* New York: Penguin Books, 1977.

MARX, KARL, and FRIEDRICH ENGELS. *Selected Correspondence, 1846–1895.* New York: International Publishers, 1942.

MOSS, BERNARD H. *The Origins of the French Labor Movement, 1830–1914.* Berkeley and Los Angeles: University of California Press, 1976.

NEYER, JOSEPH. "Individualism and Socialism in Durkheim." In Émile Durkheim et al., *Essays on Sociology and Philosophy,* edited by Kurt Wolff. New York: Harper & Row, 1960.

NISBET, ROBERT. *The Sociology of Émile Durkheim.* New York: Oxford University Press, 1974.

PARSONS, TALCOTT. "The Life and Work of Émile Durkheim." In Durkheim, *Sociology and Philosophy.* New York: Free Press, 1974.

―――. *The Structure of Social Action.* Vol. 1. New York: Free Press, 1968.

PERRIN, ROBERT. "Durkheim's Misrepresentation of Spencer: A Reply to Jones' 'Durkheim's Response to Spencer.' " *Sociological Quarterly,* 16 (1975).

POGGI, GIANFRANCO. *Images of Society.* Stanford, Calif.: Stanford University Press, 1972.

RÉMOND, RENÉ. *The Right Wing in France*. Philadelphia: University of Pennsylvania Press, 1966.

RICHTER, MELVIN. "Durkheim's Politics and Political Theory." In Durkheim, *Essays on Sociology and Philosophy*, edited by Kurt Wolff. New York: Harper & Row, 1960.

RUGGIERO, GUIDO DE. *The History of European Liberalism*. Boston: Beacon Press, 1966.

SABINE, GEORGE. *A History of Political Theory*. New York: Holt, Rinehart & Winston, 1965.

SMITH, PRESERVED. *A History of Modern Culture*. Vols. 1–2. New York: Collier Books, 1962.

SOLTAU, ROGER. *French Political Thought in the Nineteenth Century*. New Haven: Yale University Press, 1931.

STURGESS, PERRY M. "Social Theory and Political Ideology: Célestin Bouglé and the Durkheimian School." Ph.D. dissertation, City University of New York, 1978.

TIRYAKIAN, EDWARD. "Émile Durkheim." In *A History of Sociological Analysis*, edited by Tom Bottomore and Robert Nisbet. New York: Basic Books, 1978.

TRAUGOTT, MARK. "Introduction." In Durkheim, *On Institutional Analysis*. Chicago: University of Chicago Press, 1978.

WEBER, EUGENE. *Peasants into Frenchmen: The Modernization of Rural France, 1870–1914*. Stanford, Calif.: Stanford University Press, 1976.

ZEITLIN, IRVING. *Ideology and the Development of Sociological Theory*. Englewood-Cliffs, N.J.: Prentice-Hall, 1968.

PART FOUR: Weber

ABRAMOWSKI, GÜNTER. *Das Geschichtsbild Max Webers*. Stuttgart: Ernst Klett, 1966.

ALEXANDER, JEFFREY. "Formal and Substantive Voluntarism in the Work of Talcott Parsons." *American Sociological Review*, 43 (1978).

———. *Theoretical Logic in Sociology*. Vol. 3. Berkeley and Los Angeles: University of California Press, 1983.

ARATO, ANDREW. "The Neo-Idealist Defense of Subjectivity." *Telos*, 21 (1974).

ARENDT, HANNAH. *The Human Condition.* Chicago: University of Chicago Press, 1971.

BECK, LEWIS WHITE. *Early German Philosophy.* Cambridge, Mass.: Harvard University Press, 1969.

BEETHAM, DAVID. *Max Weber and the Theory of Modern Politics.* London: Allen & Unwin, 1974.

BELLAH, ROBERT N. "Religious Evolution." In *Beyond Belief.* New York: Harper & Row, 1970.

BENDIX, REINHARD. *Max Weber: An Intellectual Portrait.* New York: Doubleday, 1962.

―――. "Two Sociological Traditions." In Reinhard Bendix and Guenther Roth, *Scholarship and Partisanship: Essays on Max Weber.* Berkeley and Los Angeles: University of California Press, 1971.

BRUNN, H. H. *Science, Values, and Politics in Max Weber's Methodology.* Copenhagen: Munksgaard, 1972.

BURGER, THOMAS. "Max Weber, Interpretive Sociology, and the Sense of Historical Science: A Positivist Conception of *Verstehen.*" *Sociological Quarterly*, 18 (1977).

―――. *Max Weber's Theory of Concept Formation.* Durham, N.C.: Duke University Press, 1976.

COHEN, JERE; LAWRENCE E. HAZELRIGG, and WHITNEY POPE. "On the Divergence of Weber and Durkheim." *American Sociological Review*, 40 (1975).

COLLINS, RANDALL. "Weber's Last Theory of Capitalism: A Systematization." *American Sociological Review*, 45 (1980).

COSER, LEWIS. *Masters of Sociological Thought.* 2nd ed. New York: Harcourt Brace Jovanovich, 1977.

DAHRENDORF, RALF. *Society and Democracy in Germany.* New York: Anchor Books, 1967.

ERMARTH, MICHAEL. *Wilhelm Dilthey: The Critique of Historical Reason.* Chicago: University of Chicago Press, 1978.

FLEISHMAN, EUGENE. "De Weber à Nietzsche." *Archives Européennes de Sociologie*, 2 (1965).

FREYER, HANS. "Die Romantiker." In *Gründer der Soziologie*, edited by Fritz Karl Mann. Jena: G. Fischer, 1932.

———. *Soziologie als Wirklichkeitswissenschaft*. Berlin: B. G. Teubner, 1930.

GERTH, HANS, and C. WRIGHT MILLS. "Introduction." In *From Max Weber: Essays in Sociology*. New York: Oxford University Press, 1946.

GIDDENS, ANTHONY. *Capitalism and Modern Social Theory*. Cambridge, England: Cambridge University Press, 1971.

———. "Marx, Weber, and the Development of Capitalism." *Sociology*, 14 (1970).

———. *Politics and Sociology in the Thought of Max Weber*. London: Macmillan, 1972.

GOULDNER, ALVIN W. *The Coming Crisis of Western Sociology*. New York: Avon Books, 1971.

HEIDEGGER, MARTIN. "The Age of the World Picture." In *The Question Concerning Technology, and Other Essays*. New York: Harper & Row, 1977.

HOLBORN, HOJO. *A History of Modern Germany, 1840–1945*. New York: Knopf, 1973.

HONIGSHEIM, PAUL. "Max Weber: His Religious and Ethical Background and Development." *Church History*, 19 (1950).

HUGHES, H. STUART. *Consciousness and Society: The Reorientation of European Social Thought, 1890–1930*. New York: Knopf, 1958.

IGGERS, GEORG. *The German Conception of History*. Middletown, Conn.: Wesleyan University Press, 1968.

KALBERG, STEPHEN. "Max Weber's Types of Rationality: Cornerstones for the Analysis of Rationalization Processes in History." *American Journal of Sociology*, 85 (1980).

———. "The Search for Thematic Orientations in a Fragmented Oeuvre: The Discussion of Max Weber in Recent German Sociological Literature." *Sociology*, 13 (1979).

KRIEGER, LEONARD. *The German Idea of Freedom*. Boston: Beacon Press, 1959.

KRONMAN, ANTHONY. "Autonomy and Interaction in the Thought of Max Weber." Ph.D. dissertation. Yale University, 1972.

LANDSHUT, SIEGFRIED. *Kritik der Soziologie*. Munich: Duncker & Humboldt, 1929.

LEVENSON, JOSEPH, AND FRANZ SCHURMANN. *China: An Interpretive History*. Berkeley and Los Angeles: University of California Press, 1969.

LEVINE, FREDERICK. *The Apocalyptic Vision: The Art of Franz Marc as German Expressionism*. New York: Harper and Row, 1979.

LEVINE, DONALD. "Rationality and Freedom: Weber and Beyond." *Sociological Inquiry*, 51 (1981).

LICHTHEIM, GEORGE. *Marxism*. New York: Praeger, 1961.

LINDENLAUB, DIETER. *Richtungskämpfe im Verein für Sozialpolitik*. Wiesbaden: Franz Steiner, 1967.

LOADER, COLIN. "German Historicism and Its Crisis." *Journal of Modern History*, 48 (1976).

LOEWENSTEIN, JULIUS. *Marx Against Marxism*. London: Routledge & Kegan Paul, 1980.

LÖWITH, KARL. "Entzauberung des Welt durch Wissenschaft." *Merkur*, 5 (1964).

―――. "Max Weber und Karl Marx." *Archiv für Sozialwissenschaft und Sozialpolitik*, 67 (1932).

LUKÀCS, GEORG. *History and Class Consciousness*. Cambridge, Mass.: MIT Press, 1973.

MEINECKE, FRIEDRICH. *Cosmopolitanism and the National State*. Princeton, N.J.: Princeton University Press, 1970.

MERLEAU-PONTY, MAURICE. "The Crisis of the Understanding." In *The Primacy of Perception*. Evanston, Ill.: Northwestern University Press, 1964.

MITZMAN, ARTHUR. *The Iron Cage*. New York: Grosset & Dunlap, 1969.

―――. *Sociology and Estrangement*. New York: Knopf, 1973.

MOMMSEN, WOLFGANG. *The Age of Bureaucracy*. Oxford: Basil Blackwell, 1974.

―――. "Max Weber als Kritiker des Marxismus." *Zeitschrift für Soziologie*, 3 (1974).

―――. "Max Weber's Political Sociology and His Philosophy of World History." *International Social Science Journal*, 17 (1965).

MOSSE, GEORGE L. *The Crisis of German Ideology: Intellectual Origins of the Third Reich*. New York: Grosset & Dunlap, 1964.

MULLER, GERT. "The Notion of Rationality in the Work of Max Weber." *Archives Européennes de Sociologie*, 20 (1979).

NELSON, BENJAMIN. "Max Weber's 'Author's Introduction': A Master Clue to His Main Aims." *Sociological Inquiry*, 44 (1974).

————. "On Orient and Occident in Max Weber." *Social Research*, 43 (1976).

NIETZSCHE, FRIEDRICH. *The Gay Science*. New York: Vintage Books, 1974.

NIGG, WALTER. *Geschichte des Religiosen Liberalismus*. Zurich and Leipzig: Max Neihaus, 1937.

OAKES, GUY. "Introduction." In Max Weber, *Critique of Stammler*. New York: Free Press, 1977.

————. "Introduction." In Max Weber, *Roscher and Knies*. New York: Free Press, 1975.

OLLIG, HANS-LUDWIG. *Der Neukantianismus*. Stuttgart: Metzler, 1979.

PARSONS, TALCOTT. "Capitalism in Recent German Literature." *Journal of Political Economy*, 37 (1929).

————. "Introduction." In Max Weber, *The Sociology of Religion*. Boston: Beacon Press, 1964.

————. "Social Structure and Democracy in Pre-Nazi Germany." In *Essays in Sociological Theory*. New York: Free Press, 1954.

————. *The Structure of Social Action*. Vol. 2. New York: Free Press, 1968.

RINGER, FRITZ. *The Decline of the German Mandarins*. Cambridge, Mass.: Harvard University Press, 1969.

ROTH, GUENTHER. "The Historical Relationship Between Weber and Marxism." In Reinhard Bendix and Guenther Roth, *Scholarship and Partisanship: Essays on Max Weber*. Berkeley and Los Angeles: University of California Press, 1971.

————. "History and Sociology in the Work of Max Weber." *British Journal of Sociology*, 27 (1976).

————. "Introduction." In Max Weber, *Economy and Society*. New York: Bedminster Press, 1968.

————. *The Social Democrats in Imperial Germany*. New York: Arno Press, 1977.

————. "Weber's Generational Rebellion and Maturation." In Reinhard Bendix and Guenther Roth, *Scholarship and Partisanship: Essays on Max Weber*. Berkeley and Los Angeles: University of California Press, 1971.

SALOMON, ALBERT. "Max Weber's Political Ideas." *Social Research*, 2 (1930).

SCHLUCHTER, WOLFGANG. "Excursus: The Selection and Dating of the Works Used." In Wolfgang Schluchter and Guenther Roth, *Max Weber's Vision of History*. Berkeley and Los Angeles: University of California Press, 1979.

————. *The Rise of Western Rationalism*. Berkeley and Los Angeles: University of California Press, 1981.

SCHROYER, TRENT. *The Critique of Domination*. Boston: Beacon Press, 1975.

SCHUMPETER, JOSEPH. *Capitalism, Socialism, and Democracy*. New York: Harper & Row, 1942.

SEIDMAN, STEVEN, AND MICHAEL GRUBER. "Capitalism and Individuation in the Sociology of Max Weber." *British Journal of Sociology*, 28 (1977).

SHANAHAN, WILLIAM O. "Friedrich Naumann: A Mirror of Wilhelmian Germany." *Review of Politics*, 13 (1951).

SHEEHAN, JAMES J. *The Career of Lujo Brentano: A Study of Liberalism and Social Reform in Imperial Germany*. Chicago: University of Chicago Press, 1966.

————. *German Liberalism in the Nineteenth Century*. Chicago: University of Chicago Press, 1978.

SIMEY, T. S. "Max Weber: Man of Affairs or Theoretical Sociologist?" *Sociological Review*, 14 (1966).

SOKOL, WALTER. *The Writer in Extremis: Expressionism in Twentieth-Century German Literature*. New York: McGraw-Hill, 1964.

STAMMER, OTTO, ed. *Max Weber and Sociology Today*. New York: Harper & Row, 1971.

STARK, WERNER. "Max Weber and the Heteronomy of Purpose." *Social Research*, 34 (1967).

STERN, FRITZ. *The Failure of Illiberalism: Essays on the Political Culture of Modern Germany*. New York: Knopf, 1972.

————. *The Politics of Cultural Despair: A Study of the Rise of the Germanic Ideology.* Berkeley and Los Angeles: University of California Press, 1961.

TENBRUCK, FRIEDRICH. "Formal Sociology." In *Georg Simmel,* edited by Kurt Wolff. Columbus: Ohio State University Press, 1959.

————. "Das Werk Max Webers." *Kölner Zeitschrift für Soziologie,* 27 (1975). A slightly abridged English translation appeared as "The Problem of Thematic Unity in the Work of Max Weber." *British Journal of Sociology,* 31 (1980).

TROELTSCH, ERNST. *Der Historismus und seine Probleme.* Tübingen: J. C. B. Mohr, 1922.

————. "The Ideas of Natural Law and Humanity in World Politics." In Otto Giercke, *Natural Law and the Theory of Society, 1500–1800.* Cambridge, England: Cambridge University Press, 1934.

TURNER, BRYAN S. *Weber and Islam.* London: Routledge & Kegan Paul, 1974.

VOGEL, ULRIKE. "Einige Ueberlegungen zum Begriff der Rationalitat bei Max Weber." *Kölner Zeitschrift für Soziologie und Sozialpsychologie,* 25 (1973).

WARNER, R. STEPHEN. "Toward a Redefinition of Action Theory." *American Journal of Sociology,* 83 (1978).

WEBER, MARIANNE. *Max Weber: A Biography.* New York, Wiley, 1975.

WEBER, MAX. *The Agrarian Sociology of Ancient Civilizations.* London: New Left Books, 1976.

————. *Ancient Judaism.* New York: Free Press, 1952.

————. *Critique of Stammler.* New York: Free Press, 1977.

————. *Economy and Society.* Vols. 1–3. New York: Bedminster Press, 1968.

————. *From Max Weber: Essays in Sociology.* New York: Oxford University Press, 1946.

————. *General Economic History.* New York: Collier Books, 1927.

————. *Gesammelte Aufsätze zur Religionssoziologie.* Vols. 1–3. Tübingen: 1920–1921.

————. *Gesammelte Aufsätze zur Soziologie und Sozialpolitik.* Tübingen: Mohr, 1924.

———. *Gesammelte Politische Schriften.* 2nd rev. ed., Edited by Johannes Winckelmann. Tübingen: Mohr, 1971.

———. *The Methodology of the Social Sciences.* New York, Free Press, 1949.

———. *The Protestant-Ethic and the Spirit of Capitalism.* New York: Free Press, 1958.

———. *The Religion of China: Confucianism and Taoism.* New York: Free Press, 1951.

———. *The Religion of India.* New York: Free Press, 1958.

———. *Roscher and Knies.* New York: Free Press, 1975.

———. *Selections in Translation.* Ed. Walter Runciman. Cambridge, England: Cambridge University Press, 1978.

———. *The Sociology of Religion.* Boston: Beacon Press, 1964.

WEINER, JONATHAN. "Max Weber's Marxism: Theory and Method in *The Agrarian Sociology of Ancient Civilizations.*" *Theory and Society,* 11 (May 1982).

WILLEY, THOMAS E. *Back to Kant: The Revival of Kantianism in German Social and Historical Thought, 1860–1914.* Detroit: Wayne State University Press, 1978.

YANG, C. K. "Introduction." In Max Weber, *The Religion of China.* New York: Free Press, 1951.

ZEITLIN, IRVING. *Ideology and the Development of Sociological Theory.* Englewood Cliffs, N.J.: Prentice-Hall, 1968.

Conclusion and Appendix

ALEXANDER, JEFFREY. *Theoretical Logic in Sociology.* Vol. 1. Berkeley and Los Angeles: University of California Press, 1982.

ANDRESKI, STANISLAV. "Introduction." In Herbert Spencer, *Principles of Sociology,* edited by Stanislav Andreski. Hamden, Conn.: Archon Books, 1969.

BECKER, ERNEST. *The Structure of Evil: An Essay on the Unification of the Science of Man.* New York: Free Press, 1968.

BUTTERFIELD, HERBERT. *The Origins of Modern Science: 1300–1800.* New York: Collier Books, 1962.

CAMIC, CHARLES. "On the Methodology of the History of Sociology: A Reply to Jones." *American Journal of Sociology,* 86 (1981).

————. "The Utilitarians Revisited." *American Journal of Sociology*, 85 (1979).

CASSIRER, ERNST. *The Philosophy of the Enlightenment*. Princeton, N.J.: Princeton University Press, 1951.

CLARK, TERRY. "Émile Durkheim and the French University." In *The Establishment of Empirical Sociology*, edited by Anthony Oberschall. New York: Harper & Row, 1972.

COBBAN, ALFRED. *Burke and the Revolt Against the Eighteenth Century*. London: Allen & Unwin, 1960.

COLLINS, RANDALL. *Conflict Sociology*. New York: Academic Press, 1975.

DALLMAYR, FRED, and THOMAS McCARTHY, eds. *Understanding and Social Inquiry*. Notre Dame, Ind.: University of Notre Dame Press, 1977.

DAWE, ALAN. "Theories of Social Action." In *A History of Sociological Analysis*, edited by Tom Bottomore and Robert Nisbet. New York: Basic Books, 1978.

DILTHEY, WILHELM. "Das Achtzehnte Jahrhundert und die Geschichtliche Welt." In *Gesammelte Schriften*, vol. 3. Stuttgart: Teubner, 1957.

DUNN, JOHN. "The Identity of the History of Ideas." In *Philosophy, Politics, and Society*, series IV, edited by Peter Laslett, W. C. Runciman, Quentin Skinner. London: Oxford University Press, 1972.

EISENSTADT, S. N., with M. CURELARU. *The Form of Sociology. Paradigms and Crisis*. New York: Wiley, 1976.

FEYERABEND, PAUL. *Against Method*. London: New Left Books, 1974.

FOUCAULT, MICHEL. *The Order of Things*. New York: Vintage Books, 1973.

GADAMER, HANS-GEORG. *Truth and Method*. New York: Seabury Press, 1975.

GAY, PETER. *The Enlightenment*. New York: Norton, 1977.

————. *The Party of Humanity*. New York: Norton, 1963.

GIDDENS, ANTHONY. *Capitalism and Modern Social Theory*. Cambridge, England: Cambridge University Press, 1971.

————. *Central Problems in Social Theory*. Berkeley and Los Angeles: University of California Press, 1979.

————. "Positivism and Its Critics." In *Studies in Social and Political Theory*. New York: Basic Books, 1977.

GOULDNER, ALVIN W. *The Coming Crisis of Western Sociology*. New York: Avon Books, 1970.

HABERMAS, JÜRGEN. *Knowledge and Human Interests*. Boston: Beacon Press, 1972.

HAWTHORN, GEOFFREY. *Enlightenment and Despair: A History of Sociology*. Cambridge, England: Cambridge University Press, 1976.

HIRSCH, E. D. *Validity in Interpretation*. New Haven: Yale University Press, 1967.

HOLTON, GERALD. *Thematic Origins of Scientific Thought*. Cambridge, Mass.: Harvard University Press, 1973.

HORKHEIMER, MAX. *Critical Theory*. New York: Seabury Press, 1972.

HOY, DAVID. *The Critical Circle*. Berkeley and Los Angeles: University of California Press, 1978.

HUSSERL, EDMUND. *The Crisis of European Sciences and Transcendental Phenomenology*. Evanston, Ill.: Northwestern University Press, 1970.

JONES, ROBERT ALUN. "Durkheim's Response to Spencer: An Essay Toward Historicism in the Historiography of Sociology." *Sociological Quarterly*, 15 (1974).

————. "On Understanding a Sociological Classic." *American Journal of Sociology*, 83 (1977).

LAKATOS, IMRE. *The Methodology of Scientific Research Programmes*. Edited by John Worrall and Gregory Currie. Cambridge, England: Cambridge University Press, 1978.

LINDENLAUB, DIETER. *Richtungskämpfe im Verein für Sozialpolitik*. Wiesbaden: Franz Steiner, 1967.

LÖWITH, KARL. "Max Weber und Karl Marx." *Archiv für Sozialwissenschaft und Sozialpolitik*, 67 (1932).

LUKÀCS, GEORG. *Die Zerstorung der Vernunft*. Neuwied: Luchterhand, 1962.

MANNHEIM, KARL. *Ideology and Utopia.* New York: Harcourt, Brace & World, 1936.

MEINECKE, FRIEDRICH. *Historism.* London: Routledge & Kegan Paul, 1972.

MERTON, ROBERT. *Social Theory and Social Structure.* Glencoe, Ill.: Free Press, 1949.

PALMER, RICHARD. *Hermeneutics.* Evanston, Ill.: Northwestern University Press, 1969.

PAREKH, BHIKHU, and R. N. BERKI. "The History of Political Ideas: A Critique of Quentin Skinner's Methodology." *Journal of the History of Ideas*, 34 (1973).

PEEL, J. D. *Herbert Spencer.* New York: Basic Books, 1971.

PEPPER, STEPHEN. *World Hypotheses.* Berkeley: University of California Press, 1942.

POLANYI, MICHAEL. *The Tacit Dimension.* New York: Doubleday, 1966.

RABINOW, PAUL, AND WILLIAM SULLIVAN, eds. *Interpretive Social Science.* Berkeley and Los Angeles: University of California Press, 1979.

RADNITZKY, GERARD. "Life Cycles of a Scientific Tradition." *Main Currents of Modern Thought*, 32 (1975).

RICOEUR, PAUL. "The Model of the Text: Meaningful Action Considered as a Text." *Social Research*, 38 (1971).

ROBERTSON, ROLAND. "Major Axes in Sociological Analysis." In *Approaches to Sociology*, ed. John Rex. London: Routledge & Kegan Paul, 1974.

———. *Meaning and Change.* New York: New York University Press, 1978.

SHAPERE, DUDLEY. "Meaning and Scientific Change." In *Mind and Cosmos*, edited by Robert Colodny. Pittsburgh, Penn.: University of Pittsburgh Press, 1969.

SHILS, EDWARD. *Tradition.* Chicago: University of Chicago Press, 1981.

———. "Tradition, Ecology, and Institution in the History of Sociology." *Daedalus*, 99 (1970).

SKINNER, QUENTIN. *The Foundations of Modern Political Thought.* Vol. 1. Cambridge, England: Cambridge University Press, 1978.

――――. "Hermeneutics and the Role of History." *New Literary History*, 7 (1976).

――――. "Meaning and Understanding in the History of Ideas." *History and Theory*, 8 (1969).

――――. "Motives, Intentions, and the Interpretation of Texts." *New Literary History*, 3 (1972).

――――. "Some Problems in the Analysis of Political Thought and Action." *Political Theory*, 2 (1974).

STOCKING, GEORGE. " 'Cultural Darwinism' and 'Philosophical Idealism' in E. B. Tylor: A Special Plea for Historicism in the History of Anthropology." *Southwestern Journal of Anthropology*, 21 (1965).

――――. "On the Limits of 'Presentism' and 'Historicism' in the Historiography of the Behavioral Sciences." *Journal of the History of the Behavioral Sciences*, 1 (1965).

TIRYAKIAN, EDWARD. "Émile Durkheim." In *A History of Sociological Analysis*, edited by Tom Bottomore and Robert Nisbet. New York: Basic Books, 1978.

――――. "The Significance of Schools in the Development of Sociology." In *Contemporary Issues in Theory and Research*, edited by William Snizek et al. Westport, Conn.: Greenwood Press, 1979.

TÖNNIES, FERDINAND. *Community and Society.* East Lansing: Michigan State University Press, 1957.

WARNER, R. STEPHEN. "The Uses of the Classic Tradition." In R. Stephen Warner and Neil Smelser, *Sociological Theory*. Morristown, N.J.: General Learning Press, 1976.

WHITEBOOK, JOEL. "Saving the Subject: Modernity and the Problem of the Autonomous Individual." *Telos*, 50 (1981–1982).

WITTGENSTEIN, LUDWIG. *Philosophical Investigations.* New York: Macmillan, 1958.

Index

Abramowski, Günter, 239, 246
Abrams, M. H., 92
Absolutism, 15, 16, 196, 312n55, 356n38
Action Française, 56, 155, 157
"Address of the Central Committee to the Communist League," 115, 117
Adorno, Theodor, 340n5
Aesthetics, 27, 49, 133–134
Agrarian France, 71, 152, 161
Agrarian Germany, 210, 346n3
Agrarian Sociology of Ancient Civilizations, 238
Ahistorism, 7, 8, 9, 122–123
Alexander, Jeffrey, 2, 290, 322–323n11, 334n6
Alienation: counter-Enlightenment and, 47–48, 49, 75, 273–274, 276; Durkheim and, 14, 49; Marx and, 14, 49, 130–131, 137–138, 246; Weber and, 14, 49, 246
Alpert, Harry, 146, 150, 151
America, 114, 359–360n88; liberalism in, 237, 306n44;

Marxists in, 142; Weber interpretation in, 246–249. *See also* Anglo-American social theory
Analytical realm, 5, 6–7, 11, 179, 296–297, 302–303n19; counter-Enlightenment and, 43–49, 50, 75; Durkheim and, 148, 149, 167, 169, 178, 180–197, 199, 206, 278; Enlightenment and, 7, 8–9, 11, 31–32, 34, 43–49, 50, 74–75, 94, 95, 273; Marx and, 11, 94, 95, 138, 140, 141–142, 297, 324n26; Weber and, 206, 207–208, 222, 223–224. *See also* Methodology
Anarchism: in France, 12, 71, 76, 155, 157, 159, 198, 203; in Germany, 203; Marx and, 84
Ancient Judaism, 247
Anglo-American social theory, 6–7, 13, 355n38; individualism of, 7, 34, 74, 273; instrumentalism of, 7, 34, 74, 273; rationalism of, 7, 273; social contract theory in,

8, 40, 74, 275. *See also* English liberalism

Anomie, 14, 185, 196

Anthropology, 76; Durkheim and, 196; Enlightenment and, 29, 40; Marx and, 88–90, 132, 133

Anti-Semitism, 157, 235

Apollonian notion, 61

Archiv für Sozialwissenschaften und Sozialpolitik, 236

Arendt, Hannah, 333*n*35, 39

Aristocracy, 207–210, 211, 276

Aristotle, 101, 136, 325–326*n*1

Aron, Raymond, 1, 335–336*n*22, 347*n*12

Atomistic individualism, 7, 22–23, 44

Authoritarianism, 152, 155, 273–274; Durkheim and, 167, 181, 182, 186, 196, 198, 203; Marx and, 84, 103, 109, 140; Weber and, 61, 148, 203

Author's intention, 286, 287, 288, 289, 291, 294

Autonomy, individual, 14, 333*n*32; Durkheim and, 73, 150, 163–164, 172–173, 203; Enlightenment and, 32, 33, 59, 86, 94, 131, 132; Marx and, 12, 73, 84, 86, 88, 94, 97–100, 104, 131, 132–133, 138; Weber and, 73, 203, 205, 225, 232, 239, 348*n*12

Avineri, Shlomo, 102, 117, 326*n*2, 328*n*12

Babeuf, François, 52, 53, 64, 68–70, 148

Babouvism, 12, 64, 68–69, 71, 85, 103

Baden Kantians, 204

Barrès, Maurice, 157

Bastiat, Frédéric, 153

Baudrillard, Jean, 11

Bauer, Bruno, 83

Bayle, Pierre, 32

Becker, Ernest, 8, 275, 300*n*4

Beeghley, Leonard, 3–4, 300*n*4

Below, Georg von, 226

Bendix, Reinhard, 62, 247–249, 342–343*n*12, 354*n*36

Bentham, Jeremy, 15, 31

Bergson, Henri, 157

Berlin, Isaiah, 14, 313*n*1

Berlin, University of, 82–84, 320*n*5

Bernstein, Eduard, 148, 205, 235

Bierstadt, Robert, 308*n*1

Bildung tradition, 278

Bismarck, Otto von, 209, 215, 216

Blanc, Louis, 159

Blanqui, Louis Auguste, 12, 103, 124, 148, 159, 319*n*67

Blanquism, 53, 147; Marx and, 103, 106–107, 108, 109, 114, 116, 117–118; and vanguard party, 106–107, 116, 117, 330*n*51

Bloch, Ernst, 141

Böhm-Bawerk, Eugen, 343*n*1

Bonald, Louis, 42, 43, 52, 54, 104, 167

Bonapartist dynasty, 152

Bottomore, Tom, 306*n*39

Bouglé, Célestin, 173

Boulanger, Georges Ernest, 154

Bourbon dynasty, 152

Bourgeois, Leon, 159

Bourgeoisie, 4–18 passim, 70, 152–159 passim, 276–278, 307*n*49, 319*n*67; Durkheim and, 49, 70, 73, 77, 148–149, 160, 177, 198, 204, 277; Marx and, 10–13 passim, 49, 70–77 passim, 84–115 passim, 121, 122, 123, 130–131, 140, 142, 145, 277, 278, 322*n*11, 324*n*19, 328*nn*11, 12, 13; Weber and,

13, 49, 70, 73, 77, 204–241 passim, 269–270, 277

Boutroux, Emile, 151, 162, 173, 190

Bureaucracy, 203, 269; Durkheim and, 150, 278; Weber and, 212, 232, 237, 239, 278, 355–356n38

Burke, Edmund, 52, 54, 291

Cabet, Etienne, 71

Calvinism, 220. *See also* Puritanism

Camic, Charles, 312n52

Capital, 133, 276, 291; and capitalism, 124, 126, 127, 128, 291; and democracy, 327n9; and the dialectic, 328–329n16; and freedom, 135

Capitalism, 4–5, 15, 49, 203; Marx and, 90–106 passim, 120–140 passim, 291, 292–293, 322–323n11, 343–345n1; Weber and, 147, 203–220 passim, 237–245 passim, 252, 269, 292–293, 343–345n1, 355–356n38

Carlyle, Thomas, 169

Cartesianism, 142, 181, 196

Cassirer, Ernst, 8, 43, 275

Catholicism, 152; conservatism and, 56, 155, 157; Enlightenment and, 9, 37, 42, 275; Weber and, 220, 252

Catholic Renaissance, 56, 155, 157

Censorship laws, 16

Charity, 338–339n29

China, 232, 244, 249, 355n38

Christianity, 14, 32, 92–93, 111, 167–168, 313n60; Enlightenment and, 9, 30–42 passim, 275, 276, 312n55; Marx and, 82, 92–93; Weber

and, 210, 241, 244, 248, 252. *See also* Catholicism; Protestantism

Christian Socialism, 235

Churches. *See* Christianity

"Circular Letter to Bebel, Liebknecht, Bracke, et al.," 114

City, Occidental, 239, 241

Civic morality, 188, 189

Civilizations, compared, 235–268, 356n38

Civil religion, 67, 70, 160, 173

Class: aristocracy, 207–210, 211, 276; conflicts, 155, 176, 196; consciousness, 207, 211, 214, 217, 221, 269; divisions, 11, 70, 90, 161, 176; domination by, 17, 277, 278. *See also* Bourgeoisie; Working classes

Classical economics, 18, 31, 34, 60; in Anglo-American theory, 6, 34, 74, 75, 76, 162, 163, 345n1; Durkheim and, 158, 162, 163, 180, 182, 186; Marx and, 10, 11, 94, 95, 96, 121–131 passim, 322n11; Weber and, 218

Classic works, 293–294, 297, 363n4

Closure, 36, 37, 38–39, 40–41, 312n55

Code de la Nature, 68

Cohen, Hermann, 204, 205, 342n11

Cole, G. D. F., 67

Coleridge, Samuel Taylor, 169

Collected Essays in the Sociology of Religion, 238, 242, 249, 256

Collective beliefs, 160, 168, 169, 174–175. *See also* Religion

Collective life, 45, 50, 149, 179–197. *See also* Social solidarity

Collective norms, 335–336n22. *See also* Morality

Collectivism: counter-Enlightenment and, 44, 52–53, 55, 57, 65, 66; in English liberalism, 7, 76; French tradition of, 76; of German ideology, 225, 226, 230, 233; of Romanticism, 52–53, 55, 57, 316n27

Collectivist historicism, 204, 270

Collectivist idealism, 205

Collins, Randall, 243, 282, 355n36

Commerce, 101, 153, 169, 203, 208, 325–326n1. *See also* Capitalism; Market economy

Communards, 152, 154, 204

Communism: egalitarian, 66–73 passim, 102, 103, 104–105, 120; Marx and, 12, 72, 73, 85, 92–93, 102–111 passim, 277, 327n10

Communist Correspondence Committee, 108, 327n5

Communist League, 108, 109, 117

Communist Manifesto, 113, 119, 126; and Blanquism, 117, 118; and democracy, 110, 327n9; and vanguard party concept, 107–108

Communist party, French, 335n11

Communists, contemporary, 116

Communitarianism: counter-Enlightenment, 7, 48–73 passim, 120, 273, 276; Durkheim and, 52, 56, 149, 150, 160, 175, 178, 198; Marx and, 63, 84, 120

Community and Society, 291

Commutative justice, 338n29

Competition, 7, 15, 51

Comte, Auguste, 131, 141, 145, 293, 305nn35, 37; conservatism of, 55–56, 75,

145, 154, 158, 166–170 passim; Durkheim and, 55–56, 150, 151, 158, 165–171 passim, 180, 199

Condillac, Etienne Bonnot de, 24

Condorcet, Marquis de, 23–24, 28, 32, 159, 173

Conflict, 7, 15, 51, 155, 176, 196

Confucianism, 232, 251, 355n38

Consciousness, 57, 58, 139, 191, 193–194. *See also under* Class

Conservatism, 10, 13, 17, 39, 76, 315–316n23; of Comte, 55–56, 75, 145, 154, 158, 166–170 passim; counter-Enlightenment, 10, 52–61 passim, 70, 274, 313–314n2; Durkheim and, 55–56, 152–159 passim, 168–180 passim, 203, 274, 278; Marx and, 81, 89, 101, 277, 278; of Marxism (post-Marx), 11, 140; Weber and, 13, 148, 203, 210, 214, 215, 216, 221, 235, 236, 269, 270, 278

Constant, Benjamin, 153

Constitutions, 85, 110, 153

Contextualism, 285–286

Continuity, historical, 282, 291–293, 294, 295, 363n4

Contractarianism. *See* Social contract theory

"Contribution to the Critique of Hegel's Philosophy of Right," 84

Cooperative socialism, 129, 147, 155

Coser, Lewis, 56

Cosmological world-view, 39, 41, 51, 157, 167–169, 175

Counter-Enlightenment, 7, 8, 10, 42–75 passim, 273–276, 313–314nn1, 2, 361n1

Credit system, 129

Crisis of liberalism, 154, 156–158, 161, 180, 206
Crisis of Western Sociology, 5
Critical Marxism, 132, 142
Critique of Hegel's Doctrine of the State, 84, 94–95, 110
Critique of Judgement, 133
Crocker, Lester, 8
Cult of personality, 175
Cultural pessimism, 61, 259, 262–263, 268
Culture, 16, 153, 157; Durkheim and, 149, 158, 160, 161, 174, 185–186, 190–191, 195; Enlightenment and, 28–30, 33–34, 44–45, 47; Marx and, 81, 120, 233; Weber and, 61, 205, 211–270 passim, 347n4, 356n38

D'Alembert, Jean le Rond, 28–29, 38, 310n30
Darwinism, social, 17, 73, 159. *See also* Evolutionism
Dawe, Alan, 293
Deductionism, 163–165
Deleuze, Gilles, 11
Democracy, 16, 17, 152, 167, 178, 278; Durkheim and, 13, 73, 151, 158–185 passim, 198, 199, 204, 339n5; Germany and, 12–13, 204, 205, 213–234, 235, 236, 269, 270, 347n8, 351n1; Marx and, 12, 73, 84, 86, 97, 103–119 passim, 140, 142, 147–148, 320n10, 327nn9, 10, 329n32, 330n51; totalitarian, 64, 103, 114–119; Weber and, 12–13, 62, 73, 205–206, 213–234, 235, 236, 237, 269, 270, 342n11, 348n12, 351n1. *See also* French democratic tradition; Liberal democracy; Social democracy
Democratic-socialism, 113
Descartes, René, 35, 36, 142, 181, 196
Determinism: Durkheim and, 194, 195; Enlightenment, 7, 31, 34, 50; Kant and, 136; Marx and, 88, 97; neo-Kantians and, 204–205
Deutsche-französische Jahrbücher, 102
Dialecticism: Durkheim and, 192; Marx and, 9, 89, 94, 102, 105, 322–323n11, 328–329n16
Dialogue, historical interpretation in, 289, 294, 363n4
Dictatorship, 70, 115–116, 330n51
Diderot, Denis, 31, 38, 311–312n47
Dilthey, Wilhelm, 8, 43, 275
Dionysian element of action, 232
Discontinuity, historical, 285, 290, 291, 294, 295
"Discourse on Universal History," 28
"Discourses," 21, 25, 171
Distributive justice, 175–176, 338n29
Division of Labor in Society, 163, 168, 170, 185–192 passim, 334n6
Divisions, 51, 90, 93, 138; class, 11, 70, 90, 161, 176; of governmental powers, 65; ideological, 11; of labor, 90–91, 134, 175–176, 185–188, 189, 265
Doctors' Club, 83
Dogmatism: Durkheim and, 196; Enlightenment and, 36, 37, 38–39, 40–41, 312n55; Marxist, 93, 270
Dreyfus Affair, 154, 155
Draper, Hal, 329n32

Dualism, 32–33; Durkheim and, 189–190, 191, 194, 195, 199–200; Enlightenment and, 31, 32–33, 40, 57, 87, 93, 94, 189, 311–312n47; Marx and, 87–88, 90, 93, 94, 136–137; romantics and, 57, 58, 87, 93

Dumont, Louis, 324n26

Dunn, John, 282

Durkheim, Emile, 13, 143–200, 276, 293, 294; and alienation, 14, 49; communitarianism of, 52, 56, 149, 150, 160, 175, 178, 198; and conservatism, 55–56, 152–159 passim, 168–180 passim, 203, 274, 278; and individualism, 149, 150, 160–180 passim, 194, 195, 198–199, 335–336n22, 338n28; intellectual traditions affecting, 146–151, 157, 158–159, 206, 274, 339–340n5; and justice, 148, 150, 159–160, 172–180 passim, 198, 338–339n29; and liberalism, 12–18 passim, 56, 70–77 passim, 150–189 passim, 197–206 passim, 277, 278, 279, 306n44, 337n15; and Marx, 145–147, 334n6, 335n9; and morality, 68, 149, 150, 151, 160–163 passim, 169–196 passim, 335–336n22, 338n29; and organicism, 45, 169; and revolution, 12, 13, 56, 68–77 passim, 147–182 passim, 197, 198, 204, 277, 278; and Weber, 203–204, 206, 342–343n12

East Elbian social conditions, 147, 243

Economic history, 226, 270, 345–346n1

Economics, 16, 70, 149, 153, 222, 326n1; Durkheim and, 158–166 passim, 173, 175, 180, 182, 186, 192–196 passim, 276; Enlightenment, 34, 65 (*see also* Classical economics); historical, 45, 226, 229, 339n5; Junkers and, 208–209; Marx and, 94, 95, 96, 121–131 passim, 276, 322n11; vulgar, 17, 122; Weber and, 214, 218, 226, 233, 237, 276, 343–345n1, 346n3

Economy and Society, 238–249 passim, 291

Education: conservatism and, 155, 210–211, 226; Durkheim and, 150, 192–193; Marx and, 82–84, 111, 320n5; Weber and, 210–211, 214–215

Egalitarian communism, 66–73 passim, 102, 103, 104–105, 120

Egalitarianism. *See* Equality

Egalitarians, 12, 53, 66–69, 71; Durkheim and, 148, 173; Marx and, 120

Egoism, 7, 120, 162, 180, 196, 338n29

1844 Paris Manuscripts, 84, 89, 92, 124–125, 126, 132–133

Elections, Reichstag (1903), 236, 350–351n1

Elementary Forms of the Religious Life, 191, 194

Emanationism, 45, 229

Emergence of Sociological Theory, 3–4

Empiricism: counter-Enlightenment, 44, 47, 273–274; Durkheim and, 165; Enlightenment and, 25–28, 36–37, 39, 40, 45, 309n22; in historiography, 40, 47, 285,

290, 294, 295, 309*n*22
Engels, Friedrich, 85, 104–118
    passim, 305*n*35
England, 114, 153, 169. *See also*
    Anglo-American social theory
English liberalism, 6–7, 15, 16,
    75, 76, 215, 276, 304*n*29;
    Durkheim and, 152–185
    passim, 198, 199, 306*n*44,
    337*n*15; Marx and, 306*n*44;
    Weber and, 62, 270, 306*n*44,
    345*n*1
English Marxists, 142
Enlightenment, 9, 4–11 passim,
    21–41, 49, 74–75, 76,
    152–153, 308*n*1, 361*n*1; Comte
    and, 131, 166–167; counter-
    Enlightenment and, 42–53,
    57, 59, 63, 64–65, 75,
    273–276, 314*n*2; Durkheim
    and, 189; and history, 7, 8–9,
    17–18, 24–34 passim, 40–49
    passim, 74, 275, 309*n*22,
    310*n*30; Marx and, 8, 10, 11,
    81–88 passim, 93, 94–100,
    101, 122–124, 131–139, 142,
    274; and natural law, 9, 24,
    50–51, 304*n*29; and
    Romanticism, 42, 43, 52, 57,
    59, 63, 87, 93, 131–139,
    314*n*5; and social contract
    theory, 7–9, 17–28 passim, 35,
    40, 44, 74, 94, 275, 276,
    304*n*29, 361*n*1; Weber and,
    225, 231, 233, 246, 247, 255.
    See also Liberalism
Enlightenment and Despair, 5–6
Epistemology, 6; of counter-
    Enlightenment, 45; of
    Enlightenment, 26, 27, 40,
    133, 309*n*22, 314*n*5; Marx
    and, 12, 45, 88, 89–90, 133;
    neo-Kantian, 204, 205, 270; of
    Romanticism, 89–90, 133,

314*n*5; Weber and, 45, 205,
    222, 223–224, 239, 270
Equality, 16, 17, 39, 65–73
    passim, 103, 167; Durkheim
    and, 73, 148–149, 160,
    171–180 passim, 198–199,
    338*n*29; Marx and, 73, 84, 120
Erfurt Program, 215, 270
*Essay on the Manners and Spirit of
    Nations*, 28
Ethics, Weber and, 205, 239, 244,
    251–252, 255, 264, 270,
    356*n*48
Evolutionism, 7, 17, 18, 73, 76,
    159; Durkheim and, 165, 166;
    Weber and, 218, 228,
    246–247, 250, 354–355*n*36
Evolution of Educational Thought,
    191
Existentialism, 262, 359*n*81
Explanation, 3, 6, 241
Expressionism, 58, 59–60, 61,
    333*n*32; Marx and, 63, 82,
    132, 133–134; Weber and, 60,
    262

Factories, cooperative, 129
Fallibilism, 15, 16
Faustian images, 61, 63, 265, 266
Ferguson, Adam, 22, 23, 25–26,
    44–46
Feudalism, 59, 208, 211
Feuer, Lewis, 141
Feuerbach, Ludwig, 83, 84, 88,
    133
Feyerabend, Paul, 281
Fichte, Johann Gottlieb, 45,
    52–53, 225; idealism of, 57,
    58, 59, 82, 85, 88, 183, 326*n*2;
    Marx and, 82, 85, 88, 326*n*2
Formalism, 9, 59, 136, 205,
    238–239
Foucault, Michel, 361*n*1
Fouillée, Alfred, 159

Fourier, Charles, 76, 141; and egalitarian communism, 71; Marx and, 121, 124, 132–133, 134, 135

France, 77, 169, 203, 275; conservatism in, 17, 52, 152–159 passim, 173, 180, 203, 274, 277; counter-Enlightenment and, 44, 75; Enlightenment in, 53, 101, 153, 225, 275, 304n29; humanism in, 32, 103, 190; liberalism in, 13, 17, 76, 77, 104, 150–166 passim, 198, 203, 277; Marx and, 81, 113, 145 (*see also under* French revolutionary tradition); revolutions in, 11, 71, 105, 106, 115, 273; sociology in, 10, 55, 169 (*see also* Durkheim, Emile; Saint-Simon, Comte de); structuralism in, 141–142, 288. *See also* French democratic tradition; French revolutionary tradition; Third French Republic

Franco-Prussian War, 155

Frankfurt School, 11

Freedom, individual, 15–16, 18, 167, 203, 225, 263; counter-Enlightenment and, 65–66, 67; Durkheim and, 149, 159–160, 171–172, 174, 177, 190; Enlightenment and, 48, 50, 65, 94, 97, 98, 142; Marx and, 94, 97, 98, 104, 134–138, 142; Weber and, 231, 262, 264–265, 266–268, 348n12. *See also* Autonomy, individual

Freiburg address, Weber's, 213, 236

French Constitution of 1793, 110

French democratic tradition, 13, 76, 152, 155; constitution in, 110; Durkheim and, 13, 51, 158, 159–160, 171, 172–173, 178, 180, 185, 198, 199, 204, 339n5

French revolutionary tradition, 12–13, 53, 64–76 passim, 203, 319n67, 335n11; Durkheim and, 13, 56, 147–160 passim, 172, 173, 182, 198; Greeks and, 67, 101, 326n1; Marx and, 12, 84, 86, 101–124 passim, 277, 328n12, 335n11

Freyer, Hans, 60, 240, 245

Gadamer, Hans-Georg, 288, 289, 292, 314n5

Gans, Eduard, 320n5

Gay, Peter, 8, 43, 275, 304n29, 308n1, 312n55

Gemeinschaft, 61

General Economic History, 243

Generality, historical, 290–291, 292

George, Stefan, 62, 262, 317n37

German Historical School, 42, 56, 165–166, 184–185; of Economics, 45, 226, 229; of Jurisprudence, 52, 226

German idealism, 15, 57–59, 204; Durkheim and, 183–185; Marx and, 10, 13, 82–83, 85, 88–89, 94, 102, 141, 326n2; Weber and, 218, 222, 226, 233, 245, 246, 345n1

German ideology, 222–234, 349n20. *See also* German Historical School; German idealism; Romanticism

German Ideology, 85, 112, 222, 291

German Sociological Meetings, 267, 347n4

Germany, 77, 81–84, 149, 169, 275, 339–340n5; bourgeoisie of, 115, 207–233 passim,

269–270; conservatism in, 13, 17, 52, 56, 81, 148, 203–221 passim, 235, 236, 269, 270, 277, 315–316n23; counter-Enlightenment and, 44, 52–53, 58, 59–60, 61, 75; cultural pessimism in, 61, 259, 262–263, 268; and democracy, 12–13, 204, 205, 213–234, 235, 236, 269, 270, 347n8, 351n1; Expressionism of, 58, 59–60, 61, 82, 262, 333n32; liberalism in, 13, 17, 18, 64, 76, 203–236 passim, 269, 277, 320n10, 342n10, 347n8; Marxism in, 61, 73, 109, 118, 141, 147–148, 205, 215, 270; materialism in, 204–205, 207–212, 213, 226, 345–346n1, 360n1; positivism in, 204, 226, 270, 360n1; Prussian hegemony in, 13, 61, 81, 148, 206–216 passim, 221, 226, 230, 235, 269, 270; Reichstag elections in, 236, 350–351n1; and science of man, 44, 75; sociology of, 55, 60–64, 147, 317n31 (*see also* Weber, Max). *See also* German ideology
German Youth Movement, 259
Gesammelte Aufsätze zur Religions Soziologie. See *Collected Essays in the Sociology of Religion*
Gesellschaft, 61–62, 64
Gibbon, Edward, 46
Giddens, Anthony, 55, 146, 290, 292, 299n2
Goethe, Johann Wolfgang von, 266
Goldschmidt, Levin, 226, 346n1
Gottschalk, Andreas, 328n13
Gouldner, Alvin W., 5,

302–303n19, 305n37
Goux, Jean-Joseph, 11
Greeks, 14, 59, 255, 264, 326n1
Grundrisse, 96, 124–136 passim
Guattari, Felix, 11
Guesde, Jules, 147
Guild socialism, 146
Guizot, François, 153, 159

Habermas, Jürgen, 10, 323–324n19
Hamelin, Octave, 151, 162, 190
Harrington, Michael, 113, 117, 327n9
Hartmann, Eduard von, 226
Havelock, Eric, 14
Hawthorn, Geoffrey, 1, 5–6
Hedonism, 31, 120, 149
Hegel, George Wilhelm Friedrich, 14, 45, 53, 60, 131; Durkheim and, 183, 186; idealism of, 58, 82–83, 85, 88–89, 183, 204, 326n2; Marx and, 10, 82–89 passim, 102, 105, 106, 139, 225, 320n6, 326n2, 328–329n16; Weber and, 229
Hegelianism, Proudhon's, 95
Helvetius, Claude Adrien, 31, 34, 153
Herder, Johann Gottfried von, 46, 47, 52, 205, 225, 291
Hermeneutical theory, 288
Herr, Lucien, 173
Hess, Moses, 83, 102
Hierarchy, 15, 16, 54, 150, 167, 312n55. *See also* Class
Hinduism, 251
Historical School, 42, 56, 165–166, 184–185; of Economics, 45, 226, 229; of Jurisprudence, 52, 226
Historicism, 1–2, 8–15 passim, 204, 291–292, 297, 342n10; counter-Enlightenment, 7, 8,

47, 273–274 (*see also* Historical School); Durkheim and, 185; Enlightenment, 24, 43, 47; new, 281–282, 283–294, 295; Weber and, 62, 205–206, 222, 225, 226, 267, 270, 345n1, 354–355n36

Historiography, 1–6, 45, 281–297, 362–363n4; Enlightenment and, 8–9, 25–28, 34, 40, 45–46, 47, 275, 309n22; Weber and, 345–346n1. *See also* Historicism

History, 1–6, 7, 9, 74, 281–297, 299–300n4, 363n4; counter-Enlightenment and, 7, 8, 44, 46, 47, 48, 273–274; Enlightenment and, 7, 8–9, 17–18, 24–34 passim, 40–49 passim, 74, 275, 309n22, 310n30; liberalism and, 15, 17–18, 49, 62, 92, 159, 169, 205–206, 225, 291, 342n10; Marx and, 9, 85–105 passim, 122–123, 130–131, 243, 278, 291, 321n14; new, 281–282, 283–294, 295; presentism and, 281–282, 283–284, 286, 294, 295, 362–363n4; Weber and, 62, 205–206, 222–270 passim, 345–346n1, 352nn12, 14, 354–355n36, 356n38. *See also* Historiography

History and Nature of Sociological Theory, 4

Hobbes, Thomas, 6, 23–24; Durkheim and, 162, 186, 194; on introspection, 25; materialism of, 31, 32, 88

Hobhouse, Leonard Trelawney, 76, 293

Holbach, Baron von, 31, 34, 88, 153

Holism, 8, 11; counter-Enlightenment, 45, 47, 273–274; Durkheim and, 149, 178, 278; Enlightenment and, 9, 23, 74, 275; Marx and, 11, 95–96, 138, 140, 145; Weber and, 262, 278

Holy Family, 102

Honigsheim, Paul, 342n11

Humanism, 32; Durkheim and, 190; Marx and, 82, 83, 88, 103; Weber and, 63

Humanity, in German ideology, 227, 228

Human nature, 21–33 passim, 44, 45, 133–137 passim, 194–195

Humboldt, Wilhelm von, 81; and German ideology, 225–226; and Greek *polis*, 59; historicism of, 15, 205, 291; individualism of, 205, 225

Hume, David, 304n29; idealism of, 34; and metaphysics, 36; and progress, 310n30; and science of man, 21–22, 23, 26, 27, 29, 30, 46, 47, 275

Hunt, Richard, 118, 320n10

Hutcheson, Francis, 32

Idealism, 8, 9–10, 11, 15, 76, 204–205; counter-Enlightenment and, 7, 8, 47, 57–59; Durkheim and, 149–163 passim, 173–197 passim, 340n5; Enlightenment and, 9, 32, 33–34, 47, 74, 87, 93, 275; Marx and, 10, 11, 13, 81–95 passim, 102, 117, 132, 139–145 passim, 278, 322n11, 323–324n19, 326n2; neo-critical, 150, 151, 162, 163, 190, 340n5; vulgar, 259; Weber and, 205, 208, 213–234, 236, 245, 246, 252,

259, 270–271, 278, 345*n*1
Ideological realm, 5–14, 75–76,
179, 276–297; of counter-
Enlightenment, 48, 49–73; of
Durkheim, 75, 77, 148,
161–178, 180–181, 187, 189,
197, 206; of Enlightenment,
35–41, 48, 49–73; of Marx, 75,
77, 93, 94, 100, 140, 142, 297;
reductionist, 3, 4–6; of Weber,
75, 77, 206, 207, 217, 219,
236–237. *See also*
Epistemology; Intellectual
traditions; Metaphysics;
Morality; Politics
*Ideology and the Development of
Sociological Theory*, 4
Iggers, Georg, 205, 342*nn*10,11
Immaturity, political, 213, 214,
230–231
Imperialism, 348*n*12
India, 232, 249, 355*n*38
Individualism, 7–18 passim,
153–157 passim, 203, 326*n*1;
counter-Enlightenment and,
7, 51, 52, 57–58, 59, 63, 67;
Durkheim and, 149, 150,
160–180 passim, 194, 195,
198–199, 335–336*n*22, 338*n*28;
Enlightenment and, 7, 9,
22–23, 34, 44, 48, 63, 74, 232,
273; Marx and, 11, 84, 91–103
passim, 120, 133, 140, 324*n*26;
Weber and, 63, 205, 225–237
passim, 267, 271, 278. *See also*
Freedom, individual
"Individualism and the
Intellectuals," 187
Individuality, historical, 44, 45,
46, 47, 241
Industrialism, 155, 276–277;
Durkheim and, 73, 167–168,
182; Marx and, 12, 73, 91, 93,
121, 134, 135, 142, 306*n*43;

Weber and, 73, 208, 211, 212,
213
Industrial revolution, 11, 71, 273
Inequalities, 175, 176, 338*n*29. *See
also* Equality
Inheritance, 149, 150, 176–177
Instrumentalism, 7, 75; Durkheim
and, 160, 162, 167, 181–183,
185–189, 192, 199;
Enlightenment and, 7, 30–34,
44, 74, 273; Marx and, 11,
133–134, 138; Weber and,
218–219
Intellectualization, 258, 260
Intellectual traditions, 6–14,
75–77, 274–275; affecting
Durkheim, 146, 148–151, 157,
158–159, 206, 274, 339–340*n*5;
affecting Marx, 10–12, 81–86,
274, 320*nn*5,10, 326–327*n*5;
affecting Weber, 206, 218–219,
222–234, 238, 270, 342*n*11,
344*n*1. *See also* Conservatism;
Enlightenment; Liberalism;
Romanticism; Revolution
Intentionalism, 286, 287–289, 294
Internalization theory, 22
International Working Men's
Association, 108, 109–110,
113, 127

Jacobins, 71, 152, 153; Marx and,
72, 103, 105, 113, 116, 140
Jaffe, Edgar, 236
James, William, 157
Jaspers, Karl, 359*n*81
Jaurès, Jean, 159, 173
Joint-stock companies, 128–130
Jones, Robert Alun, 282, 284,
337*n*15, 363*n*4
Judaism: Enlightenment and, 36;
Romanticism and, 92; Weber
and, 241, 244, 247, 252, 253,
354*n*36

July Monarch, 152
July Revolution of 1830, 106
Junker class, 207–210, 211
Justice, social, 16, 70; Durkheim
    and, 148, 150, 159–160,
    172–180 passim, 198,
    338–339*n*29; Weber and,
    348*n*12. *See also* Equality

Kant, Immanuel, 15, 16, 32–38
    passim, 59, 150; Durkheim
    and, 162, 183, 190,
    339–340*n*5; Marx and, 81, 82,
    85, 88, 132–133, 136–137,
    326*n*2; Weber and, 205, 225,
    231
Kantianism, 204. *See also* Neo-
    Kantianism
Kautsky, Karl Johann, 148
Knies, Karl, 63, 224–225, 226,
    227–228, 229, 270
Kolakowski, Leszek, 324*n*21
Köppen, Karl, 320*n*5
Kuhn, Thomas, 281

Labor, division of, 90–91, 134,
    175–176, 185–188, 189, 265.
    See also Working classes
Labor process, 127–130, 133–138
Labriola, Antonio, 147, 334–335*n*9
LaCapra, Dominick, 147
Lachelier, Jules, 151, 190
Lagarde, Paul de, 56, 259, 262
Lakatos, Imre, 281
Lamartine, Alphonse de, 159
La Mettrie, Julien de, 31, 88
Landshut, Siegfried, 244–245,
    352*n*16
Langbehn, Julius, 56, 259, 262
Lange, Friedrich, 205
Lasky, Harold, 307*n*49
Laws: civil/moral/political, 24, 44,
    184; theoretical, 3. *See also*
    Natural law

Laws of motion, of capitalism,
    123, 124
League of the Just, 108
Leibniz, Baron von, 35, 36
Lessing, Gotthold Ephraim, 81
Levenson, Joseph, 355*n*38
Leviathan, 25
Liberal democracy, 64; Durkheim
    and, 171, 173, 204; in France,
    159, 171, 173; in Germany,
    204, 205, 213–234, 270; Weber
    and, 62, 64, 205, 213–234
Liberalism, 6–18 passim, 274,
    276–279, 307*n*49, 320*n*10;
    conservatism and, 13, 17, 53,
    54, 56, 101, 145, 152–156
    passim, 203, 216, 235, 236,
    277–278, 315–316*n*23;
    counter-Enlightenment and,
    48–56 passim, 64–66, 75;
    crisis of, 154, 156–158, 161,
    180, 206; defined, 14–18;
    dilemma of, 14–18, 214,
    277–278; Durkheim and,
    12–18 passim, 56, 70–77
    passim, 150–189 passim,
    197–206 passim, 277, 278,
    279, 306*n*44, 337*n*15;
    Enlightenment, 9, 10, 17–18,
    21, 39, 40, 41, 49–54 passim,
    64–66, 81–88 passim, 101,
    142, 152–153, 166–167, 189,
    231, 233, 274; in France, 13,
    17, 76, 77, 104, 150–166
    passim, 198, 203, 277; in
    Germany, 13, 17, 18, 64, 76,
    203–236 passim, 269, 277,
    320*n*10, 342*n*10, 347*n*8; Marx
    and, 12–18 passim, 70–92
    passim, 101–110 passim, 140,
    142, 145, 277, 278–279,
    306*n*44, 320*n*10,
    327–328*nn*11,12; Weber and,
    12–13, 14, 18, 62, 64, 70–77

passim, 203–237 passim, 270,
271, 277, 278–279, 306n44,
342n11, 360–361n2. *See also*
Liberal democracy
Liberal-socialist alliances, 205,
215, 217, 235, 269, 270
Liberty. *See* Freedom, individual
Lichtheim, George, 102, 113
Liebknecht, Karl, 216, 361n2
Lindenlaub, Dieter, 292, 343n1
Linguet, Simon-Nicolas-Henry, 68
Lively, Jack, 43
Locke, John, 6, 15, 16, 152–177
passim
Logic, 223–225, 229, 286
Louis XIV, 44
Löwith, Karl: on Marx, 92, 243,
292; on Weber, 239, 243, 245,
246, 266–267, 292–293
Lübbe, Fritz, 316n27
Lukács, Georg, 141
Lukes, Steven, 150, 151, 339n5
Lutheranism, 210, 211, 220–221,
222, 230–231, 233
Luxemburg, Rosa, 216, 361n2

Mably, Gabriel Bonnot de, 64, 66,
67, 68
Machtpolitik, 347–348n12
McLellan, David, 320n6
Magic, 251–252, 253, 258, 356n48
*Main Currents in Sociological
Thought*, 1
Maine, Henry Sumner, 14, 169
Maistre, Joseph de, 42, 43, 52, 54,
104, 167
Malon, Benoît, 159
Mandeville, Bernard, 31, 304n29
Manifesto of Equals, 85
Mannheim, Karl, 4, 43, 302n11
Marburg school, 204
Market economy, 65, 186, 276. *See
also* Capitalism

Martindale, Donald, 301–302n10
Marx, Heinrich, 81
Marx, Karl, 4, 81–142, 276, 291,
293, 294, 325n1; and
alienation, 14, 49, 130–131,
137–138, 246; Arendt and,
333nn35,39; and capitalism,
90–106 passim, 120–140
passim, 291, 292–293,
322–323n11, 343–345n1; and
democracy, 12, 84, 86, 97,
103–119 passim, 142,
147–148, 320n10, 327nn9,10,
329n32, 330n51; and
dialecticism, 9, 89, 94, 102,
105, 322–323n11, 328–329n16;
and dictatorship of the
proletariat, 115–116, 330n51;
Durkheim and, 145–147,
334n6, 335n9; and
Enlightenment, 8, 10, 11,
81–88 passim, 93, 94–100,
101, 120–124, 131–139, 142,
274; and Hegel, 10, 82–89
passim, 102, 105, 106, 139,
225, 320n6, 326n2,
328–329n16; and idealism, 10,
11, 13, 81–95 passim, 102,
117, 132, 139–145 passim,
278, 322n11, 323–324n19,
326n2; ideological realm of,
75, 77, 93, 94, 100, 140, 142,
297; and individualism, 11,
84, 91–103 passim, 120, 133,
140, 324n26; and
industrialism, 12, 73, 91, 93,
121, 134, 135, 142, 306n43;
intellectual traditions
affecting, 10–12, 81–86, 274,
320nn5,10, 326–327n5; and
liberalism, 12–18 passim,
70–92 passim, 101–110
passim, 140, 142, 145, 277,
278–279, 306n44, 320n10,

327–328nn11,12; and
materialism, 8, 10, 11, 63,
85–89 passim, 94, 102, 140,
145, 278, 321n14; and
organicism, 45; and
revolution, 12, 70–86 passim,
93, 101–126 passim, 142, 145,
277, 328n12, 335n11; and
Romanticism, 60, 63, 82–93
passim, 101, 131–139,
147–148, 277; and socialism,
10, 101–104 passim, 112,
113–114, 120–138 passim,
147, 148, 156, 206, 278,
327n10, 328n12, 329n32,
335n11; and sociology, 8,
9–14, 70, 96, 145–148, 274,
304n30, 305–306nn35,37;
Weber and, 12–13, 147–148,
207, 216, 218, 222, 233, 243,
244, 246, 270, 292–293,
343–346n1

Marxism (post-Marx), 11, 61,
131–132, 138–139, 140–142,
205; Critical, 132, 142;
Scientific, 132, 142; and
sociology, 279, 304n30,
305–306nn37,39; Weber and,
138, 244, 270

Massis, Henri, 56, 155, 157

Materialism, 11, 17, 153;
Durkheim and, 181–195
passim, 278; Enlightenment
and, 9, 10, 31, 32, 33, 34, 74,
87, 94, 153; Marx and, 8, 10,
11, 63, 85–89 passim, 94, 102,
140, 145, 278, 321n14; Weber
and, 63, 204–213 passim, 218,
226, 237, 270–271, 278,
345–346n1, 360n1

Maturity, political, 224, 230

Maurras, Charles, 157

Meaning, 185, 239, 257–266
passim

Mechanical materialism, 17, 32,
88

Mechanistic model, Marx's, 126,
127, 128, 130, 132, 138

Mechanistic view, Enlightenment
vs., 7, 44

Mehring, Franz, 216

Meinecke, Friedrich, 8, 43, 275,
316n27, 342n11

Meitzen, August, 226, 346n1

Merleau-Ponty, Maurice,
360–361n2

Merton, Robert, 282, 297

Meslier, Curé, 64, 66, 68

Metaphysics, 6; counter-
Enlightenment and, 47;
Durkheim and, 196;
Enlightenment and, 36, 37,
38, 41, 94, 276; existentialist,
262

Methodology, 6; Durkheim and,
149, 162–165, 192;
Enlightenment and, 25–28,
34, 45, 46, 47, 94, 95, 96, 97,
273; Marx and, 94, 95, 96, 97,
141, 142; new historicist, 282,
283, 285, 295; presentist, 282,
283, 295; Weber and, 222,
223, 224, 240. *See also*
Empiricism

Meyer, Eduard, 270

Michelet, Jules, 159, 173

Middle Ages, 243, 255

Middle classes. *See* Bourgeoisie

Militarism, 203

Mill, John Stuart, 15, 16, 131, 169

Millenarianism, 92–93, 141

Millerand, Alexandre, 159

Mitzman, Arthur, 61, 62, 63–64

Modernism, 13, 315–316n23;
counter-Enlightenment and,
42, 51–64 passim, 70, 71, 72,
274; Durkheim and, 14, 49,
157, 185–186, 198;

Enlightenment, 39–40, 41, 65, 246–247, 274; Marx and, 12, 14, 49, 71, 91, 93, 134, 142, 277; Weber and, 13, 14, 49, 62, 63–64, 219, 235–268, 317*n*37

Mommsen, Wolfgang, 238–239, 347*n*12

Monism, materialistic, 88

Monopoly, 15, 18, 203, 237

Montaigne, Seigneur de, 32

Montesquieu, Baron de, 304*n*29; Durkheim and, 186; English liberalism and, 153; and progress, 310*n*30; and science of man, 21–34 passim, 44, 46, 275

Moral autonomy, 32, 33, 172, 203, 225, 232, 348*n*12

Moral idealism, 15, 160, 173, 177, 190

Moral individualism, 7, 162–163, 205, 271

Morality, 6, 10, 67–68, 76, 94; Durkheim and, 68, 149, 150, 151, 160–163 passim, 169–196 passim, 335–336*n*22, 338*n*29; Enlightenment and, 7, 22, 30, 65; Marx and, 84; Weber and, 262. *See also* Ethics, Weber and

Moral law, 24

More, Thomas, 67

Morelly, Abbé A., 64, 66, 67, 68

Morris, Colin, 14

Müller, Adam, 45, 291

Multidimensionality, 2, 6, 74, 295–296, 297; in Durkheim's theory, 188, 190, 194; in Enlightenment thought, 30–34; in Marx's critiques, 322*n*11; in Weber's theory, 242, 243–244, 253–254

Mysticism, 157, 220

Napoleon, 81, 152, 225

Narration, in historiography, 26, 27

Nationalism: French, 155, 157; German, 218, 225, 278, 347–348*n*12; of Weber, 218, 278, 347–348*n*12

National Liberals, 216, 270

National Social Association, 235

National Social Party, 215, 236

Nation-state, 252. *See also* State

Natorp, Paul, 204, 342*n*11

Natural determinism, 31, 88, 136, 194, 195

Naturalism, 32, 65, 204, 229, 262

Natural law, 58, 66, 72–73, 105; Enlightenment and, 9, 24, 50–51, 304*n*29; historicism and, 24, 205–206, 342*n*10

Natural man, pre-social, 21–22, 25

Natural rights: bourgeois, 85; equality as, 174; liberty as, 15, 18, 50, 174; to property, 66

Nature: Durkheim and, 181, 194–195; Enlightenment and, 21–25, 29–33, 44, 45, 132; human, 21–33 passim, 44, 45, 133–137 passim, 194–195; Marx, 132, 133–134, 135, 136–137; social, 21–25. *See also* Naturalism

Naumann, Friedrich, 205, 215, 235, 236, 344*n*1, 351*n*1

Nelson, Benjamin, 249–250

Neo-Kantianism, 204–205, 225; of Renouvier, 150; of Weber, 62, 64, 205, 229, 242, 270

Neo-Marxisms, 141

Neo-Romanticism, vulgar, 203

New Critics, 286

New historicism, 281–282, 283–294, 295

Newspapers, French socialist, 155

Newton, Isaac, 153

Nietzsche, Friedrich: and German ideology, 226; Romanticism and, 58, 59–60; Weber and, 264, 349n20, 357–358n57

Nietzsche cults, 61, 262

Nisbet, Robert, 5; and conservatism, 53, 274, 313–314n2; and counter-Enlightenment, 8, 43, 53, 313–314n2; and Durkheim, 146, 274, 338n2

Nonempirical dimensions, 2–3, 136, 137

Noninterventionist state, 153

Nonlogical components, of human nature, 30–31, 44

Normative action, 47, 218–219. *See also* Morality

Noumenal self, 136, 137

Novalis (Friederich von Hardenberg), 52, 58, 59

Objectivism, 44, 58, 165, 273–274, 288–289

Occident: and liberalism, 14; Weber and, 239–248 passim, 355–356n38

Oikos, 326n1

On the Aesthetic Education of Man, 133

"On the Jewish Question," 84, 95

Order: conservatives and, 167; ideology of, 10, 11, 17. *See also* Social order

Organicism, 7, 44, 45, 169, 226–229, 233

Organism, human as, 194–195

Oriental civilizations, 232, 240, 241, 244, 249, 355–356n38

Orleanist dynasty, 152

Orthodox mandarins, 61, 211, 259

Orthodox Marxism, 141, 142, 233

Other-worldliness, 220–221, 230

Pan-German Union, 270

Paris: Marx and, 102, 107, 111–112, 113, 145; University of, 192

Paris Commune, 111–112, 113, 154, 155

Parliamentary government, 215, 216, 348n12

Parsons, Talcott, 6–7, 305n35; on Durkheim, 146, 189, 339n5, 342–343n12; and Enlightenment, 6–7, 34; presentism of, 282; and utilitarianism, 7, 312n52; on Weber, 62, 246–247, 342–343n12

Particularity: counter-Enlightenment and, 46, 47; Enlightenment and, 45–46, 47; liberalism and, 16–17, 307n49; new historicism and, 290, 291, 292

Parties. *See* Political parties

Passion, 30–31, 232

Peasantry: French, 71, 152, 161; German, 210, 346n3

Peel, J. D. Y., 282, 284, 285, 290

Péguy, Charles, 157

Perrin, Robert, 337n15

Personality: Durkheim and, 174, 175, 194, 195; Marx and, 87; Weber and, 221, 227, 228–229, 231–232, 234, 251–252, 348n12

Pessimism, 30, 61, 218, 259, 262–263, 268

Petty, William, 304n29

Phänomenologie, 89

Phenomenal self, 136

Physiocrats, 34

Plato, 23–24, 67, 326n1

Pluralism, 7, 15, 153; counter-Enlightenment and, 51; Durkheim and, 73, 198, 203;

Enlightenment and, 48; Marx and, 73, 84; Weber and, 73, 203, 205, 225, 271

Poggi, Gianfranco, 315*n*19, 325*n*37, 340*n*8

Polis, 59, 326*n*1

Political economy. *See* Classical economics

Political Ideas of Marx and Engels, 118

Political laws, 24

Political parties (general): bourgeois, 104; Durkheim and, 173; Marx and, 104, 107–109, 115, 116–117, 330*n*51; socialist, 155; vanguard, 70, 107–109, 116, 117, 330*n*51; Weber and, 215; workers', 115, 116–117, 214

Political philosophy, presentist historiography in, 363*n*4

Political will, 217, 218

Politics, 6, 18, 61, 70, 71, 154–158; Durkheim and, 156–165 passim, 173, 203; Marx and, 83–126 passim, 147–148, 278, 328*n*12, 329*n*32; Weber and, 62, 64, 148, 203–239 passim, 269–270, 347–348*n*12, 350–351*n*1, 360–361*n*2. *See also* Democracy; Political parties; Revolution

Politics of the will, 104, 105

Popper, Karl, 103, 141

"Positive Critique of Historical Materialism," 147

Positive Philosophy, 55, 131, 145, 168

Positive Polity, 131, 145, 168

Positivism, 3–4, 9, 179, 204, 226; of Comte, 55, 131, 145, 166, 168, 305*n*35; of Enlightenment, 10; in Marxism, 11, 140, 141; in new

historicism, 289; and presentism, 282; Weber and, 270, 360*n*1

Possessive individualism, 7, 149

Postpositivism, 2, 295–296, 300–301*n*5

Poverty of Philosophy, 119

Pragmatism, 157

Praxis-oriented model, 132, 138

Preliminary Discourse to the Encyclopedia of Diderot, 28–29

Presentism, 281–284, 286, 294, 295, 297, 362–363*n*4

Primeval amoral human nature, 30

"Principles of 1789," 156, 160, 178, 180, 186–187, 204

Private property: Durkheim and, 148–149, 150, 176–177; Enlightenment and, 65, 123; French revolutionary tradition and, 66, 67, 70, 120, 148–149, 159; liberalism and, 15, 65, 66, 307*n*49, 328*n*11; Marx and, 104, 120, 123, 125, 328*n*11

Productivism, 11, 182

Professional Ethics and Civic Morals, 187

Progressivism, 74, 326*n*1; Durkheim and, 14, 156, 171, 173; Enlightenment and, 8, 39, 47–48, 49, 65, 81, 310*n*30; Marx and, 8, 14, 81, 97–104 passim, 142, 306*n*43; Weber and, 14, 205, 223, 235, 270

Proletariat. *See* Working classes

Property: collective, 149; without inheritance, 149, 176–177; socialized, 128–130. *See also* Private property

Protestant Ethic and the Spirit of Capitalism, 217, 218–221, 222, 236–249 passim, 270, 271,

276; and rationalization, 245, 246, 247, 248, 249, 254; and unitary world-view, 263; and vocational specialization, 265

Protestantism: social reform movement of, 62, 205, 225, 235; Weber and, 63, 147, 210, 211, 218–222 passim, 230–254 passim, 263, 265, 266, 354*n*36, 355*n*38

Protestant Reformation, 219–220, 247

Proudhon, Pierre-Joseph, 12, 71, 147, 335*n*11; Durkheim and, 148, 149, 159, 160, 173; Marx and, 12, 71, 95, 102, 121, 124

Prussian hegemony: Marxism and, 13, 61, 81, 148, 270; Weber and, 13, 61, 148, 206–216 passim, 221, 226, 230, 235, 269, 270

Psychoanalysis, 287

Puritanism, 63, 219, 220–221, 231–232, 245, 266

Rachfahl, Felix, 226

Racialism, 157

Radical Party, French, 155

Ranke, Leopold von, 43, 45, 204, 226, 229, 291

Rationalism, 7, 11, 18, 155, 166–167, 335–336*n*22; counter-Enlightenment, 42, 56, 64; Durkheim and, 149, 150, 156–157, 169, 181–203 passim, 335–336*n*22; Enlightenment and, 4, 8, 9, 23, 24, 25–28, 35–46 passim, 273, 276; Marx and, 8, 10, 11, 81, 83, 85, 98, 99, 132, 133–134, 142; Weber and, 62, 203, 205, 219, 231–271 passim, 353–355*n*36

Realism, 60, 138

Realpolitik, 218, 235, 270

Reason. *See* Rationalism

Reductionism, 3–6, 11, 74, 302*n*11

Reformation, Protestant, 219–220, 247

Reformist politics: Marx and, 83, 84, 85; Weber and, 62, 205, 215, 225, 235, 236, 269

Reichstag elections (1903), 236, 350–351*n*1

Reification, 14

Reign of Terror, 105, 153, 155

Religion, 16, 54, 167, 250–251; civil, 67, 70, 160, 173; Durkheim and, 168–169, 173, 184; Enlightenment and, 37–38, 41; Marx and, 97; Marxism as, 141; Oriental, 251–252; Weber and, 63, 218–221, 229, 243, 251–261 passim, 356*n*48. *See also* Christianity; Judaism

"Religious Rejections," 63

Renaissance, 192; Catholic, 56, 155, 157

Renouvier, Charles, 150, 151, 159, 162, 173, 190

Republic, French. *See* Third French Republic

Republicanism, 65, 151, 173, 203, 320*n*10

Republic of Equality, 69–70

"Revelations Concerning the Communist Trial in Cologney," 109

Revisionism: in Enlightenment historiography, 8–9, 43, 275; in German socialism, 61, 205, 215, 235, 236

Revolution, 76; counter-Enlightenment, 52, 53, 64–73; Durkheim and, 12, 13, 56, 68–77 passim, 147–182 passim, 197, 198, 204, 277,

278; Marx and, 12, 70–86
passim, 93, 101–126 passim,
142, 145, 277, 328n12,
335n11; Weber and, 12–13,
71–77 passim, 204, 215, 269,
277, 278, 361n2. *See also*
French revolutionary
tradition; Socialism
Revolutions, French, 11, 71, 105,
106, 115, 273
Rheinische Zeitung, 102
Ricardo, David, 122, 123
Rickert, Heinrich, 204, 205, 224
Ricoeur, Paul, 288
Rights. *See* Natural rights
Ringer, Fritz, 61, 211, 317n31
Rise of Totalitarian Democracy, 64
Robertson, Roland, 290
Roman Empire, 14, 147, 244, 264,
345n1, 356n38
Romanticism, 10, 13, 76, 316n27,
317n31, 326n1; counter-
Enlightenment, 42, 43, 52–53,
55, 56, 57–64, 70; Durkheim,
70, 197; and Enlightenment,
42, 43, 52, 57, 59, 63, 87, 93,
131–139, 314n5; Marx and,
60, 63, 82–93 passim, 101,
131–139, 147–148, 277; Weber
and, 60, 61, 62–64, 70,
147–148, 222, 262. *See also*
Communitarianism; Idealism;
Unity
Roscher, Wilhelm, 63, 224–229
passim, 270
Rossides, Daniel, 4–5
Roth, Guenther, 351–352n12
Rousseau, Jean-Jacques, 21, 25,
53, 309n18; Durkheim and,
148, 149, 171–173; and
revolutionary tradition,
64–66, 68, 71, 148, 149, 160
Royer-Collard, Pierre Paul, 153
Ruge, Arnold, 112

Rules of a Sociological Method,
165
Russia, 237

Saint-Simon, Comte de, 159, 182,
305n37; Durkheim and, 150,
182; Marx and, 10, 72, 83,
103, 121, 320n5
Saint-Simonians, 121
Sand, George, 119
Savigny, Friedrich Karl von, 45,
54, 83, 291, 320n5
Say, Jean-Baptiste, 153
Schelling, F. W. J., 52, 57
Schelsky, Helmut, 60
Schiller, Friedrich, 52, 59, 133,
134
Schlegel, August Wilhelm von, 52,
58, 59, 82
Schlegel, Friedrich von, 52, 58, 59
Schleiermacher, Friedrich, 52, 225
Schluchter, Wolfgang, 354–355n36
Schmoller, Gustav, 216, 226, 235,
343n1
Schopenhauer, Arthur, 226
Schurmann, Franz, 355n38
Science, 9, 10, 11, 155, 203,
295–296; Durkheim and, 45,
156–157, 163, 165, 166–168,
190; Enlightenment and, 7,
35, 38, 41, 65, 132, 255; Marx
and, 10, 11, 45, 63, 121,
122–124, 127–128, 132, 142;
new historicism and, 281–282,
283–294, 295; presentism and,
282–283, 295; Weber and, 45,
63, 212, 222–225, 232, 252,
258, 261–262, 269
"Science as a Vocation," 63, 232,
259, 260, 263
Science, Class, and Society, 4
Science of man, 9, 21–35, 40, 74,
275; Becker and, 8–9, 300n4;

counter-Enlightenment and, 44, 45–46, 47, 75, 276
Scientific Marxism, 132, 142
Scottish philosophes, 49, 275, 304*n*29
Sectarianism, 121
Secularism, 316*n*23, 319*n*67; counter-Enlightenment and, 42; Durkheim and, 156, 167, 168–169, 187, 198; of Enlightenment, 39, 41, 42, 48, 273; Marx and, 97–98, 142; of Weber, 63, 64, 234, 255–265 passim
Seidman, Steven, 352*n*20
Self-consciousness, 57, 58, 191, 194
Shaftesbury, Earl of, 32
Shils, Edward, 292
Simmel, Georg, 13, 61, 148, 245
Sismondi, Jean de, 121
Skinner, Quentin, 282, 287, 288, 290, 291, 363*n*4
Smith, Adam, 122
Snell, Bruno, 14
Social Contract, 171
Social contract theory: Durkheim and, 162, 176–177; Enlightenment and, 7–9, 17–28 passim, 35, 40, 44, 74, 94, 275, 276, 304*n*29, 361*n*1
Social Darwinism, 17, 73, 159. *See also* Evolutionism
Social democracy, 171; contemporary, 112–113, 114, 117; Durkheim, 73, 171, 173; in France, 159–160, 171, 173; in Germany, 205, 214, 215, 216, 235, 236, 269, 270, 351*n*1; Marx and, 73, 112–113, 114, 117; Weber and, 73, 205, 214, 215, 216, 235, 236, 269, 270, 351*n*1
Social Democrats: Marx and, 114;

Weber and, 205, 214, 215, 216, 235, 236, 269, 270, 351*n*1
Social development: Durkheim and, 165, 166, 167; Enlightenment and, 28–29, 44–45; Weber and, 218, 240–241, 246–247, 250, 253, 354–355*n*36. *See also* Evolutionism
Socialism, 4, 15, 67, 215, 277, 335*n*11; Durkheim and, 68, 145–147, 155–156, 158, 160, 172, 173, 180, 182, 203; Marx and, 10, 101–104 passim, 112, 113–114, 120–138 passim, 147, 148, 156, 206, 278, 327*n*10, 328*n*12, 329*n*32, 335*n*11; Weber and, 61, 203, 205, 215–216, 217, 226, 235, 245, 269, 270, 342*n*11
Socialism (Durkheim), 68
Socialism and Communism in Present-Day France, 102
Socialization theory, 22
Social justice. *See* Justice, social
Social nature, of man, 21–25
Social order, 17, 167, 203; counter-Enlightenment and, 47–48, 75, 276; Durkheim and, 175, 177–178, 180, 185, 189; Enlightenment and, 39, 50; Marx and, 87. *See also* Democracy; Hierarchy; Morality; Pluralism
Social realism, 60, 138
Social reform movement, 62, 205, 225, 235
Social solidarity, 159; Aristotle and, 326*n*1; Comte and, 168; Durkheim and, 149, 150, 173, 174, 175–176, 178, 185, 190
Social theory, 1, 2–6, 74
Société Universelle des

Communistes Révolutionaries, 116
Society, Weber's concept of, 232–233. *See also* Collective life; Communitarianism; Culture; Organicism
Sociological Tradition, 5
Sociology, 1–2, 4–5, 17, 276, 278, 279; Conservatism and, 10, 54–55, 56, 274 (*see also* Comte, Auguste); English (*see* Spencer, Herbert); in Enlightenment thought, 40; French, 10, 55, 169 (*see also* Durkheim, Emile; Saint-Simon, Comte de); German, 55, 60–64, 147, 317*n*31 (*See also* Weber, Max); historiography in, 106, 281–297, 363*n*4; Marx and, 8, 9–14, 70, 96, 145–148, 274, 304*n*30, 305–306*nn*35,37,39
Solidarity, worker, 126–127. *See also* Social solidarity; Working class associations
Sombart, Werner, 61; on Enlightenment, 304*n*29; and Marxism, 13, 148, 343–344*n*1; Weber and, 236, 343–344*n*1, 347*n*4
Sorel, Georges, 147
Southwest Kantians, 204
Spencer, Herbert, 7, 75, 76, 158–172 passim, 180, 199, 337*n*15
Spinoza, Baruch, 31, 35, 360*n*1
Spirit, 36–37, 57, 82, 125
Spirit of the Laws, 23, 26–27, 28, 33
Stabilisationswissenschaft, 10
State, 7, 15, 16, 103, 152, 153, 252; counter-Enlightenment and, 54, 70; Durkheim and, 149, 150, 173; Marx and, 85;

Weber and, 212. *See also* Authoritarianism; Bureaucracy
State socialism, 61
Stein, Lorenz von, 102
Stern, Fritz, 315–316*n*23
Stirner, Max, 133
Stocking, George, 282, 283–284, 297
Stoecker, Adolf, 235
Structuralists, 141–142, 286, 288
Structure of Scientific Revolutions, 281
Structure of Social Action, 189
Subjectivism: Durkheim and, 164; and German ideology, 226; of liberalism, 14; Marx and, 94; of Romanticism, 42, 57–58, 59
Suffrage, universal, 112, 214, 215, 348*n*12
Suicide, 187, 188, 189, 196, 276
Sumner, William Graham, 293
Syndicalism: in France, 12, 71, 76, 147, 155, 157, 159, 203; in Germany, 203
Systematic idealism, 208
Systematic spirit, 36–37

Talmon, J. L., 64, 67–68, 103, 141
Tar, Zolton, 305*n*35
Tarde, Alfred de, 56, 155, 157
Taylor, Charles, 333*n*32
Technology, 203, 347*n*4. *See also* Industrialism
Tenbruck, Friedrich, 248–255 passim, 353–354*n*36
Terrorism, 153, 155, 157
Textualism, 286
Theocracy, 54
"Theoretical Interlude," 259
Theory, 3–4
Therborn, Göran, 4, 5
"Thesis on Feuerbach," 88
Third French Republic, 72, 157; Durkheim and, 72, 154, 156,

158, 160, 161, 171, 173, 178, 180, 198; revolutionary tradition and, 12, 71, 154, 155–156

Tiryakian, Edward, 335*n*11

Tocqueville, Alexis de, 159, 173, 306*n*44

Tolerance, 16, 39

Tolstoy, Leo, Count, 63, 261

Tönnies, Ferdinand, 13, 61, 148, 291, 343*n*1

Totalitarian democracy, 64, 103, 114–119

Toulmin, Stephen, 281

Trade unionism, 62, 147, 155, 214. *See also* Working class associations

Traditionalism, 152, 157, 167, 278, 292; counter-Enlightenment and, 42–43, 54, 59, 61; Durkheim and, 161, 185, 203; Enlightenment and, 39, 41, 49; Weber and, 203, 210–211, 212, 219, 220, 226, 269–270

"Tragedy of Culture," 245

Transcendental idealism, 57–58, 82, 88, 183, 190, 326*n*2

Traugott, Mark, 334*n*6

Treatise on Human Nature, 27

Troeltsch, Ernst, 43, 225, 342*n*11, 344*n*1

Tucker, Robert, 92

Turgot, Anne Robert Jacques, 28, 32, 153, 304*n*29

Turner, Jonathan, 3–4, 300*n*4

Ulam, Adam, 327–328*n*11

Uniformitarianism, 7, 51, 165

United States, 359–360*n*88. *See also* America

Unity: Durkheim and, 149, 188–189, 196; Marx and, 82–93 passim, 131, 132–133;

Weber and, 263–264. *See also* Social solidarity

Universal history, 28, 235–268, 356*n*38

Universalism, 16–17, 98, 99, 307*n*49

Universal suffrage, 112, 214, 215, 348*n*12

University of Berlin, 82–84, 320*n*5

University of Paris, 192

Urbanization, 71

Utilitarianism, 7–18 passim, 73, 76, 153, 312*n*52; Durkheim and, 162, 182, 194, 195; Marx and, 11, 94; Weber and, 266

Utopianism, 67, 155; Durkheim and, 68; Marx and, 8, 10, 93, 121, 123, 131–139, 246; Weber and, 246

Value form, of labor, 127–128

Values, Weber and, 222, 239, 264–266

Vanguard party concept, 70, 106–109, 116, 117, 330*n*51

Verein für Sozialpolitik, 216, 235, 236, 270, 343*n*1

Viewpoints (Weber's term), 222–223, 224

Violence, 112–119 passim, 153, 155, 157

Voegelin, Eric, 92

Volk, 61, 227–229, 233

Vollmar, Georg von, 235

Voltaire, François Marie Arouet de, 49, 304*n*29; and Christianity, 30, 313*n*60; and English liberalism, 153; and science of man, 21–34 passim, 44, 46–47, 309*n*21, 310*n*30

Voluntarism, 15, 16, 17–18, 155; counter-Enlightenment, 273; Durkheim and, 160, 169, 173, 183–189, 199, 278;

Enlightenment and, 33; Marx and, 126, 130, 132, 138; Weber and, 267

Wagner, Adolf, 216, 226, 343n1
Weber, Marianne, 205, 317n37, 360n1
Weber, Max, 203–271, 276, 291, 347n4, 351–352nn12, 14, 359–360n88; and alienation, 14, 49, 246; and capitalism, 147, 203–220 passim, 237–245 passim, 252, 269, 292–293, 343–345n1, 355–356n38; and Durkheim, 203–204, 206, 342–343n12; and economics, 214, 218, 226, 233, 237, 276, 343–345n1, 346n3; and existentialism, 262, 359n81; and history, 62, 205–206, 222–270 passim, 345–346n1, 352nn12,14, 354–355n36, 356n38; intellectual traditions affecting, 206, 218–219, 222–234, 238, 270, 342n11, 344n1; and liberalism, 12–13, 14, 18, 62, 64, 70–77 passim, 203–237 passim, 270, 271, 277, 278–279, 306n44, 342n11, 360–361n2; and Marx, 12–13, 147–148, 207, 216, 218, 222, 233, 243, 244, 246, 270, 292–293, 343–346n1; and Marxism (post-Marx), 138, 244, 270; and materialism, 63, 204–213 passim, 218, 226, 237, 270–271, 278, 345–346n1, 360n1; and modernism, 13, 14, 49, 62, 63–64, 219, 235–268, 317n37; nationalism of, 218, 278, 347–348n12; and Nietzsche, 264, 349n20, 357–358n57; and organicism, 45, 226–229, 233; and

positivism, 270, 360n1; and rationalism, 62, 203, 205, 219, 231–271 passim, 353–355n36; and religion, 63, 218–221, 229, 243, 251–261 passim, 356n48; and revolution, 12–13, 71–77 passim, 204, 215, 269, 277, 278, 361n2; and Romanticism, 60, 61, 62–64, 70, 147–148, 222, 262
Weiner, Jonathan, 345n1
Weitling, Wilhelm, 102, 326–327n5
Westermarck, Edward Alexander, 76
Westphalen, Baron von, 81, 320n5
Whiggish histories, 281, 283–284, 295. *See also* Presentism
Will, 104, 105, 217, 218, 234, 237
Willey, Thomas, 347n8
Windelband, Wilhelm, 204
Wissenschaft, 13, 222, 225
Wissenschaftslehre, 58
Wordsworth, William, 58
Working class associations, 62, 147, 149, 155; Durkheim and, 173, 187; Marx and, 102, 107, 115, 116–117, 126–127; Weber and, 214
Working classes, 16; Durkheim and, 77, 177, 187, 204, 277; Marx and, 10, 11, 70, 77, 102–138 passim, 322n11, 330n51; Weber and, 77, 204, 213–214, 215, 216, 236, 269, 270, 277

Yang, C. K., 355n38
Young Hegelians, Marx and, 10, 83–89 passim, 139, 225, 320n6

Zeitlin, Irving, 4, 145–146, 274

Laski

Designer: Marian O'Brien
Compositor: Imperial Litho/Graphics
Printer: Vail-Ballou Press
Binder: Vail-Ballou Press
Text: 10/12 Aster
Display: Aster